WATER SECURITY FOR PALESTINIANS AND ISRAELIS

WATER SECURITY FOR PALESTINIANS AND ISRAELIS

Towards a New Cooperation in Middle East Water Resources

Christopher Ward
Sandra Ruckstuhl
Isabelle Learmont

BLOOMSBURY ACADEMIC
LONDON • NEW YORK • OXFORD • NEW DELHI • SYDNEY

BLOOMSBURY ACADEMIC
Bloomsbury Publishing Plc
50 Bedford Square, London, WC1B 3DP, UK
1385 Broadway, New York, NY 10018, USA
29 Earlsfort Terrace, Dublin 2, Ireland

BLOOMSBURY, BLOOMSBURY ACADEMIC and the Diana logo
are trademarks of Bloomsbury Publishing Plc

First published in Great Britain 2022
This paperback edition published by Bloomsbury Academic in 2023

For legal purposes the Acknowledgements on p. xiii constitute an extension of this copyright page.

Cover image: Aerials and water tanks on the rooftops of houses in Jerusalem's Old City, Israel. (© Dieter Telemans/Panos Pictures)

A catalogue record for this book is available from the British Library.
A catalog record for this book is available from the Library of Congress.

ISBN: HB: 978-0-7556-3794-2
PB: 978-0-7556-3798-0
ePDF: 978-0-7556-3796-6
eBook: 978-0-7556-3795-9

Typeset by Deanta Global Publishing Services, Chennai, India

To find out more about our authors and books visit
www.bloomsbury.com and sign up for our newsletters.

Dedicated to the memory of our late teachers Tony Allan, Albert Hourani, Roger Owen, Robert Mabro, Donald Russell, Adrian Sherwin-White, Freddie Beeston and Dennis Sandole

And in love and gratitude to our friend and guide, the late William St Clair, scholar and mentor to so many

CONTENTS

ILLUSTRATIONS

Figures

Tables

Maps

ACKNOWLEDGEMENTS

The authors are entirely responsible for the content of this book, but we must mark our great appreciation of the many friends, colleagues and interlocutors who have helped us to understand the challenges or have provided invaluable information.

The very many people in the Palestinian territories and in Israel who helped us are too numerous to mention by name but we would like to extend our thanks to every one of them. We must, however, record our huge thanks to Gidon Bromberg and his colleagues of EcoPeace who have long laboured in the vineyard in which we now trespass. We also acknowledge the generous cooperation of many Palestinian communities, including in Jenin, Falamyeh, Jayyous, Yatta, Aqraba and Farkha, and in Gaza City and Khan Younis.

Several experts have unstintingly supported us in aspects of this endeavour, including Dr Mark Zeitoun, now professor at the University of East Anglia, the late professor Tony Allan, the doyen of Middle East water studies at King's and SOAS, London, and Dr Shimon Tal, former water commissioner of Israel. We also thank Professor Eugene Rogan of St Antony's College, University of Oxford, and Dr Marc Valéri and his colleagues and students at the Institute of Arab and Islamic Studies of the University of Exeter. We also acknowledge the inspiring work of Professor Ilan Pappé and of Dr Seth Siegel, both of whom have made dry stories come alive.

Colleagues from the World Bank have over the years been an inspiration and a support, and on the subject of this book in particular we learned much from Salah Darghouth, Sabine Beddies, Pier Francesco Mantovani and Adnan Ghosheh.

We acknowledge the sterling work of our editors, our insightful and dedicated commissioning editor David Stonestreet at I.B. Tauris, and at Bloomsbury, Tomasz Hoskins and Nayiri Kendir, and Sophie Campbell, Dhanuja Ravi and the excellent Bloomsbury production team.

We must also pay tribute to Wikipedia and its branches, great organs of truth and open access.

We thank all those individuals and organizations who have allowed us to use their material. Where we have been unable to track down copyright holders, we request that they contact us so that we may correct matters accordingly.

In researching and writing this book and its companion volume, we have clambered awkwardly onto the shoulders of giants. But if we have wavered there, it has been from our own weaknesses of understanding or of confidence. All failings or errors of fact or judgement are ours alone. And none of the people who so generously helped us in any way endorses the content of this book, which is our sole responsibility.

PREFACE

Security is an essential need of the soul.

Simone Weil, The Needs of the Soul

In our companion book, *The History of Water in the Land Once Called Palestine*, we looked at the water resource of the land defined by the borders of Mandate Palestine and traced the history of the development and management of water since Ottoman times up to 2020, a history characterized by a divergence between the two peoples in respect of water as strong as their divergence in other spheres.

The present book, *Water Security for Palestinians and Israelis*, carries on the theme to first examine in detail the current security situations of Israelis and Palestinians in respect of water. We take adequate water as a necessity not only for life but for the development of a modern society and economy, and we take water security as a good that all people aspire to in a world where water is increasingly scarce. We start from the premise that two peoples with common water resources would share those resources in a fair way and cooperate in their management. We argue that the development of a modern economy and society requires a certain amount of water and that both Palestinians and Israelis should have the use of that amount, provided the water is available and does not deprive others. Our reasoning is not based in politics, which often seem intractable in the situation we are discussing, although political processes are essential to achieving outcomes. Our reasoning is from the principles of good water management, and from historical, practical, economic, legal and ethical considerations.

We use this concept of water security as our framework for analysis, supported by two fundamental tenets – that water security for people sharing a common resource requires cooperation based on the principles of equity, efficiency and sustainability, and second that no one state or people sharing a common resource has a superior entitlement to water security. In the final part of the book, we propose what we earnestly and humbly hope may be a workable scheme for putting into practice a new form of cooperation in a way that would benefit both peoples and strengthen their water security.

Plainly this result will not be achieved without political will and compromise from the respective leaderships.

Christopher Ward, *University of Exeter*
Dr Sandra Ruckstuhl, *International Water Management Institute, Colombo*
Dr Isabelle Learmont, *Hennock, Devon*
May 2021

INTRODUCTION

THE DIVERGENCE OF TWO PEOPLES AND THE NATURE OF WATER SECURITY

Our first volume, *The History of Water in the Land Once Called Palestine*, described how the paths of two peoples sharing the same land and the same water a century ago began to diverge.

Today enormous economic disparities have sprung up between the two peoples who only a hundred years ago had much the same standard of living. In 2019 Israelis had a GDP per capita of $35,000,[1] twelve times that of the average Palestinian (about $3,000) and twenty times that of the average Palestinian in Gaza ($1,600).[2] While the Israeli population of 8.7 million lives at a standard resembling that of Europe or the United States, nearly one quarter of the Palestinian population of 4.8 million are classified as poor.[3] An estimated 1.6 million Palestinians and almost one third of households across the Palestinian territories are food insecure.[4] The situation is worst in Gaza, where over two thirds of households – about 1.3 million people – are food insecure and 16 per cent cannot afford the minimum caloric intake, the basics of survival.[5] Life expectancy at birth is eighty-two years (2016) for Israelis, above that of Americans (seventy-nine years), while the Palestinians trail nearly nine years behind their Israeli neighbours at seventy-four years (2018).

Living conditions for Palestinians are poor and are actually deteriorating. In 2018, GDP in the Palestinian territories declined by 8 per cent from an already miserable level. The economy has very little strength or resilience. Restrictions on trade and on access to resources in the West Bank, along with a decade-long blockade of Gaza, have hollowed out the productive base. The share of manufacturing in the economy has halved in the last twenty-five years, while agriculture is only one third of its previous size. Crumbling basic infrastructure and frequent interruption of key services such as water and electricity curtail business operations and drive up production costs. The economy is import-dependent, with imports over three times the size of exports and a trade deficit close to 40 per cent, one of the highest in the world.[6]

Almost one Palestinian in three in the labour force is out of work, compared to one person in twenty-seven in Israel.[7] Only one Palestinian young person in six has a full-time job.[8] In Gaza more than half the working-age population is unemployed – and two thirds of Gaza's youth have no work to go to. Never having had a job, young people grow angry and restive. This compares to Israeli youth, where only one young person in fourteen has no job.[9] Today, Gaza essentially lives off transfers – remittances, donor aid, transfers from the Palestinian Authority. Together these transfers make up three quarters of Gaza's GDP. Four fifths of Gaza's residents depend on humanitarian aid.[10]

The gap between the two peoples is nowhere more striking than in the question of water. The Israeli people have today achieved a water security that is near complete. With over 250 cubic metres of water for each Israeli every year, water is available for all human and economic needs and an enviable level of water services is provided for (almost) everyone[11] in every corner of the territory. Israelis have achieved complete water autonomy, controlling all their water resources. Water systems are proof against drought and against hostile action, and all of this in a dry and progressively drier land prey to climatic vagaries and extremes. Today the Israelis are so efficient in production and use of water that they export their lessons and their technology around the world. Every precious drop of natural water is valued, used and reused. New water is made from the sea in huge plants ranged along the Mediterranean. Water is stored and despatched as needed to every corner of the land and to every use through a national grid of pipes. One network carries drinking water to households; another carries clean recycled wastewater for farmers to grow food and produce for a rich export trade and to green the environment and create river parks. Israel has been called a 'water superpower' and encouraged to use the almost limitless water the nation controls or can create through desalination as an instrument of policy with its arid neighbours.[12]

Alongside, in the same land, are two small territories where the Palestinians live in conditions in respect of water that are in some ways world-beating too. West Bank Palestinians have access to rather scanty natural water, about 40 cubic metres a head annually. Expensive water purchases from Israel bring the per capita ration up to 65 cubic metres, one quarter of Israeli levels and a small fraction of the water needed to develop a modern economy like Israel's. Water services are often poor, sometimes terrible. The average amount coming out of the tap in the West Bank is about 50–60 litres a day for each person, compared to the Israelis' 260 litres. People in Palestinian towns like Dura and Yatta are lucky if they get 25 litres a day on average, and households in these towns count themselves fortunate if they get tap water every month or two. Their water systems are corroded from disuse. Households disconnect and harvest water from the roadway instead.

Lacking access to water, West Bank Palestinians must buy from their strong neighbour. Although they are the poorest people in the region and have ample groundwater beneath their feet that they could pump out at relatively low cost, they are obliged to buy water from Israel at the high cost of desalination and pay for pumping from the coast up to the highlands. In West Bank towns which buy all their water, tariffs run as high as NIS 7 per cubic metre (about \$2.20), little less than the \$2.55 that the well-off Israelis pay – and three times higher than the cost would be if the West Bank Palestinians could meet their needs from local wells.[13]

The West Bank Palestinians live within the constraints of an interim agreement on water made with Israel in 1995 for a five-year period which has now lasted for twenty-five years. The quantity they may pump from beneath their feet is controlled. The infrastructure they may build to move water around the West Bank and provide water services in towns is controlled. The construction of sewage networks, of sewage treatment infrastructure and of the works required for the reuse of treated wastewater is controlled.

There is, too, another more fugitive and slow-moving dimension of loss that has become apparent as the turbulent, state-building period which saw the acquisition of water resources and the development of water services came to a close. This is the environmental dimension, the cost and the impact of that cost on the lives and well-being of the inhabitants of the land.

The Jordan River system has been exploited without limit. The river itself 'deep and wide',[14] where Saint John the Baptist baptized the Christ, is now a vestigial drain polluted with nitrates. The great sea of Galilee, Lake Tiberias, has shrunk. As the level of water drops, the risk is of wholesale salination from the salty springs that lie beneath the surface. The Dead Sea, the Jordan's sump, the lowest point on earth, is no longer fed by the river's waters and is in constant retreat, this natural wonder another drying sea. The land suffers too. Tiberias water piped over two hundred kilometres south to irrigate the Negev brings sterilizing salts that accumulate in the soil.

The waters of the aquifers that lie beneath the West Bank highlands charge the seasonal and the base flow of the many streams that flow east and west from the watershed. The race to pump out these sweet waters to supply the burgeoning population depleted the aquifer. The water table dropped and the rivers dried up. As the flow of freshwater towards the sea shrank, seawater began to intrude, bringing salt into the aquifer. Fresh water in the streams was replaced by sewage flows and the accumulation of municipal rubbish. So polluted was the Yarkon stream that when a footbridge collapsed during an international sporting event, four athletes from Australia fell in and died. One drowned, the other three died later, infected by a fungus that thrived in the filthy water.

The Gaza aquifer has been the worst affected. With 2 million people drawing water for all their needs from the slim resources of this Coastal Aquifer, seawater rushes in. Today Gaza water is undrinkable; the aquifer is ruined as a potable resource.

As these problems emerged over the years, Israelis started to recognize the consequences of their intense development of natural resources and, like other developed countries, began to devise many remedies. Israel is, by and large, getting on top of the problem – at least of the most visible aspects within its borders. Some flow has been restored to certain streams; there are jogging trails along the banks – even clean water in a special Jordan River baptismal site.

The Palestinians by contrast have done little – not from lack of wishing or caring, but from lack of the powers and resources needed. They have a somewhat free hand in only one tenth of the land of historic Palestine, in the 700 fragments of territory where they have jurisdiction. The great swathes of the environment, the vast majority of the land and water of historic Palestine, lie beyond their hand. Even what lies within their remit – domestic water supply, sanitation – is hedged with rules and constrained by their impoverishment.

What sewage the Palestinians collect goes largely untreated. It courses raw down the wadis, polluting the environment and streaming across the Green Line into Israel. When the hot summer comes, everything gets worse. Water is cut off for days; the sewage stinks in the water courses. In Gaza the tap water is so salty that it is undrinkable, and raw sewage is stored untreated in great lakes or released to foul the beaches and waters of the Mediterranean.

What is water security?

The purpose of the first two parts of the book (Parts I and II) is to assess the water security of Israelis and of Palestinians today, to compare the two and to suggest reasons for what are evidently considerable gaps between the situations of the two peoples. In the Preface we sketched out the notion of water security in very general terms but now, as we embark on a detailed assessment of the current water security status of Israelis and Palestinians, we refine our definition.

We break water security down into three interdependent components: security of water resources, security of water services and security through the management of risks and threats. The wheel below – *Elements of Water Security* – is taken from a World Bank publication. It shows the three components and some of the elements that make up security for each of the components. There are other interpretations of water security and we shall come back to these – and also to what lessons about the concept of water security we may learn from the Israeli and Palestinian experiences – in Part III, right at the end of this book.

In summary, to achieve *water resource security*, renewable water resources must be available in adequate quantity and quality to meet all present and future needs. The key element is, first and foremost, securing control of enough water to meet human needs, to develop the economy and to maintain the environment.

Here we will come up against the question, *How much water does an economy or a society actually need?* Much of the discourse is about scarcity, with some fairly arbitrary cut-off points about what constitutes scarcity – usually so many cubic metres per capita of water each year. But this begs the question of what a nation does with its water. A fast urbanizing and industrializing economy that has allocated all its water to agriculture may well find itself water scarce. This is not, however, a natural scarcity, but one produced by past decisions. So in our analysis, we try to avoid this definition of scarcity. Instead, we ask, *How much water does a nation need in order to develop a modern economy, and what is the most economical source of that water*?

An important consideration here is 'water autonomy' – how much water resource does a jurisdiction actually control. This is usually judged by what share of a nation's resources arises in its territory. A nation like Turkey, for example, has complete water autonomy: almost its entire resource comes from springs, rivers and groundwater which lie within its territory. Iraq, by contrast, has more limited water autonomy because rainfall is scanty and most of the waters of the

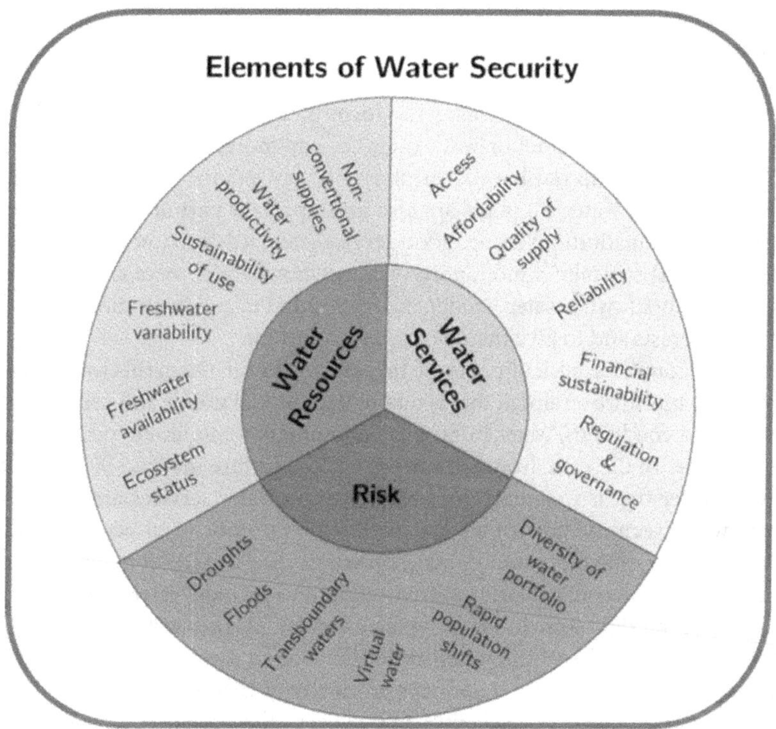

Figure 0.1 Elements of Water Security.

Tigris and Euphrates arise outside its borders, upstream in Turkey, Syria and Iran.

What a nation does with its water is also a cornerstone of water resource security. Does the nation use its water efficiently and productively to get the maximum value from every drop? Is the quantity of water that is diverted from watercourses or pumped from groundwater sustainable, or is the resource being depleted? Are aquifers being drained, are springs and streamflows dwindling and disappearing, are inland seas and lakes drying up, are great rivers no longer reaching the sea?

A more recent concern for water resource security is water quality. In many countries, pollution is a massive problem – from sewage, from urban garbage, from industrial pollutants and heavy metals, and from agricultural drainage water loaded with nitrates and pesticides. Water in many rivers has become so polluted that it is no longer usable without first being scrubbed clean. Groundwater has become unsafe, contaminated by sewage and by agricultural residues percolating down, or spoiled by saltwater intruding into the aquifer from the sea.

Security of water services is about fair access of all to good-quality water services. A benchmark for domestic water supply would be permanently available water of assured potable quality piped into households, rich and poor, urban and rural, seven days a week without interruption at a price that is affordable given the local standard of living. How much domestic water is a fair amount? The World Health Organization suggests a minimum of 100 litres a day. Where costs are high and incomes low, provision for the better off to help reduce the cost to the less well-off would be usual. Often this takes the form of a lifeline tariff. Those who use more water to fill their pool or wash their car pay more, and those who use less water because they do not have a car or a pool pay less for just a basic quantity of water. Efficient water suppliers are also an important part of security of water services. Sound institutions assure good service standards and low prices. Because water supply is typically a monopoly – almost nowhere is there competition to supply households with water – independent regulation and institutions to protect citizens' interests and to give them voice are important.

In many countries, agriculture is the biggest water user. Often this water is in the form of soil moisture – rainfall that is retained in the soil profile and used by crops. In more arid conditions, water from rivers or aquifers is mobilized to complement soil moisture. In these environments, irrigated agriculture may use 90 per cent or more of water that is mobilized for use. Irrigation water services are thus a vital part of water security. Often they are the lifeline for poor rural people, and also the motor of profitable agricultural economies. These irrigation services must work within the overall agricultural environment to provide water sustainably and efficiently at the right time in the cropping calendar. The key criteria are irrigation efficiency – what share of the water mobilized from a river, for example, actually reaches the plant roots – and crop water productivity, that is '$ per drop'.

Security from water-related risks has always been a preoccupation in the dry Middle East. Arid lands face the risk of drought. Water-abundant lands suffer floods. But today new risks have arisen and old ones have intensified. As populations have grown and demand for water services has shot up, the risk of water shortages and of conflict between water users has risen. As upstream countries or communities have diverted more and more water, their downstream neighbours have been under threat of diminishing access. Aquifers have suffered the 'tragedy of the commons' as a free-for-all well drilling has led to competitive overpumping and a race to the bottom. As the needs of towns have grown, the large quantities of water that agriculture uses have come under question and countries have faced important trade-offs between water supply to households or industry and the needs of agriculture and of food production. More recently, the spectre of climatic change and variability has threatened secular shifts in hydrological patterns and heralded warming that can only push up demand for water and reduce its availability through increased evaporation. Finally, there is the risk to the precious water-related ecology as the hand of man or natural changes threaten flora and fauna and menace whole ecosystems and the services they provide.

It is against these three yardsticks that we assess the water security of the two peoples who share the common natural resources and environment. As we have already suggested, the contrast will be a stark one. Our intention is that by revealing all aspects of this contrast, we will make a forceful case for change. Then in Part III of the book, we will explore how change may be accomplished – to mutual advantage.

Water security for all

How did two peoples who set out very roughly from the same point a century ago arrive at so different a result today? For a hundred years Palestinians have struggled against the takeover of their land and water, and they have lost. Dunam by dunam, cubic metre by cubic metre, they have lost the land and water which they once held. A relentless logic has for over a century added to Israel's water inventory and strengthened Israel's water security and in the old zero-sum game of water, Israelis' gain has been Palestinians' loss. Successive new realities, new facts on the ground have become well established. Palestinians are accorded only controlled and limited access to just enough water to scrape by.

The new realities are imposed by the country that is now by far the most powerful state in the Middle East and supported by the most powerful country ever, the United States. No strong political current in the world is rooting much for change. Israel and America call the shots. The 'peace process', the idea of a 'two-state solution' – these notions look quite remote. Almost nobody with any clout in either country appears to care anymore. The discourse is 'Get over it. You lost. Get on with it'.

Amongst all the 'facts on the ground', where is the lever that might move change? In water there may just be such a lever. One new fact on the ground, as we shall see in this book, is the coming of desalination. A new possibility has arisen – that if we can now *make* water, then water need no longer be a reason for struggle. It may instead be part of a solution to struggle.

And that is the justification of our book. Israel now makes water from the sea. This relaxes the old zero-sum game. Already this has helped to bring a kind of peace between Jordan and Israel. In our first book we told the story of loss, about how Palestinians come to be so dispossessed of water. And how, for Israelis, it was a contrasting history of the step-by-step and successful consolidation of a water inventory and of resulting water security. In this book we tell a more hopeful story. We try to answer the question, *How can Israelis consolidate their hard-won water security – and how can Palestinians achieve the same?* What are the conditions in which the water security of both peoples can be obtained in a framework of fairness and justice and of good water management?

Water drove Israeli development – could it now drive that of the Palestinians?

All else set aside, nobody would deny that the Palestinian Arab inhabitants of the land are entitled to a fair share of the water resources of that land and to the right to develop those resources as they see fit for the benefit of the people and their economy.

The historical narrative in our companion volume *The History of Water in the Land Once Called Palestine* opened in the twilight of the Ottoman era and traced the development and use of water resources through the Mandate and

Independence periods, and through the Occupation up to Oslo and after. Now in the present volume we take the neutral concept of water security – security of water resources and services and the ability to manage risks to the resource – to look at the status of Israeli water security today, and at the current water insecurity of Palestinians. The huge gap between the two peoples then drives the analysis and the argument of the final part of the book which explores options for bringing the water security of Palestinians up to the level enjoyed by Israelis – *and without compromising Israelis' own hard-won water security.*

Five principles for action

A century ago, in the dusk of the Ottoman era and at the time of the creation of Mandate Palestine, the water resources of the land were little exploited. There had been scant investment to develop the waters of the aquifers that underlay the hills and the coastal plain, or the springs and streams that ran down either side of the north to south watershed, or all the waters of the Jordan basin from above Lake Tiberias right down to the lowest sink on earth, the Dead Sea.

Today, a hundred years on, almost every last drop of these waters has been developed. The Israelis have the lion's share and have developed absolutely world-beating water services. The Palestinians have a rather negligible share and have water services that in some cases rival the worst in the world.

The purpose of this book is to examine in detail the gap in water security between the two peoples, and to explore options for rebalancing that will strengthen Palestinian water security while not diminishing that of Israel.

In the first two parts of this book (Parts I and II) we look in detail at how water secure the Israelis have made themselves, and at the corresponding water insecurity of the Palestinians, both in the West Bank and in Gaza. In the third part (Part III), we explore options for change and for cooperation between Israelis and Palestinians based on five water management principles which we suggest are axiomatic:

First, *the basis for sharing a common water resource should be spelled out clearly and fairly amongst the parties.* Here we suggest that the riparians of a transboundary resource take into account all relevant factors and circumstances, including the physical characteristics of the resource, who has physical access, where does the water come from and flow to, or, in the case of an aquifer, where is the recharge, where is the outflow, where can it most economically be tapped; the level of dependence on the resource of any one segment of the population; the availability of alternatives for each party, and the cost and affordability of those alternatives; the degree of autonomy of water resources that access could provide; and the social and economic needs of each party, not only lifeline or basic needs but the amount of water needed to develop a modern economy.

Second, *arrangements for sharing and developing the resource should be economically efficient.* Where possible, investment should be optimized at the basin scale and infrastructure should exploit economies of scale. The valuation of water should reflect its marginal value, which would be much greater in the socio-economy of the water scarce, and should take account of the relative affluence or poverty of the parties. The poorer people should not, other things being equal, be required to exploit the most costly resource.[15]

Third, arrangements should *respect the water security of both parties and should allow for cooperation on an equal footing*. Where possible and relevant, as in the case of the Jordan Valley, cooperation should include other riparians.

Fourth, arrangements for future water management should be constructed on the basis of *best practices in basin management, integrated water resource management and environmental sustainability*. An important part of this should be to ensure the sustainability of the shared resource in terms of both quantity and quality, and the protection of the ecological setting and the broader environment. Where options are energy intensive and have a high carbon footprint, as with desalination, consideration should be given to renewables, particularly to solar energy.

Finally, arrangements should allow *rational, least-cost development of water infrastructure*. Where possible, infrastructure should provide for an integrated joined-up system of water conveyance from source to the point of use, and allow for the collection, treatment and reuse of wastewater.[16]

Part I

WATER SECURITY FOR ISRAELIS

Chapter 1

THE THREE COMPONENTS OF ISRAELI WATER SECURITY[1]

Although Israel is a small country with scant natural resources, it has achieved a remarkable degree of water security. This security drives a dynamic modern economy that has carried Israel high in the ranks of developed countries. The water resources Israel has come to control are adequate to supply water to households, industry and a thriving agricultural sector. By dint of astute planning and management, technological and institutional innovation and massive investment, the country has been able to bring assured and adequate water supplies to everywhere in the country. Unparalleled performance on wastewater treatment and reuse has recovered and reused almost all wastewater and so almost closed the urban water circuit.

Research, development and now huge investment in desalination have increased water availability – at the time of writing (2020) desalination supplies over four fifths of domestic urban water consumption and two fifths of the country's total water consumption. The adjacent unbounded sea and abundant offshore energy reserves open the prospect of almost limitless future water resources and secure water autonomy.

Water services to households, industry and agriculture are provided through an integrated nationwide grid that can flow water from Tiberias in the far north to the Negev in the south. Demand management through technology and pricing has made all uses and users of water highly efficient. A policy of charging full cost for water services has sharpened incentives to water saving and underwritten the financial viability of the service providers. Water productivity and efficiency in agriculture are world-beating, thanks to technological advances like drip irrigation, to commercialization and to a switch to high-value crops.

Despite the evident maturity of Israel's water economy and infrastructure and the high degree of security of water resources and services, risks remain. Underwritten by the prospect of 'creating' all the water the country could need through desalination, Israel's risk management is a combination of far-sighted planning to protect existing resources against both climatic and geopolitical risks, and continued promotion of innovation and investment.

One negative consequence of Israel's success in water security has been the damage to the environment – the fall in the water table of the Mountain Aquifers and the related drying up of streams where sewage and rubbish took the place of seasonal freshwater flows, the overpumping of the coastal groundwater wells and the intrusion of saltwater into the aquifer, the dangerous drop in levels of Lake Tiberias and the consequent risk that the precious resource will become increasingly salinized, the parlous state of the lower Jordan River, now a filthy drain, the newly moribund, shrinking Dead Sea.

The retreat of the spectre of water scarcity has today allowed Israelis to turn their attention to the restoration and protection of this bruised water-related ecology and environment. Within Israel a new environmental awareness has prompted the start of clean-up of the polluted streams. Efforts at reviving the ecology of the Jordan River require cooperation across frontiers and a start has been made on this. Protection of the environment requires cooperation with the Palestinians, but there are continuing political impediments to this and, at the moment, it is largely cross-border NGOs which are active.

The institutional support for Israel's remarkable performance in the water sector is equally striking, although characterized by what might appear to be quite contradictory policies. On the one hand, policy since the foundation of the state has been nationalization of water resources and services. On the other hand, Israel has one of the most privatized and commercially minded water industries in the world. This unique combination of public interest and private business has brought huge capital investment, promoted innovation and entrepreneurship, and developed a large and thriving export business in water technology.

It may be that Israel's current water security might just begin to saw away at the Gordian Knot that binds up the water issues between Israelis and Palestinians. Could it open up the possibility of a new cooperation on water with Palestinians, as it has already done for cooperation with Jordan? Will the logic that environmental protection requires cross-border cooperation drive a new understanding between Israelis and Palestinians? These possibilities will be explored in the third part of this book.

* * *

Achieving water resource security in Israel

Our conquest in water was like winning a second war of independence.

Ori Yogev, senior Israeli civil servant, quoted by Siegel[2]

Israel faces three considerable natural impediments to water security. One is the limited natural water resource which poses challenges in simply sourcing enough water for human consumption and for the development of the economy. The second is variability of the resource between seasons and between years which raises challenges of how to store water economically until it is needed and of how to mitigate the risks of prolonged drought. Finally, geographical imbalance – water is needed throughout the country, but the bulk of the natural resource is at its northernmost tip.

This chapter assesses how Israel has faced up to these challenges and by dint of a long national effort has achieved water security on all three criteria: *water resource security, security of water services* and *security from water-related risks*. In this first part of the chapter, we seek to assess how far Israel has achieved security of water resources by first examining the institutions the state has set up for the governance and management of water resources. We then discuss the wide range of often highly innovative measures Israel has deployed to protect and increase its natural water endowment.[3]

Water governance in Israel

Water belongs to the nation[4] The very high value that the Zionists had always placed on water since the earliest migrations in the nineteenth century was reflected after the foundation of the state of Israel by the early nationalization of the resource. This move not only reflected the culture of common property that had from the outset characterized the Zionists' approach to settling and working the land. It also reflected a far-sighted understanding that water was so scarce and so valuable a resource that decisions on its development, allocation and use were better taken by a wise government rather than by a myriad of users.

As a result, water was progressively brought into public ownership during the first decade after independence. A first law, in 1955, imposed regulation on the precious groundwater resource, which was at the time the main source of water. Experience in other countries was already showing that leaving groundwater development and management to farmers, industries and households led to competitive overpumping. The risk increased with the advent of the tube well and powerful electric pumps that allowed well owners to drill deeper and extract much more water. Israel acted early enough to prevent this anarchic development. Under the 1955 law, a licence was needed for all groundwater development, quotas were allocated and all extraction was to be metered and controlled. A second law, in 1957, extended regulation to all other water sources – springs and surface water flows, rainwater and rainwater harvesting, and even to the collection, treatment and reuse of wastewater. No diversion of any water source was allowed without a permit, and water quotas and use were subject to check and control. Finally, the comprehensive Water Law of 1959 declared water to be the property of the nation and all private rights were extinguished.

This nationalization was innovative mainly in that it was effective. The notion of water belonging to a nation and being held in trust is a common one. Many countries have legislation that imposes state ownership and control over water resources in this way, and central control of water resources has been practiced by states in the Middle East since the beginning of history. In Israel, however, there were several differences. The first was that, whereas in most countries a whole baggage of inherited laws, property rights and practices obscured the situation, Israel as a brand-new state could readily declare *tabula rasa* and start over, and the approach had considerable support at least from the Jewish inhabitants who had a sense of common property and common effort that had characterized the Zionist settlement process. This general support contributed to broad respect for the law and encouraged compliance with it. The views of the Palestinian Arabs, who had been dispossessed of their land and now saw any chance of claiming water rights extinguished, would certainly have been very different.[5]

A second difference from laws of common ownership of water resources in other countries was that control was asserted and effective over *all* water resources, not just over surface water but also over the Protean groundwater resource and over traditional resources like rainwater, as well as over non-conventional resources like wastewater. Important, too, was the effectiveness of the Israeli administration in implementing the law. A final, important difference was that Israel matched provision for centralized control with an infrastructure plan that essentially gave the state perfect capability to exercise that control.

As a result of its nationalization of water, Israel was able to plan, invest in and manage its water cycle centrally. Water management in Israel became completely centralized. Seth Siegel[6] quotes Uri Shani, former head of the Israel Water Authority (IWA): 'We govern the whole cycle of water, from the first drop to final use.' There is a unified national approach to water, with a single national utility, Mekorot, and a single integrated infrastructure system organized around the National Water Carrier (discussed herein). Access to water is available to all, limited only by price, and nationwide water tariff schedules apply to households and businesses across the entire country.

The notion of water as a national resource is embedded in social attitudes. This 'all-in-it-together' sentiment supports a common water-saving culture and even the idea that water is emblematic of the strengthening and expansion of the state of Israel and of its achievements. Water is, in many ways, a source of national pride and – it must be admitted – water is seen by Israelis as an indication of superiority over other nations which, facing the same water constraints, have failed to achieve the same measure of water security. Seth Siegel appositely quotes Professor Arnon Soffer: 'With water, collective ownership is one of the reasons why we are able to be a villa in a surrounding jungle.'[7] At the level of political economy, Israel has been able to make a social compact in water: surrender of power and ownership to the state in return for guaranteed quality services. The trade-off is clear: that Israelis have consented to give government power to manage water, regulate prices and allocate water in exchange for water security.[8]

Sound, independent institutions[9] At the apex of Israel's water institutions stands the Israel Water Authority (IWA). The germ of this body lay in the 1959 Water Law which provided for a Water Commission headed by a water commissioner, responsible for planning and regulation of all water activities. However, one drawback with this arrangement soon emerged – the Commission came under political jurisdiction, first of the Ministry of Agriculture – which naturally oriented water investment and supply towards farming – and later of the Ministry of Infrastructure, which had an engineering and water supply bias.[10]

Eventually, the government decided to keep politics out and to reorient the Water Commission so that it could take a long-term view independent of sectoral or political interests. Hence, in 2006, the Water Law was amended and the Commission was re-established as an autonomous government agency, the Israel Water Authority, combining planning and regulatory responsibilities for the entire water sector (water resources management, potable water and sanitation, wastewater treatment and irrigation) with full powers to plan and regulate the water sector without political interference. Other regulatory bodies which previously existed in the water and sanitation sectors were absorbed into the IWA.[11]

Water infrastructure and bulk water supply are the responsibilities of Mekorot. Mekorot (which means *Sources* in Hebrew) had been established in 1937 during the Mandate period. In today's Israel, it is responsible for water infrastructure development, bulk water supply, desalination and wastewater treatment. In a set of reforms in 2007 designed to improve the efficiency of the water sector, Mekorot was corporatized and transformed into a regulated public company. It has been successful in operating with this new status. It has a strong balance sheet, with a AAA credit rating in the United States and sound operating results. Annual turnover is in excess of the equivalent of $1 billion. Sound finances have enabled it to borrow an average of the equivalent of $300 million a year for investment over the last decade.[12]

The infrastructure that Mekorot manages is vast and complex. In addition to the works to extract water from Lake Tiberias and the management of the National Water Carrier (discussed herein), the company also runs over 2,500 pump stations and 1,200 wells as well as more than 100 large earth reservoirs.[13] Mekorot has entered into a number of international partnerships for developing water resources and supply in foreign countries, including India, Cyprus and Uganda.[14]

Integrated water management supported by infrastructure and knowledge

Israel's pioneering water planners were faced with a massive water management challenge. Water resources were very limited and geographically concentrated, but water was needed throughout the country. The main resource – Lake Tiberias – was in the extreme north of the country, so the question was how to ensure the supply of water to all points of demand. In particular, how to bring water to the main towns along the coast? How to supply the desert south of the country where the new state had set both strategic and food production objectives which required the development of population centres and irrigated agriculture?

The answer was first, as we have seen, to nationalize all the water resources that the nation controlled,[15] and to manage them in an integrated way, allocating water both according to demand and in line with government policy. This approach required an infrastructure to realize it and the decision was taken to construct the National Water Carrier (NWC).[16] By 1964, this giant pipeline connected all major water resources, and in particular the water of Tiberias and the lion's share of the water from the Mountain Aquifers, to points of use throughout the country. The NWC allowed water to be stored until it was required and then despatched throughout the country to the point of demand. Subsequently, the system was completed by conveyance infrastructure branching off to points of use in all corners of the country.

A separate line was constructed in 1989 to convey treated wastewater from the Tel Aviv area to supply irrigated agriculture in the Negev. More recently, the NWC has been extended by 100 kilometres of 2–2.5-metre diameter pipeline to convey 'new' water from the five desalination plants along the coast. The last branch, a new pipeline to Jerusalem, will be in place by 2021. In 2019 a decision was also taken to construct a second pipeline between Tiberias and the coast – but this time to carry water back up to replenish the lake.[17]

Connecting almost the entire country, with the exception of Eilat, this complex web of water infrastructure today conveys 95 per cent of Israel's natural and desalinated water from all sources to the regional providers that supply end users (domestic, industrial, agriculture). Despatching of water through the 12,000 kilometres of transmission pipelines is controlled from ten main command centres across the country, with very low losses – about 3 per cent. This water transmission infrastructure has been the basis for Israel's astute and provident management of the water resources it controls. National ownership of the resource allows government to conceive a rational strategy for water allocation and the infrastructure allows that strategy to be implemented. Depending on hydrological conditions and on demand, water can be stored, released and despatched throughout the country as it is required. The infrastructure has also allowed the seamless incorporation of the two new resources – treated wastewater and desalinated water – into water management.

The efficient management of this infrastructure is based on knowledge of the resource and of patterns of supply and demand. Israel has two competent agencies for collecting the necessary comprehensive and timely data. The Hydrological Services Unit within the Israel Water Authority monitors long-term trends, collecting, analysing and modelling water data and detecting trends in hydrology, and setting out the scheme of allocation of natural, recycled and desalinated water to remain within sustainable limits. Mekorot collects, analyses and interprets data on a day-to-day basis in order to manage allocations across the network.

Making the most of natural water resources

On the supply side, Israel has used multiple ways to maximize its natural water resources. These ways include conventional means like rainwater harvesting and the construction of hill dams as well as innovative technologies in groundwater management. Early in its existence, the new state developed a series of check dams that captured seasonal run-off and spate flows in the many wadis that run from the mountains to the sea. The objective was not to store water but to promote infiltration and so increase the volume of groundwater available for subsequent use. Recharge volumes vary enormously with precipitation patterns. The maximum recorded was 62 million cubic metres in 1980, a substantial contribution to the national water budget. In a lean year, the contribution may be negligible – the drought year of 1990 yielded only 4 million cubic metres. It has been estimated that recharge promoted in this way averages 8 per cent over and above natural replenishment.[18] A further contribution to infiltration is provided by Israel's afforestation programme, which has increased tree cover from 2 per cent of the country in 1948 to 8 per cent.[19]

A significant innovation has been Israel's systematic use of rechargeable aquifers as reservoirs. When Israel established its integrated water supply system in the 1960s, it relied on the storage capacity of Lake Tiberias and the Mountain Aquifers to balance supply and demand throughout the year. More recently, as desalinated water and treated wastewater have been added to the mix, Mekorot has devised more complex mechanisms to store water until it is needed. The countrywide network based on the NWC allows water to be stored when aggregate or local demand is less than supply and then drawn down when demand increases. The reservoir of choice for this is the aquifer as it is more reliable and much cleaner than surface storage and has virtually zero losses to evaporation.

Groundwater aquifers are thus used not just as sources of supply but as rechargeable reservoirs, typically drawn down in hot, dry summers and recharged in the wet season. They may also hold water over from wetter years to subsequent dry years. The water can then be pumped out into the NWC when it is needed. Groundwater has always served as a reserve and as a buffer against dry spells. Israeli recharge techniques have expanded these roles and have also eliminated the problem of evaporation which bedevils surface storage in hot dry climates.[20]

Management of aquifers as reservoirs is, however, a tricky business and requires close measurement, monitoring and management. Groundwater levels are measured in 1,500 wells across Israel. Some of these wells are regular pumping wells; others are specifically observation wells drilled for monitoring purposes. The data is uploaded to a central database. Each aquifer requires its own dedicated operating rules, but the management of all the aquifers is coordinated with the management of other sources. For example, the principal surface reservoir – Lake Tiberias – can support only a 4-metre difference in its water level. Below that level – the Red Line – saline springs will intrude and permanently damage the resource.[21] Hence, aquifer operations have to complement the drawdown or filling of the lake, releasing water to the NWC if no more water can be drawn from the lake, or storing Tiberias water if levels in the lake are too high and there is a risk of spilling water downstream into the Jordan River. Aquifer management along the coast also has to ensure that there is enough fresh water maintained in the aquifers to prevent the intrusion of saline water from the sea that would impair the quality of the groundwater.

Advanced techniques are used for groundwater recharge. Israel has developed technologies of recharge, both injection through wells drilled for the purpose, and surface spreading where water is flooded into a basin to infiltrate into the aquifer. Economic analysis shows that when water of potable quality is used for recharge, well injection is better than surface spreading as it does not require scarce land and the losses to evaporation are virtually zero. For lower-quality water, however, surface spreading may be preferred, as the slow percolation through soil, sand and rock can do much to cleanse impurities.[22]

Desalination as a means of 'creating' new water[23]

One area where Israel has emerged as a world leader is in desalination. For almost two decades it has been Israel's official policy to develop desalination as the basic source of water for household and industrial use. The rationale is twofold: to develop what is an almost limitless source of water to remove the spectre of water shortages; and to manage the risk to conventional water supplies from climatic variability or geopolitical threats.

What is desalination – and why is it expanding fast?[24] Desalination removes salt from water, typically for municipal or industrial uses. Desalinated water is produced either from brackish water[25] or from seawater, which typically has a salt content of between 30 to 50 grams per litre. The world's oceans contain over 97 per cent of the planet's water resources and thus provide an essentially unlimited raw material for seawater desalination.

There are two main desalination methods: thermal and membrane. Thermal desalination is a process of boiling and evaporating saltwater and condensing the resulting vapour. The two commonly used thermal processes are multistage flash distillation (MSF) and multiple effect distillation (MED). Both work in a similar way as an evaporation process, with the saline water passing through a series of chambers, with each successive chamber operating at a progressively lower pressure. By contrast, membrane methods adapt the natural process of osmosis, with reverse osmosis (RO) the most commonly used form. Membrane technologies can also be used for treating wastewater.

Typically, desalinated water is much more expensive than natural water. Despite significant reductions over the years, the costs of desalination are almost always higher than the costs of obtaining fresh water from rivers or groundwater, water recycling, water conservation and even water transfer between basins. Desalination is typically the option of last resort, essentially for markets that require high-quality water and complete reliability of service and where customers can afford to pay the higher cost. Desalination thus suits the needs of large cities where there are high concentrations of people who demand a quality 24/7 water service and who are prepared to pay for that service. Desalination can also provide a reliable supply of large volumes of water to high-value industry, commerce and tourism. In these uses, demand is going up in pace with incomes, demographics and urbanization. It is also in these uses that the value of water is typically the highest and where there is the highest willingness to pay. Desalination is also of specific interest in certain locations where the alternatives are also high cost or where the risk of supply failure is high.

Desalination is, however, demanding in terms of location. Water has a very high ratio of bulk to value and is very expensive to lift or transport. This drives the location of a desalination plant – it should be near to its raw material, the sea; it should be close to its market or point of use; and it should be not too far in altitude below its market, as pumping up to heights is very expensive indeed. Hence, the typical location of a desalination plant is alongside a coastal city or coastal industrial zone. In these locations, desalination can supply a relatively well-off industrial, commercial and domestic demand. In fact, already over one third of the world's population lives in suitable locations – in urban centres bordering the ocean. In many arid parts of the world such as the Middle East, Australia, Northern Africa and Southern California, the population concentration along the coast exceeds 75 per cent.

Desalination is also an excellent tool of risk management. With unlimited raw material – the ocean – desalination is drought-proof and it is an excellent way to deal with climate change risks. Desalination is also a good response to exogenous risks such as dependence on other jurisdictions for water supply. It can bolster self-sufficiency and procure water autonomy for a city or territory where this is politically or economically important. Singapore, for example, opted for large-scale desalination to reduce its dependence on increasingly expensive water imported from Malaysia. The stable, efficient supplies of urban and industrial water that desalination provides can help governments to manage a range of economic, social and political risks. Where the physical and socio-economic conditions are right, seawater desalination provides a strategic solution for the sustainable, long-term satisfaction of a particular segment of water demand.

Increasing global interest in desalination – and its rising feasibility and use With growing water scarcity, interest in desalination has risen in recent decades. Large-scale interest started in a few rich but very water-short states, particularly in countries of the Gulf Cooperation Council (GCC), where the availability of low-cost energy also facilitated adoption. Driven by rising demand and commercial innovation, the cost of desalination has decreased significantly over the years. As a result, desalination is becoming an increasingly feasible option, with a growing number of plants around the world (see Figure 1.1). In 2018, 18,426 desalination plants were reported to be in operation in over 150 countries, producing 87 million cubic metres of clean water each day and supplying over 300 million people.[26] Almost half this capacity (44 per cent) is in the still-growing Middle East market, but other regions are expanding even faster, notably Asia (and in particular China), the United States and Latin America.

Desalination in Israel

Israel has invested heavily in desalination Israel has been enormously successful in its efforts to increase its water security from natural resources in the region – resources not only within the state itself but those of the Jordan basin and Mountain Aquifers. But from early on it was apparent that more might be needed. Even with the extra supplies from Lake Tiberias that were coming on stream through the NWC in the 1960s, water demand for the burgeoning economy and population was outstripping the limits of the natural supply. The search for new sources and supplies – both conventional and unconventional – was on. A number of alternatives for increasing the potable supply were considered, including water

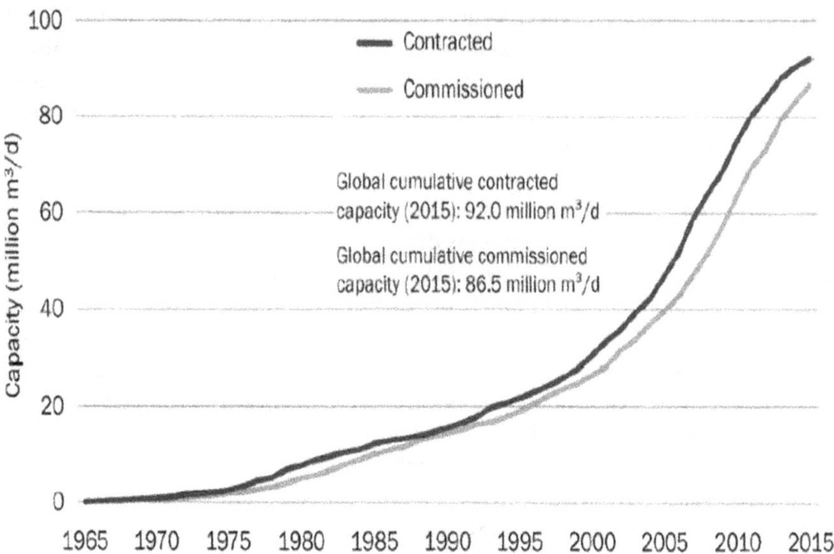

Figure 1.1 Global cumulative installed contracted and commissioned desalination capacity, 1965–2015. *Source*: GWI Desaldata / IDA, 2015.

imports from the Turkish 'water terminal' at the mouth of the Manavgat River.[27] But in the vulnerable geopolitical environment, sources within Israel's immediate control offered the most chance of security of water supplies. Thoughts turned to seawater desalination, the new technology that could actually create water from a boundless raw material under Israel's immediate control.

Interest in desalination began very early on. Even before the foundation of the state of Israel, Zionists showed interest in its potential. According to Shimon Peres, David Ben-Gurion, Israel's first prime minister, talked constantly about the idea of turning seawater into fresh water[28] and Ben-Gurion's diaries are full of references to the 'scientific prospects and societal implications' of desalination.[29] As early as the 1960s, Israel sought a technical and financial partnership with the United States to develop the technology. This bore fruit in 1964 when President Johnson and the Israeli prime minister Levi Eshkol made an agreement to cooperate on desalination.[30] Seth Siegel quotes LBJ as saying: 'Mr Prime Minister. you told me . . . that water was blood for Israel. So we shall make a joint attack on Israel's water shortage through the highly promising technique of desalting. Indeed, let us hope that this technique will bring benefit to all the peoples of the parched Middle East.' He agreed that the United States would 'help Israel on this [desalination proposal] as much as possible'.[31] Subsequently, Johnson appointed George Woods, who had been the first president of the World Bank, to lead talks on desalination with Israel.[32]

Beginning with a trial plant in the mid-1980s, Israel became a desalination pioneer. This first plant, at Ashdod, was co-financed by a US grant and used the thermal multiple effect distillation (MED) technology. Subsequently, work in Israel and elsewhere on seawater reverse osmosis (SWRO) developed this technology to the point where it has become the technology of choice for certain conditions, particularly for temperate and not too turbid or dirty waters.[33]

In the early 2000s, the government made the strategic decision to develop desalination plants on a large scale. Despite applying all the improved management, technological innovation and conservation measures for conventional water resources that it could muster, Israel saw demand continuing to rise and a gap between supply and demand threatened to emerge. No new supply sources were available and Israel was heavily overdrawing on both the Coastal Aquifer and the Mountain Aquifers.[34] There were also fears of threats to existing supplies from climate change. In addition, the government had a regional strategic objective – to eliminate any possibility that geopolitical threat to the precious resources of the Jordan Valley and Lake Tiberias would interrupt Israel's water supply. With these factors driving policy, the government decided that the bulk of water for household and industrial use would in future come from desalinated water. The view was that this would ensure the water resources component of water security.

In fact, Israel well fitted the profile for adopting desalination – water scarce and vulnerable but with a high-income population and profitable industry and commerce located largely along the seaboard. The main stumbling block was cost, particularly energy cost which makes up as much as half to two thirds of the cost of desalination. However, the opportune discovery of offshore gas reserves from 1999 offered the prospect both of greater energy security and of lower costs of desalination.

Government's strategic decision prompted investment and the subsequent development of five further desalination plants, all of which use the seawater reverse osmosis (SWRO) technology. These plants have been built along the Mediterranean coast, with a total capacity of 585 million cubic metres per year (see Table 1.1). In the process, Israel has become a world leader in seawater reverse osmosis technology which is now used for almost two thirds of desalination capacity worldwide. Seeing the commercial potential of this, the Israeli government established a company to market the technology overseas. This company, IDE, which built and currently also manages three of the plants in Israel, has now constructed more than 300 desalination plants around the world.[35]

Israel is not stopping there. In 2018 the government decided on construction of a further, even larger, plant at Sorek, together with an associated dedicated power plant. When completed in 2023, the plant will provide 200 million cubic metres of desalinated water each year, even more than the present plant which produces 150 million cubic metres. Tenders were also expected to be launched in 2020 for a seventh plant, in Western Galilee, to produce 100 million cubic metres annually.[36]

The benefits of desalination in Israel Desalination has had a transformative effect on Israel's water sector – and beyond. Israel now produces every day nearly 2 million cubic metres of desalinated water, which meets over three quarters of the country's domestic water needs and accounts for 40 per cent of the country's total water consumption.[37] This flexible and expanding source not only directly supplies

Table 1.1 Major Seawater Desalination Plants in Israel

Project	Year of operation	O&M duration	Concessionaires	Business model	Price per m^3 (US$)	Production capacity (million m^3)	Estimated capex (US$billion)
Ashkelon	2005	25 years	IDE (50%) Oaktree (50%)	BOT	0.78	119	0.27
Palmachim	2007	25 years	Derech HaYam (100%)	BOO	0.86	90	0.16
Hadera	2010	25 years	IDE (50%), Shikun U'Binui (50%)	BOT	0.72	127	0.43
Sorek	2013	25 years	IDE (50%), Veolia (50%)	BOT	0.54	150	0.41–0.54
Ashdod	2016	25 years	Mekorot (100%)	BOT	0.65	100	0.41–0.54

Source: *World Bank 2017, drawing on:* (a) The Israeli Desalination Sector, Internal Research Paper by Variance-Ascola Economic Consulting, Tel Aviv, March 2017; (b) Ministry of Finance of Israel website, http://www.mof.gov.il/, Jerusalem, Feb. 2017; (c) Financing Projects of Desalination in Israel, Midroog Credit Rating Agency, Tel Aviv, 2012; (d) Global Issues in Water Policy: Desalination in Israel-Erica Spiritos and Clive Lipchin, Springer Dordrecht Heidelberg New York London, January 2013, (e) The National Inquiry Commission on water management in Israel, Government of Israel, Jerusalem, 2009; (f) Annual Report of Water Authority Activity, Israel Water Authority, Tel Aviv, 2015.

Note: BOO = build-own-operate; BOT = build-operate-transfer; capex = capital expenditure; O&M = operations and maintenance.

Figure 1.2 The Ashkelon desalination plant, with permission from IDE Israel.

municipal, industrial and domestic customers but also underwrites supplies to agriculture and nature as well as to Jordan under the 1994 peace treaty. Desalination effectively consolidates the water resource component of Israel's water security and ensures its water autonomy.[38] Today, with the apparently limitless possibilities of desalination, Israel has achieved self-sufficiency and access to any extra water it may need in the future. Siegel quotes Ilan Cohen, the former director general of the prime minister's office: 'Desalination means you don't have to rely on others. Important for us as long as we are surrounded by enemies.'[39]

Desalination also proofs Israel against any climatic changes that affect its other sources. This is important because it is likely that climate change will bring hotter, drier weather to the region, and greater uncertainty in the timing and quantity of rainfall which will affect the volume of groundwater and streamflow. Higher temperatures and increased aridity will also increase demand from both agriculture and households. Shimon Tal, the former Israeli water commissioner,[40] says that desalination prepares Israel to withstand a long drought. 'We have gotten ahead of the climate change question', he says, predicting an end to the threat of drought or water shortages. So far advanced is this thinking, says Shimon Tal, that

> another recent decision (2019) stemming from lessons from the last five drought years, is to build a pipeline that can convey desalinated water to [Lake Tiberias] from south to north, as opposed to the traditional flow from north to south. It will be done during long and severe droughts, but we expect to use this system more often since the effect of global warming on natural water resource in the watershed of the lake.[41]

There are also some water-quality benefits from desalination. Levels of sodium, chlorides, nitrates and industrial contaminants in the aquifer water which was previously the main potable water source have been on the rise with agricultural and industrial development. The desalination process removes not only salt but also most other minerals. As a result, desalination has reduced the overall salt and nitrate content in Israel's drinking water.[42] On the downside, a recent study found some links between use of desalinated water and iodine deficiency.[43]

Why seawater desalination in Israel is low cost The five recent SWRO desalination plants have achieved good performance in terms of efficiency and cost. The ex-plant price of desalinated water started low and has dropped with each subsequent plant – from US$0.78 per cubic metre in the first Ashkelon plant commissioned in 2005 (see Table 1.1) down to only US$0.54 per cubic metre in the 2013 plant, Sorek (which is also the largest one).[44] Israel's prices for desalinated water are now amongst the lowest in the world. For plants constructed worldwide over the last two decades, the average cost of water produced (in constant 2016 US$) was around US$1.40 per cubic metre for thermal plants and, depending on location, between US$0.98 per cubic metre and US$1.38 per cubic metre for SWRO plants.[45] The low prices achieved by Israel have been key to ensuring the financial viability of the whole system. Desalinated water remains affordable for customers despite Israel applying full-cost recovery through tariffs.

There are several key determinants of desalination cost, and Israel has benefitted from some – and taken advantage of others through strategic choices. Costs for SWRO have been dropping fast everywhere, largely due to advances in membrane technology. By using the latest technologies – some of it developed within Israel – Israel has been able to reduce production costs which a decade ago were still averaging over US$1.00 per cubic metre to very near to half that. Energy costs have been dropping, too, as new technologies in pre-treatment, filter design and energy recovery have reduced energy consumption per unit of water by a factor of ten since the 1970s.

Israel has also benefitted from the location of its plants close to both the sea and water demand. As we said earlier, the cost of water transfer is very high and desalination plants are best sited not only right next to their raw material, seawater, but also close to large centres of demand. All of Israel's plants are right on the sea, and are adjacent to the NWC which conveys the water over the short distance to the concentrations of population and business along Israel's crowded coastline.

A further location benefit is the quality of the Mediterranean feedwater. The costs of SWRO technology are sensitive to salinity and turbidity, and to both temperature levels and temperature variability. Situated on the relatively low-salinity Mediterranean, which is also relatively cool and has relatively low suspended solids, Israel is able to produce desalinated water at considerably lower investment and O&M cost than are incurred in warmer, saltier, more turbid environments.[46]

Size – and operating mode – matter One key factor in achieving low prices in Israel is the large size and 24/7 operational mode of the plants. Desalination plants are most economic when they are large – because there are considerable economies of scale – and when they operate full time at maximum capacity, The integrated nature of Israel's water system within a small, densely populated territory means that a few very large plants could be sited at intervals along the coast and feed into the NWC which conveys the water to population centres countrywide. The decision to make desalinated water the primary source of municipal and industrial water means that demand is constantly high and the plants could usually be operated 24/7 and close to full capacity.[47] Thus the large size and the continuous operation allow the Israeli plants to achieve significant economies of scale and to absorb large fixed costs, which in turn contributes to low unit costs.

Project delivery method Israel's plants were largely built and are run by the private sector. Four of the plants were developed through public–private partnerships (PPPs) with private concessionaires under build-operate-transfer (BOT) and build-operate-own (BOO) schemes. The approach was first adopted for the 2005 Ashkelon plant and then for Palmachim (2007), Hadera (2009) and Sorek (2013).[48]

The use of public–private partnerships was a significant factor in low costs. The government opted for this approach because it believed that private know-how would better master the technology and operating challenges and that private business would be able to source finance and construct and run the plants more efficiently. To attract the maximum high-quality competition and to secure private financing on the best possible terms, it was important to design the packages so as to maximize incentives to efficiency for the private sector but also to minimize the level of private sector risk. Design of the proposals needed an experienced and astute negotiating team and the government set up the Water Desalination Administration under the IWA to handle all aspects of desalination public–private partnerships. Over time, the use of the public–private partnership approach has had a significant impact on costs. Today, the growing maturity of Israel as a desalination market and its role as a technological leader have created a high level of confidence and a low perception of risk, which have contributed to some very advantageous deals.

The build-operate-transfer (BOT) approach, which was used for three of the plants (although not for Palmachim), was designed to give incentives to efficiency and low cost. Israel essentially offered a standard BOT package in which the private firm takes responsibility for all capital and operating costs over a twenty-five-year period, after which the plant is handed over to government. In return, government contracts to buy water produced in determined quantities at a fixed price. This approach builds in incentives for the contractor to minimize both capital and subsequent operating costs, with flexibility to make technological choices. All cost overruns are borne by the concessionaire, and there are stiff penalties during operations if the plant does not deliver the contracted amount and quality of water.

In order to reduce costs further, the Israeli government assumed some risks usually borne by the concessionaire and provided more government guarantees to private investors than is typical for such public–private partnership projects. Government contracted to bear any risk of interest rates changing and allowed bidders to propose their own formulae for adjusting prices according to changes in various indexes. In addition, BOT arrangements usually specify a minimum fixed payment to the concessionaire for a fixed minimum volume of water to be delivered. Israel introduced a formula in the tender to allow bidders to optimize the proportion of fixed to variable fees based on their own cost structure, allowing each one to propose its own optimal mix. Finally, and perhaps most importantly, the cost of land was borne by the government, a significant factor given the high cost of land in Israel's coastal areas.[49] These provisions helped Israel to get bid prices for desalinated water that are amongst the lowest in the world, in turn making large-scale access to desalination financially viable.

Bidders also had some flexibility over source and cost of energy. Because energy is such an important component of cost, bidders had a strong incentive to be energy efficient and in fact Israeli plants have proven to be energy efficient.[50] Low energy costs have derived in part from the relatively low price of energy in Israel, which uses gas from fields in the Mediterranean to fire its power plants. In addition, although desalination plants do not benefit from preferential electricity prices from the grid, plants have managed their operations so as to benefit to the maximum from lower off-peak rates. The Sorek plant, for example, uses spurts of off-peak electricity throughout the day and night. In some projects, bidders were given the option to build gas-based power plants to reduce the energy supply cost under a parallel independent power producer contract.

The superiority of public–private partnerships is held to be proven by the poorer results from the most recent large seawater desalination plant, Ashdod, which started operation in 2016. In this case, the build-operate-transfer (BOT) contract was signed not with a private firm but with the public agency Mekorot. Analysts suggest that under this arrangement 'the transfer of risk to an outside private partner that normally takes place under a BOT was not fully effective. This project has experienced major construction delays, cost overruns, and operational problems.'[51]

Another factor in keeping costs down is experience of all partners – of the project promoters, of the administration and of the professionals. Where there is experience on both sides, more competent contract administration and execution lower the need for oversight. It is reported that the total engineering oversight costs for the Sorek project in Israel were fifty times lower than for a similar-sized SWRO plant in Melbourne.[52] This is in part attributed to Israel's long track record and considerable competence, both on the owner's side, with extensive government experience and expertise in developing, financing and regulating desalination projects, and on the project delivery side, with extremely experienced engineers and contractors.

Environmental impact Desalination is not costless from an environmental perspective. There are direct environmental impacts on the marine environment caused by the intake and outlet facilities and by the elevated content of salinity, the high temperature and the residual treatment chemicals in the plant discharge. A particular challenge is disposal of the brine which in the case of reverse osmosis technology is particularly concentrated and requires careful management. Israel has dealt with this by disposing of the brine well out to sea. The Sorek plant, for example, takes the brine back out to sea to an outfall 20 metres below the surface of the Mediterranean, so that the salt is well dispersed and does not affect the ambient salinity.[53] There is, nonetheless, an effect on marine fauna and flora, and the mitigation of this can be very costly. For example, in California the Coastal Commission required the huge Carlsbad project to implement an intake impingement and entrainment mitigation programme, constructing 64 acres of coastal wetland to create a substitute marine habitat and coastal ecosystem. The requirement added 5 per cent to both capital and operating costs. The main indirect environmental impact of desalination is the relatively high carbon footprint from the energy intensity of the process and the consequent emissions.[54]

Wastewater treatment and reuse

Wastewater collection and treatment For a century after modern systems of piped water supply began to spread across urban centres globally, wastewater collection and treatment were the poor relations. Priority was everywhere given to piped water supply. Piped sewerage came a distant second. Only as countries grew richer was wastewater treatment a concern, with the idea of reuse a far-off idea.[55] Today the picture is much changed. There are over 100,000 wastewater treatment plants worldwide, and wastewater reuse is on the agenda of many countries, particularly the arid countries of the Middle East.

In the time of Mandate Palestine, as we saw in *The History of Water*, sanitation was largely rudimentary. After 1948, piped water to households developed rapidly, and piped sewerage was soon engineered in the growing cities. However, for long the sewage collected went untreated. Volumes of sewage rose rapidly. Most wastewater and sewage were discharged raw or at best partially treated to the environment, and there was concern about the impact on the land and marine environment of the dumping of raw sewage. From the 1960s, flows in the streams which run down from either side of the West Bank watershed were largely composed of sewage and untreated wastewater, harming ecological systems and becoming an environmental nuisance and health hazard.

As late as the mid-1980s, only half of Israel's wastewater was treated at all, and most of it only received primary treatment. Israel reacted eventually. Responsibility for pollution control was transferred to the newly established Ministry of the Environment. New standards were set for wastewater treatment. A massive wastewater treatment plant makeover and construction plan began.[56]

A leading preoccupation was the Greater Tel Aviv area, with its large population and high production of domestic and industrial wastewater. Israel's first large modern treatment plant – the Dan Region Centralized Sewage Plant – was completed in 1973 to treat all the wastewater from this agglomeration. Treatment capacity greatly expanded in the 1980s. The large-scale immigration from the former Soviet Union in the early 1990s brought a huge increase in demand for water and, with the consequent increase in supply, the volume of wastewater also rose. Wastewater treatment plants became overloaded, operational problems developed and pollution from wastewater was said to have caused a number of outbreaks of infectious diseases. Popular and political pressure mounted, demanding better wastewater treatment. As a result, Israel invested in significant new capacity. Today, the country has sixty-seven large wastewater treatment plants,[57] including ten very large plants which together treat more than half (56 per cent, 300 million cubic metres) the total volume.

The idea of reusing treated wastewater As treatment expanded and as the water crises that affected the country in the 1980s and 1990s persisted, policy makers and technicians turned their attention to the potential for reuse of treated wastewater. So was born another non-conventional resource. Over time, Israel has come to treat and then reuse almost all of its wastewater, so eking out a precious resource and coming close to a closed urban water system. Wastewater and sewage have gone over the last thirty years from being a waste product discharged raw into the streams and the Mediterranean Sea to being a vital component of the nation's water inventory.

The share of reused treated wastewater has risen from approximately 10 per cent of the 130 million cubic metres of wastewater collected in the early 1960s, to

Figure 1.3 The Shafidan Dan Region Central Sewage Plant, Photograph by courtesy of Igudan.

87 per cent of the 500 million cubic metres collected in 2015. The treated effluent has become a major source of water for farmers, supplying two thirds of the water used in irrigation. According to Siegel, sewage is today a 'treasured national resource' and recycled wastewater is seen by Israelis as a 'valued parallel water system'.[58]

One of the challenges of using treated wastewater in agriculture is that approximately equal volumes are produced every day of the year, but farmers need it only at certain points of the cropping season. Israel has therefore developed an innovative system under which the effluent is treated and then conveyed to storage areas where it is allowed to infiltrate into aquifers until it is needed – for the techniques involved see the section on *Innovation*. When the water is needed, it is pumped out into a separate dedicated 'national wastewater carrier' which conveys the treated effluent to agricultural areas, particularly to the Negev, over 50 miles away from Tel Aviv.[59]

In addition to underground storage, over 400 plastic-lined reservoirs have been constructed around the country for holding treated wastewater. Much of the treatment and reuse is, in fact, local, with regional effluent systems and local distributors of treated wastewater, all of which minimizes the need for costly pumping.[60]

In this way, from being a waste product and environmental and health hazard, wastewater has become a major component of Israel's water resources, with its own dedicated system of storage and distribution (Table 1.2).

Reuse today Israel now treats 95 per cent of its wastewater – only about 5 per cent is still disposed of through on-site systems like septic tanks – and almost all (85 per cent) of the treated wastewater is reused in agriculture. Treated wastewater now accounts for one fifth (20 per cent) of Israel's total water supply and for nearly two thirds (62 per cent) of all the water used in agriculture.[61] These levels of reuse are truly world-beating, well ahead of any other major country. Only tiny urban Singapore achieves 100 per cent reuse, and Cyprus recycles about 70 per cent of its treated wastewater. After that, amongst major countries, Spain is the next best

Table 1.2 Wastewater treatment in Israel (2015)

Treatment plant	Treated effluent 2015	Population (thousands)	Type of treatment
Shafdan	134,188	2,500	Tertiary
Haifa	37,960	550	Secondary(a)
Jerusalem (Sorek)-	33,772	635	Secondary(a)
Ayalon	20,173	358	Secondary(a)
Netanya	15,796	236	Tertiary
Beer Sheva	15,025	256	Secondary(a)
Ashdod	11,544	216	Tertiary
Hadera	10,420	184	Secondary
Kfar Saba – Hod Hasharon	10,145	162	Tertiary
Carmiel	9,508	200	Tertiary

Source: Israel Water Authority 2015. (a) being upgraded to tertiary treatment.

performer globally, with reuse at around just one quarter of wastewater produced. The United States is way behind that, with only one tenth of its wastewater treated and reused.[62] Today, Israel is planning to up the share of wastewater that is reused even further, from 85 per cent to 90 per cent.

Most wastewater must now undergo tertiary treatment. Only plants serving fewer than 5,000 people equivalent can continue to treat to secondary level, except where a supplementary treatment is provided, as in the case of Israel's largest plant, Shafidan (see the section 'Innovation'). Today much of the water is so clean that it can be used for all crops – in fact for anything except drinking – without any risk to public health. Reuse in agriculture is subject to strict health and environmental controls, with comprehensive standards and guidelines developed to ensure that there is no risk either to farmers or to consumers, and no harm to the environment or to aquifers.[63] However, wastewater that has only been treated to secondary level is restricted in its use, limited mainly to inedible crops and, in order to protect groundwater, to certain locations.[64]

Farmers took quite some persuading. Even though water shortages and the effects of changing rainfall patterns and increasing aridity were pressing hard on them, Israeli farmers were reluctant at first to accept what they saw as dirty water. It took education and financial incentives to get them to change their minds. The government did a deal – *take wastewater and your water quota will be increased*: farmers get 20 per cent more wastewater than their old freshwater ration. Prices were lowered too[65] and subsidized, as wastewater treatment is a costly business and storing it underground, pumping it out and then conveying it around the country is very expensive. The tariff recovers only about one third of the capital costs of treatment and storage. Up to 2017, this represented an aggregate investment subsidy of as much as the equivalent of $800 million. Storage is a particular expense, as wastewater is produced and treated every day of the year, but agricultural demand is largely confined to a few months a year.[66]

After a rocky initial ride, farmers became enthusiastic, saying that reclaimed sewage was a more reliable, fixed supply than the old freshwater deliveries, which might be cut in a drought year. The price was a strong incentive, too. Even the water quality, suspect at first, is now seen as an advantage, as the water is rich in nitrogen.[67]

Innovation The largest plant – Shafidan – in fact only treats wastewater to secondary level. Treatment to tertiary level is provided by natural filtration through the soil. The wastewater Shafidan produces is discharged into recharge basins where it naturally filtrates through the sand to an aquifer below. This may take between six and twelve months. The filtration through sand further cleans the water, which is then stored as a source of clean water for agriculture.[68] To separate the treated wastewater from adjacent natural water, an artificial water level depression is created (see Figure 1.4). The resulting 'hydrologic trough' prevents the treated wastewater from spreading. The reclaimed wastewater may stay underground for up to a year, and, when it is required, it is pumped out via peripheral reclamation wells. It is reported that in the hot, dry summer months,

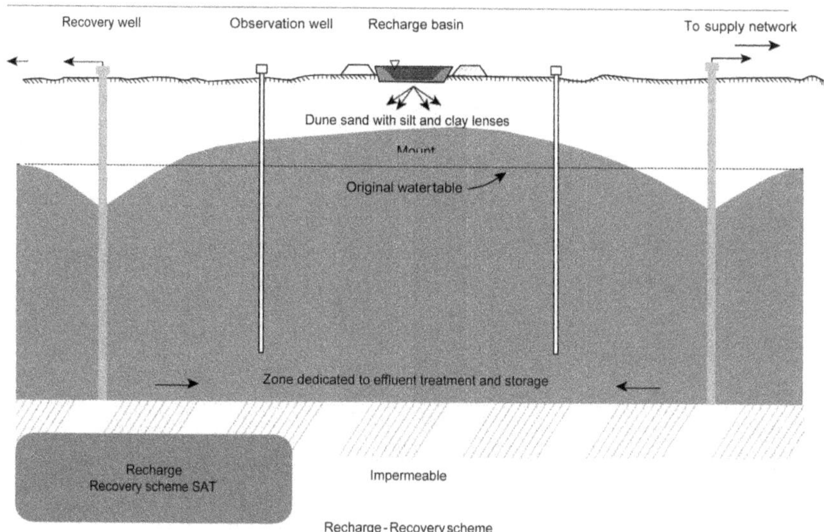

Figure 1.4 Shafidan soil aquifer treatment method, Israel. *Source*: Mekorot 2016; World Bank 2017.

Mekorot may supply farmers in the Negev with more than 130 million cubic metres of this water.

Israeli technological inventiveness and business sense did not stop with simple treatment, storage and reuse. Energy recovery has been progressively built in – the biogas produced in the treatment process now powers almost two thirds (60 per cent) of wastewater plant processing. Costs are also being turned into business lines through recovery of oils and heavy metals from sewage. Even the cellulose is being extracted from the sewage before treatment, reducing the bulk to be treated by almost a third, minimizing sludge and creating value from resale of the cellulose by-product to the pulp and paper industry.[69]

* * *

Managing overall supply of water[70]

Total water supply In the first decades after independence, Israel's total water inventory was composed entirely of natural water. By dint of aggressive development of the aquifers and Lake Tiberias, this inventory increased from around 1.3 BCM in the late 1950s to a peak of over 2.0 BCM once the NWC came on stream – see Figure 1.5. The droughts of the early 1990s produced a crisis; annual water availability plummeted to 1.4 BCM in 1991. It was from this point that innovative sources began to be developed in earnest, first treated wastewater from the late 1980s and then desalinated water from the mid-2000s. The result was remarkable: although these were years of highly erratic rainfall and declining availability of

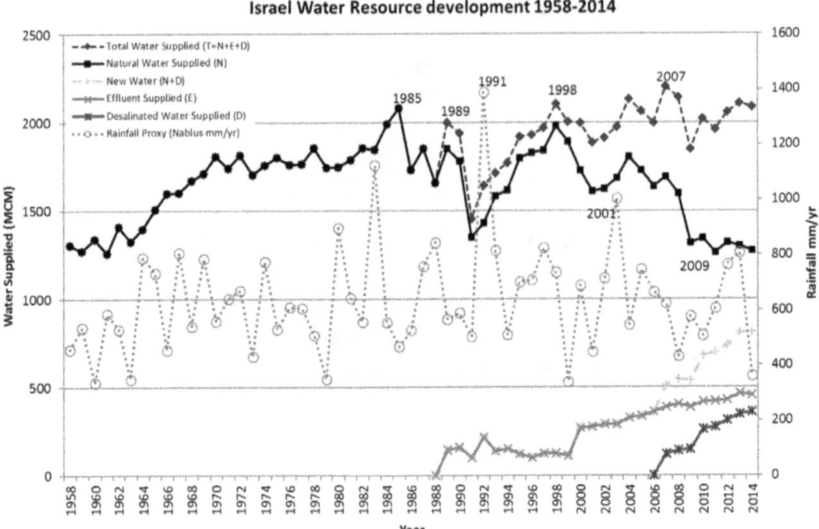

Figure 1.5 Israel's water resource development, 1958–2014. *Source*: WANA 2017, based on Gilmont 2014, with additional data from Israel CBS 2016.

natural water resources, Israel was able to maintain its annual water supply at or above the 2.0 BCM level. At the same time, as we shall see, demand management allowed the satisfaction of the water needs of a fast-growing population and a thriving and vibrant agricultural sector.

Water allocation State ownership and control of water resources combined with the unique national water infrastructure allow Israel to allocate water on an annual basis. Each year the IWA determines the total amount of water available for supply and how much should go to each sector – domestic, industrial, agriculture – and to each geographical area. The Ministry of Agriculture then determines allocations amongst the agricultural regions and the regional agricultural water unions. Domestic uses and industry take priority over agriculture, which is in effect the residual.

In recent years there have been some (minor) allocations to the environment. However, the largest 'environmental allocation' is simply the reduction in the use of natural water. This reduction will, over time, help the replenishment of the aquifers and of Lake Tiberias. Indeed in 2021, the heavy rains of two recent years may even cause water to be spilled from an over-full Tiberias into the lower Jordan River for the first time in twenty-five years.

* * *

It will be clear from this discussion that today Israelis enjoy water resource security – and of a most striking kind – 'natural' fresh water now represents only half of total supply. This achievement is remarkable, unparalleled in the world. We now turn to the question of what use the nation makes of this carefully constituted water resource security to ensure the secure provision of water services to the population and the economy.

Security of water services

This section looks at the ways in which Israel has achieved high standards of supply of water to most domestic, industrial and agricultural users through a mix of institutional, economic and technological measures. It looks first at water supply to domestic uses, and then at water supply to agriculture.

Water supply to domestic consumers

Up until the turn of the century, Israel's municipalities ran water and sanitation services through a plethora of large and small municipal providers. These were of varying standards. Although many were relatively efficient, many were not, and they were generally too small to achieve the economies of scale vital to efficient water and sanitation services. They were not independent of local councils or of local politics, and their finances were mixed up with general municipal finances. The municipalities collected fees – and sometimes used the proceeds elsewhere.

In 2001, government moved to increase efficiency by mandating 'aggregation' of these providers into corporatized regional utilities reporting to their own board of directors. The utilities were to have financial autonomy and to reserve financial surpluses for reinvestment in improving services. Initially, there was considerable reluctance from the municipalities to let go of what some councils saw as a 'cash cow', and, although the utilities were set up, the expected gains in terms of efficiency and quality of service were slow to emerge.

However, from 2009 the utilities came under the regulatory authority of the IWA, which required them to provide an efficient service, including fixing leaks promptly, or face stiff fines.[71] A 'carrot-and-stick' approach rewarded good performers with needed tariff increases, while poor performers were subjected to sanctions. Thereafter, performance improved gradually, although close regulatory supervision from the IWA has been essential and there remains scope for improvement. Essentially, the regionalization of utilities has been successful, but the process has been slow to bear its fruits and is still incomplete more than two decades after the reforms were launched. Nonetheless, the growing efficiency of the providers is a cornerstone of security of water services for most of the population

Who in Israel does not benefit from world-class water supply and sanitation facilities? In contrast to the quality services provided to most of the population, water supply and sanitation services for Israel's minorities trail behind. One fifth of Israel's population is Arab – about 1.9 million people (2019), of whom Moslems, including Bedouin, make up four fifths (82 per cent), the Druze 9 per cent and Christians 9 per cent. A number of towns and villages have a predominantly Arab population – notably Lower Haifa, the city of Nazareth and the Old City of Acre. Inequality in public funding has left a deficit in water and sanitation infrastructure and services for these communities.[72] The Druze in the Golan, most of whom have refused to take Israeli citizenship, experience similar neglect in access to quality water and sanitation services.

Worse affected are Israel's Bedouin minority who number about 170,000 – 110,000 in the Negev, 50,000 in Galilee and about 10,000 in central Israel. The government has moved to settle the Bedouin of the Negev in 'development towns' and about half of the Bedouin live in these towns – described by *The Guardian* as 'sprawling urban dumps',[73] where water and sanitation infrastructure and services are very poor. The other half of the Bedouin population live in what the government terms 'unrecognized villages' which are not connected to the electricity grid or to water or sewerage networks.[74]

Managing demand for domestic water As we have seen, securing water resources was a strategic priority in Israel's early years, and water development was a key element in building the state and the economy. Economics and the thorny questions of water pricing and cost recovery that dog so many poor nations were important but secondary considerations. As this development and state-building phase was completed and Israel began to prosper, the questions of demand management and water pricing became more prominent. Cheap water and implicit subsidies had three drawbacks – there was no incentive for people to save water and fast-rising demand began to place stress on supply sources; revenues were far from covering the running costs of the system – including the very high-energy cost of pumping water up from Lake Tiberias, so that government was having to underwrite the costs; and there was no incentive to innovation or even to efficiency in water supply, as the water utilities received a subsidy to cover their deficits.

Increasing shortages of water, particularly with the protracted drought of 1987–91, came at a time of wholesale immigration and a huge increase in demand for water. Government needed not only to find new supplies but also to restrain demand. As household consumption was a relatively important part of total consumption (about one third of the total), it was an area where savings could make a difference. Several mechanisms to reduce demand were available. For example, more than one third of household water use (35 per cent) in Israel was for flushing, and dual flush systems had the potential to reduce flush use by half, yielding 50 million cubic metres a year saving in household consumption. So, as part of a programme to get householders to reduce domestic water use, the government promoted the installation of water-saving devices in bathrooms, toilets and kitchens. More than half (55 per cent) of all households and public buildings adopted these measures.

However, it was pricing that promoted the greatest water saving. From 2008, a new financial framework was gradually put in place under the direct control of the IWA, which as national water regulator set water tariffs. Tariffs for all users were gradually increased to approach full-cost recovery for the overall water chain, while the regulator set the utilities performance targets for improved efficiency. In the first place this approach was applied to the household sector, where incomes were at a level that people could afford to pay. The average price of water rose by 40 per cent, and a two-tier tariff structure was introduced for potable water and sanitation services. The idea was to give consumers a price incentive to save water. Since 2010, the lower (lifeline) consumption block has been set at 115 litres per person each day, amounting to 3.5 cubic metres per person each month.[75]

At the same time, a media campaign (2008–10) was launched to raise awareness and educate consumers about water use. The campaign was based on the notion that change would happen only if there was buy-in from an informed public. A combination of education and media activities targeted different groups.[76] These measures had a remarkable effect on water saving.[77] Together the campaign and the rise in tariffs were successful in reducing average per capita consumption: overall consumption dropped by 20 per cent, with total domestic consumption down from 750 million cubic metres in 2007 to 650 million cubic metres in 2011. It is estimated that about one third of the reduction was the result of the education campaigns and two thirds the effect of the price hike.[78] However, demand has risen again in recent years. According to a 2018 Knesset report, by 2016 total domestic consumption was up to 809 million cubic metres, with per capita consumption averaging 96 cubic metres (263 lcd).[79] These levels of use are in line with other warm, dry environments in developed countries. In water-stressed Los Angeles, for example, daily domestic water use averages 296 litres per person.[80]

One extra incentive for consumers was a promise that all water revenues would be spent on water infrastructure and service delivery, that the water charges would be ploughed back into improving water services, especially investing in infrastructure and in leak plugging.[81]

Full-cost recovery has also been a prime means of promoting increased efficiency and accountability of the water supply utilities. Prices are regulated so that utilities have incentives to keep costs down and to innovate for greater cost efficiency. Amongst the innovations that this approach promoted has been 'distance meter reading', with cell phone technology used to transmit reports on consumer use every four hours. This has allowed not only reduction in the cost of reading meters but an exceptional ability to profile customer usage and to detect and chronicle leak history. The success of this approach is shown by the extraordinary reduction in 'unaccounted for water' – either losses or thefts. In 2006, unaccounted-for water stood at 16 per cent. By 2013, the level had fallen below 11 per cent. Today the target is 7 per cent.[82]

After many years of reforms and massive investment, the Israeli water sector has now achieved almost full financial autonomy. Almost all the costs of investing and operating the water infrastructure are now paid by users through tariffs.

Water for agriculture

In the early years, food security for the growing population was interpreted as trying to achieve the maximum self-sufficiency in basic food products. Farmers were encouraged to produce lower-value cereals and other commodities for the domestic market rather than high-value crops for export. Cheap water was a prime means to provide the needed incentives. Other motives also drove this impulse to favour agriculture through favourable terms on water: the Zionist concepts of attachment to the land and the pioneer virtues of collaborative effort in agriculture, together with the strategic, demographic and spiritual thinking that sought to people even the driest corners of this new land.

Despite agriculture's central place in the Zionist conception and in Israel's final realization of that conception, the sector was continually threatened by growing water scarcity in the decades after 1948, as towns developed and business and amenity demanded more and more water. The state strove to increase the natural water endowment with resources from the Jordan basin and the Mountain Aquifers but these improvements on the supply side were not enough to sustain and develop Israel's productive and profitable agriculture. As household demand went up and industry and services became ever larger parts of the economy, agriculture was faced with calls to give up water to supply the cities.

Given the importance of agriculture in the national economy and in employment and exports, and its historic role in nation building, letting agriculture shrink was not an option. But as early as the 1960s, Israel made a strategic decision to go for a 'virtual water' approach – to import agricultural produce where the value of water 'embedded' in a crop was low in relation to the crop value, and to use scarce and costly agricultural water within Israel to produce crops that returned the highest value to each drop of water.[83] The strategy provided for import of products like cereals, cotton and even oranges that could be brought in from countries that had more abundant water and lower labour costs. Israel then specialized in products which returned the highest value to each drop of water, for example, off-season vegetables for markets in Europe in winter.

One factor was increasing water scarcity resulting from the growing incidence of climatic variations and drought in the region – for example, the protracted drought of 1987–91. The impact within Israel was considerable. Water resources were under increasing stress and at the same time fiscal resources to subsidize water were being squeezed. As the largest water-using sector, agricultural water use became an increasing concern as demand from other sectors continued to rise.

Government began measures to manage demand. As early as 1991, as the drought dragged on, measures were brought in to ban cotton cultivation. Water allocations to agriculture were cut by half. This resulted initially in some painful costs of transition – but ultimately the measure has had a transformative impact on the sector. Farmers began to invest in water-saving technology and to switch to higher-value crops. Even the Jaffa orange, which was relatively water intensive, became less profitable and some farmers began to uproot citrus groves. Ironically the winter rains of 1991–2 were heavy. Lake Tiberias was full to the brim and flood damage was a greater concern than water shortages. However, the need for an agricultural transformation remained clear. The spectre of water shortages had not gone away, and farmers continued their migration towards higher water productivity farming systems and crops.[84]

Change thus came through rapid reorientation of the agricultural sector towards higher-value crops that returned more shekels per cubic metre of water, the scarce factor, combined with more efficient irrigation technology and higher productivity crop husbandry techniques and choices. A highly efficient agricultural extension service and regional irrigation companies promoted and facilitated these changes.

Ultimately, the development of wastewater treatment brought a whole new resource. With the progressive replacement of limited fresh water with treated wastewater, water supply to the agricultural sector was secured. The profitability of agriculture also allowed the government to raise prices progressively towards full-cost recovery levels, sweetened by assurances that farmers would get all the water they needed. Farm water prices went up, but farmers had assured quotas and no reductions in time of drought. Nor were farmers out of pocket, because they switched to the water-saving hi-tech production systems and equipment that were by then readily available.[85] A block tariff system encourages limited water use. For fresh water, the first 50 per cent of the quota is priced at NIS 1.650 ($0.49); the next 30 per cent at 1.902 ($0.56) and the final 20 per cent at NIS 2.411 ($0.71). Farmers may exceed their quota, but at a much steeper tariff. Treated wastewater is about half the price of fresh water (NIS 0.803 per cubic metre, $0.24), with the better quality Shafidan effluent priced a little higher, at NIS 0.934 ($0.27).[86] Overall, pricing agricultural water at full cost had multiple beneficial results, promoting conservation; cost recovery; and efficiency and innovation.

Actual quantities of water for agriculture have not increased for forty years or more. The peak was 1,465 MCM in 1985, but use has averaged 1,110 MCM in recent years. By contrast, crop water productivity – the value of output of crops per unit of water – has grown sevenfold while water use per hectare went down from 7,000 cubic metres in 1990 to just 5,000 cubic metres today. Measures to achieve these efficiency gains included the widespread application of pressurized irrigation, particularly drip irrigation and fertigation, as well as adoption of high-yielding crops and varieties. New generations of technology feed fertilizer to the plant roots along with water, controlled by moisture-sensitive automated sensors, often with computer control. The effect is to ensure the most cost-effective dose of water and nutrients to the plant roots. Drip irrigation systems can reach 90 per cent efficiency in water use.[87] Intensive research and plant breeding have produced water-saving varieties too – a new short-stem wheat, tomato varieties with fewer leaves, short-root plants and plants that tolerate or even thrive on brackish water.[88] Much of this high-value agriculture is in protected environments like glass or plastic houses or plastic tunnels. A beneficial side effect of Israel's innovative agricultural technology has also been the rise of a profitable export industry in irrigation equipment. Some 80 per cent of irrigation equipment made in the country is now exported. These changes have brought crop water productivity – shekels per drop of water – to world-beating levels. As a result, agriculture has

Figure 1.6 Israel's hi-tech agriculture: hothouses at Ein Yahav, Wikimedia Commons.

maintained its share in the fast-growing Israeli economy and become ever more hi-tech and focussed on the efficient use of water (Figure 1.6).

Security against water-related risks

From the foundation of the state onwards, Israel has always been alert to risks to water. Much effort has been put into planning to manage and mitigate these risks – both strategic planning for infrastructure and military and diplomatic planning to defend water resources against threats. Measures to manage water shortages and the risks of a changing climate and apparently more frequent droughts have been both institutional, particularly demand management, and technological, developing innovative approaches to water saving and to boosting water productivity and efficiency. In this, partnerships between a highly risk-aware government and a highly entrepreneurial water sector have been invaluable. Most recently, as water resources and water services have become more secure, Israel has turned to managing risks of pollution and threats to ecosystems and to amenity.

Risk management through far-sighted planning

From the outset, Israel showed intense commitment to planning for water resources and services. Beginning in the 1950s, there was always a rolling water master plan. Currently planning is underway with horizons as far off as 2050. In the past, the focus of these plans was on the water sources and services aspects of planning. Now, however, there is an understanding that these two pillars of water security are essentially in place. The focus of thinking today is more the third pillar of water security – risk management. In particular, there is a growing awareness of environmental risk – pollution, aquifer depletion and salinization – and of the risks of climatic change. These risks can go unseen for long but then suddenly emerge. As Seth Siegel says, they 'can spell doom over a generation'. Israel's planning philosophy is thus to think long term but act in the short term, to make plans mandatory and to stick to them – but with flexibility to change in the light of changing circumstances, and to identify the scope for new technology and to adapt plans as new ways of working emerge.

Measurement and monitoring are constant imperatives. The habit of focussing on measurement at the retail and local levels – in leak detection, for example – is scaled up to quality and contamination control for water supply and beyond, to measurement and monitoring of key parameters of water quantity and quality in the main water sources, the aquifers and Lake Tiberias. For monitoring of the aquifers, for instance, the Hydrological Service divides each aquifer into cells with similar hydrogeological properties and identifies representative wells in each reporting cell. Groundwater levels are measured in 1,500 wells across the country at a frequency varying from monthly to annually. Water quality in both springs and production wells is measured monthly, with more than 800 samples taken. Measurements are uploaded to the central database. Forecasts of demand and plans for supply are constantly updated.[89]

Encouraging innovation to manage risks

Israel has fostered innovation and developed a sizable global business by promoting new ideas and start-ups through incubators and grants, becoming a world leader in several technologies and gaining a global export trade in innovative practices.[90] The first innovations were in agriculture, notably drip irrigation. More recently, the advent of information and communications technologies has enabled academia, private companies and individual entrepreneurs to develop many high-technology concepts – for example, algorithm- and cloud-based leak detection.

The leading water utilities, including Mekorot, have formed collaborative partnerships with the private sector, allowing inventors and businesses to test their innovations under real operating conditions before they are introduced to the market. The government has underwritten these partnerships with programmes that specifically support water innovation.[91] Partnerships are also in place with EU and US research programmes. This proactive policy to support innovation in the water sector has resulted in a profitable export business for equipment, technology licences and services.

Working with the private sector

One important strategy Israel has used to build water security and to manage risks has been to tap all available sources and technologies. In this, partnerships with science and with entrepreneurship have been key. Despite the character of water as a public good and the public ownership of the resource, Israel has not been shy to treat water as an economic commodity and to associate the private sector where it is can be shown to be more efficient.[92] Thus, over the last two decades, a number of partnerships have been established between the public sector and private business. The aim has been to improve water services and to raise investment finance. The most notable example is the massive desalination programme. As we have seen, this has largely been developed through partnership arrangements with private concessionaires who have financed the investments and are responsible for managing the plants for up to twenty-five years. The four plants developed in this way – Ashkelon, Palmachim, Hadera and Sorek – have together mobilized $1.3 billion of private capital.

Another example of an innovative public–private partnership is the independent power production (IPP) contract put in place for biogas production at the wastewater treatment plant of Kfar Saba-Hod Hasharon in the centre of Israel. The treatment plant itself is run by the public utility and the partnership is limited to the biogas production process. The biogas plant, which began operation in 2016, uses the biogas produced by the anaerobic digestion process to provide about 80 per cent of the electricity needed by the plant, saving about 20 per cent of the energy costs.

Beyond this, the water utilities are increasingly obtaining their investment capital from financial markets. The financial viability of Mekorot and the corporatized regional utilities has allowed them to raise market finance either through commercial debt with private banks or by issuing bonds, without the government having to provide guarantees.

At a more local level, private contractors now perform many operational tasks. The water utilities outsource or subcontract many O&M tasks in the plants and networks to the local private sector, as well as commercial services such as meter installation and reading, billing, debt collection and call centre operation.[93]

Managing environmental risks

During the mandate, the Zionist ideal was rural and agricultural. Water along with the land was the essential resource that would enable Zionist settlement and economic progress. As in the expansion of the United States, resources had value only if they were harnessed and put to use. Water was for use, not for its ecological services or recreation or spiritual value. Thus Israel's priority from the outset was to secure control over a water inventory adequate for its needs and to use that water to bring world-class water and sanitation services to its people and to develop its agriculture, industry and commerce.[94]

Israel's 1959 Water Law captured this perfectly, listing the priorities for water use but overlooking what we call nowadays environmental uses or the sustainability and protection of water resource. This determination to put water to work was interpreted in the huge projects for the development and transfer of water the length of the country and in the reclamation of vast areas of desert for irrigated agriculture.[95]

There was, however, a price to be paid for this single-minded pursuit of water security. Inevitably there have been costs. One of these costs has been to the environment. Specialists in water were long concerned about the environmental effects of the development and use of water – about depletion of the Coastal Aquifer and the risk of saline intrusion, about the overpumping from the Mountain Aquifer and the consequent harm to the groundwater balance.

The most glaring example has been that of the depleted springs and polluted wadis. The natural ecosystems of these periodically flowing streams are by their intermittent wet/dry character already under considerable stress. These systems largely disappeared in Israel in the 1950s and 1960s as flows there began to be diverted for irrigation and the dry channels were filled with untreated municipal sewage and household and industrial refuse. Less water entered the system anyway as Israel's aggressive pumping from the upstream Mountain Aquifer dried up springs and depleted the headwaters. Streamflow dwindled to negligible levels. The Yarkon River, which flows through Tel Aviv, shrank to just 2 per cent of its natural flow. Where water did flow or ponded it was contaminated by nutrients and bacteria. The vegetation either disappeared or took on a new character adapted to the polluted environment. Streams like the Kishon and the Na'aman that flowed through industrial zones carried a toxic cocktail of untreated factory effluents. Often more than half of this melange of water-borne contaminants percolated to the water table and polluted the aquifer (Tal and Katz: 320).

As often with environmental deterioration, few were aware of the degradation of the riverine environment until it was well advanced. Only extremes made people sit up and take notice – the death of several Australian athletes in 1997 – see the section 'Cleaning up the Yarkon' – and cancer amongst veterans who had dived years earlier at the mouth of the heavily polluted Kishon River.[96]

New attitudes and policies on the environment Driven by the views of specialists and by growing public concern, Israel began to turn its attention to the environment. As a developed country, and with the constraint of water scarcity apparently lifted, Israel now has the resources and the expertise to pay attention to environmental problems.

One priority is cleaning up the rivers. The legal framework is provided by the 1959 Water Law and by the Streams and Springs Authorities Law of 1965. Although the 1965 law established the legal basis, the first river authority was established only in 1988 (for the Yarkon), followed by the Kishon Authority in 1994 and – a full decade and a half later – the Besor Authority. Eventually, eleven river authorities have been set up, responsible for all thirty-one Israeli rivers and streams. The main purposes of these organizations are to monitor the environmental health of the watercourses and to progressively clean them up. The principal problems have been upstream diversion of water, depletion of the groundwater table that fed springs and streamflow, and pollution both from sewage and wastewater and from solid waste dumped into or near to watercourses (Tal and Katz 2012: 322).

Cleaning up the Yarkon Work began, starting with the clean-up of the Yarkon,[97] which became a national priority at the time of the 1997 Maccabiah games, where a disaster prompted a time of shame and national reflection. A temporary bridge over the Yarkon River collapsed and three of the four Australian athletes who died were actually rescued but died later of infections. The polluted river got the blame. It had, in fact, long been in terrible shape. Ever since 1955 almost all the natural streamflow had been diverted upstream into the National Water Carrier. The only regular flow was partially treated sewage. The ecology was in a dire condition, the unique flora and fauna long gone, and the river bed covered in toxic polluting chemicals.

The Yarkon River Authority, set up in 1988, produced a river recovery plan but government dithered. It was only six years after the extreme event, in 2003, that the government finally gave the green light to the plan and $50 million was mobilized to back it. The principal actions were to dredge the watercourse, to introduce clean water from the National Water Carrier upstream, to improve the treatment of wastewater along the river's course and to stem the flow of industrial waste into the river. The private sector was required to finance 60 per cent of the cost of dredging, based on the 'polluter pays' principle.

But little of the water that flowed in the river would go to the sea – nothing so wasteful. As the river approaches the coast, the water is siphoned out to the Sheva Tahanot wastewater treatment plant facility near Ramat Gan and then reused for irrigation.[98]

This closed system has created a much cleaner river and environment. With the clean-up came efforts to restore the riverine ecology along a 7.5-kilometre stretch of the Upper Yarkon near Rosh Ha'ayin together with the improvement of downstream amenities for sailing, fishing and even swimming. The river bed and banks were cleaned up, the banks reinforced and raised, hiking and bicycle paths were established, and trees and vegetation were thinned. The plan calls for a series of further parks and open spaces the length of the river. The Yarkon Park is already said to serve as a 'green lung' for some two million inhabitants of the Dan metropolitan region.[99]

Despite all the attention, there have been occasional small disasters. In October 2017, the *Times of Israel* reported, 'White foam covers sections of Yarkon River despite clean-up efforts. As residents complain, authorities say phenomenon caused by first winter rains flushing dust, oils into waterway.'[100] Six months previously, thousands of fish had been found floating dead in the river after sewage was inadvertently released into it.

Replicating the Yarkon experience What has been done on the Yarkon is being replicated elsewhere in the country. Twelve coastal rivers are currently undergoing rehabilitation according to approved master plans. More than twenty projects have been launched, from simple clean-ups to widening of riverbeds, from drainage and soil conservation to landscape and park development.[101]

A major help came from the huge improvement in the quality of treated wastewater released into the streams. Wastewater treatment guidelines and effluent standards improved, and between 1990 and 2010 Israel invested $2 billion in secondary wastewater treatment plants.

In addition, in 2000 government approved for the first time an allocation of 50 million cubic metres of water for environmental flows in Israeli streams. This allocation has been slow to materialize – by 2011 only 10 million cubic metres had actually been allocated, almost all for the Yarkon. However, now that the advent of desalination has relieved some of the pressure on the natural resource, Israel has growing ability to reallocate water to the environment. Simply reducing abstractions will help to stabilize groundwater levels and the level of Lake Tiberias. Ultimately this may restore some measure of natural spring flow into the streams. Already it has triggered the release of a small environmental flow from Tiberias into the Jordan (Tal and Katz 2012: 322, 326).

An irony that goes with this is the cost. The restoration of Israel streams is estimated to cost over $1 billion, and even this rich country is allocating only a fraction of the budget needed. The innovative financing of the dredging of the Yarkon River, where the private sector bore 60 per cent of the cost on the 'polluter pays' principle, is grounded in the capacity of a prosperous country and private sector to afford the clean-up. The Palestinians have no such luxury.[102]

The challenge of the Jordan River

> *Jordan River too polluted for baptisms . . . In recent years the flow of the river has slowed to a dirty trickle as fresh water has been replaced with sewage . . . severe mismanagement . . . diversion of 98 per cent of its fresh water . . .*[103]

One environmental concern became very public in Israel in June 2015 when it was announced that Britain's Prince George was baptized with water from the Jordan River. Although the little prince was in fact baptized with a vial of very much cleansed water from the Jordanian side of the river, the headlines in Israel read 'Baptism by Mire? In Lower Jordan River, Sewage Mucks Up Christian Rite.'[104] Gidon Bromberg, head of the Israeli branch of the cross-border environmental activism group EcoPeace,[105] was reported as saying, 'The water quality is anything but holy in nature . . . a mixture of untreated and partly treated sewage, agricultural runoff, fish pond waste, and saline waters from springs.'[106]

In truth the whole of the lower Jordan River has been reduced to a dirty stream. Nowhere is this more flagrantly apparent than at the Qasr al Yahud baptism site on the western bank of the Jordan River, near Jericho. This is thought to be the actual spot where John the Baptist baptized Jesus.[107] Although the site is managed by the Israeli Ministry of Tourism as a national park, the site is in fact not in Israel but in the Palestinian West Bank in Area C, under Israeli military control.[108] In 2014, the Israeli Environment Ministry reported a faecal coliform count for the site of 2,300 per 100 millilitres. This is six times the level allowed for swimming in Israel – the Israeli Health Ministry closes beaches when the count exceeds 400 per 100 millilitres.

Although the pollution levels in the river vary considerably over the seasons with changes in the levels of fresh water and return drainage water and with the inflow of pollutants, the fact is that development by the three upstream riparians – Israel, Syria and Jordan – has completely changed the ecology of the river, virtually eliminating the minimum environmental flow needed to retain any of the river's former character and loading the stream with pollutants. Essentially all riparians divert as much water as they can and return only dirty water and domestic, industrial and agricultural effluents to the stream. Salinity is extreme in part because of Israel's diversion of saline springs around Tiberias in order to reduce the salinity of the water it abstracts for the NWC and irrigation. The saline water is dumped back into the Jordan River below Tiberias (Figure 1.7).

One stimulus to action has been pressure from environmental groups. In 2010 EcoPeace published a report[109] estimating that full rehabilitation of the river would require as much as 400–600 million cubic metres of annual freshwater flow – almost half of the old natural flow – to remain in the river. It would also require higher

Figure 1.7 The River Jordan as a dirty drain, with permission from Faith-Notre Dame.

standards for treatment of wastewater and better management of pollution from chemicals in agricultural drainage water throughout the catchment. EcoPeace followed this up in December 2012 with a study stressing the economic benefits of rehabilitation, particularly from tourism.

It is clear that increasing the flow of fresh water in the river is essential to cleaning the river and reviving the riverine ecology. This, of course, is the hardest action of all, as all three riparians have long since been diverting to human use every last drop they can. From the start of Jordan River development in the 1950s no account has been taken of the need for environmental flows. The Johnston Plan from the 1950s made no provision for the environment, and the latest agreement on division of the river – the 1994 Peace Treaty with Jordan – makes no mention of the environment or water quality.

Nonetheless, the Israeli government did take notice, deciding on a master plan for the section of the Jordan Valley that it controls and on provision of significant investment to develop tourism. The National River Administration included in its priority list for rehabilitation a 30-kilometre section of the lower Jordan River from Tiberias to the Naharaim Bridge. In 2013–14, three new wastewater treatment plants came into operation along the river, reducing pollution from domestic effluent. Some rehabilitation projects are underway: the Ein Gedi Oasis, some springs in Galilee.[110] There has been attention to the environmental disaster caused by the draining of the Huleh wetlands in the 1950s, where the peat soils had oxidized and turned to infertile dust and sub-surface fires had raged. A reflooding project – on just 1 square kilometre – has been a small-scale success. The exiguous new ecosystem provides a magnet for migratory birds and attracts 400,000 visitors a year, demonstrating the economic value of environmental restoration.[111]

Most significantly, from May 2013, Israel also began to release an extra 9 million cubic metres of fresh water annually from Tiberias to the lower Jordan. Releases were to gradually increase to 30 million cubic metres – a far cry from the proposed 400–600 million cubic metres but at least a start. This plan has been aided by the more abundant rains of 2019–20 which can allow the spillage of excess water from Lake Tiberias.

Plainly real change could come about only through cooperation amongst all the riparians. This has long been talked about, often in the context of a Middle East 'peace' process, but with scant result. The Jordanian government did set up a Jordan River Committee, and the Palestinian Water Authority supported a regional master plan for the lower Jordan River basin, but Israel's security preoccupations and its activities in Area C of the West Bank place severe constraints on both the will to cooperate and the practicality of cooperative action, particularly for the Palestinians.

The most progress has been made by NGOs, notably EcoPeace which created the first transboundary integrated masterplan for the valley and, in November 2016, piloted a 'model basin commission', with a governance structure based on best practices. EcoPeace has also operated its Good Water Neighbours (GWN) programme in communities along the Jordan, linking neighbouring Israeli, Palestinian and Jordanian communities on either side of the river and developing

'Neighbours Paths', trails along the river that highlight the cultural and natural heritage of each community as well as their individual water resources.[112]

It must be said, however, that the voice of the West Bank Palestinians has been faint in all this. As the Palestinian director of EcoPeace, Nadeer al-Khateeb, said, 'We may not be able to return the Jordan to its original state, but we can create an economic engine in the Jordan River, not keep it a closed military zone.' EcoPeace's idea is to bring the Palestinians in as full partners in environmental action, setting up a trilateral working group to work on cleaning up the river and to promote the Jordan as a 'valley of peace, with a healthy Jordan River at its centrepiece'.[113] But there is little sign of Israel giving such an idea much traction.

Future directions Overall, Israel has seen a change from the development phase where water was viewed simply as a resource to be developed to the limit and put to work. Gone are the days when environmental values were altogether neglected, and streams were seen simply as convenient conduits for sewage. Today a modern environmental consciousness has begun to emerge that recognizes the multiple benefits of a thriving revitalized ecology. Some first steps are being taken towards restoration.

However, the cost is enormous. The restoration of Israel's streams is estimated to cost over $1 billion, and, even though the involvement of the private sector in the Yarkon restoration gives some hope of cost-sharing, this rich country is allocating only a fraction of the budget needed.

Another question is whether there is enough water to restore the environment. Money is one thing – but water is another. Any number of projects can be undertaken but to restore the environment requires vast quantities of water. A government policy brief of 2003, *Nature's Right to Water*, estimated that an extra 600 million cubic metres a year were needed to restore coastal streams and nature reserves, and a further 200 million cubic metres for the Jordan River. The total is more than half of the natural fresh water available to Israel. It is estimated that, costed at the price of desalinated water, this would require an investment of half a billion dollars a year.

Climate change too poses a question over future water resources. Predicted changes are likely to include longer periods between rainfall events, increasing storm intensity, and more frequent and longer droughts. Despite the more plentiful rains of 2019–20, a decrease in precipitation of 10 to 30 per cent is expected by 2030 and of up to 50 per cent by 2080. The annual availability of natural water is expected to decrease by one half during this century. When reduced water availability is combined with projected temperature increases of between 2°C and 4°C, the land will become increasingly arid. Demand for water will shoot up, at the same time as supplies dwindle.

A final challenge remains the need for regional cooperation. Unless Israel can work together with the Palestinians and with Jordan, it will struggle to overcome the persistent environmental challenges. This is a theme to which we return in the last part of this book. Cooperation on the environment poses many challenges – but it may also indicate pathways to a wider cooperation.

Israel is water secure

Israelis live in a quite dry land with a fast-growing population and a water-intensive economy. Demand for water has constantly threatened to outstrip supply. In fact, the entire history of the nation has been characterized by rapid increases in demand and by technical and strategic responses both to contain demand and to increase supply. Much of the geopolitical and military history since 1948 has resulted in increased and more secure supplies. More recently, technology has greatly increased water use efficiency and progressively added to the nation's water inventory.

As a result, Israel is today water secure by all and any standards. Israel has come to control all the water to which it has access, and has through foresight, ingenuity and investment recycled or simply created enough extra water to meet all its current needs. In fact, through desalination it has created the possibility of almost limitless new resources and has turned the age-old strategic challenge of water in the Middle East into as much an economic matter as a geopolitical one.

By providence and long-range planning, Israel has ensured that water is stored and distributed throughout the country and is available to meet all needs at a price that encourages conservation and prudent use but which is also affordable. Management of demand and technical innovation have allowed the country to run efficiently today on little more water per capita than it used in 1985. Water agencies are generally efficient and self-sustaining financially. Only wastewater recycling still requires subsidy, and there is a public good rationale for that in terms of environmental protection.

Planning, infrastructure and 'new water' today provide the means of managing risks. In a semi-arid environment with limited natural resources, Israel has developed the instruments of knowledge and the practical responses that will enable it to cope with prospective climate change. From near-total dependence on natural water three decades ago, Israel now has a balance between natural water, recycled water and desalinated water (see Figure 1.8). This balance allows it to meet demand sustainably despite a considerable drop in the availability of natural

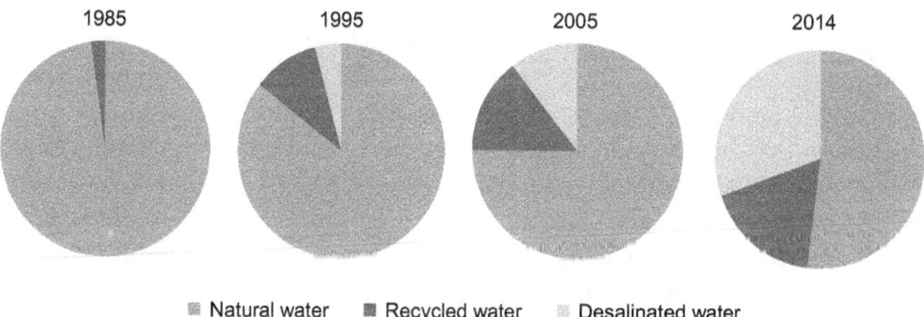

Figure 1.8 Breakdown of water sources in Israel, 1985, 1995, 2005, 2014. *Source:* IWA 2015; World Bank 2017.

water – for example in the drought of 2014. Today the country has achieved the level of wealth that allows it to begin to tackle the last risk of water development, the management of pollution and the protection of the natural environment and ecology.

Of course, nothing is perfect and everything comes at a price. Critics point to the fact that rights to most of the natural water resources Israel controls are contested and Israel has asserted its claims forcefully. The Palestinians maintain that much of Israel's accumulation of its water inventory has been to their cost, that Israeli gains from the Mountain Aquifers and the Jordan Valley have caused corresponding Palestinian losses. There are the economic questions, too. Was the huge investment cost to create a nationwide water network more justified by political and strategic goals than by economic ones? Does the adoption of single national water tariffs for potable water supply and (separately) for irrigation water distort economic incentives for users? Could the rather bumpy process of aggregation of municipal providers into regional utilities have been handled more efficiently? Is there a way to reduce or offset the relatively high carbon footprint of energy use and other negative environmental impacts of seawater desalination? Trade-offs are inevitable in struggling with water scarcity, and these economic and environmental costs are set against the gains in water security. It also has to be said that this high level of water security is not for all – not so much, at least, for Arab Israelis, the Bedouin in the Negev and the Druze in the Golan.

So what are the factors that have allowed Israel to achieve this world-beating water security? Here we will try to summarize these factors under three headings: *integration*, *institutions* and *investment*.

Integration

The integrated water network From the outset, Israel set about creating a network of transmission lines which allows water to be conveyed, just as electricity is conveyed, along a 'national grid' which connects 95 per cent of the country's water resources, not only natural water but also treated wastewater and desalinated water. This, combined with national ownership of the resource, allows a very high level of control and flexibility. Water can be allocated both in line with demand and in line with policy. Supply can be planned, but also altered flexibly in case, for example, of drought. The nationwide network allows new water supplies, for example from a new desalination plant, to be factored in with little extra infrastructure.

The network also helps the country to manage its natural water for sustainability. When levels in Lake Tiberias or in groundwater approach dangerous lows, water can be switched around the system. Israel is even now creating a mechanism for restoring levels in Tiberias by transferring desalinated water back to the lake.

This integrated national water conveyance system essentially allows optimization of water management, matching supply and demand and ensuring resource sustainability under conditions of extreme scarcity. Such a system is well adapted to Israel's needs, and also to its relatively small size. It is costly but it facilitates sustainable access to water resources which is the first pillar of water security. In addition, it allows the country to manage risks of drought and climate change, as well as strategic risks, the third pillar of water security.

Wastewater treatment Israel is far and away the world leader in wastewater treatment and reuse. It treats virtually all the wastewater collected to the highest standards, uses advanced techniques to further cleanse and store the treated wastewater underground, and reuses about nine tenths of the treated wastewater productively in agriculture. It has effectively engineered a new water resource, developed means to store the water until it is needed, and to convey it over distances to the point of demand, and has integrated it into the agricultural economy of the country. The downside is that treatment and reuse on this scale are expensive. Even in Israel where the economic value of water is very high and where capacity to pay in Israel's high-value horticulture industry is also very high, large public subsidy is required. This said, the near-total reuse of this resource is a key element in strengthening Israel's water resource security.

Desalination Israel's strategy on desalination – cutting-edge technology, focus on cost reduction, economies of scale and efficient partnerships with the private sector – has resulted in amongst the lowest-cost desalinated water in the world. The cost remains higher than that of natural water, but the policy of allocating desalinated water to potable use, with a target of all potable water coming from desalination, assures security of supply for this priority need and also enables desalination to be run as a business. The domestic market can afford to pay full price for desalinated water. A significant co-benefit is the large and growing export business Israel has developed in desalination technology. Desalination has finally guaranteed Israel security of water resources. The country can create water. This creates the possibility that Israel may be a water-surplus nation and could use that surplus in pursuit of other policy goals in the region. Already agreements with Jordan on water contained an element of 'water for peace' – or at least were branded so. Desalination, with its prospect of surplus water, may facilitate other such negotiations – we discuss the effect of desalination on regional water relations and the likely winners and losers in the last part of this book.

Institutions

Capacity and consent Israel has built up a series of highly competent water agencies. More recently a vibrant private water sector has sprung up, partnering with government and bringing the entrepreneurial and innovative characteristics of private enterprise. Alongside these capacities comes an invaluable support to good water management – public consent. Since the days of the foundation of the state, all Israelis have valued water and been aware of the need to manage it wisely. Nationalization of the resource and construction of the National Water Carrier hardened that awareness into a support for public water management. When scarcity began to press and this basic loyalty seemed to erode, demonstration of good management and an education campaign led to acceptance of tough measures of demand management, steep price hikes and reduced personal consumption. This combination of agency capacity and popular consent to what is understood to be for the common good and in the national interest has enabled the good water management, including demand management, that underwrites Israel's water security.

Command and control Extreme water scarcity and Israel's strategic vulnerability have since independence driven strong planning and top-down management. Israel's water plans see far into the horizon and a combination of rigorous management of supply and demand and intensive investment, together, where necessary, with subsidy, has kept supply and demand in equilibrium. For some difficult years, particularly the drought years of the late 1980s, the country teetered on the brink of a major imbalance. Tiberias approached the tipping point at which irreversible salination would ruin the resource. The Coastal and Western Aquifers were heavily overdrawn. But long-range planning, integrated management and massive investment managed the risks. Government's prudent application of demand management measures and cost recovery, together with supply-side development of desalination and wastewater treatment and reuse, brought demand and supply back into equilibrium.

Knowledge Knowledge characterizes all aspects of Israel's water management, particularly knowledge of the resource. It is a truism that *You can't manage what you can't measure*. Some of this is risk management, long-term understanding of the changes in hydrology that are likely to come with a changing climate which threatens to be ever warmer and drier and less predictable. Some of it is shorter-term risk management, understanding the relations between water sources in a fully integrated system, watching over aquifer levels and the famous red lines in Tiberias which indicate possible emergency, then compensating for excessive drawdown from Tiberias or an aquifer with non-conventional water. First-rate knowledge is essenial for the quotidian, too, for example for ensuring releases of treated wastewater are available for farmers 50 miles away precisely when the crops are in need of water; or for simply ensuring the provision of sufficient volumes of operational water to meet demand, taking account of seasonal peaks and troughs and reflecting actual rainfall which will determine, for example, irrigation requirements from day to day. Israel has the institutional capacity for collecting the comprehensive and timely data essential to integrated water resources management under scarcity conditions and for interpreting that data as knowledge to back up policies, plans and investment programmes. The generation, interpretation and application of this knowledge are an essential part of Israel's water security, protecting and allocating the resource, ensuring supply and managing climate and other risks.

Separation of roles Best practice in water management globally calls for the separation of three functions. At the top is government which has to decide basic policy and allocate public money. There is then the function of planning, allocation of water resources and regulation of water services. Finally there are the service providers who operate the infrastructure and bring the water to consumers.

Israel has placed all the powers of regulation and planning in one agency, the Israel Water Authority, which enjoys a high degree of autonomy. The IWA plans for and regulates all aspects of the sector, water resource management, water supply, wastewater treatment and reuse, irrigation and environmental management of rivers. It promotes efficiency of the service providers – water utilities, Mekorot or build-operate-transfer [BOT] concessionaires – by a series of contractual targets. It has, for example, the power as a regulator to fine the water service providers if they fail to meet efficiency targets. This separation of roles, particularly IWA's role in regulating the utilities, is critical to ensuring security of water and sanitation services.

Financial viability A key achievement has been to make the Israeli water system as a whole financially viable and sustainable. After decades in which the undeclared watchword was 'water security at any price', Israel concluded that it should move towards an economic approach where users paid tariffs that reflected the costs of the whole system. Fortunately in this approach big investments, for example, in the NWC and in wastewater treatment, had already been made and were essentially 'sunk costs'. There has also always been considerable outside financing from foreign supporters for aspects which might otherwise require public subsidy, particularly for environmental protection. From 2007 Israel began to apply principles of cost recovery that targeted the financial viability and sustainability of the whole system and the progressive elimination of public subsidy. This has not only relieved the exchequer of the burden, it has also greatly promoted efficiency, helped manage demand and obliged service providers to be cost-conscious and to target financial viability. A valued side effect has been to promote innovation and entrepreneurship. Today the financial viability of the water system is a cornerstone of security of water services.

Investment

Public and private investment in infrastructure From the outset, high levels of prudent public investment allowed Israel to realize its ambitious plans for water infrastructure. Recently, the development of public–private partnerships with government guarantees and some government support, for example over land acquisition, has allowed major investment in desalination with limited cost to the public purse. The involvement of the private sector has contributed to efficiencies that make the cost of desalinated water affordable to domestic customers while assuring full-cost recovery through tariffs. This remarkable development, which has essentially abolished the water resource frontier and done so in an economically efficient manner, has been aided by the exploitation of offshore natural gas fields which provide an assured source of moderately priced energy. Overall, the enormous investments that Israel has made in its water systems are the fundamental guarantor of its water security.

Part II

WATER (IN)SECURITY FOR PALESTINIANS

Part I of this book described how, by judicious exercise of the power, authority and resources of the state, by high levels of national commitment, ingenuity and investment, and by the development of appropriate institutions and competent agencies, Israel has been able to achieve water security – security of water resources and services, and security from water-related risks.

Part II now describes a quite different picture, essentially one of water insecurity in which, in the parts of the West Bank over which Palestinians exercise a measure of control, an administration with scant power, authority or resources and with access to very little water, struggles to bring even the basics of water security to its people. And in which the residents of the Gaza Strip exhaust their natural resources to enjoy water that is so salty as to be undrinkable.

In this part of the book, we set out the characteristics of this poor situation and try to explain how it has come about. Chapters 2–5 assess water security for Palestinians in the West Bank, and Chapter 6 discusses the plight of the Gaza Strip. What may be done to align the two peoples who live in the same land and to bring both Palestinians and Israelis to the same degree of water security is the subject we then broach in the last part of this book.

Chapter 2

SECURITY OF WATER RESOURCES FOR WEST BANK PALESTINIANS

In the West Bank, water for survival, water for swimming pools

One day in late 2008 we arrived to visit a newly built school on a dry and dusty hilltop in the Palestinian West Bank. The headmaster Kassem was waiting to receive us. 'Before we start the tour', my colleague Paolo asked, 'might I use the cloakroom?' Kassem looked embarrassed, and Paolo muttered something apologetic about his prostate. Kassem made a vague gesture of male solidarity, and the two of them went off round the back of the school.

When Paolo returned, he was fuming. 'There was nothing, just a stinking wall! When we built this school, did we forget the toilets?' Kassem raised his hand to calm Paolo down. 'No,' he said, 'no, we did not forget the toilets. There they are!' He indicated a fine-looking building, adjacent to the main school.

'But then, why on earth. . .?' Paolo is Italian, he has a short fuse. He is an education expert who cares deeply about education as the means of bringing people out of poverty. To him it was an affront that there should be a newly built school without the proper facilities.

'There is just no water, you see', Kassem said, 'so we cannot use the new block.'

'You mean, the block is not connected to the water main?'

'No, everything is connected. It is just . . . well, there is no water here.'

'But whyever. . .'

Kassem said nothing, but took Paolo by the sleeve and led him to the edge of the playground. We followed. From there, we could see across the dry land, to Ramallah, and as far as Jerusalem in the haze on the horizon. Still silent, the headmaster pointed to a hill opposite, half a mile away across the deep valley.

This other hill looked quite different from the one we were standing on. It was a hill occupied by Israeli settlers. The hill was green. There were neat white stuccoed villas set amongst luxuriant trees. There was a large swimming pool, the blue water sparkling under the bright noon sun. Children were doing back flips from the high board. You could hear their happy cries across the valley as they splashed down into the deep water.

The World Health Organization recommends a minimum of 100 litres of clean water daily for each person. The average West Bank Palestinian receives about two thirds of that minimum – about 65 litres a day. Some households regularly consume only one fifth of that. The 20 litres per person these households have each and every day is just 5 litres more than the minimum ration the UN provides after a disaster. Yet over the Green Line in Israel, and in the Israeli settlements across the West Bank, average consumption of domestic water in 2016 was, as we saw in Chapter 1, 263 litres for each citizen daily, four times as much as Palestinian per capita consumption. [1]

The disparity is just as large if we consider total water resources available, including all the water that goes to agriculture, industry and commerce. Total annual water consumption per person in Israel in 2016 was 257 cubic metres, or 704 litres a day. For the West Bank Palestinians it was 39 cubic metres of their own water, plus a further 26 cubic metres bought from Israel, for a total of 65 cubic metres, or 178 litres a day, a quarter of the water Israelis consumed.

Israelis and Palestinians both drink from the same overstretched aquifer. The Palestinians are demanding their rights on a broad front. The demand for access to enough water is one that everyone can understand and support.

* * *

The fact is that West Bank Palestinians are short of water – and they are not doing too well in managing what they have. The solution in the short term is disagreeable to the Palestinians – more costly water purchases from Israel, and consequently more dependence on Israel.

The Israelis advise management measures to get more out of the existing – efficient agriculture, release of some water from agriculture to domestic and industrial uses, leak plugging in water supply, wastewater treatment and reuse. The Palestinians agree with some of these points and disagree with others. But they point out the constraints to actually doing these things. Water resources development is subject to strict limitations under the Oslo Accords which, even though long outdated, still govern Palestinian water resources management.[2] With Palestinian jurisdiction restricted to small islands in the ABC mosaic of the West Bank, integrated planning and investment are well-nigh impossible. Infrastructure development and operation are hobbled by Israeli security preoccupations. It is true that investments in wastewater treatment and reuse could give Palestinian irrigated agriculture a boost, but many political and economic hurdles have first to be surmounted, not least that almost all the infrastructure for treatment, storage and reuse can be built only in Area C, where Israeli control is at present absolute.

The Palestinians return always to the basic question on water resources security – that they need more water, full stop. They need water autonomy, the control of their own water resources. They need to be empowered as water managers over some meaningful hydrological unit. They seek essentially to have management – or co-management – authority over the Mountain Aquifers. And they seek, as riparians, a fair share of Jordan River water.

They need also to be able to construct and manage the infrastructure for developing water resources and for storing it until needed, for conveying water efficiently to the point of use, and for then collecting, treating, storing, conveying and reusing the effluent wastewater.

They argue that only in this way can they achieve water resources security as the Israelis have done. Only in this way can they manage their own water resources in an efficient, equitable and sustainable way.

The question starts from Article 40 of the Oslo Interim Agreement, known as Oslo II, the five-year agreement that was concluded in 1995 pending a final resolution of the Palestinians' status.[3] The Palestinians propose far greater access to the water beneath their feet than they got in that temporary arrangement, together with the development of an integrated grid for bulk water transfer around the West Bank. They have plans for the needed institutions and infrastructure, but political agreement is a prerequisite.

So in this chapter we look at the first component of water security, security of water resources, this time from the Palestinian viewpoint. We ask the basic questions – why is access to water of two peoples living in the same land so different, and why are West Bank Palestinians not making better use of the resources they actually do have? In the following chapters, we look at the other aspects of Palestinian water security in the West Bank – water supply and sanitation services in Chapters 3 and 4, and water for agriculture in Chapter 5. Throughout, we also consider Palestinian access to the tools needed to manage water risk, including the risks of water shortages, the risks from an increasingly hot, dry and uncertain climate, and the risks of harm to the ecology and the broader environment.

Because the problematic of Gaza is largely distinct from that of the West Bank, most questions of water security for Palestinians in Gaza are discussed in a separate chapter (Chapter 6). The present chapter, and Chapters 3–5 touch on issues of the Gaza Strip only where common ground exists, for example in the legal and institutional framework.

* * *

The institutional framework

Palestinian water law

Article 40 of the 1995 Oslo Accords proposed to return to the Palestinians some measure of control over water resources and some power to manage those resources for the benefit of the Palestinian people.[4] The newly established Palestinian Authority (PA) therefore set about establishing institutions for water resources management, including a legal framework and public agencies. Initially the legal framework comprised a motley of legal instruments from the Ottoman, British and Occupation eras. The public agencies were those inherited from the Occupation period – the West Bank Water Department and the local service providers – and a new water agency, the Palestinian Water Authority (PWA), set up in 1995.

The Palestinian Authority then passed two successive water laws that sought to establish a revised institutional framework. In line with good practice, the first Water Law (2002) provided for separation of the three functions of water resource management. *Policy* was to be with the cabinet and a National Water Council; *regulation* was with the Palestinian Water Authority (PWA), working with the Joint Water Committee (JWC), the Palestinian–Israeli committee set up under Oslo;[5] and *operations* were to be with a national utility to be established on the lines of Mekorot, working with regional utilities. But a telling question was attributed at the time to Yasser Arafat: *Why should there be a law at all when the Palestinian Authority has such limited control over the resource?*[6]

In practice, the institutional structure changed little from the status quo before the law. The cabinet and the PWA continued to share the policy-making role. The PWA shared the regulatory role with the JWC and with Mekorot; and water operations were delivered by the existing bulk providers – Mekorot and the West Bank Water Department (WBWD), by the 300 or so existing utilities and municipal and village providers, and by traditional agricultural water providers.

Following a process of national debate and agreement on a sector reform programme – see the section *Sector reform* in Chapter 3 – a revised Water Law was passed in 2014 confirming the separation of the three functions but with a new configuration, and mandating a new organizational structure. The idea was to return the PWA to a role of policy and planning, to set up a national water carrier and company, and to re-establish water services on an enterprise basis with an independent regulatory body to protect consumer interests. Services were to be consolidated under four regional utilities (three in the West Bank and one in Gaza). By 2020, the independent regulator had been set up (although not fully empowered). Considerable study work had been done on the other components of the new structure – but no actual change had yet taken place.

The Palestinian Water Authority (PWA)

The PWA was first set up in the wake of Oslo to develop water policy and to oversee the allocation, development and management of Palestinian water resources and services. When the Water Law was updated in 2014, PWA's responsibilities were clarified.[7] Essentially, it plays the role of a water ministry, responsible for drafting policy and legislation, for water resources allocation and protection, and for investment planning. In practice, it has also taken a role in project implementation. PWA has about 100 staff and is financed by the state budget and by donors. The organization has received extensive capacity-building support over the years under various programmes, again supported by donors. There is a branch in Gaza (see Chapter 6), but its effectiveness has been sorely constrained by a parallel PWA set up by the Hamas administration.[8]

From the outset the PWA was charged with a daunting mandate and it is not surprising that it has struggled to fulfil its mission. In short order it had to develop the skills needed to manage a water sector which was underdeveloped and in need of considerable investment. Water services for the four million or so

Palestinians in the West Bank and Gaza were of poor quality. Water management was of a scanty and scattered resource defined and limited by the Oslo Accords. PWA's powers in water resources management and regulation were closely limited, leaving scant room for manoeuvre. The rules were fixed by Article 40, which effectively made Israel the co-manager of Palestinian water resources (but not vice versa), with a power of veto over water resource development, infrastructure investment and water abstractions. The circumscribed and fragmented geography and water resource controlled by Palestinians made an impossibility of integrated management. PWA's power of decision was super-restricted by the exiguousness of the resource and by the skewed nature of the JWC and its project approval and licencing procedures.[9]

In the event the Palestinian Authority and the PWA have had little success so far in putting in place the new sector organization mandated by the 2014 law. Essentially, the idea, which was heavily promoted by donors, was to model the Palestinian water sector on that of Israel. This has proven largely unimplementable, for reasons that we will see. The PWA was to be an autonomous water resources management agency, charged with an 'IWRM development mission'[10] according to the rules agreed in Dublin in 1992. The essence of Dublin is that water resources are managed in an integrated way across all uses within a hydrological unit – a river basin or an aquifer – with the responsibility for water allocation and management separated from the interests of water users. Immediately the paradox for Palestinians sticks out. The PWA has never had a discrete hydrological unit to manage, just a small quota of the three aquifers that lie beneath the West Bank, with no geographical identification of which bits of the aquifer Palestinians had rights to. Nor has it had the power to allocate or manage water within those aquifers – the rules had been laid down by Article 40 and have been enforced by the Israelis.

So from the start, the PWA could not pretend to be the 'autonomous manager' the donors had conceived. It was tied hand and foot. It could only ever be an executing agency, obliged to work within the tight confines of Article 40 and doing the best it could to develop water resources and services for the benefit of its people. Not surprisingly, critics have seen the PWA seen as a 'donor construct', a creature of aid agencies and international experts, called to high things in the name of the Dublin principles but in reality able only to do little more than turn out reports aimed at a donor audience and to coordinate donor-financed projects. Critics point out that even the staff are mostly there because the donors pay for them – most staff are employed on a project basis.[11]

PWA's role as an autonomous resource manager is further constrained by Palestinian policies. It is called on to fight the fight for water rights and water autonomy. This means avoiding any action that would compromise future Palestinian claims to water resources or which would recognize the Occupation or the settlements. This mission inevitably precludes any pretence at the cooperation with Israel which would be required for integrated management of the water resource.[12] Recall the Palestinian official quoted in *The History of Water* who told us in 2008, 'It is hard to plan when you have 400,000 settlers who have to leave.'

Internal Palestinian politics do not help either. Within the PA, there are divergent interests on water and inevitable power struggles. The most obvious is the tug-of-love between the PWA, which seeks to centralize water resource management and reorganize water supply on a new efficiency model in line with the 2014 Water Law, and the Ministry of Local Government and the municipalities, which seek to retain local control over water and the financial flows it generates.[13]

However, in some ways, the PWA has adapted to the difficult environment. In the early years, policy, regulation and operations all appeared to be confusedly merged in the PWA. It was against the principles of Dublin that the water resources management agency should be so focussed on water project implementation and donor funding. But in an embryonic institutional environment, where skills were scarce and everything was an apprenticeship, a degree of non-conformity was understandable. At least some things got done, even if results were far short of expectations.

In fact, aided by donor money, PWA has presided over some considerable achievements. In the run-down situation of the West Bank water sector, investment in infrastructure has been perhaps the most critical function and the PWA has overseen a sizable investment programme over the last two decades: $830 million of donor money was invested 1996–2002. By 2018 there were 114 water projects being implemented in the West Bank and Gaza valued at nearly NIS 3 billion ($770 million).[14] Water services have improved, with total water available to Palestinians in the West Bank and Gaza up from 331 million cubic metres in 2010 to 375 million cubic metres in 2017,[15] an increase in network coverage, and a 5–10 per cent reduction in network losses.[16] Nonetheless, huge and growing problems remain. Resources from the Mountain Aquifers are dwindling, per capita consumption has dropped, water and sanitation services are often terrible, 200,000 people in 100 communities remain without piped water supply at all, agriculture is parched and water quality has deteriorated, especially in Gaza.[17]

Overall, the PWA has struggled to gain legitimacy in the eyes of the Palestinian population. Battling with conflicting and sometimes impossible missions, PWA has often been seen as weak. When things go wrong, particularly when there is no water for months or there are long intervals between water service in the hot summers, it is the PWA which gets the blame. When the limits on water use set out in Article 40 are strictly enforced, it is the PWA which gets the blame even when it is the Israelis who are doing the policing. When sorely needed infrastructure or new bulk water supplies are not delivered, it is the PWA which is said to be at fault. All this contributes to a popular view that the PWA can do little either to control the resource or to ensure good water services.

A population that is as disappointed by the failure of Oslo to result in Palestinian sovereignty as it is frustrated at poor water services will just see a 'weak PWA weakly presiding over less than one quarter of West Bank water production and consumption' and a strong occupier helping itself to the lion's share of the resource and closely controlling what the Palestinians do with the residue. The perception is that Israeli planning goes unchallenged by a compliant PWA, and that essentially it is the Israelis who continue to manage the water resources of the

West Bank. That this is not far from the truth makes the implied rebuke the more stinging.[18]

The Water Sector Regulatory Council (WSRC)

The establishment of the independent regulatory body, the Water Sector Regulatory Council (WSRC), is the only institutional provision of the 2014 Water Law to have actually been carried out to anything nearing completion. The Council has the mandate of sector regulator, approving tariffs, licencing and regulating service providers, and protecting consumers.[19] However, most of these statutory functions have not yet been legally transferred to WSRC. The official reason for the delay is that the sector restructuring should first be completed, with the new configuration of the National Water Company and the regional water utilities in place. In practice, there is suspicion that the PWA is reluctant to let go.

As a result, the WSRC's main activity since its establishment in 2014 has been data gathering and monitoring of service provider performance – it has constituted a useful time-series on key performance parameters. The Council has published annual reports which give a good insight into the state of water service provision. WSRC has a small, skilled staff, all located in Ramallah, with correspondents in Gaza. It is financed by the state budget and by donors.

Other actors

There is a range of other ministries and actors dealing with water. Other state actors at the centre include the Ministry of Local Government (which oversees most local authority water and sanitation service providers), the Ministry of Agriculture, the Ministry of Finance and Planning, the Ministry of Health and the Environmental Protection Agency.[20] A large number of donors operate in the sector. The most prominent are USAID; KfW/GIZ; AFD; the World Bank; Swedish SIDA; and UNICEF. Numerous national and international NGOs also support development and service delivery in the sector. Many are long-established, even from the beginning of the Occupation in 1967. Their effectiveness has often stemmed from the fact that they have greater agility and capacity to respond to the multiple constraints than do official agencies or donors. They are particularly active in Area C, where official agencies find it virtually impossible to operate.[21]

Water resources and uses

Palestinian water ownership and allocation

Water resources in the West Bank are in both public and private hands. Public resources comprise the wells around towns and villages managed by public agencies for water supply. Private resources are the water resources developed and managed by individuals and communal groups for agriculture and rural settlements.

Table 2.1 West Bank: Allocation of Water Resources of the Three Shared Aquifers under Article 40 (million m^3)

		Article 40 allocation		
Aquifer	**Estimated potential**	**Total Palestinian**	**Total Israeli**	**Total**
Western	362.0	22.0	340.0	362.0
North Eastern	145.0	42.0	103.0	145.0
Eastern	172.0	54.0	40.0	94.0
Eastern (unallocated)				78.0
Total	**679.0**	**118.0**	**483.0**	**601.0**
Percentage of estimated potential		**17**	**71**	**88**

Sources: Article 40, Table 2.

Article 40 of the Oslo Accords set out an agreed allocation of water from the aquifer, divided between Palestinian and Israeli uses – see Table 2.1. With this agreement set to last for a maximum of five years, the Palestinian Authority received what was effectively a temporary water right to the quantity of internal renewable water resources that Palestinians were permitted to develop and extract in West Bank. This quota was the amount which Palestinians had already developed and were already using, plus a modest extra quantum to be developed. In total, this Palestinian water right came to about one fifth of the total resources from the three shared aquifers.[22]

Israel also contracted to provide water through Mekorot, its National Water Company. At the time of the 1995 agreement, the West Bank was already being supplied with 27.9 million cubic metres by Mekorot. Under Article 40, it was agreed that an extra quantity of 3.1 million cubic metres of fresh water from Mekorot for domestic use was to be made available to the Palestinians in the West Bank during the interim period, bringing the total of water imports from Mekorot to 31 million cubic metres a year. Five million cubic metres was also to be supplied by Mekorot to Gaza – see Chapter 6.

Palestinian under-abstraction – and Israeli over-abstraction

As we saw in Chapter Seven of *The History of Water*, actual Palestinian abstractions from the Mountain Aquifers have, for the last decade, been running well *below* the levels agreed at Oslo – 113 million cubic metres in 2007, 104 million cubic metres in 2013, 109 million cubic metres in 2017, against a total allocation from the Mountain Aquifers of 138.5 million cubic metres (see Tables 2.2 and 2.3). The lion's share of water from the West Bank aquifers was allocated under Oslo to Israel, which abstracts it both within the West Bank and west of the Green Line. The numbers for 1999 illustrate a pattern of over-abstraction, with Israel withdrawing 872 million cubic metres from the three shared Mountain Aquifers

Table 2.2 Abstractions from the Three Shared Aquifers within West Bank and Israel 1999 (million m³)

		Abstractions			Excess over Article 40 allocation		
Aquifer	**Estimated potential**	**Total Palestinian**	**Total Israeli**	**Total abstracted**	**Palestinian**	**Israeli**	**Total over-extraction**
Western	362.0	29.4	591.6	621.0	7.4	251.6	259.0
North Eastern	145.0	36.9	147.1	184.0	(5.1)	44.1	39.0
Eastern[a]	172.0	71.9	132.9	204.8	(2.6)	92.9	90.3
Total	**679.0**	**138.2**	**871.6**	**1,009.8**	**(0.3)**	**388.6**	**388.3**

Sources: Estimated potential from Article 40. Other numbers from Table 1, Shuval and Dweik: 24 Figure 2.9.
[a]For the Eastern Aquifer, the Article 40 Palestinian allocation was the 54.0 million cubic metres (Schedule 10) – see the table *West Bank: Allocations*, plus 20.5 million cubic metres 'immediate needs' under Section 7, making a total of 74.5 million cubic metres allocation.

Table 2.3 Palestinian Abstractions from the Three Shared Aquifers 1999 and 2007 (million m³)

Aquifer	Article 40 allocation	1999	2007
Western	22.0	29.4	27.9
North Eastern	42.0	36.9	26.8
Eastern	74.5	71.9	58.8
Total	**138.5**	**138.2**	**113.5**

Sources: Article 40 allocation from Schedule 10 and Section 7. 1999 numbers from Table 1 and Figure 2.9 in Shared Management of Palestinian and Israeli Groundwater Resources by Amjad Aliewi and Karen Assaf, in Water Resources in the Middle East, edited by Hillel Shuval and Hassan Dweik, Berlin, Springer 2007. 2007 numbers from Water Sector Status in West Bank, PWA October 2008.

in that year, 388 million cubic metres or 80 per cent above its Oslo allocation of 483 million cubic metres.

Most of this over-abstraction (259 million cubic metres) was from the Western Aquifer, where the dense concentration of Israeli wells in the foothills along the line of the National Water Carrier – see the Map 2.1 – makes this overpumping an easy task and one of which the Palestinians may have no direct knowledge, and certainly no control.[23]

Reasons for Palestinian under-abstraction

The Palestinians cite four factors for the decline in Palestinian abstractions of West Bank groundwater even below the levels attributed in Article 40: Israel's long-term over exploitation of the aquifer; the impact on Palestinian wells of Israel's new deep wells in the West Bank; the technical difficulty of developing the new wells in the Eastern Aquifer that formed part of the Article 40: agreement and the closing off of access to many wells which are the wrong side of Israel's Separation Barrier.

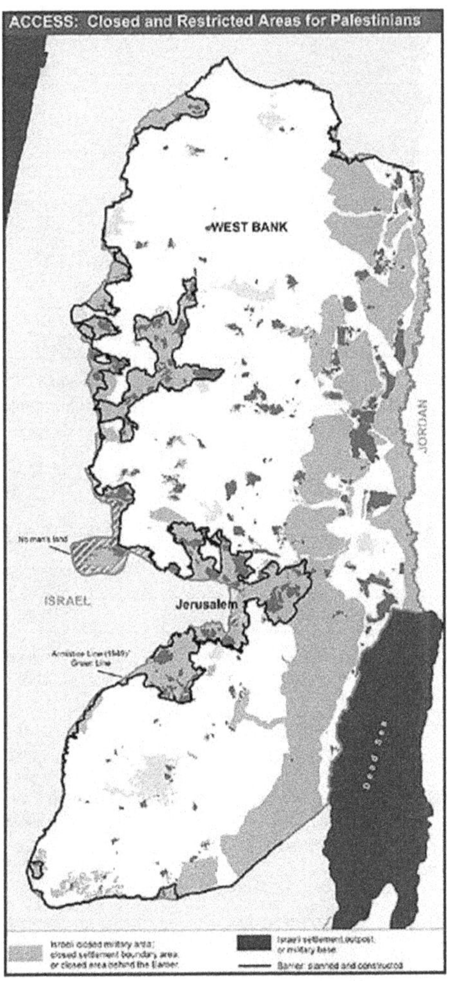

Map 2.1 West Bank ABC, UNOCHA.

On the first factor, the Palestinians assert – and the Israelis have not denied – that the consistent pattern of Israeli over-abstractions over many years has led to a secular decline in the water table. Israel was not unaware of the potentially damaging effect of this over-abstraction and the consequent decline in the water table.[24] The problem was raised as long ago as the 1990s by the Israeli State Comptroller[25] and has been openly acknowledged much more recently by the IWA.[26]

The effect of Israeli over-abstraction is much more profound for the Palestinians whose wells are upstream, than it is for the downstream Israelis. As the water table has dropped, Palestinian wells have simply dried up as excess abstraction causes water levels in the upper part of the aquifer beneath the West Bank to drop.

Palestinian reports are that between 1967 and 2005, 446 of the West Bank's 774 wells had gone out of operation, a reduction of 58 per cent. The restrictions on Palestinian well deepening or new drilling mean that as wells have dried up, their capacity has not been restored by deepening or by drilling of a substitute well.[27] This effect has considerably reduced the amount of water that could potentially be exploited within the West Bank.

On the second factor, a glance at the map *Israeli wells* shows how Israeli wells have proliferated in the West Bank, particularly in the Eastern Aquifer and in the Jordan Valley. There is evidence of these deep Israeli wells directly affecting Palestinian wells and springs. [28]

The third problem for the Palestinians is that there have been considerable technical difficulties in developing the new Palestinian wells in the Eastern Aquifer that were agreed under Article 40. The fourth factor cited by Palestinians is that access to a large number of both agricultural and domestic wells has been lost to Palestinian communities due to the Separation Barrier. It has been estimated that access to almost one third of West Bank water resources has thereby been lost.[29]

Currently, internal water resources are well below demand

Through the combination of declining aquifer yield and rapid population growth, internal water resources available to each Palestinian for all purposes in the West Bank have fallen sharply. We saw in *The History of Water* how per capita availability of internal resources dropped from 1999 levels of 190 litres per capita per day to 123 litres in 2007. By 2017, this had dropped further, to only 107 litres.[30]

As a result, Palestinians now have very low access to water which lies within their control, far below that of Israelis. Water withdrawals per capita for Palestinians from natural water in the West Bank are about one quarter of those available to Israelis. Today, Palestinians have the lowest access to internal water resources in the region: Lebanon has almost 2,600 litres per person per day; Syria, about 2,350; Egypt, 2,000; Israel has 500 litres per day of fresh water and even dry Jordan has about 470 litres against the 107 litres available to the Palestinians.[31]

The allocation of internal water to domestic uses is low, with most internal resources going to agriculture. Of the available internal resources, almost two thirds – about 60 per cent – is allocated to agriculture and the balance to municipal and industrial (M&I) uses – see Table 2.4. As a result, in 2013 only about 42 million cubic metres, equivalent to about 40 litres per capita per day, was available from internal resources for domestic, commercial and industrial uses.

The low availability and high cost of water have led to shortages and coping strategies, with some West Bank Palestinian communities carrying out unlicenced drilling to obtain drinking water – see the case of Arrabona in Chapter 3. The incidence of illegal connections and unauthorized tapping into supply lines has also increased.

Table 2.4 Sources and Uses of Water for Palestinians in the West Bank, 2013

	million m³	%	M&I	%	Agriculture	%
M&I wells	35.8	22	--	--	--	--
Agricultural wells	28.5	17	--	--	--	--
Springs	39.5	24	--	--		
Subtotal – Internal resources	**103.8**	**64**	**41.6**	**40**	**62.2**	**60**
Purchase from Mekorot	59.3	36	59.3	--	--	--
Total availability	**163.1**	**100**	**100.9**	**62**	**62.2**	**38**

Source: PWA 2014c.

Bulk water supply

The problem

The history of the last twenty years demonstrates challenging conditions, with several factors combining to create a crisis in water resources availability for the West Bank Palestinians. Since 1967, water resources development and water use in the West Bank has been strictly controlled, first unilaterally by the Israelis during the Occupation up to the time of Oslo, and subsequently by the limitations of Article 40. PWA has not been able to develop even all the water resources agreed under Article 40, while Israel has been overdrawing the resource and depleting the aquifers. The rules of the JWC and the way they have been applied have constrained new Palestinian water development and rehabilitation of older structures. Israeli movement and access restrictions[32] and the tight constraints within Area C which covers nearly two thirds of the West Bank have further held back development both of new water sources and of the conveyance structures needed to transfer water to the point of demand. Water available for domestic and industrial use is very unevenly distributed.

At the same time, on the demand side, agriculture – a vital economic sector – has continued to use the bulk of the water resources available to Palestinians in the West Bank (60 per cent, see Table 2.4), while water allocations to M&I uses have become increasingly inadequate as demand has gone up much faster than supply. With a growing gap between supply and demand, dependence on costly water purchased from Israel and subject to Israeli decision and control has increased. Rising from zero in 1967 to 28 million cubic metres in 1993, water purchases from Israel for the West Bank reached a new high of 72.6 million cubic metres in 2017 (see Table 2.5). As a result, 'water autonomy' – the share of total water use provided from internal renewable water resources – has declined to just 60 per cent in the West Bank. Some towns are very short of water throughout the year. Others are water-short at times of drought when both internal resources and supplies from Israel may reduce. A few towns – Jericho, for example – have abundant local water supplies.

Sources for municipal and industrial (M&I) supply

Current supply levels fall far short of demand for potable water. In 2016, average supply levels to Palestinian households in the West Bank were about 115 litres per person –

Figure 2.1 Israeli water tanks, Palestinian water bowsers in the West Bank, with permission from Irish Central.

Table 2.5 Annual Available Water Quantity in Palestinian Territories by Source, 2017 (in million m³)

	Purchases from Mekorot	Desalinated water	Spring discharge	Pumped from Palestinian wells	Total
West Bank	72.6	-	23.5	85.8	181.9
Gaza Strip	10.6	4.0	-	178.7	193.3
Total	**83.2**	**4.0**	**23.5**	**264.5**	**375.2**

Source: Palestinian Water Authority, 2017. Water Information System. Ramallah – Palestine.

see Table 2.6. However, of that more than two fifths (44 per cent) is 'unaccounted for water' – losses from the system, illicit connections, water delivered but not billed. As a result, total supply per person was no more than 65 litres per person – compared to the PWA ambition of increasing supply towards what is thought to be 'actual unconstrained demand' of 150 litres of potable water for each person each day. The current actual consumption of 65 litres is well below the World Health Organization (WHO) benchmark minimum of 100 litres for domestic consumption to achieve full health and hygiene benefits. It is also only one quarter (25 per cent) of 2016 consumption in Israeli households of 263 litres per person per day.

Even the present low levels of per capita domestic supply have been maintained only by growing water purchases from Mekorot – dependence on Israeli sources has increased to nearly two thirds of total domestic supply. As Table 2.6 shows,

Table 2.6 Domestic Water Supply and Demand for Palestinians in the West Bank, 2016

	Million m³	Litres per person per day*
Domestic demand	**152**	**150 litres**
Water available for domestic supply		
• Groundwater and springs	48	47 litres
• Mekorot purchase	69	68 litres
Subtotal	**117**	**115 litres**
Unaccounted-for water	51	50 litres
Total supply (supply less unaccounted-for water)	**66**	**65 litres**
Supply gap (domestic demand less total supply)	**88**	**85 litres**

**Based on a West Bank Palestinian population of 2.8 million.*
Source: PWA. Adapted from Securing Water for Development (World Bank 2018).

in 2016 only 47 litres per person – 40 per cent of water available for domestic purposes – came from Palestinian-controlled groundwater and springs within the West Bank and the rest – 68 litres per person, 60 per cent – came from Mekorot purchases.

Variations in supply – and in tariffs

There is wide variation in quantities supplied for domestic purposes per capita between locations, with extremely low supply in some towns. The best-served towns benefit from an ample domestic supply. In Jericho, for example, consumers receive 257 litres each on an average day, and in Qalqilya 161 litres. These towns are those that have good supplies from wells that they control or which have good access to supplies from Mekorot. The worst served towns have only a fraction of those levels of supply. In Yatta, for example, consumers receive just 27 litres per day on average, and Dura just 28 litres. In some cases, supply has shrunk markedly: in 2009, Bethlehem was supplying 142 litres per person each day. By 2015, this had fallen by half to 71 litres.[33]

Varying levels of dependence on purchased water lead to wide variations in water tariffs in the West Bank. Tariffs are much lower in towns that have their own wells than in towns that must purchase their water.[34] The average tariff in the West Bank in 2015 was NIS 5.05 per cubic metre ($1.40), but towns with their own water were able to charge less than one third of the average, as little as NIS 1.59 per cubic metre ($0.45) – and to supply higher quantities of water. By contrast, consumers in towns without their own wells and dependent on water transfers from elsewhere and on purchases from Mekorot were paying as much as NIS 7.04 per cubic metre ($2.00), more than four times as much as the lowest tariffs.[35]

The distribution of bulk water is not efficient

Up until 1967, bulk water for municipal and industrial water supply came exclusively from wells around towns. The source was one of the three aquifers which lie beneath the West Bank. Under the Israeli occupation from 1967, all

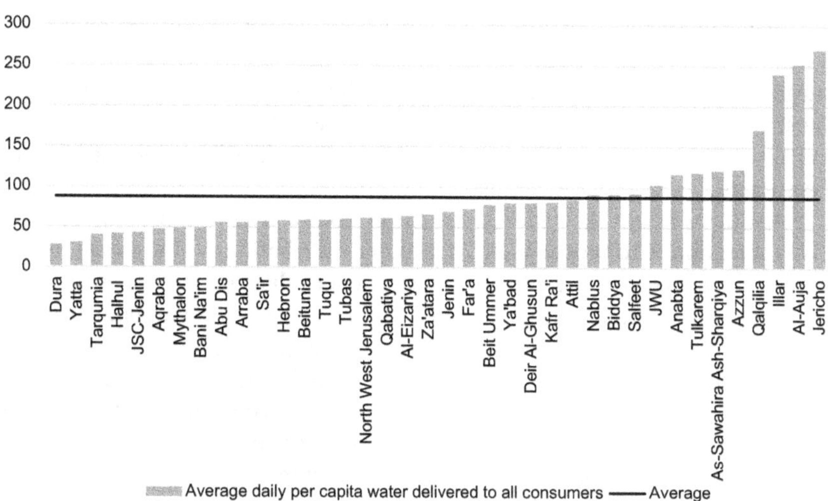

Figure 2.2 Average daily per capita water delivered to all consumers, West Bank, 2015. *Source*: Water Sector Regulatory Council.

water points had to be licenced and regulated, and abstractions were limited by quotas.[36] The West Bank Water Department (WBWD) was set up to organize bulk water supply, either from local deep wells or through a bulk transmission network between towns. Over time, this network was linked to the Israeli bulk water system, so that water could be delivered from Israel to the West Bank. A largely parallel bulk network served the Israeli settlements in the West Bank as these sprang up.

Today bulk water provision in the West Bank remains the responsibility of the West Bank Water Department (WBWD), which was transferred from Israeli to Palestinian control in 1996.[37] WBWD manages wells and purchases water from Mekorot. It then distributes and sells bulk water to service providers. A number of studies over the last decade have faulted the technical and financial performance of the WBWD. There are proposals for institutional restructuring of bulk water supply – as we have seen, the 2014 Water Law provides for the establishment of a National Water Company (NWC) on a business basis (on similar lines to the Israeli company Mekorot) that would be the bulk provider for both West Bank and Gaza. In March 2016, PWA drafted a road map (*National Water Company Draft Action Plan*) for setting up the NWC by a phased transformation of the WBWD into the new company. However, no decision has yet been made to implement the road map – see the section *Sector reforms* in Chapter 3 for detail on the proposals and on progress to date.

However, it is not clear that institutional change alone will solve the problem of efficient distribution. At present, the West Bank's infrastructure for bulk water supply is fragmented, linked piecemeal with the Mekorot network and with scant connections between towns across the West Bank. The result is a confused pattern of Palestinian bulk water mains that convey water from Palestinian wells to towns and villages – see Map 2.1. This fragmentary Palestinian bulk water system is plugged in at points to the elaborate network by which Mekorot has integrated Israeli settlements in the West Bank into its national water grid, linking the settlements ultimately to Israel's National Water Carrier – see Chapter 1 – and also providing the opportunity to sell water from Israel's national grid to the Palestinians.

Palestinians would like to develop an integrated water grid on the Israeli model. PWA's intention is to model West Bank water distribution on the Israeli model, with an integrated network of bulk water pipelines that transfer water to points of demand economically and at least cost. The advantages of this approach, which have been amply demonstrated by Israel's integrated network, are complete control over despatching of water, and the possibility of linking all sources with all points of demand in a high-connectivity water grid. Non-conventional sources like desalinated water together with water imports could also be readily factored in.

Plans for this kind of grid in the West Bank are stymied by the difficulty of long-range planning and by Israeli restrictions. In the absence of a clear and equitable agreement on future water resources for the West Bank and on the Palestinians' right to develop water infrastructure all across the West Bank, the PWA is unable to plan for the related infrastructure. This is well illustrated by the most recent proposals for purchase of water,[38] where the PWA has had to go to the drawing board to prepare hasty plans for new pipelines and capacity to accommodate the proposed extra water.

In addition, a glance at the map of the West Bank divided into Areas A, B and C will show that Palestinian-controlled areas (A and B) are essentially fragmented islands of authority, separated by large tracts of Area C, by settlements and by the increasing levels of segregated east–west infrastructure – roads, power lines, water pipes, soon light railway tracks – designed to serve the settlements and reinforce Israeli control of the West Bank. Planning a rational, cost-effective Palestinian water network would be well-nigh impossible under current dispensations. In the absence of a new agreement, the West Bank's infrastructure for bulk water supply will remain fragmented, linked piecemeal with the Mekorot network, and with a rising level of dependence on water imported from Israel.

How could the West Bank increase its water resource security and reduce risks?

With rapidly rising demand and constrained supply, the West Bank is facing a large and growing gap between supply of water and the demand for it. This is particularly acute for water for M&I uses. According to PWA calculations, this gap amounts to 66 million cubic metres, two thirds more than current supply. With less than 50 litres of domestic supply per person per day from internal resources (see Table 2.6), anything approaching an adequate level of resources for domestic supplies is being maintained only by making up the balance from water purchases.

However, even with purchases from Israel, current levels of domestic water supply in the West Bank are below PWA target levels – currently 120 litres daily for each person, rising over time to 150 litres. The population is growing and with it demand for water, so that ever more bulk water is required. The World Bank has estimated that by 2030 total demand for domestic water will reach 209 million cubic metres, nearly double the current availability and more than four times the water currently available internally for domestic supply from groundwater and springs. If there is no change, within a decade West Bank Palestinians would be dependent on Israel for nearly 80 per cent of their domestic water requirements. Moreover, internal supplies are likely to be further constrained as the yield of groundwater aquifers and springs continues to drop. Thus the Palestinians are a very long way from realizing the kind of 'autonomy' in water resources that Israel has achieved.

Bridging the gap

PWA's blue skies planning PWA's Strategic Development Plan (SDP)[39] targets water resources development as the main way to bridge the large and growing gap between supply and demand in the West Bank – see Table 2.7. The plan proposes a doubling of total water availability between 2014 and 2022, from 164 million cubic metres to 327 million cubic metres. The extra water would come from conventional water production from springs and wells, which would more than double, from 104 million cubic metres to 213 million cubic metres; from desalination (22 million cubic metres); and from a further 50 per cent increase in purchases from Mekorot, which would rise from the 2014 level of 60 million cubic metres to 92 million cubic metres.[40]

It is clear at once that an extraordinary revolution in water development and management would have to take place for these targets to be achieved. For conventional water production to more than double over the eight-year period, the Israelis would have to give up each year 109 million cubic metres of Mountain Aquifer groundwater or Jordan River water that they at present control. For the West Bank to have its own production of 22 million cubic metres of desalinated water there would have to be elaborate and expensive infrastructure built to

Table 2.7 Sector Targets According to the 2016 SDP: West Bank (million m^3)

Indicator	Actual 2014	Target 2022
Water resources		
Conventional water production – MCM	104	213
Desalinated water production – MCM	0	22
Purchased water – MCM	60	92
Total available water – MCM	***164***	***327***

Source: National Water Sector Strategic Plan and Action Pan (2017–22) Part 1: Strategic Development Plan. Table 13. PWA May 2016.

desalinate seawater at the coast and to pump up to the West Bank. Even if this were technically and financially feasible, it would demand a level of agreement and cooperation with Israel which until today has remained a distant prospect.[41] Only increased purchases from Mekorot look feasible today – these would require only Israeli agreement and new bulk conveyance (see the section *Water purchases*).[42]

In the current circumstances of the constraints of Article 40, the SDP responds to aspirations and to need rather than to feasibility. The plan is inevitably more a statement about recovering control over natural resources that Palestinians consider their own than it is about practical planning. It is understandable that the PA plans on assumptions which remain unconfirmed – including sovereignty over land and water within Palestinian territory, an end to the Occupation, complete Israeli withdrawal from the West Bank, and an end to the multiple constraints of movement and access. But it is also not surprising that so far little progress has been made in implementing the planned steps. Only a resetting of the whole basis of cooperation on water would make these targets attainable – and this is precisely what we explore in Part III of this book. But in the meantime, are there other possible steps, and what are the potential and constraints to realizing them?

Reducing losses

The high rate of unaccounted-for water in the Palestinian water system in the West Bank has been noted earlier – it approaches 45 per cent.[43] Much of these losses are purely physical, water escaping from leaking networks. This problem is prevalent because networks are old and the terrain often hilly. When water is pumped uphill under pressure it often springs a leak, and this problem becomes much worse when supply is intermittent and a surge of water goes clanging up rusty old pipes. All too often new leaks erupt and much precious water is wasted.

There is plainly scope for technical measures and investment to reduce these losses. Estimates (World Bank 2018) are that 15 per cent of the unaccounted-for water occurs in the bulk supply system and 29 per cent occurs at the domestic delivery level. These levels are way above those that prevail in Israel, but nonetheless the Israeli example indicates the potential of reductions in 'unaccounted for water': as we saw in Chapter 1, in 2006, unaccounted-for water in Israel stood at 16 per cent. By 2013, this was down to 11 per cent, well on the way to the target of 7 per cent.[44]

There is not only a question of water availability at play here. It is also a financial and economic question. As the cost of bulk water supplies goes up, reducing system losses will become increasingly the cheapest source of extra water for many towns. According to the PWA's current plans, realistic targets for 2030 are to reduce losses in the bulk system to 8 per cent and in the retail system to 22 per cent. This reduction from over 44 per cent to an average 30 per cent could increase water availability to Palestinian consumers by 16 million cubic metres, equivalent to one quarter of current actual domestic supply of 66 million cubic metres – at relatively low cost compared to the high price of importing desalinated water.[45]

A significant but unknown share of 'unaccounted for water' is not actually due to physical losses at all. It is water actually consumed but not billed for one reason or another. This includes considerable volumes of water abstracted through illegal connections. Most of this occurs in the southern West Bank, particularly in Hebron Governorate, where the population receives the poorest official water service. The average per capita supply in the governorate is in the range 15–35 litres per person per day. A typical reaction to such poor service is to help oneself by illegally connecting to supply lines. Reducing this component of the losses requires a tough stance by both the administration and service providers. Palestinian authorities may be reluctant to take such a stance, particularly in volatile Hebron. There may be some political will to tackle water theft, but this is tempered by a general awareness of the unfairness of the current water allocation. In any case, much water theft is thought to occur in Area C, where it would require cooperation with Israel to address the problem.

There are thus two political economy questions. Internally, within the Palestinian administration and society, water theft may be seen as an almost venial sin, or even as a just act. Even if water theft is reprehended, would Palestinians want to be associated in its repression? In the view of Palestinians, water is scarce, the Occupier controls it. Article 40 is outdated, 'Occupier's Law'. Tapping in to a Mekorot line may be seen not as a crime but as somehow regaining what is one's own. It might even be seen as an act of justified resistance. Certainly images flashed around the world of Israeli soldiers roughing up poor Palestinian peasant families who have been trying to help themselves to what they see as their own patrimony suggest there are ways of seeing the act other than as outright theft (see Figure 5.9). To have Palestinian police standing by, associated with the Occupier, is almost insupportable for the PA.

The second political economy question concerns Area C. In 2017 a new agreement with Israel was made to revive the Joint Water Committee (JWC), and one element of this has been interpreted as allowing the Palestinian Authority (PA) a freer hand to intervene in Area C. It may, of course, be that even willingness to cooperate in the JWC may not overcome restrictions imposed by the Civil Administration on Palestinian ability to act within Area C. But even so, the question remains posed: in the vexed politics of water in the West Bank, would the Palestinian administration or security forces wish to be associated with arresting Palestinians and accusing them of water theft? It may be that they are more comfortable with the status quo where Israelis do the enforcement.

Transferring water out of agriculture

One option always considered when water is scarce and finite is inter-sectoral transfer, from 'lower value' uses to higher-value ones. In the West Bank, nearly two thirds of internal resources have been allocated to agriculture (see Table 2.4). Although this allocation is usually treated as fixed and non-negotiable, the question inevitably arises as to whether water might be reallocated from lower-value agriculture to higher-value M&I uses. Here there is an essential question of feasibility – and of law

– because most agricultural water in the West Bank is in private hands. Individuals, groups and communities have developed and used the resource, often for decades or centuries, and they remain to all intents and purposes the owners of the water that comes from the water source they control and exploit. Although the Palestinian water laws have declared water a national resource, the PA has never applied this in practice by taking over water sources held in private hands. In any case, agricultural water is not an easily fungible resource that can be physically reallocated wholesale elsewhere.

But even if it were possible, in terms of equity, legal and institutional arrangements and infrastructure, to siphon water out of agriculture and transfer it to urban uses, would it be the best policy? This is a debate familiar from many countries but one which is very controversial in the highly charged political atmosphere of the West Bank. In the relatively poor West Bank, agriculture is important economically, as we shall see in Chapter 5. The sector contributes some 6 per cent of GDP and 12 per cent of employment, so clearly the idea of reducing water allocations would be questionable economically and socially. It would also be contentious politically, threatening the prosperity of the sector and undermining the PA's policy of sustaining the rural economy for economic and food security purposes. Agriculture is also the prime means of maintaining occupancy of land which is constantly under threat from Israeli land grab. In Area C, even the constrained agriculture that is allowed remains a vital mechanism for asserting Palestinian ownership.

One approach used in Israel, as we have seen, was to make agricultural water use more efficient and productive by combining technology like piped conveyance, drip irrigation, fertigation, protected agriculture in plastic houses and so on with adoption of a commercial production and marketing system of high-value crops that return the maximum '$ per drop'. In fact, West Bank farmers, like their colleagues on the Jordanian East Bank, have long since acquired many of these techniques. They could certainly do more if they did not face constraints of costs, capital, market outlet and so on (on which see Chapter 5). But even if further efficiency gains saved water in agriculture, would it be a prudent policy to abstract these savings from the sector and transfer them elsewhere? In the eyes, of the Palestinians, certainly not. For Palestinians the priority would be to use the saved water to expand the irrigated production area – for exactly the same reasons that Israel has always promoted its agriculture: occupation of the land, making unused lands productive, security, rural economic development, maintenance of traditional land use, protection of the environment, food security.

Palestinians question why their own agricultural sector should be artificially limited when that of their neighbour has benefitted from quite different treatment.

Managing risks through storage and conveyance

Water sources in their undeveloped state rarely match demand either temporally or spatially, hence the predominant risk in water resources management that water is not available when and where it is required. The solution is to ensure the means to store water for when it is needed and to convey it to the location where it is needed. Storage is needed to carry water over from the rainy season so that it can be distributed to farmers in the summer when irrigation requirements are at their highest or to convey it more evenly throughout the year to households and business needs. Storage is also required to hold treated wastewater, which is produced every day, until it is needed for agriculture or the environment, usually only in summer. In addition, onveyance infrastructure is essential to carry stored water to its point of use in towns, villages or fields.

Apart from natural lakes and wetlands, there are three main ways to store water – in the soil profile, in aquifers, and in constructed retention infrastructure like ponds, tanks and reservoirs. In all these ways of storing water, the West Bank Palestinians are constrained. They have only limited and controlled access to the soil moisture of Area C and are constrained by restrictions from developing the same means of enhancing soil moisture that Israelis regularly employ – such as new terraces and run-off-run-on techniques of water harvesting.

Groundwater is a first-class tool of risk management for farmers. It provides a perennially available, high-quality resource ideal for hi-tech irrigated farming, and it also acts as a just-in-time resource for supplementary irrigation and as a buffer against drought. Aquifers can also form part of an integrated storage and water resource management system as the Israelis have well demonstrated with their investment in recharging aquifers with fresh water, desalinated water and treated wastewater, and then pumping out and conveying the stored water when and where it is needed. However, these options are not available or even of use to the West Bank Palestinians, who are limited to their small quantities of groundwater and that is it. There is no point enhancing recharge or replenishing the aquifer artificially or even in conservation as there is no benefit to be derived because of the quota limitations of Article 40. In time of drought a Palestinian farmer cannot increase pumping. When groundwater yields dwindle, he is barred from deepening an agricultural well or drilling a new one. Storage of water in aquifers – for example, the treated wastewater expected from the new plants to come on stream in the coming years (see Chapters 4 and 5) – would require extensive infrastructure development in Area C, unlikely to be permitted by the Israelis. The same goes for surface water storage, which has been systematically rejected by the Israelis.

Wastewater reuse in agriculture

We saw in Chapter 1 how Israel has brilliantly succeeded in transferring fresh water out of agriculture by replacing it with treated wastewater – today nearly two thirds of water used in Israeli agriculture is treated wastewater. This kind of exchange has also been practiced in neighbouring Jordan for over thirty years. In its *Strategic Development Plan*, the PWA has actually proposed that where it is economically and technically feasible, water might be transferred out of agriculture, with compensation in the form of return of treated wastewater.

At present, West Bank Palestinians produce very little treated wastewater and reuse almost none of it, at least officially. The reasons for this have mostly to do with lack of the necessary treatment and conveyance infrastructure – see Chapter 4. In any case, little real thought has been given up to now to the institutional or economic mechanisms that would allow such a transfer to take place. As we saw earlier, it would also pose practical problems of storage and of conveyance from towns to farming areas, and require the laying of pipe networks which so often run afoul of Israel's visceral security concerns.

It may be that as new wastewater treatment plants come on stream, reuse in agriculture may become more practiced – see the discussion on Hebron in Chapter 4, for example. But reusing wastewater is one thing, swapping it for fresh water is quite another. Small-scale experiments in the West Bank to date suggest that transfer of water from agriculture compensated by allocation of treated wastewater would be furiously resisted by farmers and would strike at the image of the farmstead and traditional Palestinian rural life. The experience in Israel shows that it is not impossible, but that it requires steady policy, guaranteed availability, and strong institutions and incentives. Again Israel was dealing with a centrally managed nationalized resource. In the West Bank, most agricultural water is private and managed at the level of the farm or of groups of farmers.

Water purchases

The easiest solution, although in many ways the most problematic, would be to buy more water from Mekorot. This is the only really practical solution in the short term, and it is a realistic possibility, as Israel has increased its desalination capacity considerably and is now in a position to become a commercial net water exporter. The PA has recently re-engaged with Israel in the Joint Water Committee (JWC) and negotiations are underway for an extra 30 million cubic metres purchase. In addition, the proposed 'Red–Dead' deal also includes a commitment by Israel to provide an extra 34 MCM of desalinated water to the Palestinian territories. However, the terms of these purchases are not yet clear, and they may prove expensive. In addition, purchasing more water from Israel will further reduce Palestinian water autonomy.

The lack of water autonomy for Palestinians and the increasing dependence on Israel are particularly invidious issues. Palestinians look at Israel's long struggle to establish water autonomy and conclude that this is a valid goal, a source of independence and sovereignty – but that their chances of achieving it ebb away with every increment in water imports.

The question of the source of imported water is important too. Palestinians reason that the water they are required to import comes from one of two sources In the case of fresh water, they consider it is from regional water resources – the Mountain Aquifers and the Jordan River basin – of which they consider themselves at least part-owners. In particular, the fresh water that can be delivered most economically would be from the groundwater under their feet, and that is a resource to which they feel entitled. So why must they buy it – and why pay high prices when it can be produced locally at a much lower cost?

In the case of desalinated water, the Palestinians consider it wrong that they should be required to replace water that is available beneath their own territory with water desalinated at the coast at high cost and then pumped all the way up to the highlands. They also consider it wrong that one of the poorest peoples in the region should be required to pay the highest price for water, especially when four fifths of the low-cost groundwater resource arising in their own land is denied to them.

The political economy of increasing water purchases is highly charged. From the Palestinian perspective, extra purchases would increase dependency and would be seen as recognizing the perpetuation of Israel's de facto control of West Bank water resources and the allocation of water rights under Article 40. Beyond that, water resources are one of the five 'final status' issues, and concessions on water resources are seen as compromising Palestinian future claims to sovereignty over West Bank water resources.

The complement to this on the Israeli side is that water sales to the West Bank will never be a politically neutral commercial transaction. Since the dawn of Zionism, water has been a political, strategic issue. Israel is likely to enter into a commitment for extra water sales to the Palestinians only if it were seen as being within its own political interests: that is, bringing some advantage beyond the benefit of sale of surplus water.

Article 40 and security of water resources for West Bank Palestinians

At the time of Oslo, Article 40 was considered by some as a breakthrough for Israeli–Palestinian cooperation. Others saw it as a prelude to a surrender of Palestinian water rights, part of a larger surrender of most of the rights for which Palestinians had struggled over for more than a century. Whatever one's views of the virtues and vices of Article 40 at the time that it was negotiated, it is generally agreed, even by those who see it through an Israeli lens, that over the years the agreement and the way in which it has been implemented have failed to correspond to Palestinian needs. Water resources are insufficient, water services remain poor. Any semblance of good practice cooperation over the management of shared water resources has vanished.

The way it looks to Palestinians is that after waiting nearly three decades for a fair and final resolution of their claims to water resources and to the right to manage them, they have in truth achieved *less* water resources security rather than more. They believe that any measure of water autonomy they enjoyed in the past has receded ever further; that there is no equitable mechanism for joint planning and management; and that governance arrangements give Israel a veto over Palestinian water sector development and services but not vice versa. The West Bank has become a client, going continually cap in hand to Israel for ever-increasing quantities of Mekorot water.

From a human rights point of view, they believe that the water resources that lie under their feet should be used for the benefit of their people; that the Israelis have no right to drill wells in the West Bank and pump out West Bank water for their own benefit; and that a fair share of the water in the international river that flows past Palestinian territory should belong to them for their sovereign use.

From an economic point of view, they believe that extra water should come from the cheapest available source – surface water, groundwater, springs, water harvesting within the West Bank – and not from seawater desalinated at high cost many miles away and then pumped over a long distance and to high elevation at considerable economic, financial and environmental cost. They believe, also, that it is unfair for wealthy Israelis and developed Israel to enjoy the low-cost and high-quality groundwater that arises in the West Bank while the comparatively poor Palestinians, with one tenth of the income per person and all the handicaps of a lesser developed country, should be asked to pay top dollar for artificial water (with a high carbon footprint) which is far and away the most expensive source of water in the region.

From the viewpoint of both water security and national security, the Palestinians also believe that water resources within their national territory, both surface water and groundwater, belong to them and should be under their management. How else can they manage water resources in an integrated and sustainable way for the benefit of their people and with respect for the interests of their neighbours?

Yet at present there appears little prospect of moving forward on these issues. Water has become a part of the fractured Oslo deal, a politicized issue that lacks either a political dialogue or an institutional mechanism to resolve it. Palestinians do not feel powerful over outcomes and cannot see how to move forward. Water resources management and water services have become emblematic of a wider disempowerment.

The result is a highly politicized context that makes it hard to treat water in a pragmatic way. 'Peace' negotiators often say *Let's start with water, a low hanging fruit*, as though water security for a people was simply a matter of delivering a commodity. Yet in the politicized context, Palestinians are very reluctant to see water just as a commodity like cake, or to see water services as simply a business. They aspire to a view of water as a national resource, just as the Zionists and then the Israelis have done for a hundred years or more.

This is one reason why Palestinian water planning looks so unrealistic. The Palestinian Water Authority's plans for water resources development and management reflect a vision of water security for Palestinians which includes recovery of control over the resource. But as we said, these plans respond to Palestinian claims to the resources that lie close to their hand and to aspirations to water autonomy that do not look feasible under present circumstances.

But are there other circumstances in which Palestinians might have more realistic hopes of matching Israel's level of complete autonomy in water resources, and of having the same level of access to resources to supply their people and their economy as Israelis have? We shall come back to this question in Part III of this book.

Chapter 3

SECURITY OF WATER SERVICES IN THE WEST BANK[1]

In 2008, we visited West Bank villages in the north-eastern corner of Jenin Governorate, along the border with Israel. Straight out the local leader, Khaled Abu Farha, said, 'We don't have enough water even for drinking – and we are an agricultural and pastoral area, we rely on water for our livelihood. Even when we pay 12 shekels a cubic metre (about $3.50) for drinking water, the quality is very poor. Water is our number one problem.' In Khaled's village, Deir Abu Daif, the water source was mainly tankers but villagers were also buying from unlicenced wells because it was cheaper. However, quality was very poor. Khaled told us, 'There is a lot of diarrhoea and vomiting, especially during the summer. But what can we do? This is a poor village where agriculture is the only employer. Water is so short that the farm workers often get paid in water.'

In nearby Faqua, Ali Abu Dukar says,

> The Israeli water pipe supplying their settlements is a few metres from our village. But we have to get our water by tanker. You have to wait two weeks to get a tanker, as demand is so great, and in summer it's worse. For sanitation, we all use cess pits, but with our permeable soils we know that the sewage is polluting the aquifer, and perhaps our cisterns too.

The low availability and high cost of water oblige Palestinians to adopt coping strategies. In this part of Jenin Governorate, the JWC did not licence further wells and coping strategies became extreme. In *The History of Water* we told the story of Arrabona whose villagers ran out of all alternatives for access to safe water at a reasonable cost. They dared to drill an unlicenced well for drinking water. They spent 90,000 shekels ($25,000) on the well, but still the Israeli military came and filled it in. They told us laconically, 'All we wanted was safe water for our children. Now we have a very expensive play park – and the same contaminated expensive water.'[2]

* * *

Arrabona and the other villages are at one end of quite a broad spectrum of experience in the Palestinian West Bank. In fact, over the half century since 1967, many West Bank Palestinians have come to experience greatly improved water services. Today, most towns and villages – but not all – have been connected to piped water supply. About half of households get at least some water most days and some communities have ample water at reasonable prices. Other communities, however, have a very poor service indeed.

This chapter will tell the story of the highs and the lows. It looks at overall delivery and impacts of water service provision in the West Bank, at the general and specific constraints and their causes – and at the possible solutions that would enable West Bank providers to emulate their Israeli counterparts and provide a first-rate water service. We examine the plethora of suppliers, which range from large urban utilities to small village operations. Some of these are as good as they can be in the West Bank context; others are weak technically or financially, or both. The chapter looks at how these operations are run, at why some succeed and others fail. A big financial issue is that many of the municipal providers do not pay their bulk water bills. Sizable arrears have built up and Israel simply deducts the amounts due to its National Water Company, Mekorot, from the Palestinian Authority's import tariff revenues which it collects.

We look too at the Palestinian Authority's aspirations to bring water supply services up to twenty-first-century standards and to provide efficient 24/7 service by obtaining enough bulk water and by reforming water institutions along the lines of the Israeli model. The proposal is to set up a single bulk supplier and four regional utilities – three in the West Bank and one in Gaza. A water grid network would connect all communities, just as the National Water Carrier does in Israel. In addition, the idea is to resolve all the technical and financial problems in retail supply by building up financially and managerially autonomous providers at the municipal and local level. However, progress on this agenda has been limited. Added to the challenges the plan poses for the capacity of Palestinian institutions are the multiple constraints imposed by the Occupation. The chapter ends by considering what options the Palestinians have in the current context – and what would have to change for them to be able to have the quality water services that their Israeli counterparts enjoy.

Service provision for West Bank Palestinians today

Policy on water and sanitation service provision[3]

Since the Palestinian Authority (PA) was set up in 1994 under the Oslo Accords, its policy has been to provide quality and affordable water and sanitation services to all the people of the West Bank and Gaza. Since some responsibility for water resources, infrastructure and services in West Bank and Gaza was transferred to the Palestinian Authority (PA) under the Accords, policy has been what any government would wish to do – to connect all households to continuous potable water supply; to provide access for all to safe sanitation and sewerage networks and to wastewater treatment; to supply these services to all in an adequate quantity and quality at an affordable price; and to provide services through efficient and financially viable service providers.

Following the Oslo Accords, rates of connection improved. At the time of Oslo, about 87 per cent of the West Bank population was connected to water supply and about 31 per cent to sewerage networks – these are 1995 figures. Over the more than two decades since then, the population has increased and household connections have more than kept pace. Today 93 per cent of households in the West Bank are connected. Network sanitation rates have, however, only kept pace with population growth.[4]

However, the quality of service has not kept pace with connection rates. The imbalance between supply and demand for water has increased and a series of problems has emerged at both the bulk and retail service levels. Water service is often intermittent, physical losses are high and service provision is uneven across the West Bank, with many consumers facing high costs and low supply quantities. The performance of the plethora of service providers, over 300 in total of differing sizes and capacities, is highly variable.

These problems alarmed the government, which started taking steps towards the comprehensive reform of the water and sanitation sector. A process of national debate and study resulted in agreement in 2009 on the need for comprehensive reform based on best-practice guiding principles. As we saw in Chapter 2, sector reform and the resulting *Action Plan for Water Sector Reform* were incorporated in the 2014 Water Law. In water supply, the reforms provided for a single national water company, and for consolidation of water supply services under regional utilities – three in the West Bank and one in Gaza. The bulk of the reforms were planned to be completed by 2022, but this now looks unlikely, for reasons that will become apparent later in this chapter. In the meantime, services continue to be provided by a host of service providers, largely under the aegis of the Ministry of Local Government (MoLG).[5]

The plethora of suppliers[6]

West Bank water and sanitation services have grown up in different political and institutional contexts – under Jordan from 1948 to 1967, under Israeli Occupation from 1967 to 1995, and under the framework of the Oslo Accords since then, within the complex jurisdictions of ABC. Different ideas and policies have shaped the institutions which today take various forms, each with its history and its strengths and weaknesses.

The first of these forms of service provider is what is more or less a classic water utility. In the West Bank, about a quarter of the population is served by two of these bodies which have been formally established as autonomous utilities. The Jerusalem Water Undertaking (JWU) provides water services to East Jerusalem and surrounding communities, and to much of Ramallah and al Bireh governorate. The Water Supply and Sanitation Authority (WSSA) provides water services to the Bethlehem area.

Most of the rest of the West Bank population – about 72 per cent – are serviced by providers under the aegis of the Ministry of Local Government (MoLG). Larger towns have *municipal water departments,* which provide water and, in some cases, sanitation services – there are seventy-six of these municipal departments in the West Bank. A number of smaller West Bank municipalities and villages have joined together to form *Joint Service Councils*, of which there are thirteen so far set up. These councils provide water services to their local area, and sometimes also deal with wastewater. Some 162 *village councils* also deliver water and wastewater services to their local communities.

In addition there are other, non-state, providers. Services to some refugee camps are provided by the United Nations Relief and Works Agency for Palestine (UNRWA). In the West Bank, there is also an active private sector of water-purifying plants and private water tankers. One purely private network provider (in the Rawabi luxury housing complex) serves a few hundred high-end consumers.

Case studies of service providers

In a quest to see for ourselves what exactly are the problems of water supply for the Palestinian people that need to be solved, we visited a number of the more than 300 West Bank water suppliers. Our visits took place over a decade, between 2008 and 2017. We found the best of cases and the worst of cases. Some providers were working efficiently, providing good-quality water round the clock at a reasonable price. Others were in a dire state, providing some of the worst services to be found anywhere in the world, barely able to justify the name of water service provider at all.

Amongst the best were large providers, providing good services to a demanding, relatively well-off urban clientele. There were also smaller providers serving smaller communities or rural villages with comparative efficiency. At the other end of the spectrum there were municipal and community providers which were failing to deliver even the most basic level of service. We looked in detail at four of these providers as a way of illustrating achievements and constraints. Our objective was to describe the quality of water services in the West Bank and to pinpoint the types of challenge that providers face.

The Jerusalem Water Undertaking

We went first to the largest of the West Bank suppliers, the Jerusalem Water Undertaking (JWU). This is a well-run utility by any standards. JWU owes its relatively good performance to its status as an autonomous utility and to the related good governance and dynamic and forward-looking management. In its service area, which includes the Palestinian administrative capital of Ramallah, there is a high concentration of middle-class civil service and professional households. Set up over fifty years ago, on the eve of the 1967 Occupation, JWU serves a third of a million people, delivering a fairly good quantity of water of high quality, albeit at a fairly high price. Operating efficiency is about average for the West Bank and financial viability is relatively good, with sales and collections covering costs. Water shortages mean that full service cannot always be maintained in the summer.

In 2008, we asked Dr Ibrahim Safi, the general manager, what the strengths of the JWU operation were. His answer was, 'a combination of good governance and good management'. Governance is helped by JWU's autonomous status. Established in 1966 by separate statute under Jordanian law, it is governed by an independent board and prides itself on its efforts at transparency and accountability to the municipalities it serves. The utility has good customer relations, with broad outreach and communications, a dedicated customer service department and transparent complaints procedures.

'Management is driven by our practice of focussing on both the short term and the longer term', Dr Safi said.

> We have short-term programmes – technical ones to keep the water flowing and minimize system losses, and financial ones to control costs and ensure people pay their bills. Longer term, we are aiming to increase our supply of bulk water and to apply ways to keep demand within reasonable limits – for example by ensuring our tariffs reflect the real costs and by introducing technical fixes like low-flush toilets.

JWU puts a lot of effort into its financial and business management. They are aware that this is a classic area of weakness of water supply utilities. The usual crowd-pleasing populist politics of low tariffs are an ever-present risk in the highly charged Palestinian environment. JWU tries to ensure its tariffs are set at full-cost recovery levels. It endeavours to keep costs down while working to maintain a relationship of mutual responsibility with consumers. Its cost recovery policy is backed up by vigorous collection of current and past dues. Finally, although Dr Safi did not say this, JWU recognizes the importance of good leadership, businesslike management and motivated and qualified employees.

Although JWU enjoys good relations with the Israeli authorities, it has still encountered difficulties. In 2008, JWU had a problem with operating one of their wells.

> This kind of thing is a headache as it means we have go to the Israelis. We call Shahal (an Israeli company). If we need spares or replacement parts, everything has to come through Israel. There can be problems getting equipment or goods in. We call the Germans (JWU's main donor supporter) and they help, or we call an Israeli fixer – or we speak to the Civil Administration direct. We discuss the goods – whether it's pipes or whatever.

But despite these arrangements, JWU can have major problems: in 2008, water meters arrived from the UK, and stayed at the docks for six months. Dr Safi explained: 'We had to pay NIS 400,000 ($120,000) in customs and demurrage.

They did this to force us to buy meters from them. So usually we must get our spares from Israeli companies.' These restrictions add to costs. The JWU reckons the extra cost is 10–12 per cent above what prices would be under competition. 'And the checkpoints make business harder generally.'

Getting enough bulk water has become increasingly hard. JWU operates six wells, pumping from a depth of 1,500 metres, but most of JWU's water, about 80 per cent, now has to be purchased from Mekorot. Dr Safi commented in 2008: 'We suffer from water shortages every summer. Mekorot does not give us enough water. Until 2008, Mekorot used to deliver 32,000 m^3 a day, but now Mekorot has decreased the amount to 26,500 m^3.' When water resources were getting short, JWU applied for permission to drill a new well. Permission was granted but they still faced many difficulties – we come back to this later in this chapter.[7]

Returning to JWU a decade later, in 2016 and 2017, we found the utility still operating well – but within some pressing constraints. On the one side, demand had been growing very fast. On the other side, bulk water availability was getting to be ever more of a problem. Costs of bulk water supply had increased, so tariffs were on the rise. Today, JWU is having to work hard to persuade consumers that service remains good value. So far, it appears that the emphasis on accountability and the relatively good service have created a sense of ownership amongst stakeholders and have helped protect JWU's autonomy. Despite the ever-present risk of politicized interference, indications are that JWU's autonomous status, its good governance and dynamic and provident management will enable it to weather the current constraints and continue to provide good services.

* * *

Is Yatta municipal water department the most stressed water supply operation on the planet?

The JWU stands out as the largest of the West Bank suppliers. It is certainly amongst the best performers. But for most West Bank households, water is supplied by their local municipality. The 1997 Local Authorities Law assigned responsibility for water and sanitation services to local government under the jurisdiction of the Ministry of Local Government (MoLG). There is no specific provision for organizing or managing these services, and each municipality is free to organize services as they see fit. As we said, larger towns usually do this through a municipal water department.

Performance and results of the departments vary widely, and we wanted to find out why. So on a grey November day in 2017 we went to the town of Yatta, where the water supply operation contrasts in every way with that of the JWU. Yatta is a populous and fast-growing municipality in the southern part of the West Bank, to the south of Hebron.[8] Our visit to the municipal water department was a depressing experience. This must be one of the most stressed water supply operations in the world.

The fact is that Yatta is just desperately short of water. It has one of the lowest per capita supply rates in the country, less than 30 litres per person per day.[9] We ask the obvious question. *What's the problem?* The head, who valiantly manages the operation, says: 'Simple. We don't have our own wells. We depend on buying our bulk water from Mekorot through the West Bank Water Department which handles bulk supplies. The line that comes in from Mekorot has a delivery capacity of 1,100 m^3 an hour. That would more or less meet our needs – but we only get a fraction of that amount.' On average, Yatta receives only 200 cubic metres per hour, less than a fifth of the capacity of the line. That means that the Yatta water department can deliver water to its customers only *once every two or three months*. A lot of the water leaks out anyway. He points out that the network is ageing and Yatta is quite hilly. 'When we try to pump water up through the rusty old pipes, the whole system starts vibrating and springing leaks.' The cost is high, too – NIS 5.90 per cubic metre($1.65), compared to the already quite high West Bank average of NIS 5.00 per cubic metre ($1.35) – and the water is of poor quality.

We surmise that customers must not be too happy, which he ruefully confirms. 'We have a complaints procedure but most people don't bother complaining', he says. 'Actually, most households have given up and disconnected from the system altogether. They reason that if they remain subscribers, they are billed quite a high fixed fee each month. As they don't get any water, why stay connected and have to pay the fee?' When we visited, there were only 3,800 subscribers. Yet the population is 87,000 people living in about 14,000 households. Only a quarter of households have found it worthwhile to remain connected.

Even those who are connected often do not pay their water bill. The collection rate – the share of bills that people actually pay – is 40 per cent.[10] The municipality receives only 40 cents for every shekel they bill to customers. This has been going on for twenty years, so that one would expect the municipality to be totally bankrupted.

We are nervous about asking, *how, under these appalling conditions, does the department make ends meet?* But we ask anyway and the manager smiles and is happy to reply. In fact he laughs.

> Ends meet! You have to understand that the system is running at a huge loss. But you can't actually see that because we work on a cash basis.[11] And we don't have separate accounts. Our money is mixed in with the general municipal accounts.

Yet in fact the local council has been quite happy to let this go on – at least until recently. The water department is embedded within the municipality and reports to the mayor and municipality council rather than to a dedicated water services board. The council's attitude is that if Mekorot or the West Bank's bulk supplier, the West Bank Water Department (WBWD), provide so little water, why should they pay for it at all? So for twenty years, they have simply not paid the bulk water bills sent to them by the West Bank Water Department – and the Water Department in turn has not paid Mekorot. As a result, Yatta Municipality has actually been getting positive cash flow from their desperate and loss-making water operation.

They have spent the revenue on other municipal projects and services, because without more water there is no point spending it on improving the water delivery system.

Sadly, Yatta is now having to rethink this ostrich policy. The Israelis deduct Mekorot's unpaid water bills from the customs revenues that they collect on behalf of the Palestinian Authority. Which means that it is the PA which has been subsidizing Yatta for not paying its water bill. But this changed in 2017 when the Palestinian Ministry of Finance decided to act. The PA started deducting both past and current unpaid bills for bulk water from the transfers they make to subsidize Yatta municipality. As a result, the municipality is entering a financial crisis.

We come back to the question, *How on earth do people cope with so little water being supplied? What do they do for water in the two or three months when they don't receive any water at all from the municipality?* The manager says, 'Come and see'. We go to the area on the outskirts of town where he and his extended family live. They have four houses there, two are finished and two are in that state of half construction that can last for years, or decades, as the money to finish each stage comes in bit by bit. He shows us how the family have constructed channels to collect water from the hillside above and from the tarmac road that runs down the hill past their houses. Beneath each house is a huge water storage tank and all the tanks in the houses are connected to each other by pipes. The water flows by gravity to the tanks and from tank to tank. When the water is needed, it is pumped through a filtration system and up to metal tanks on the roof. He actually collects so much water in this way that he even sells some of it to neighbours. Almost all houses in Yatta harvest rainwater in one way or another, and they have extensive private storage. When households run out of this private supply, they cope by buying tanker water, but this is very expensive.

The situation of the Yatta water department and its piped supply seems desperate, even hopeless. Yet the water team is dedicated and the city council earnestly wants to do something to improve. The question is – *what*? The manager says they have been considering upgrades like prepaid meters to increase collections and action to reduce leaks. In fact, the investment programme accompanying PWA's 2017–22 *Strategic Development Plan* (SDP)[12] provides for a $20 million project for rehabilitation of the Yatta internal network and construction of water tanks. Apparently, the United States Agency for International Development (USAID) has expressed interest in financing this project.

But the manager agrees that all of this would be pointless under present circumstances. The first and essential step to improving the situation is more water. Yatta is simply hoping that PWA will allocate the municipality extra water. If the extra water comes, then the rehabilitation project would be excellent. Institutional changes could be made to put the water operation on a business footing through ring-fenced finances, separate accounting, cost recovery and payment of the WBWD/Mekorot bills. But if there is no more bulk water, then no amount of rehabilitation or institutional strengthening can improve the situation for Yatta's population.

* * *

Aqraba Joint Service Council

As we noted earlier, for the smallest communities, particularly rural ones, village councils may provide services, or a joint service council (JSC) may provide water to groups of villages. The idea of a JSC is to help smaller communities group together to provide services more efficiently. JSCs enjoy legal status similar to that of utilities. They report to a governing board; they maintain separate accounts and bank accounts which are ring-fenced, so that money cannot be siphoned off to other community activities. Generally, they balance their books and build up reserves for replacements.

To date, thirteen JSCs have been set up in the water and sanitation sector, with varying results. In December 2016, we visited the Aqraba Joint Service Council. This, it soon appears, is one of the best, a modern, efficient service provider which seems to be solving the problem of bringing affordable water supply to scattered rural communities.

We are greeted by the engineer in charge of water supply, an extremely dynamic and motivated young woman. She explains that the water operation supplies fifteen communities in the area. The scheme was set up in close cooperation with the authorities in Ramallah. They worked with the PWA to obtain financing and with the WBWD on project design and engineering. The money came from KfW, the German capital aid organization. Although rural-based, the JSC is no small operation – and no slouch. It has set up an efficient network to supply over 40,000 people in 8,000 households on a 24/7 basis. The scheme is run by five technical staff under the engineer's management. Governance is provided by a board of nine members made up from the larger Village Councils that own the JSC. None of the Village Councils derive any revenue from the water operation – all the revenue remains within the water operation. The JSC is accountable to local leadership, but, perhaps most importantly, it is close to and accountable to its customers.

From the start, the engineer and her team recognized the challenge of supplying relatively high-cost water to quite poor communities. Investment costs worked out at about €1,500 per household connection, which is a lot for the residents of the service area. There was initially considerable reticence amongst consumers, and a risk that the scheme would not attract enough subscribers. The board responded. They negotiated with the KfW and got agreement that the connection fee would be set at a lower level that would cover only about one third of the cost. The JSC then recruited a team of eleven customer relations officers who discussed the proposal with the communities. In the end almost all households in the service area agreed to subscribe. One strong motivation was how unattractive the alternative was – before the network came along, residents were buying water from tankers at NIS 10–14 per cubic metre ($2.80–3.90).[13] The water source is a single well, managed by the West Bank Water Department. The water is pumped to five reservoirs. Usually pumping is for about eighteen hours a day and thanks to the reservoirs the system remains pressurized and gives a 24/7 service.

'The running costs are on the high side', the engineer says. 'It's hill country around here and the villages are quite scattered.' Yet to make ends meet and keep the scheme going, the board has set tariffs which recover the full costs of operation and maintenance and contribute to building up a capital reserve for major repairs and replacements. ‘The Water Department charges us NIS 2.60/m^3 ($0.70) at the well head. We have a block tariff, with the lowest block for domestic customers at NIS 4.98/m^3 ($1.35) and the highest at NIS 9.00/m^3 ($2.40). Industrial and commercial customers pay a flat NIS 8.00/m^3 ($2.15).’ The question came up, *What about those who can’t afford to pay?* The engineer replied, ‘In Palestine we never ask widows or the families of martyrs to pay for water. But the JSC can’t afford to subsidize like that, we would go bust. So the local communities decide who is to get free water. We send the bill to their Village Council to pay.’

For other consumers, the JSC requires payment in advance. There are prepayment meters installed for all domestic and business customers. ‘People were really reticent about that’, the engineer says.

> But we have kept on the team of customer relations officers, basically one in each village who help explain to people. There are charging points in each community and the relations officers are there to show people how to charge their cards. After some discussion, everyone accepted and it is going well. Our collection rate is about 95 per cent.

The 5 per cent who are not paying turn out to be public bodies, like the fifty-eight schools and the thirty-three mosques in the service area. Public finance rules forbid advance payment, so these customers are on mechanical meters and slow procedures mean that these bodies are often behind in paying their water bill.

‘But slow and sure. In the end we get the money’, the engineer says.

There is one more problem – and one success to recount. She tells us that the West Bank Water Department well is in Area C where the Israeli military usually restrict entry.

> Even the Water Department can only access the well with a special permit. We found that we were getting less water than we were being billed for. There was endless back and forth with the Civil Administration until in the end the West Bank Water Department was able to go and check. They found that the metering at the wellhead was indeed incorrect and the bills were reduced.

And the success? She says that the JSC has managed to hook up 265 households within Area C which, considering that the Israelis usually forbid any pipework in this military-controlled area, is indeed an achievement.

So it seems all is going pretty well for now. We look at the installations which are clean and well maintained. Then in comes a thick set man who is introduced as the mayor of Jurish, one of the communities that take part in the scheme. He confirms that by and large his people are happy with the service. The cost was considered on the high side, but everybody is happy with the quality and with the 24/7 availability.

'This is a project for all the community', he says. 'For the first time, we have continuous supply.'

* * *

Farkha Village Council (VC)

Last but not least, in late 2016 we visited the smallest operation in our tour, the Farkha Village Council. One of the principles of good water management is 'subsidiarity' that you delegate the management to the lowest level at which it can be done efficiently. Often for water supply this is not very low, as there are big economies of scale. But in the Palestinian hills there can be advantages to very local management and our visit to the village of Farkha a few miles outside of Salfeet seems to bear this out.

Under local government legislation, village councils are empowered to supply water services to their community. In Farkha, we found the elected Village Council running a small scheme supplying adequate water at a reasonable price. The energetic young manager explains that the network connects 380 households through 315 metres, serving a total population of 1,685 people. He says that the NGO Hydrologeia/Oxfam financed the project. The scheme is fed by two sources of water. There is a pipeline which carries Mekorot water from Salfeet Municipality with a capacity of 200 cubic metres daily. There is also a spring which they have recently rehabilitated and which provides 50 cubic metres a day. Both sources are potable, after chlorination, and the water quality at the spring is checked by Ministry of Health officers. Water is stored in a tank to which water is pumped.

The council provides round the clock service of up to 150 litres per person per day. In the summer, however, the quantity provided by Salfeet declines, and Farkha receives water only every one to two days. The mayor's view is that this is because 'Mekorot serves the Israeli settlements first'. Demand is high, as people also use water for their animals. When summer water shortages occur, residents may buy a tanker of water or two, paying as much as NIS 10 per cubic metre ($2.80). Nine out of ten households have also invested in harvesting rainwater from the roofs of their houses, and this is now a condition for the issue of a building permit.

In this small community, the council's accountability to its electorate for the water operation is direct. Residents can confront their elected councillors at any time, and the council offices where the water operation is located are open every day.

The council runs the water operation on a businesslike basis but does not seek any financial gain from it. The tariff, which is close to the national average, covers costs and raises a small surplus which is put in a reserve for replacements and major repairs. The water operation has its own accounting, separate from the Village Council accounts, and maintains its own separate bank account. The collection rate is 100 per cent – all villagers pay their bills in full and on time. We ask how this is achieved. In most Palestinian communities, the only sanction for non-payment is to cut off supplies – and cutting off a basic essential like water is seen as simply not right. The manager's answer is clear – 'you can't cut off water but you can cut off electricity if the bill is unpaid. So when villagers come to the Council office to pay for electricity, they are first required to pay their water bill.'

There are, however, disadvantages to being small. The scheme is largely dependent on the Mekorot water piped via Salfeet Municipality. To link the village with an operation with economies of scale and to provide for more rational planning of bulk water distribution, the Ministry of Local Government has encouraged the Village Council to link up with Salfeet town and other villages in a Joint Service Council operation. However, the Farkha villagers are not keen to do this.

> Frankly, we are nervous about becoming more dependent on Salfeet Municipality. We feel the municipality's interests would dominate. There was a proposal for the village to merge into the municipality which was rejected by 80 per cent of the population in a ballot.[14] We see that Salfeet is the dominant partner in the current Joint Services Council. We are very afraid that Salfeet would cream off all the benefits.[15]

So the Village Council would prefer to increase its water autonomy rather than rely on Salfeet's doubtful willingness to cooperate. They would also like to reduce costs by developing another local water source. Attempts to drill an unlicenced well have proved costly failures. The current mayor has twice tried to drill for water within Area A land. These were informal operations in search of water autonomy. They were not sanctioned by PWA. The contractors charged a very high price for undertaking this unlicenced drilling. Both times, the Israeli authorities called a halt. On the first occasion, the Israeli army confiscated the drilling rig and filled in the well, even though Area A is supposed to be entirely under PA control.

The council has now identified a nearby spring as a possible new supply. However, tapping this source would require the agreement and cooperation of PWA, and the PWA would have to ask for Israeli approval under the joint water management arrangements set up at Oslo.[16] The village also lacks the money to develop the new source by itself. They are thinking of contacting an non-governmental organization (NGO) or a grant donor. However, the community already had NGO financing for their existing water supply scheme and the council fears that the village is too small to qualify for further support. Also, they are apprehensive that a donor might think that Farkha already has a reasonable level of service and is not really a priority.

So it seems that a Village Council can run an efficient operation with a high degree of consumer satisfaction. This model of water supply appears to be able to provide the governance, accountability and financial autonomy needed to provide a good service. In this case, 'small is beautiful'. However, in a pervasive context of water shortages, communities are anxious wherever possible to develop local water resources – and here they run up against the water resources management regime which was agreed as part of the Oslo Accords. There is more water available locally, but the villagers – and the Palestinian Authority – cannot touch it.

Service provider performance

There are two tests of a good water supply system. One is technical – the organization of adequate bulk water supplies, service to consumers of an adequate quantity of good-quality potable water available on demand around the clock, a customer service responsive to needs and ready to solve problems. How Palestinian service providers perform on this technical criterion is discussed in this section. The second test is equally important – the efficiency of the service provider and the related question of the provider's financial viability. These aspects of service provision are discussed in the next section.

Measuring the quality of water supply service – a review of key performance indicators

Relying on the old adage that *You cannot manage what you cannot measure*, we adopt a quantitative approach, measuring performance against benchmarks. The case studies gave snapshots of four service providers out of the more than 300 which serve the West Bank. A more comprehensive bird's-eye view of water services across the board can be constructed from the excellent database compiled by the Water Sector Regulatory Council (WSRC).[17] Using this data we were able to compile Table 3.1 to show the average performance and range of performance for the forty largest service providers in West Bank.[18] Taken together, these data cover services to about 80 per cent of West Bank households. Table 3.1 also compares service provision for Palestinians in the West Bank with the median performance of the more than 1,000 utilities worldwide in the database of the International Benchmarking Network for Water and Sanitation Utilities (IBNET). We also give comparator figures for neighbouring Jordan and Egypt, and for Israel. Based on Table 3.1, we then discuss access, quantity, quality and affordability.

From the data, it appears that connection rates are relatively high by world standards. The reported connection rates of around 93 per cent in the West Bank compare favourably with the IBNET median of 89 per cent, although falling short of the essentially 100 per cent access reported in neighbouring Jordan and Egypt, as well as in Israel. Unconnected households in the West Bank are largely in Area C, where movement and access restrictions prevent communities from being connected to the network.

By contrast, the average quantities delivered are low by global standards, confirming chronic water shortages, although the average figures mask very wide variations. Average supply of 80 litres per person each day falls well short of the average 162 litres which is the global median, and also falls below levels in Egypt, with its abundant Nile resource. However, average supply in Jordan is below the

Table 3.1 Water Service Key Performance Indicators for the West Bank (KPIs), 2014

Purpose of KPI	Definition of KPI	West Bank Average	West Bank Range	IBNET global median[a]	Jordan	Egypt	Israel
Measuring access	Percentage of households connected to the network	93%	n.a.	89%[b]	100% (2010)	99% (2014)	100%
Measuring quantity	Quantity of water provided per person each day to households	80 litres	26–242 litres	162 litres (range 119–221 litres)	73 litres (2010)	126 litres (2010)	263 litres (2016)
Measuring quality	Percentage of samples at source free from total coliform	92%	78–100%	WSRC benchmark for 'good' performance: >95%			
Measuring affordability	Selling price	NIS 5.05/m^3 ($1.40)	NIS 1.59–7.04 ($0.45-2.00)	n.a.			NIS 6.22/m^3 ($1.73)
	Water cost as share of GNI per capita	1.30%	n.a.	0.55%[c]	0.59%	0.50%	0.64%[d]

Source: WSRC, except 'households connected', which is from the PWA Strategic Development Plan (SDP: 49), and IBNET data, which are from the IBNET Blue Book 2014.

Note: IBNET = International Benchmarking Network for Water and Sanitation Utilities; GNI = gross national income; KPI = key performance indicators; WSRC = Water Sector Regulatory Council; n.a. = not applicable.

[a] Based on data for over 1,000 utilities worldwide.

[b] IBNET Blue Book Table 1.1.

[c] IBNET Blue Book Table 1.14.

[d] The average domestic water consumption of 96 cubic metres per person per year at the average selling price of NIS 10 per cubic metres ($2.94) gives an annual per capita cost of $280, which is 0.64 per cent of GNI per capita of $44,000.

average for either the West Bank (or Gaza), an indication of the very extreme water shortages from which that arid country suffers.[19] The most glaring difference is with Israel, the Palestinians' partner in the resources of the land – Israelis receive on average over three times as much domestic water as the West Bank Palestinians. There is a very wide variation amongst service providers around the average of 80 litres per person per day, ranging from 26 litres – a level scarcely more than the survival minimum for drinking, cooking and personal hygiene – to a very high 242 litres a day. Although the table does not document continuity of service, most service providers deliver water only intermittently, with only half of West Bank households receiving water daily.

Raw water quality is generally acceptable, but sometimes poor. Groundwater quality is generally acceptable, although with localized concentrations of chlorides and nitrates. However, tap water quality is generally poor, due in part to contamination in the networks. IBNET does not provide international comparative data for water quality, so we used WSRC's benchmark – that more than 95 per cent of samples should be free from coliform at source. Against this measure, average quality of water coming out of the tap in the West Bank is poor, averaging only 92 per cent of samples free of coliforms. In the worst cases, only 78 per cent of samples were uncontaminated.

On average, network (piped) water is only moderately affordable in the West Bank. Network water costs about 1.3 per cent of average per capita income, more than twice the global median of 0.55 per cent, and also more than double the average in Jordan (0.59 per cent) and in Egypt (0.50 per cent) – and double the average in Israel, where incomes are ten times higher. The cost varies widely between West Bank locations, depending mainly on the bulk water source and on utility efficiency.[20] Where households must buy tanker water, prices are much higher. As supplies increase, costs are expected to rise rapidly, especially as new supplies at the margin may be priced based on desalination costs and on the cost of pumping up from the coast.

The efficiency and financial performance of service providers

We focus now on the second test of a good system – the efficiency of the service provider and the related question of the provider's financial viability. Two headline indicators will show what we mean. First, across the West Bank, 'unaccounted for' or 'non-revenue' water averages 29 per cent at the retail level, amongst the highest in the region.[21] Water is super scarce, yet the providers are losing almost one third of the precious resource even before it gets to the consumer. This indicates poor management, inadequate operations and underinvestment in maintenance.

Second, bill collection rates average 68 per cent. For every three shekels the providers bill to customers, they get back only two. The reason why people do not pay is mainly because they are unhappy with the service. Who does not know that feeling of bloody-mindedness when a service is very poor? The temptation is to say *To hell with it!* There is a level of customer dissatisfaction which links straight to the poor quality of service. On the side of the provider, low collections indicate both a breakdown in business management and a failure to reach out and communicate with the customers. If the customer understands the constraints that the provider faces, he or she will normally be more motivated to pay. A dry tap and an empty tank communicate only failure.

So we first look at a couple of examples – of poor and not so poor performance. Then we see how Palestinian service providers get financed and, in more detail, how efficient and financially viable they are. Finally we explore some of the ideas that have been mooted that could improve the efficiency and financial soundness of service delivery even within an environment so freighted with constraints.

Two examples

In 2008, towards the end of the al Aqsa *intifada*, we went to Jenin to talk to the municipal water department.[22] It was there that we observed 'signs of a utility close to meltdown' – see the section 'Planning and investment'. The director, Wadah Labadi, was straight with us.

> Our service is terrible. Until the German project we were losing half the water in our pipes.[23] Even now, we can only supply water every now and then. Some of our service areas have not received water for four months. We can't put tariffs up – why would people pay more for such lousy service. So what we charge doesn't even cover our operating expenses. And then, of course, people don't pay. Now our recovery rate is just 32 per cent and customer arrears are huge – NIS 16 million ($4.5 million) at the last count.

Here, as elsewhere, the city fathers were covering the deficit simply by not paying the West Bank Water Department for the water that Mekorot supplies to them.[24]

At the Jerusalem Water Undertaking in the same year we found a complete contrast.[25] As we have seen, JWU's operation efficiently serves a third of a million people with good supply standards.[26] 'Our aim', Ibrahim Safi, the general manager explained,

> is business self-sufficiency. We set our tariffs at full cost recovery levels. PWA regulates them to make sure they are fair. Fortunately our customers are relatively prosperous – and we have a first rate finance manager. Last year we actually made a surplus – NIS 0.5 million ($150,000). In fact our finances are strong enough that we can take investment loans and repay them with interest. Fortunately our lenders – German and French aid – give us very soft terms.

Already in these two vignettes we can see some of the factors that make good performance possible. The case of JWU suggests that where a utility has a certain scale, an assured source of water, investment finance and technical support for capacity building, together with good governance, a businesslike approach and a relatively prosperous and satisfied customer base, it can be run as efficiently in the West Bank as anywhere else. By contrast, the Jenin case illustrates almost the opposite, that where there is no institutional autonomy, water is scarce, relations with Israeli sector counterparts are poor, and the customer base is impoverished and resentful, the services fall into a decline which cannot be reversed even by committed staff and external aid.

Both cases illustrate the dependence of the water supply utilities on Israel and their consequent vulnerability. Both cases underline the need for adequate water supplies and easing of the problems caused by the Israeli Occupation. They also show the risks of dependence on Israel in terms of vulnerability to Israeli decisions and interventions in a conflict context, the impossibility of planning rationally when the PWA controls neither the land nor the water, and the higher financial cost and commercial risk of having to work always with Israeli partners. These concerns underline the need for a new compact between Israelis and Palestinians based on an equitable cooperation – the essential theme we will explore in the last part of this book.

The Jenin case also shows the risk that not paying for bulk water – and effectively leaving the PA to pay by deduction from tax revenues – creates perverse incentives. The provider has reduced incentives to provide a good service because customers do not pay anyway. Providers have a distorted incentive to depend more on Israeli bulk water supplies as they do not have to pay for them.

Financing of water service delivery

Tariffs and how they are set Tariffs in the West Bank for both bulk and retail water are often set at below cost, so that water operations are typically running at a deficit. The tariff for bulk water is set by the West Bank Water Department (WBWD) in consultation with the PWA. In 2017, this tariff was below cost. WBWD had set the selling price at the level of the purchase price of NIS 2.60 per cubic metre ($0.70). However, WBWD's total costs were equivalent to NIS 3.04 per cubic metre ($0.82). Thus, there was a 17 per cent loss to WBWD (and therefore a 17 per cent subsidy to service providers) on bulk water sales.

At the retail level, service providers and their governance structures set tariffs. In principle, tariffs for water out of the tap should be set at levels that at least recover all costs from consumers. On average, West Bank suppliers bill more than the cost of supplying the water (see Table 3.2). However, a significant number do not. In addition, many providers collect only a proportion of the amounts billed, reducing actual income well below expenditure.

New tariff by-laws and methodology have been approved, but WSRC's role in regulating them is not yet operational. A new regulatory framework for tariffs was established by the *Water and Wastewater Tariff By-law* approved by PWA in January 2013. The methodology was set by the *Water and Wastewater Tariff Model* approved by PWA in October 2015. In the future, WSRC is to have responsibilities for approving tariffs under the Water Law (see Chapter 2). The intention is that, once the National Water Company (NWC) is established, it will be responsible

Table 3.2 Efficiency and Financial Viability Key Performance Indicators (KPIs) for the West Bank, 2014

Purpose of KPI	Definition of KPI	West Bank KPI		IBNET global median	Jordan	Egypt
		Average	Range			
Measuring efficiency	Percentage of non-revenue water	29%	12-50%	27%[a]	36% (2010) *(43% in 2008)*	28% (2010) *(31% in 2008)*
	Operating costs per m³ of water sold	NIS 5.00 ($1.39)	NIS 1.45–8.07 ($0.40-2.44)	NIS 2.68[b] ($0.70)	$0.70 (2010)	$0.18 (2010)
	Number of employees per connection	3.4	1.2–7.7			
Measuring financial viability	Working ratio (operating costs/sales – > 1 = deficit)	0.89	0.53–1.22	0.92[c]	0.99 (2010)	1.13 (2010) *0.98 (2008)*
	Collection efficiency	68%	51–100%		109% (2010)	84% (2010) *92% (2008)*

Source: WSRC. Adapted from WB 2019.

Note: IBNET = International Benchmarking Network for Water and Sanitation Utilities; KPI = key performance indicators.

[a] IBNET Blue Book, table 1.

[b] IBNET Blue Book, table 1.9. Median $0.70/m^3 = NIS 2.68/m^3; highest quartile, $0.40/m^3 = NIS 1.53/m^3; lowest quartile, $1.12/m^3 = NIS 4.29/m^3.

[c] IBNET Blue Book, table 1.8. The median operating cost coverage was 1.09 = working ratio of 0.92; the highest quartile operating cost coverage was 1.38 = working ratio of 0.72; and the lowest quartile operating cost coverage was 0.83 = working ratio of 1.20.

for proposing a unified price for all bulk supply to service providers throughout the West Bank and Gaza.[27] WSRC will be responsible for approving both this bulk tariff and the retail price proposals submitted by service providers. For the reasons outlined in Chapter 2, the approval system has not started, although WSRC has been conducting a number of tariff studies on behalf of service providers.

Financial impacts on the sector and on the Palestinian Authority

Effective subsidies and non-payments Hidden transfers at the bulk water supply level reward West Bank service providers that do not pay their bills. At the bulk level, municipal water departments benefit from two levels of such transfers. The first is a direct subsidy because, as we say earlier, the bulk provider, the West Bank Water Department (WBWD), bills water to service providers at about 17 per cent below the cost of supply. The second is an indirect subsidy because many municipalities simply do not pay WBWD for the water.

In 2014, the under-pricing by WBWD and non-payment by municipalities provided an effective transfer of NIS 130 million ($36 million) to service providers, mainly the municipal water departments. It was the PA that had to pick up the tab for this effective subsidy of service providers. This is because it is the PA that pays for the financial deficits of the West Bank Water Department, and it is the PA which suffers a major loss of revenue when the Israelis dock the unpaid Mekorot bills from the customs and VAT receipts that they collect on behalf of the PA.

So this is effectively a subsidy from the PA to the water sector. Who benefits? First and foremost it is the municipal governments because they can keep back and spend elsewhere any surplus on the water operation that arises from not paying for bulk water. But the subsidy is not shared equally amongst municipalities. It goes proportionally to the service providers that are the worst payers, rewarding the worst performers.

At the consumer level too, the effective subsidies also disproportionately reward the worst payers rather than those who need it. Service providers are collecting only 68 cents on every dollar billed. The 32 cents unpaid – one third of total billings – represents a subsidy to the consumers who do not pay. Essentially these non-payers get water for free. But this consumer subsidy is unevenly distributed and inequitable. It goes mainly to those served by service providers with the lowest collection efficiency, such as Tulkarem, Qalqilya, Jenin and Jericho – all of which collect little over half of amounts billed. Within a service area, the subsidy goes mainly not to the poor but to consumers with the biggest bills, and to consumers who assert entitlements as a class to not pay. Their fellows who do pay their bill are the losers, paying a high price for what their neighbours are getting for nothing.

Clearly there are some highly perverse incentives washing around the system at present. Because West Bank service providers do not recover their costs from consumers, services run at a deficit and the web of hidden subsidies allow providers to cover these deficits. On average, in 2014 service providers lost roughly NIS 1.57 ($0.44) for every cubic metre supplied. As a result, the West Bank water sector experienced a total deficit of the order of NIS 110 million ($31 million), which providers covered by not paying WBWD for bulk water. Large arrears have built up. According to WBWD, in 2014 they were owed over NIS 1 billion, or $350 million, in unpaid bills for bulk water going back many years. These losses have been financed by the build-up of unpaid Mekorot water bills, which Israel currently deducts at source. In 2016, Israel deducted $70 million for unpaid Mekorot water bills and a further $24 million for sewage treatment – see Figure 3.1.[28]

Inevitably, in this tangle of 'robbing Peter to pay Paul' there are some mightily crossed wires. The PA has continually protested that the deductions made by Israel are considerably higher than what is due. The PA's calculations, based on data from the Water Sector Regulatory Council and the West Bank Water Department, show much lower levels of arrears. The Palestinian Ministry of Finance (MoF) is now recovering both current bills and arrears by deducting from transfers due to the municipalities. This is inevitably leading to a crisis in municipal finances, and will certainly squeeze water services further. In poor Yatta, for example – see the case study earlier – arrears are already returning to haunt the municipality which owes a total of NIS 27 million ($7 million). Its total annual municipal budget is about NIS 15 million ($4 million). In 2016, the Ministry of Finance (MoF) deducted NIS 6.7 million ($1.9 million, 25 per cent of arrears) from its transfers and since then

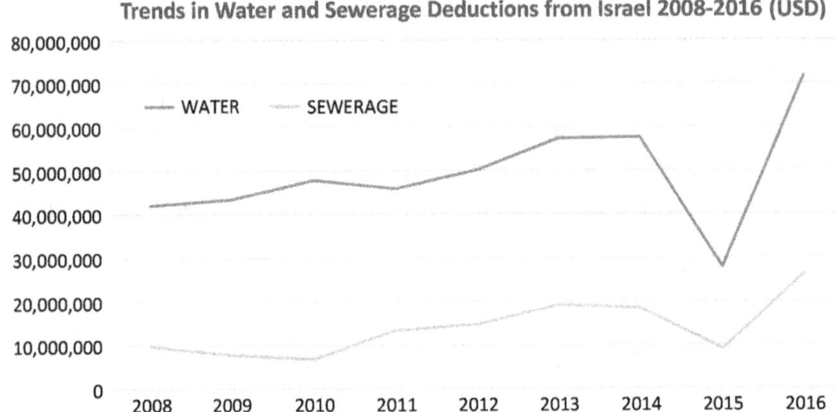

Figure 3.1 Water and sewerage deductions by Israel, 2008–16. *Source*: Palestinian Ministry of Finance and Planning.

has been deducting NIS 250,000 ($70,000) per quarter to pay current bills to the West Bank Water Department.[29]

Palestinian purchases from Mekorot are expected to rise rapidly in coming years and, unless efficiencies improve, the problem will worsen. PWA currently purchases more than 70 million cubic metres of water per year from Israel.[30] As discussed in Chapter 2, negotiations are underway for purchase of up to another 30 million cubic metres, and a further 34 million cubic metres may be delivered under the so-called Red–Dead accord, so that overall purchases may reach 135 million cubic metres annually in the foreseeable future. Unless service providers can recover their costs from consumers and pay the full cost of bulk water, the problems of non-payment and arrears will only get worse.[31]

Financial viability of service providers

Measuring the financial viability of water supply service providers – a review of key performance indicators We now follow the same methodology as we did earlier for the quality of water supply service in order to carry out an assessment of the efficiency and financial viability of service providers. We measure performance and compare it to world benchmarks for the forty largest service providers in the West Bank.[32] Selected measures of the efficiency and financial viability of service providers are presented in Table 3.2, using data from WSRC.[33]

Findings on efficiency[34] In assessing efficiency, we look at three classic measures of water utility performance. First comes one of the two headline indicators we mentioned earlier – the amount of water that is 'unaccounted for' or 'non-revenue'. Second, we look at the operating costs per unit of water sold. Finally, we see whether over-staffing – or conversely skimping on staff for operation and maintenance – may be a problem. Both practices are very common in developing countries.

Levels of non-revenue water (NRW) represent a dramatic loss for the very water-scarce Palestinian economy. Non-revenue water is the difference between the water that is supplied and the water that is billed. It has three components: actual physical losses from the system; water that is stolen either through physical theft or meter tampering; and water that is not billed because some constituency is entitled to – or claims to be entitled to – free water.[35] Depending on the service provider's policy, these claims may include refugee camps, the surviving family of those who have been declared martyrs or who are political prisoners, mosques and public buildings.

Average non-revenue water per service provider in the West Bank (29 per cent) is not far from the IBNET global median and is similar to that of Egypt (28 per cent) and considerably better than in Jordan (36 per cent).[36] The rate ranges widely, from good (12 per cent) to very poor (50 per cent). On average, non-revenue water in the West Bank equals 267 litres of precious water per day for each connection—enough water to increase supply by half.[37]

West Bank suppliers have relatively high operating costs, largely because of the cost of bringing in water from Mekorot. Total operating costs in the West Bank are almost double the IBNET median, putting the West Bank towards the bottom of the fourth quartile worldwide. The range is great, with some very expensive providers indeed. The biggest items in variable costs relate to the costs of water supplied by Israel's bulk water supplier, Mekorot, and to energy and personnel costs. At 70 US cents per cubic metre (equivalent to NIS 2.60), Jordan is a lower-cost supplier despite its extreme supply constraints and long-distance pumping, but there is presumably no resource cost being charged. Egypt, with its huge cities, flat topography and adjacent limitless supplies of Nile water, is a very-low-cost comparator.

Measuring financial viability – deficit-ridden utilities and the impact on service provision In the West Bank, some service providers' billings cover their operating and maintenance (O&M) costs but others do not. The relation between costs and billings is captured by the working ratio – a working ratio greater than 1 indicates that a provider is billing sales at less than cost. In the West Bank, the average is reasonable (0.89), slightly better than the IBNET media of 0.92. Jordan with a 2010 working ratio of 0.99 is on the cusp, and Egypt is well into deficit territory at 1.13 (2010). However, some West Bank service providers also have working ratios well above 1, guaranteeing that, even if they collect 100 per cent of sales billed, they cannot break even.

If we combine the working ratio with the second headline indicator that we looked at earlier – the bill collection rate – we can get a precise picture of the real financial viability of service providers – and on average it is a pretty bleak picture. An average working ratio of 0.89 (equivalent to billing $1.12 for every $1.00 of costs) and an average collection efficiency of 68 per cent means that the average West Bank service provider is collecting only 76 cents on each dollar of costs – and some are doing much worse. As a result, almost all West Bank service providers are running deficits which they typically cover, as we have seen, by not paying their bulk water bill. In addition, all service providers are dependent on public or donor finance for capital investment or asset replacement. Performance on collections is better in Egypt at 84 per cent in 2010 but still well short of full-cost recovery. Jordan achieved 109 per cent in the same year, through vigorous collection of past due amounts.[38]

Such low performance on basic viability leaves the entire West Bank water supply sector dependent on public subsidy and on donor finance. Most service providers cover their deficits simply by not paying WBWD for bulk water supplies (see discussion earlier). There is no scope for private provision because there is no prospect of profitability and risks are high. Given that supply costs are rising quickly and will be even higher in the future (because extra supplies will be high-cost water from Mekorot), solutions must be found.

Flaws and gaps in the current financing model

The top-down model of investment financing does not create ownership or incentives for good operations. When we were at Yatta visiting the municipal water department on that grey November day in 2016, we saw a contractor laying out water pipes. 'That's good', we said, 'laying pipes. Extending the network.' *Better water supply for the Palestinian people*, we thought. But the director of the municipal water department, shook his head. 'What's the point of it?' he asked rhetorically. 'We don't have any water. Most people have turned off their connections. Whatever is the point of extending the network?'

The problem is that here we saw the results of a way of financing of water sector investments that is quite typical of donor-dependent countries. It is a way of financing that operates where the municipalities have no money, whereas the central government and aid agencies do. Under these circumstances, investment is decided by the central government or by donors based on their assessment of needs from the top down rather than relying on the commitment and financial participation – and sweat equity – of the service providers.

While it is always nice to get a present and sometimes it may be manna from heaven, this way of deciding on investments has some huge pitfalls. First, it is local people who know best what they need, and it is local service providers who know best what they can handle and how best to improve their services. Second, projects in the West Bank and Gaza are in practice usually carried out by the PWA or by the donors themselves. The control of the local utility over how the project is designed and carried out is often quite slim, and, when it comes to operating the new infrastructure, the local staff will be quite unfamiliar with it.

While there are some advantages (mainly economies of scale) to the direct execution of projects by PWA or a donor, the lack of adequate stakeholder consultation — especially with service providers and citizens who are the intended beneficiaries of these investments — may result in these investments not responding to local priorities. This separation between the central powers – PWA and donors who are creating assets – and the service providers who will have to take over the management and maintenance of those assets makes for investment decisions that may not be a priority, may not be sustainable and – above all – may not be owned by the local community.

So what is the solution? It is essentially decentralization. Service providers should make investment decisions and the government should provide them with financial resources directly. This will make for better investment, better operations and also more direct and stronger accountability between the service providers and consumers. As the policy maker, the PWA should develop the national investment strategy – but the investment programme should be put together bottom-up, starting with local consultations.

Local people and local authorities should also take some share in the financing. We have seen how local authorities put their hands in the till of their own water operations. There is money there in the till because the municipality is not paying for the bulk water, and they need the money because financing of local government is notoriously inadequate. This chaotic system of financing has two negative consequences for water services. One is that there is no money for the water department to improve services, either investment or operations. The other is that consumers who pay their bill see their contribution going to other things while the water service remains poor and deteriorating.

Here we are reminded of the promise the Israelis made when full-cost water pricing was introduced – that all water charges would be ploughed back into improving water services, with not one shekel to be diverted. The psychology is the same everywhere – like the Israelis, Palestinian consumers are motivated to pay if they see a connection between their contribution and the service they are getting. And vice versa.

One first step to strengthening the financing of water services – or at least to keeping track of the situation – is for water departments to keep separate accounts and for the finances of water services to be ring-fenced. This would have two advantages. First, it would make municipal accounting more transparent; any shortfall in financing municipal services would be clear and would have to be dealt with. Second, it would provide clear incentives for water departments to recover their costs, as each water department would have to live within its income – and would have access to any surplus to plough back into the operation.

Water as a business[39]

Keeping separate accounts and ring-fencing finances would be first steps towards running water services on a businesslike basis. In fact, PWA policy for water services includes provision for the elements of such an approach: commercialization, ring-fencing of revenues, and full-cost recovery. This would require service providers to set tariffs on a full-cost recovery basis[40] and to follow accepted international standards for financial management and accounting, including accounting on an accrual basis with both balance sheet and income and expenditure statements; maintaining an assets register; accounting for depreciation and constituting depreciation reserves; keeping separate ledgers for receivables and payables; and accumulating and retaining working capital. A further international standard would require accounts to be audited and published within a reasonable period, normally within six months of each year end.

Planning and investment

The situation a decade ago – emerging from the al Aqsa intifada

When we were in West Bank between September 2008 and February 2009, everybody said that investment in the Palestinian water sector had practically ground to a halt. Many factors, it seemed, were combining to make investment a risky and high-cost business, including the governance arrangements for investment approval by the JWC and the Civil Administration, institutional weaknesses in planning and implementation, the inefficiencies inherent in donor aid and, above all, the more or less permanent political and security emergency. We saw many examples but just two will illustrate the problem.

During our visits to the JWU – see the case study earlier in this chapter – they told us that water resources were getting short but investment in new sources was proving very hard. In early 2008, about ten months before our visit, JWU had applied for permission to drill a new well. They were pleasantly surprised to receive the prompt approval of the JWC, which had become notorious for turning down requests to drill for water. Permission was granted for a well at Hezmah. However, Hezmah lay within Area C and so the well required Civil Administration clearance.[41] According to JWU, 'they kept saying move it 50 metres, 60 metres . . . then there was the hassle of getting approval for the pump. And so on.' Eventually the JWU got the well but late and at a higher cost.[42]

We found that even when investments had been made, that alone was not adequate to improve services in a deteriorating political and economic climate. In our second example, at Jenin municipality, we saw how, even after an investment programme, a utility may be unable to improve service delivery. Rehabilitation and improvement of water supply for this very water-short municipality had been a priority under the PWA strategy. Extra water resources were allocated at Oslo and the German aid agency KfW agreed to support a €4 million programme for rehabilitation of the network and for institutional development, building up the water department as an autonomous entity, separate from the municipality.

The investment project got underway in 1999–2000. However, the *al Aqsa intifada* broke out and life became very difficult. KfW told us that 'despite Israeli incursions and a big battle in the camp, we finished the project in a proper way, with all the accompanying measures, including training'. But then came the operational phase. Unfortunately, the security situation was so poor that little of the project gains could be sustained. When we visited in November 2008, there were signs of a utility close to meltdown. Water was being supplied very intermittently – some areas had not received any water at all for four months.

'Nobody wants to pay for such poor service', the director in Jenin said. 'Our collection rate was 75 per cent before the *Intifada*, now it's 32 per cent. Even after the German rehabilitation, we are losing more than a third of our water to leaks and theft.'

Staff were completely demotivated. The director said: 'Most staff would leave if they could find another job. Because we have a headache all the time. There is nothing on the ground that makes you hope.' He went on, making a gesture of despair, 'Why spend my life here for nothing?' In fact, he and his deputy were quite alone in the office. All the other staff were on strike. They had not been paid for three months.[43]

Looking more broadly across the water sector, we found a huge mismatch between needs and investment on the ground. This was the result of multiple constraints which had reduced investment to very low levels. At the time (2008), the West Bank was only just emerging from the bruising *al Aqsa intifada*. Investment – and investment efficiency – in West Bank water supply and sanitation infrastructure had dropped to very low levels. Investment in the sector as a whole was running at just one tenth of planned levels. Large infrastructure projects that would have improved the overall integrated regional management of resources were set aside. Wastewater treatment investments had been blocked for a decade, and only one of the seven planned new plants (al Bireh) had been commissioned and was operational. In effect, emergency projects had become the norm.

It was not only low levels of investment that were the problem. What investment was being made was inefficient. The problems were multiple – fragmented contingency planning, the high risks of delay, the political and security problems, and the resulting steep escalation in costs. Many investments never got off the drawing board, and, when they did, they encountered multiple administrative hurdles for permitting and implementation, with inevitable delays and spiralling costs.

The investment programme and disbursements were well below expectations – and were declining. Total investment needs for the water sector had been calculated in the Palestinian Water Strategic Planning Study (PECDAR 2001) at around $260 million a year. Actual investment, however, averaged only one third of that – $90 million annually 1997–2004. Subsequently investment declined further, to an average of $47 million a year 2005–7. In 2008, the investment budget for water was $138 million over three years – but according to PWA, only $20 million was disbursed for planned projects in 2008. Hardly any major projects were going ahead. As much money was being invested in small emergency projects ($26.2 million in 2008) as in major infrastructure. One donor commented to us in 2008 in Jerusalem, 'emergency is now the norm'.

Stakeholders recognized the inefficiency and high costs of such fragmented and contingency infrastructure development. Some withdrew or suspended support. Others persevered in the knowledge that much investment would be nugatory, but some might just improve the lives of the Palestinian people a little.

Planning and investment a decade on

A decade later, in 2017, we revisited the issue – and found that some things had got better, others had not. As we saw in Chapter 2, there were an extraordinary 114 water

Table 3.3 Water Sector Strategic Development Plan (SDP): Water Supply Targets

Indicator	Actual 2014	Target 2022
Unaccounted-for water	29%	26%
Litres per person per day delivered at the tap	79	88
Percentage of communities unserved	14%	3%
Percentage of households connected to the public network	93%	96%
Percentage of samples meeting specifications	95%	100%

Source: Water Sector Strategic Development Plan 2017–22 (SDP).

and sanitation projects being implemented, for a total value of nearly NIS 3 billion ($770 million).[44] This high level of investment was bringing real improvements in access to water and sanitation services. However, investment was still facing many problems. Planning for water and sanitation services remained overly ambitious and implementation was facing persistent problems, particularly getting the agreement of the Israelis on investment, and the movement and access restrictions imposed by Israel.

Again, we saw in Chapter 2 that recent Palestinian water sector planning represents aspirations and politics as much as it does real intent or need to invest. What appears to be the least realistic, most aspirational, component of the PWA's *Water Sector Strategic Development Plan 2017–22 (SDP)* is that on water resources (see Chapter 2). But in contrast to the water resource targets, the targets for supplying water to the West Bank population are much more practical (see Table 3.3). In fact, the targets for reduction of non-revenue water levels even look rather timid. Levels have remained high (29 per cent in 2014) and there are certainly many practical challenges to reduction. However, as we have seen, leak plugging and reduction in water theft could be the cheapest source of water available in many locations and PWA has already set up a task force to help the utilities and municipalities to reduce leaks in a prioritized and economic way. In this light the reduction to 26 per cent targeted over the plan period looks modest.[45]

The targeted increase in supply per person also looks at first sight quite modest. Daily availability at the tap is targeted to increase only by 11 per cent, from an average of 79 litres per person to 88 litres. However, the reality is that actual levels of supply are currently even below the 79-litre level – see the estimate of 66 litres per person per day in Table 2.6 in Chapter 2 – and any increase in these levels would face both the water resource constraint discussed in Chapter 2 and the likely growth of the population to be served. The proposed increase in network connections to 96 per cent would bring the West Bank to near-complete coverage, well above the global median of 89 per cent.[46] However, in the absence of much more water, would an increase in connections improve water service?

Sector reform

The current reform programme and planned structure for the water sector[47]

A brief history of sector reform since 2009 As we saw at the start of this chapter (see the section 'Policy'), the Palestinian Water Authority (PWA) started taking steps more than a decade ago towards the comprehensive reform of the water and sanitation sector. The PWA had identified a series of constraints to water and sanitation services: pressing water shortages, a growing imbalance between supply and demand for water, and emerging problems at both the bulk and retail service levels in providing efficient, equitable and sustainable water and sanitation services. A major concern was the 'jungle of service providers' – the several hundred service providers, large and small, operating without regulation and sourcing water haphazardly. With considerable donor support, PWA led a thoroughgoing process of national debate and study, which resulted in agreement in 2009 on the need for comprehensive sector reform based on best practice (see Table 3.4).

On 14 December 2009, the cabinet endorsed the *Action Plan for Water Sector Reform* and the main points of sector reform, which were to be enshrined in a new Water Law: establishment of an independent regulator, a national water company, and regional utilities. A memorandum of understanding was signed between national and international stakeholders in 2012. In 2014, the revised *Water Law* mandating the reforms was approved, together with a *Water Sector Policy and Strategy 2012–32*. In 2016, a three-year action plan for implementing the reforms (the *Water Sector Reform Plan 2016–18*) was adopted.

Table 3.4 Guiding Principles for Water Sector Reform

Governance principles	Water supply	Sanitation	Water resources management
• Delineation of roles (not referee and player) • Lean government (greater reliance on private sector) • Appropriate planning and prioritized investment • Separation of financing from implementation • Independent oversight • Robust data management systems	• Ring-fencing of revenues • Commercialization • Water as both a social and economic good • Equitable access to safe and sustainable water services • Separation of tariff setting from revenue collection • Full-cost recovery • Demand management first, supply management second	• Polluter pays • Wastewater treatment and reuse • Equitable access to services • Separation of tariff setting from revenue collection • Recovery of full operation and maintenance costs	• Aquifer/basin management approach • Integrated water resource management (IWRM) • Stakeholder participation in water resource management • Equitable allocation of the water resource • Conservation and protection against contamination
Cross-cutting principles			
• Public access to information • Public participation and social responsibility • Financial transparency and accountability to international standards • Sector sustainability • Needs driven and not donor driven			

Source: PWA 2012 and World Bank 2018.

The heart of the reforms: Four institutional changes

Four main changes were planned. Essentially these were to apply best-practice principles of water resources management and service delivery and to remodel the Palestinian institutional set-up on the lines of the Israeli water institutions.

The first change agreed was to strengthen sector planning and investment by building the capacity of PWA for water resources management and allocation, for planning and financing bulk water infrastructure, and for investment planning and programming within overall sector master plans. Public participation and public information were to be key characteristics of the planning process.

In line with good practice globally, the second change was to separate water resources management from water supply by transferring responsibility for bulk water sourcing and distribution from WBWD (a PWA department) to a newly created National Water Company (NWC), which would be set up on a businesslike basis similar to the Israeli water company Mekorot. The role of the NWC would be to produce raw water both from natural sources and from desalination, to buy water from Israel and to develop and manage national water carriers and distribution networks in both the West Bank and Gaza. Establishment of a sector regulator was the third reform. A Water Sector Regulatory Council (WSRC) was to be set up to regulate service provision in the interests of consumers and to separate tariff setting from revenue collection – see the section 'The institutional framework' in Chapter 2.

Finally, a set of regional water utilities was to be established to provide equitable access to safe and sustainable water services for all in a businesslike fashion with full-cost recovery. The new institutions would operate under the Water Law and the jurisdiction of the PWA and the WSRC. The utilities were to be established at a scale that could even out the current imbalances in water supply quantities and in tariffs. The new larger entities were also expected to realize efficiencies and economies of scale. Utility status would provide governance mechanisms for accountability of management to an independent board and for financial autonomy, ring-fenced finances and accrual accounting following international standards. Public accountability and public participation mechanisms were to be introduced.

According to the 2016 Strategic Development Plan (SDP),[48] current planning is to have completed the bulk of the reforms by 2022. The target by that date is to have PWA and WSRC fully staffed and functional; to have the NWC and the proposed regional utilities established; and for at least 60 per cent of the West Bank population and 90 per cent of the Gaza population to be served by JSCs or utilities operating as autonomous service providers.

Progress on the reform programme to date[49]

The role of PWA has been redefined in the 2014 Water Law, and the authority has been the object of considerable technical assistance and capacity building. PWA has produced comprehensive policy documents and strategies and plans for the short, medium and long terms. PWA has also overseen what progress has been made on implementation of the reforms so far. The WSRC has been established, although most of its statutory functions have not yet been legally transferred by PWA (see Chapter 2).

A proposal for phased transformation of the West Bank Water Department (WBWD) into the National Water Company (NWC) is on the table. The proposed new organization responds to concerns about accountability, efficiency and viability of the current structure. It would be set up as an autonomous bulk carrier, responsible to an independent board and chairman appointed by the cabinet. PWA recommends a three-phase approach for this progressive transformation of the WBWD into the NWC over a five-year period.[50] Phase 1 would restore WBWD's financial equilibrium in the near term, develop improved governance between the WBWD and customers, and improve bulk water provision. Phase 2 would strengthen WBWD though capacity building and improvements in operation and maintenance (O&M) and communications. Phase 3 would comprise the final steps to create the National Water Company.

The proposal includes detailed actions to implement the setting up of the NWC – but there are issues. The most important question is the feasibility of the proposed phasing, which depends on the ability of the existing institution to transform itself, and on WBWD being able to bring about improvements in water supply and financial performance before the NWC is actually set up. Critics point out that all these improvements have been targeted for over a decade with very little to show. A related question is stakeholder incentives. What are the incentives for stakeholders to make this new plan happen? What is different from all the other plans? Here the protracted timetable and step-by-step approach will require sustained political, public and financial support. Finally, there is some lack of clarity about what the end institution will look like. Will it, for example, be the key public water engineering resource, able not only to drill wells but also to help service providers with their infrastructure projects?

On balance, immediate creation of the National Water Company is probably a better way to manage the risks than a gradualist approach. At a meeting to discuss plans for the NWC in early 2017, donors expressed the view that more than a decade of attempts at internal reform of WBWD had not produced expected results and that it would be best to establish the NWC legally, appoint the board and then allow the board to get on with the restructuring, conducting reform steps within the new organizational structure. Experience shows that in such challenging restructuring situations, it is generally best to act decisively early on. Previous attempts to work from within WBWD have been costly and have had limited results. In any case, all stakeholders, including donors, need to align on the decision and provide sustained moral, intellectual and financial support until the job is complete.

The proposed regional utilities PWA's proposal is for a progressive 'aggregation' of service providers, with gradual progression towards grouping them under regional utilities. In February 2017, PWA published a draft proposal for the progressive establishment of regional utilities through a twin process of expansion and absorption from the top and progressive clustering and expansion from the

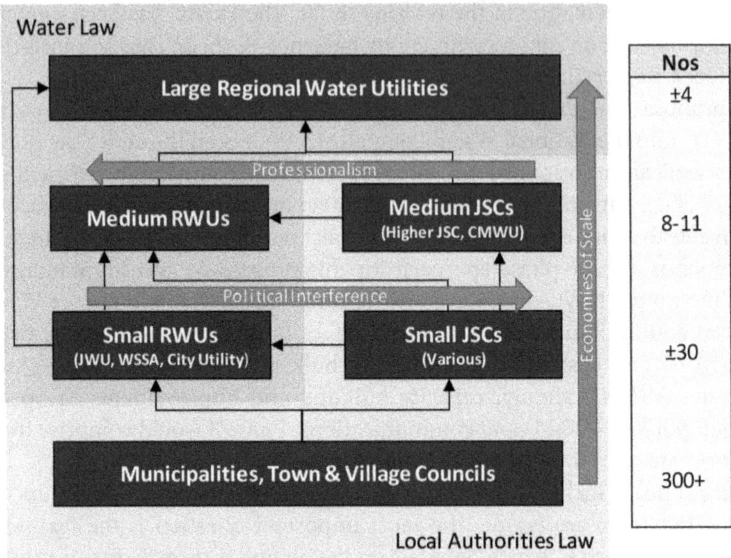

Figure 3.2 Proposed restructuring of water and sanitation service provision. *Source*: PWA/Orgut 2017.

bottom. Proposals are to begin the restructuring of service providers and provision with the 'clustering' of the current 300 or so municipal water departments and smaller providers into either smaller regional utilities (mandated by PWA) or Joint Service Councils (JSCs)[51] mandated by the Ministry of Local Government (see Figure 3.2).[52]

The objectives are to achieve economies of scale and greater professionalism and to do away with the problems of overlap between water service business and other local government business that has characterized the sector up to now. The new organizations would be autonomous and owned by the participating local government units, but they would operate under the Water Law and be regulated by the WSRC. The restructuring would thus progressively remove local government water service providers and provision from the jurisdiction of the Local Authorities Law and the Ministry of Local Government and bring them under the aegis of the Water Law and PWA/WSRC. The medium-term objective would be to have about thirty of these smaller utilities or JSCs, which would progressively be merged into larger entities. The establishment of the large regional water utilities would be a longer-term goal.

These future organizations would be financially self-sustaining, not-for-profit and not subject to taxation, and would be audited.[53] Financial sustainability based on full-cost recovery would be mandatory, as provided for under the 2013 Water Tariff Regulations. Assets would be transferred to the new organizations, and participating local governments would have voting rights and rights to distribution of any surplus in proportion to the value of their assets transferred.

The two existing utilities (the Jerusalem Water Undertaking and the Bethlehem WSSA) provide the potential nucleus of regional utilities in their area. JWU is already providing water to 200 villages in the environs of the 13 municipalities it also serves. In Gaza, CMWU also represents such a nucleus (see Chapter 6). Working from the bottom-up, a number of smaller local government units have, as we have seen, come together in Joint Service Councils (JSCs), but their coverage is so far limited. MoLG has developed a strategy to strengthen the role of JSCs to act as water service providers and has prepared standard instruments to improve water service management in local government units.

Two pilots for the clustering exercise were proposed: in North Jenin and in Salfit Governorate. For the time being, however, the vast majority of service providers are still governed under the 1997 Local Government Law, and the reform process has not yet begun to yield results, although there are efforts to encourage all service providers to strengthen transparency, accountability and financial autonomy.

Issues related to the proposed restructuring

There will be legitimate concerns over loss of control and accountability in a scaled-up service provider which need to be met by adequate governance arrangements. Inevitably there would be loss of control by local people and their local councils over local service provision and a loss of the direct accountability between consumers and local service providers that exists at present. People will feel that they no longer have a responsive partner locally to whom they can turn. They may also feel that there is a risk of 'their' water being surrendered to a common pool over which they have very little say. The PWA has assessed this trade-off and concluded that gains in efficiency from a more professional scaled-up service provider, and gains in equity from the ability to even out water rations across many communities, outweigh these concerns. But clearly governance arrangements need to take the concerns into account.[54]

Local authorities currently draw benefits from provision of water services and will be reluctant to hand over assets and responsibility unless there is some compensating benefit. In addition to having power over their own service provision, which brings both practical and political advantages, many local authorities currently benefit from transfers of a financial surplus on the water account to finance other municipal activities – see the case of Yatta described earlier, for example.

Local authorities will be loath to surrender these advantages. The example of Gaza is highly relevant here. The regional utility, the Coastal Municipalities Water Utility (CMWU) was set up in Gaza over two decades ago, – see Chapter 6 – but even today only one out of twenty-five municipalities has so far agreed to hand over its assets and full responsibility for water service provision to the CMWU.

The PWA's plan in the West Bank proposes a trade-off whereby either the assets are purchased from the local authority, providing the wherewithal for them to invest in alternative revenue raising activities, or – as an alternative – local authorities become part-owners of the new organizations, with their share based on the value of assets transferred.

This is a key issue that could become a constraint to the whole process. There is difficulty with the notion that local authorities should be compensated for handing over assets which have largely been financed by central government. There is also a natural reticence about the idea that local authorities should be compensated for the loss of access to surpluses which are in fact largely fictitious.[55]

To be financially viable, the new organizations will need to recover all costs and there needs to be careful consideration of the roles of tariffs and subsidy in this. In the longer term there will be efficiency gains which will reduce costs but in the short term, there will be a high cost of transition. In addition, in order to balance their books on the basis of full-cost recovery, the new organizations will have to recover all operation and maintenance costs at least,[56] and also recover the cost of non-revenue water and uncollected debts. If the government is not prepared to subsidize shortfalls on these three headings, tariffs will certainly have to go up to cover them. It is clearly correct that tariffs should allow service providers to balance their books, but there needs to be a plan to make this fair and politically palatable.

Could the Palestinians emulate Israel's achievements in water supply?

On water supply as on all other components of water security, the contrast between Israelis and Palestinians is striking. On the simplest indicator – access to safe drinking water – Israel is again a world leader, while the Palestinians trail behind even impoverished Yemen – see Figure 3.3. Yet we can safely say that Palestinians aspire to the same level of water services as their Israeli neighbours. This means 24/7 availability of quality potable water in quantities limited only by consent and by prudent management of demand through price and technology. It means water service providers which are efficient and responsive to consumer needs and which match supply and demand at economic levels consistent with societal goals and with limits on water availability and affordability. It requires water service providers which are financially viable, which have access to investment capital, and which invest in good service provision and in technological advances.

Some of these factors lie within the reach of Palestinians or close to their hand. Strengthening water service providers can be done by the progressive implementation of institutional reforms. If these reforms are well done, the result in the long run should be autonomous, accountable utilities with ring-fenced finances providing equitable access to safe and sustainable water services on a financially sustainable basis.

The Palestinian reforms of service providers bear a strong resemblance to those carried out in Israel which we discussed in Chapter 1. Israel started from a position nearly two decades ago in some ways similar to that of the West Bank today – a plethora of large and small municipal water and sanitation service providers whose governance and finances were entangled with those of the municipality of

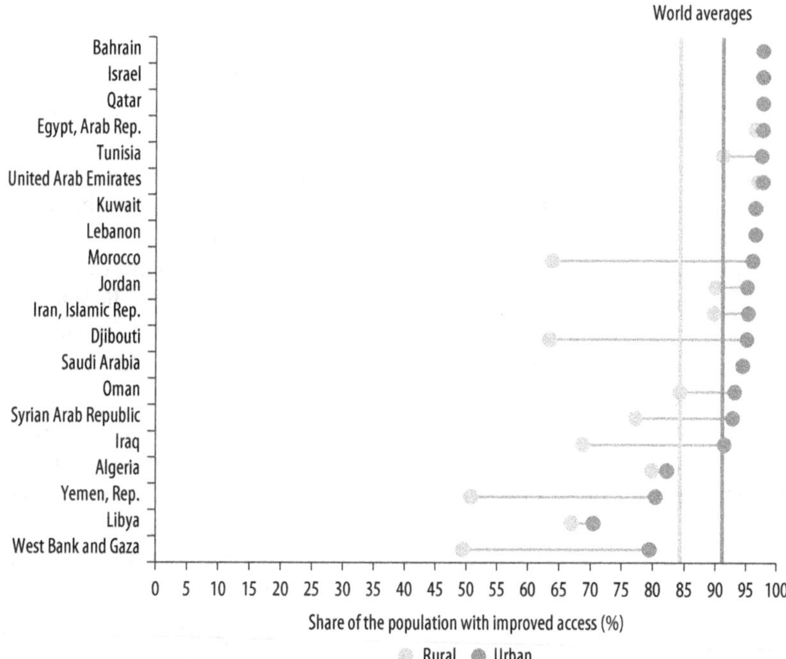

Figure 3.3 Percentage of population with access to safe drinking water in the Middle East and North Africa. *Source*: Beyond Scarcity, World Bank 2019.

which they were a part. As long ago as 2001, the Israeli government mandated an aggregation into corporatized regional utilities with financial autonomy reporting to dedicated boards of directors. For a number of years, these reforms proceeded lethargically and it was only from 2009 when the IWA assumed regulatory authority and adopted a 'carrot-and-stick' approach that performance began to improve. The conclusion is that these reforms for West Bank Palestinians will require political commitment and a firm guiding hand. They are likely to be slow in implementation and slow to bear their fruits.

The Israeli example thus illustrates some of the challenge facing the Palestinians. But there are also other constraining factors. In the Israeli case we talked about agency capacity – the skills and experience in the Israeli Water Authority, in Mekorot, and in the utilities. By contrast, it has to be said that Palestinian institutions are quite weak. We talked about balancing the books and financial autonomy of the service providers. This goal is made more difficult for West Bank service providers because of the high cost of water relative to incomes – ten times higher than in Israel – and because as long as services are poor, willingness to pay will remain low.

We talked also about the importance of the consent of society to reform. Are there constituencies that can be counted on to support reforms, as there were in Israel? On this, too, the Palestinians trail well behind. In fact, it is hard to say that there is a clear support amongst West Bank Palestinians for the reforms. The municipalities and their oversight ministry are, to say the least, reluctant. As for consumers, they might support change in the hope of better services, but they have scant institutional voice to influence events. In any case, consumers will inevitably be sceptical of reforms that will put more power in the hands of the Palestinian Authority. Certainly the PWA, which is the owner of the reforms, lacks authority and the confidence of the public. It lacks, too, much capacity to steer the reforms, which many see as devised by consultants and pushed by donors.

But perhaps most importantly, the West Bank lacks the ability to bring real benefits to consumers through the reforms. Water resources are too little to satisfy basic demands in many localities, and West Bank Palestinians lack the means to transport water from one site to another. Where Israel has developed an integrated system of production and storage (including underground and lake storage), linked to a nationwide network of transmission mains and has secured – or created – water resources adequate for all its needs, the Palestinians operate within scattered fragments of service area with no West Bank–wide network connecting Palestinian towns, working within a quantum of bulk water that is palpably too limited and with no storage to act as a buffer to manage risks of water shortages.

The big challenges are thus access to water resources and the means to get them to the point where they are needed. At the margin, where Israel can simply create new water through desalination, the Palestinians, bound still by Article 40 which has long outlived its relevance, are obliged to go cap in hand to the Israelis to buy extra potable water. Not only does this impair their water security by ever shrinking their autonomy in respect of water resources, but it constantly brings water into the political arena and also imposes unreasonably high costs. Of course it raises constantly the festering question of water rights. For the moment, too, the Palestinians are unable to create their proposed national water network. All their own supplies are local, and connectivity is not amongst Palestinian centres of population but with Mekorot.

Figure 3.4 Israeli water tanks in Hebron, the West Bank, with permission from Irish Central.

Figure 3.5 Palestinian water tanks in Hebron vandalized by Israeli settlers, Wikimedia Commons.

In order to meet current unmet demand and to supply adequate drinking water in the future in the West Bank, Palestinians will need to seek some new dispensation if they are to emulate Israelis' security of water service provision. Essentially, they need their own water inventory, just as Israel has. They will need an efficient infrastructure that underwrites their water security, just as Israel has.

We will return to these requirements in Part III of this book, where we look at these elements as part of a reset of the overall framework of cooperation on water between Israelis and Palestinians.

Figure 3.6 Swimming pool at the Israeli West Bank settlement of Ma'ale Adumim, Davidmosberg on Wikimedia Commons.

Chapter 4

SANITATION AND WASTEWATER IN THE WEST BANK

In the end we will do the right thing – but only after exhausting every other possibility

J. M. Keynes

Understanding after Oslo that the collection, treatment and reuse of wastewater and sewage were public health and environmental priorities, the Palestinian Authority (PA) made ambitious plans to develop sewer networks, construct treatment plants and treat wastewater to standards that would allow wastewater reuse in agriculture. In the second half of the 1990s, the authority prepared several treatment plant projects, negotiated financing for them and obtained approval of the Joint Water Committee (JWC). However, very little happened on the ground. By 2009, only one plant out of the eleven planned had been built and almost no new sewerage connections had been made. Raw sewage was running in the wadis and water sources were increasingly polluted. Health problems related to water, sanitation and sewage were widespread. Although most of the population had access to improved sanitation, for more than two thirds of households these were cess pits, which overflowed regularly. Reuse of treated wastewater was non-existent.

The most contentious plant was that for Hebron which suffered an on–off fate for nearly two decades. Sewage coursed down the streambeds for over a 100 kilometres across the southern West Bank and into Israel. Citizens and NGOs from both communities protested vociferously. Unwilling to agree to construction of a plant on the terms the Palestinians proposed, Israel began treating Hebron's sewage on its side of the Green Line. Only when Israel's Comptroller General intervened did Israel finally agree to construction of the Hebron plant. In 2019, almost twenty years after the project was first proposed, work finally started.

Overall, more than two decades after Oslo, there has been scant progress. Only a quarter of sewage in the Palestinian West Bank is collected; only one fifth is treated. Reuse levels remain negligible. Environmental problems persist, particularly raw sewage running in the wadis.

The PA's plans for sanitation and wastewater had been ambitious but its capacity relatively weak. However, this has not been the mean reason for the appalling situation. The real sources of the problem were fourfold. First, Israel's Civil

Administration which controls most of the West Bank opposed construction of Palestinian infrastructure in Area C, the 60 per cent of the West Bank it directly controls – yet sites for sewage treatment and reuse are necessarily almost entirely located in Area C. Second, Israel imposes tight restrictions on the materials required for building and running a wastewater treatment plant, particularly pipes and chemicals. Third, Israel has insisted that Palestinian plants in the West Bank should also treat sewage from the multiple Israeli settlements that have spread across the West Bank. The Palestinian Authority determined that any agreement to this would be a recognition of the legitimacy of settlements, breaching a clear Palestinian red line. Finally, donor aid has been subject to shifting attitudes, varying with the donors' appreciation of the political and security situation in the West Bank and the sides donors felt obliged to take in the acrimonious politics of the struggle between Palestinians and Israelis.

This chapter looks at the facts, the issues and the apparently irreconcilable policies. We start with an in-depth look at the Hebron case, we discuss plans and their results, and then we trace outcomes and costs in terms of public health, of amenity and of environmental damage.

Turning a wastewater crisis into an opportunity: The long history of the Hebron wastewater treatment plant

With a population in 2013 of about 200,000 people, Hebron Governorate is one of the largest in the West Bank, and Hebron city is a leading industrial and economic centre. It is the heart of the Palestinian stone-cutting industry – Hebron cut stone accounts for over a quarter (27 per cent) by value of Palestinian exports from the West Bank. The governorate also has one of the West Bank's largest areas of agricultural land, second only to Jenin. Water is, however, very scarce and the few small areas with access to irrigation water predominantly grow high-value vegetable and fruit crops.

The pollution problem

In Hebron city, four fifths of the houses have sewer connections, but there is no provision for sewage treatment. Every day, 10,000 cubic metres of raw sewage – 10,000 tons by weight – is discharged into the Wadi al Samen. The wadi is essentially an open sewer. The sewage currently runs untreated through populated areas and environmentally sensitive zones, towards the Green Line with Israel. This sewage stream is joined by polluted effluent from stone cutting and olive pressing. En route towards the Green Line, much of the dirty flows percolate into the soil, contaminating the Eastern Aquifer. Currently, some 104,000 people living along the wadi are affected by this polluted stream. It is reported that some poor households along the stream lack water and use the sewage water for irrigation and other purposes.

Downstream, across the border with Israel, there are more sophisticated preoccupations. Shlomit Tamari is a teacher and a member of the Council for a Sustainable Negev. Shlomit, who lives in the Israeli town of Metar, said: 'The wadi is exactly where I usually run, and a lot of people go biking there.'[1]

But probably the people worst affected by the current sewage problem in the area are the Bedouin, living in humble circumstances on either side of the Green Line, scratching a living in this polluted environment. 'Their homes are shacks, they're literally next to the stream and that stream is raw sewage', the environmental activist Gidon Bromberg told *The Jerusalem Post*. Bromberg, an advocate of cooperation on natural resource issues, went on: 'The impact is harsh on both Israeli and Palestinian communities equally.'[2]

Interim solutions

First attempts The problem of sewage pollution from Hebron was identified as a serious issue as far back as the 1970s. A first proposal for a Hebron treatment plant foundered in 1999 on Israeli insistence on too high a treatment standard. The proposal, costed at 45 million euros, was submitted to the JWC in 1999 and approved. The Civil Administration then required a series of modifications, including upgrading to tertiary-level treatment to increase effluent quality to '10:10 standards'. This meant a 60 per cent cost escalation to 75 million euros. PWA and the donor pulled out, unable to proceed with a project that had such a high capital cost and with the risk that subsequent operating costs would be unaffordable for the relatively poor population.

Proposals for a regional solution for wastewater management in the whole Hebron Governorate were then elaborated in a 2001 master plan.[3] The plan found that pollution of the Eastern Aquifer was already resulting from untreated sewage not only from Hebron municipality but also from other communities in the governorate. These communities included Israeli settlements, notably the contentious and – by Palestinians – hated settlement of Kiryat Arba. Elevated nitrate concentrations were found in some potable water wells and detailed aquifer modelling showed the increasing threat from the ongoing pollution to the potable quality of the aquifer. An extensive set of studies was then conducted under the USAID-funded West Bank Integrated Water Resources Program (2002–6) to implement the master plan.

For the first phase of implementation, the PWA decided to construct a regional wastewater treatment plant that would provide secondary treatment for around 15,000 cubic metres of wastewater per day at a site just south of Hebron city. A detailed feasibility study was done in 2004 for both the regional wastewater treatment plant and the reuse of reclaimed effluents and biosolids. In addition, a full environmental assessment was conducted. Based on this documentation, the project was submitted to the JWC, which approved the project. Subsequently the Civil Administration issued the required permits. In 2005, USAID issued a Request for Proposals for a design-build contract to construct the plant. However, with the election of Hamas that year, US attitudes changed and eventually no contract for construction was awarded.

The Shoket plant With this comprehensive solution falling afoul of politics and with the pollution and environmental health problems growing worse by the day, environmental activists on both sides of the Green Line protested. Local Israeli communities petitioned the Israeli High Court which instructed the Israeli government to find a solution. This solution was to be the unilateral decision by Israel to build a tertiary treatment plant on Wadi al Samen but on the Israeli side of the Green Line and to charge the PA with both the capital and the operating costs of sewage treatment.

However, this plant, which was sited at Shoket junction right on the Green Line, proved very costly – estimated at about NIS 100 million ($28 million). It has never operated as designed and has been the source of bitter and resentful criticism from the Palestinians both of the imposed cost, deducted at source from tariff receipts, and of the appropriation of the treated wastewater which is said to be used by Israeli farmers. In any case, the sewage stream flows for 50 kilometres before it reaches the Green Line, by which time much of the damage to the aquifer and the environment has been done.

Pre-treatment of the stone-cutting effluent With still no agreement on a comprehensive solution, the Palestinians took a risk-management approach to a pressing problem of point source pollution. The pollution was from the effluent of the stone-cutting industry along the stream. To combat this, Hebron Municipality and USAID in 2012 began a programme to manage wastewater from stone-cutting operations in Hebron's industrial area. Pre-treatment facilities at stone-cutting factories were installed and enforcement measures were put in place to control disposal of industrial wastes in the sewer network and streams. The programme successfully contained most of the stone-cutting waste and was turned over to the municipality and the PWA for management in July 2013. In the same month, USAID completed a *Hebron Industrial Discharges Study* that provides a strategic plan for comprehensive management of all industrial wastes from Hebron. Based on this, Hebron municipality and the PWA have adopted an action programme for industrial wastewater based on on-site pre-treatment and strengthened regulation.

The new project[4]

Despite action on industrial wastewater, the problem of sewage running in the stream remained unsolved. By 2013, the environmental problems had become ever more pressing, and there was willingness on both sides to revive the idea of a full-scale Hebron treatment plant. Government requested financing from the French *Agence francaise de developpement* (AFD) and from the World Bank to update the feasibility studies and PWA prepared a revised proposal in 2013–14. The proposal was for a four-stage programme to improve wastewater management and reuse. The first phase was to address the immediate needs by building a plant to treat the existing sewage stream coming from the 80 per cent of households and businesses in Hebron municipality already sewered. The plant would be constructed on an 11-hectare site owned by the PA, four kilometres downstream from Hebron city. Beneficiaries would be not only the residents of Hebron but the more than 100,000 residents of Palestinian communities living along Wadi al Samen and the Israelis living beyond the Green Line as well as the 900,000 people in the Bethlehem and Hebron Governorates who obtain part of their water supplies from the at-risk Eastern Aquifer.

The second phase would consist of an irrigation scheme adjacent to the treatment plant for reuse of the treated effluent. A third phase would build sewerage networks and associated treatment and reuse capacity for the remaining 20 per cent of Hebron municipality at present unsewered. The final, fourth phase would finance sewerage, treatment and reuse capacity for communities along Wadi al Samen such as Yatta and al Dahriyyeh.

Contracts for implementation of the first phase – the treatment plant – were finally signed in 2019.[5] Donors – AFD, the European Union, the World Bank and USAID – are financing the US$41.9 million cost of the plant. The Hebron municipality is initially to be the operator, but over time and within the framework of the sector reform process (see Chapter 3), it is expected that the plant will be transferred to the proposed regional utility.

The plant will treat the wastewater to secondary level. This has lower treatment costs than the tertiary treatment which is nowadays the norm in Israel. Effluent quality will nonetheless be greatly enhanced and the pollutant load flowing down the wadi will be significantly reduced. The treatment will be adequate to allow for reuse of the treated effluent for restricted irrigation of agricultural lands adjacent to and downstream from the plant. The agricultural development project to be financed in the second phase is expected to demonstrate for the first time in the West Bank effluent reuse in irrigation at scale, including the introduction of reuse standards and practices.

The plan is that the plant should cover its operation and maintenance costs and depreciation. In economic terms, taking into account both direct benefits, including the value of treated wastewater, and the many externalities such as public health benefits and protection of surface and groundwater resources, calculations suggest the project is economically viable with an economic internal rate of return of 12 per cent.

The agreement to construct the Hebron plant has been greeted as a success by environmentalists. Gidon Bromberg, the influential Israeli activist we cited earlier, said the plant is 'a very important first step'.[6] He stressed that cooperative solutions are essential for joint environmental problems. 'Only joint management and monitoring of the sewage by both sides will enable a real, long-term resolution for the issues of the Hebron Stream.'

Nader Khatib, Bromberg's then Palestinian co-director of Eco Peace, saw the project in an even broader context – that of collaboration leading to a wider trust. 'Sewage treatment is more than just an infrastructure project, but an opportunity for communities who jointly suffer to work together and build trust between one another. It is important that infrastructure projects involve all communities impacted from the earliest of stages, so that all come to understand the benefits of working together.' Bromberg added, 'We both drink the same water. Unilaterally, no one can solve this – we need to be working on these water issues and sanitation issues together.' [7]

Palestinian plans for sanitation and wastewater treatment: A story of largely disappointed expectations[8]

Ambitious plans following Oslo

The prospect that by 2022, the current target for project completion, the Hebron plant will be operational will finally deliver on one – but only one – of the goals that the Palestinians set themselves after Oslo more than a quarter of a century ago. As far back as 1995, with the prospect under Article 40[9] of extra water resources and a rapid rise in household connections and levels of water use, the Palestinians saw that the volumes of wastewater and sewage would also increase fast. It was clear to the new Palestinian Authority that in order to protect human health and the environment, the expected increase in water supply would have to be accompanied by an increase in wastewater collection and treatment. Also, in so water-scarce an environment, treated wastewater could become a valued resource, as it already was on the way to becoming in Israel.

So in the planning phase immediately after Oslo (1995–9), the Palestinians began studies to prepare to bring wastewater collection, treatment and reuse up to modern standards. For much of this planning, Israel was the model. In 2001, the Palestinian Authority published its ambitious wastewater treatment and reuse plans in the *Palestinian Water Strategic Planning Study* (PECDAR 2001).

The study proposed that all main towns should have full sewer coverage by 2020. Reaching this goal would bring Palestinian towns up to the level of their Israeli counterparts, where household sewerage coverage had been universal for decades. The plan was also for all the wastewater collected to be treated to the same standards as practiced in Israel. In a first phase up to 2005, this would require the four existing plants to be extended and improved and seven large new treatment plants to be constructed. These projects were incorporated in the priority investment plan. Fifteen additional plants were to be constructed by 2020, together with extensions to the original eleven, to keep pace with the extension of sewerage.

The plan also targeted treatment of all wastewater to the level where it could be reused, just as in Israel. An institutional structure was to be set up to develop and implement a wastewater reuse strategy, and all future programmes were to integrate reuse wherever possible. With this in mind, treatment plants were to be located close to agricultural lands. Where this was not possible, treated wastewater would be transported to where it *could* be reused. Ideally this would have followed the Israeli model of a dedicated national network to pipe treated wastewater to

Table 4.1 Proposed Treatment Standards

	Recharge	Reuse
Suspended solids	30 mg/l	15 mg/l
BOD	20 mg/l	10 mg/l
Nitrate	30 mg/l	10 mg/l
Faecal coliform	1,000/100 ml	200/100 ml

Source: PECDAR 87ff.

farming areas, but initially the Palestinians proposed to set up receiving stations and to tanker the treated wastewater to outlying farmlands. Research and extension programmes were to be put in place to support farmers for reuse.[10]

Treatment standards were set – see Table 4.1. These provided standards both for reuse in restricted agriculture and for reinjection of treated wastewater into the ground where it would be naturally filtered as it made its way down towards the aquifers, as is now the practice in Israel (see Chapter 1).

Multiple obstacles and scant realization

These plans proved in practice unrealistic, even wildly so. The long saga of the Hebron plant is matched throughout the West Bank, although elsewhere not yet with prospects of so positive an outcome. When we visited in 2008 and 2009, almost a decade after the PA had made its plans, we found that almost none of the hoped-for improvements had been realized. Sewerage and wastewater treatment had low coverage and reuse was virtually non-existent. Out of seven new plants that were supposed to be operational by that time, only one new plant had been built – at al Bireh. Sanitation projects had been subject to extraordinary delays and constraints. Two further plants – at Nablus and the Hebron one – had been approved in principle but no work had yet started. Little had been done to connect more households to the sewerage network. Wastewater reuse in agriculture remained a distant prospect apart from isolated pilot schemes of a few hectares.

Only ten towns were served by sewerage systems. Of these, only four had treatment plants and none had a reuse scheme. Little had been done to extend the sewer systems – according to the Palestine Central Bureau of Statistics (PCBS) surveys at the time, about 69 per cent of the West Bank population still relied on septic tanks. Only a third of sewage was being collected (31 per cent) and little of that was being adequately treated. The working plants – at Hebron, Jenin, Ramallah and Tulkarem – were performing considerably below design capacity. Efficiency was 10–30 per cent, and effluent quality was poor.

This failure to develop wastewater systems was the more damaging because under Oslo, water supply quantities – and hence wastewater quantities – had gone up. The environment and groundwater quality were proving to be the major victims. An estimated 25 million cubic metres – 25 million tons – of untreated sewage was being discharged to the environment each year at over 350 locations in the West Bank. One concerned and experienced Israeli environmental NGO representative commented: blandly, 'Since Oslo, we have not given enough attention to the environment. Yet more water leads to more wastewater, and hence inevitably to environmental problems. So the environmental problems are in a way a result of success, but the environmental implications were neglected.'

To which the Palestinians responded forcefully. After all, the 2001 plans had foreseen all this but implementation had been stymied, largely – in the Palestinian view – by Israel. The PWA commented at the time that, in addition to the constraints imposed on carrying out their plans, they 'lacked enforcement tools to regulate wastewater in Areas B and C, and certainly not to control the pollution generated from settlements'.[11]

Sometimes it seemed to the Palestinians that the Israelis simply did not care for the environment, let alone for the Palestinian people. For example, in 2008 the Dar al Khaled wastewater facility at Azmuth village had not been operating for three years. The leather factory in the nearby Israeli settlement was producing highly toxic effluent and noxious odours. Palestinian protests produced no response from Israeli authorities. Only when the Israeli NGO B'tselem complained and publicized the problem was the facility repaired. At Wadi Fukin, the Beit Ilia settlement was treating its wastewater and pumping it to the wadi. But this ultra-orthodox settlement could not work on a Saturday, and then the sewage ran raw in Wadi Fukin.[12] In another case, movement and access restrictions led to the flooding of an entire city by sewage. This was in the Palestinian city of Qalqilya, where 45,000 people were connected to the sewerage network and the outflow went for treatment to Israel. On 5–8 February 2005, the trunk line blocked and the entire city was flooded with sewage and wastewater. It took three days for the Palestinians to get permission from the army to go out to clear the blockage.[13]

* * *

Many factors were at play here. Some of them related to the overall situation which made all water-related investment in the West Bank a risky and high-cost business – the institutional weaknesses in planning and implementation, the inefficiencies inherent in donor aid, the more or less permanent political and security emergencies. A key factor was the governance arrangements for investment approval by the JWC agreed at Oslo. This constraint was further complicated by the requirements of the Civil Administration.[14] In the case of sanitation investments, the Israelis insisted that Palestinian wastewater treatment plants should treat wastewater to the high tertiary treatment standards set out in Israel. When it came to decisions on actual investment, the Palestinian Authority and its donors had concluded – as in the first attempts at a solution for the Hebron plant, for which see earlier – that the capital and running costs of this tertiary treatment were just too expensive for a relatively poor people. But the Civil Administration would not agree and the investment programme was halted.

* * *

> *The case of Salfit and Ariel* Jamal Hammad remembers when the al-Matwa spring in Salfit city was a popular destination for locals. Several decades ago, the area would often be crowded with Palestinians hiking in the valley and families picnicking alongside the clear, flowing stream. Now, however, the sewage flowing through the spring, the rancid smell that engulfs the valley and the mosquitoes swarming the area have left the valley largely deserted. 'All of this waste is coming from Israel's settlements; mostly from the Ariel settlement,' Hammad [said]. 'We are very worried about what long-term effects this pollution will have on our future.'
>
> Drowning in the waste of Israeli settlers by Jaclynn Ashly, 18 September 2017, al Jazeera

At Salfit, problems blocked construction of a wastewater treatment plant for two decades. Salfit has an ancient spring from which the town has drawn its water since time immemorial. But when we were there in 2009 there was a flood of sewage flowing in the stream bed just fifteen yards from the spring. Local people said that this was untreated wastewater flowing down copiously from the large Israeli settlement of Ariel. Recently, they said, the sewage had overflowed and flooded the spring, contaminating the town water supply. The Palestinian community had to build a four-metre-high protection wall.

For years, a treatment plant to serve Salfit had been in the PA programme. Germany had agreed to finance the 5 million euro plant. The proposal was submitted to the JWC on 28 November 1996 and approved. But, as with most proposals for wastewater treatment plants, the site was in Area C and the project had also to be approved by the Civil Administration. The Civil Administration refused permission on security grounds, and a new site had to be designated. The PA duly found a new site and presented the project again, but the Civil Administration now demanded that the plant also treat the wastewater of Ariel settlement. This was anathema to the Palestinian Authority – Palestinians reject all investments that recognize or help the Israeli settlements they loathe.

For three years the project was stalled, but eventually the Civil Administration did give its approval and construction actually started. But then the Israelis came back to say that the plant was too close to where they planned to build further settlements. In 2000, they called a halt to construction and paid 1 million shekels in compensation to Germany. A long delay ensued but eventually in 2009 the PA came back with a new site. This too was held up by 'planning considerations', because the new site was also in Area C. The patient German donor then finally withdrew its financing. When we visited in 2009, sewage was still running untreated in the wadi.

At the time of writing (2020), Salfit still lacked a treatment plant, and residents continue to attribute the responsibility for this to Israeli controls. As a coping strategy, the municipality has constructed a relief pipeline to collect the sewage and dump it further down the wadi. The upstream Israeli settlements – Ariel, Ariel West and the Barkan settlements – have invested in their own sewage treatment facilities, but Salfit residents report that these 'routinely break down or overflow, causing raw sewage to flood into the al-Matwa valley and spring'. Whatever the origins of the problem – and there is no doubt much to be said on either side – the current situation is an environmental catastrophe.[15]

The case of Nablus West In some cases, the issues were simply the security situation – and Israel's security requirements. The proposal for the 26.5 million euro Nablus West wastewater treatment plant was submitted to the JWC on 8 August 1997 and approved by both the JWC and the Civil Administration. However, security requirements in Area C during and after the *al Aqsa intifada* made access to the site and the transport of equipment and materials impossible, and this project too was shelved. The project was eventually revived and the plant came into operation in 2013, more than fifteen years after the original agreement.[16]

Al Bireh wastewater treatment plant and settler sewage The issue of settler sewage also came up in the case of the El-Bireh plant which was designed to treat the sewage of Ramallah and El Bireh.[17] Preparation of the project began in 1992 but was dogged by the usual vicissitudes. A final modified design was completed in February 1996 and construction started later that year. However, during construction, Israel decided to construct a 'bypass road' right through the site of the plant. Plans had to be modified, costs went up and project completion was delayed two years.[18]

Also during this period, Ramallah was growing fast. Towards the end of the construction period, in March 1998, revision to the expected load led the Palestinians to propose an increase in the size of the trunk main from 10 inch diameter to 14 inches. This was initially refused by the Civil Administration. Then a year later, in March 1999, the Israelis proposed that the Israeli settlements of Cochav Yacov and Psagot be connected. The Palestinian authorities and the donor, Germany's KfW, both refused. However, according to the Palestinians, the Israelis simply went ahead and made the connection from the settlements to the sewer trunk line flowing into the treatment plant without the approval of either the PWA or KfW. This was because, although the plant is owned by the Palestinian municipality of El-Bireh, it lies in Area C which is under Israeli military control and Palestinians need special permission to enter, even to go to the plant. As a result, the Palestinians were powerless to prevent this unilateral action.

Thus, despite consistent Palestinian policy, it appears that the plant actually is treating settler sewage. In 2013, plant director, Mahmoud Suleiman Abed, confirmed this. He referred to a 'political agreement' in 2000 on this between the Palestinian Authority and Israel. The deal, he claimed, was that the Palestinian Authority agreed to treat the wastewater of the settlements[19] 'in exchange for the permission from Israel to allow the construction and operating plant license for the plant'.[20]

Sanitation, water quality and public health

When we were in the West Bank in 2009, it was clear that water quality and environmental contamination were of increasing concern. There was a growing problem with biological contamination, particularly with springs and water tankers. A World Health Organization (WHO) programme to treat all West Bank spring water had been completed in 1999. Some seven years later, few of the chlorinators installed under that programme were functioning and the risk of contamination was evident. Similarly, for the more than 200,000 people without piped water who were served by rainwater harvesting and water tankers, alarmingly high rates of BOD pollution were reported. Studies by USAID in the countryside of Nablus and Hebron governorates revealed high contamination levels in tankered water – only 38 per cent of samples were free from faecal coliforms.[21] The USAID report went on to identify 'the provision of reliable, piped, treated water as the single most important intervention for increasing health and quality of life in the West Bank'.[22]

During our field visits, we found that water quality was a great concern for most village women in the countryside around Jenin.[23] At the household level the concerns and the coping mechanisms were relatively common across the different villages, regardless of whether the villages used tanker water or were connected to a network. Virtually all the women interviewed complained of poor water quality. They explained that many wells were close to sewage sources, some as close as 12 metres. Whether they obtained water from tankers or from the tap, they all boiled the water before using it. They explained that poor water quality was visible to the naked eye in most cases, especially in winter when it was cold.

Concern about the quality of tanker water was particularly acute, as the source was never quite clear, and households were generally forced to purchase what was available. 'Water boiling is costly', the women said – on average it contributed to consumption for a family of four with two children of two large propane tanks per month at the cost of 1,200 NIS ($325).

Chlorine tablets were distributed for free by local authorities, and families were using these. Filtration systems were also available, but few of the women said that they could afford to use these safer methods. The smallest filtration system available, which involved pouring water through a paper filter system and into bottles, cost 1,000 NIS ($270) up front for the equipment, and 60 NIS ($15) each month thereafter for filter replacements. To keep costs of purified water down, the women gave priority to babies and small children. This meant that many adults were consuming untreated and unboiled water, which led to health problems. Mothers estimated 3–4 litres of boiled or purified water per day per child. They reported spending up to two hours every day preparing and bottling clean water for a household with two children.

Several public health problems were reported as a consequence of poor water quality. The problems included parasites, diarrhoea and kidney stones. Residents described a recent incident when Jenin hospital reported that 75 per cent of the population of the villages in the north-east of Jenin Governorate had been afflicted with acute diarrhoea. Another resident reported: 'Two years ago [in 2005–6] there was a time when Israel did not allow [propane] gas into our area. There was a kidney stone outbreak, and 30 per cent of the population of Jalama had to have them removed. It is a very costly operation.'

Water in these villages was so precious that women reported using little or none of it for cleaning the house, and limiting clothes washing to the bare minimum. Grey water from kitchens was frequently piped to the garden for irrigation, but some wastewater collecting in pools attracted mosquitoes and bugs, which were both a nuisance and a health risk. Mosque water used for washing before prayer was also reused for irrigating nearby gardens and cleaning houses near the mosque.

It appears that all across the West Bank, there is a high incidence of water-related diseases. Epidemiological data is uneven, but there are many anecdotal stories. In Nablus, for example, where the new wastewater treatment plant was for long held up – see discussion earlier – the PWA told us: 'The wastewater treatment plant is sorely needed. Yesterday 65 cases of diarrhoea were treated in the hospital there.'[24] At Burin near Nablus, there had been recently 450 cases of hepatitis A. Students in school were infected.

The health impacts on smaller communities unconnected to the network, and for people living in Area C, appeared particularly harsh. A 2003–4 study[25] found that outside the main towns, water- and sanitation-related infections were common. Four communities in ten (41 per cent) reported infections related to poor water and sanitation services, with 14 per cent of communities reporting dysentery and 22 per cent reporting amoebic infections. More than one third (39 per cent) of the communities reporting amoeba did not have access to water treatment and more than half (52 per cent) did not have community chlorination. Only one household in eight (16 per cent) had household chlorination. Very few communities (7 per cent) had access to wastewater networks.[26]

Where closures drove up the cost of water, there were greater risks of sickness. In November 2002, the community of Jurish in Nablus district was using each day about 30 litres of poor-quality tanker water for each person. The cost was high at 15 NIS per cubic metre ($4.20), a cost driven up by the impact of checkpoints and curfew during the trip of about three kilometres from the well. In the community of 1,500, there were 300 cases of amoeba infection at the time, due to the poor-quality source and to sewage flow and cess pits near to their cisterns.[27]

The 2006 PAPFAM survey found that 12 per cent of children under five had suffered from diarrhoea in the two weeks preceding the survey. Diarrhoeal conditions are strongly associated with water quality, hygiene and sanitation. More than half (54 per cent) of these cases had required a medical consultation. Extrapolating from the nature and cost of the medical treatments involved and without accounting for the losses of adult productivity, it was estimated that the annual cost of the health impacts of poor water and sanitation on children five years old or less was NIS 72 million ($20 million), equivalent to 0.37 per cent of Palestinian GDP.[28]

The situation of sanitation and wastewater today

At the time of writing (2020), little has improved in the dismal West Bank sanitation story. Only one quarter of wastewater is collected and only one fifth is treated. A 2017 survey[29] found that on average, 94 per cent of the West Bank population has access to 'improved unshared sanitation' – but less than one third of this access was by sewered systems. Despite considerable investment in expanding wastewater networks, only 30 per cent of West Bank households are connected to sewerage networks. Rates vary widely by governorate, from zero (in Tubas) to 59 per cent (in Qalqilya). Access also varies strongly by household income: only 13 per cent in the poorest quintile are connected to sewer networks, compared to 42 per cent in the richest quintile. With such limited sewerage, sanitation for two thirds of the West Bank population is still the cess pit. These pits create a threat to human health and the environment, with high likelihood of overflow across different types of sanitation. The 2017 survey found that across all governorates, overflows of sewage were frequent or occasional for 18 per cent of the population.

Large quantities of untreated sewage are still being discharged into the environment. Overall, only about one quarter of the 62 million cubic metres – 62 million tons – of wastewater generated each day in the West Bank is being collected in sewerage networks, and only one fifth of wastewater is being treated (about 13 million cubic metres annually). Reuse of treated wastewater remains negligible. The biggest problem continues to be the 25 million cubic metres of untreated sewage being discharged into wadis each year from 350 locations. Some 15 million cubic metres of this raw sewage is still flowing into Israel, where it was being treated and reused in agriculture. Israel charges to the Palestinian Authority for treating this wastewater in 2015 were over NIS 82 million ($23 million).

With this profile, it is not surprising that the Palestinian performance in sanitation and wastewater service provision would be rated 'very poor' by global standards. There are essentially three objectives in the provision of sanitation and wastewater services, and it is possible to measure Palestinian performance against these criteria. First is the provision of access to sanitation and wastewater services for all citizens in adequate quantity and quality at an affordable price through financially viable agencies. Here West Bank performance, with only 30 per cent of households connected to sewerage networks, is very poor set against the global median of 75 per cent.[30]

Sewage and untreated wastewater are a potent hazard to the environment and to human and plant health, and so a second, complementary objective is to ensure that environmental and health standards are respected. Although there are no global benchmarks for this criterion, West Bank performance on the share of wastewater treated in plants – just 13 per cent of wastewater produced – is very poor.

Finally – and this is paramount in a water-scarce environment like the Palestinian West Bank – it is essential to ensure maximum reuse of treated wastewater. Although there is certainly some informal reuse of untreated wastewater at risk to human health, the PWA records only a handful of small-scale projects of just a few hectares at most (see further in this chapter and Chapter 5). Again, there is no international benchmark, but the record of what is essentially close to zero reuse is certainly a global low.

Recent plans for West Bank sanitation and wastewater

In May 2016, PWA produced the *Water Sector Strategic Development Plan 2017–22 (SDP)* (Table 4.2).[31] As we saw in Chapter 2, the supporting *Water Sector Investment Plan (WSIP)* included a five-year investment programme that was massive in terms of the finance required ($1.25 billion for 240 projects) and in its demands on implementation capacity.[32] The plan has laudable ambitions for expansion of sanitation and wastewater services, but achieving these would require a level of cooperation with the Israelis not previously achieved as well as a far higher priority and investment for this sector than has been accorded up until now.

The plan targets an increase in connections to sewerage networks from 31 per cent of households to 45 per cent in just eight years, a high bar. Likewise, increasing wastewater treatment from 13 per cent to 24 per cent will require considerable extra treatment capacity. The target of irrigating over 50,000 hectares with treated wastewater is also wildly ambitious – four times the current irrigated area of the West Bank and one third of its total arable land (see Table 5.1 in Chapter 5). Major investment in regulation, incentives and education would be needed. As most or all of the lands to be irrigated would lie in Area C, the ball would be very much in Israel's court to allow the necessary infrastructure development and access by farmers.

One of the challenges of wastewater collection and treatment is that it is an expensive business, but consumers are typically very loath to pay for it, especially when they have what they consider to be perfectly adequate septic tank systems. Cost recovery in the few municipalities that have working sewerage systems is extremely low and quite inadequate to ensure the financial sustainability of the service. A new regulatory framework for tariffs was established by the *Water and Wastewater Tariff By-law* approved by PWA in January 2013. The methodology was set by the *Water and Wastewater Tariff Model* approved by PWA in October 2015. WSRC is to regulate tariff setting for wastewater services, as for water supply, but this role is not yet operational. In the meantime, cost recovery and willingness to pay for sanitation and wastewater services are likely to remain low.

Decentralized wastewater treatment

For smaller communities and rural areas, simpler decentralized wastewater treatment is often the answer. NGOs have shown particular initiative in developing these decentralized systems – Table 4.3 records over 800 such schemes.

Table 4.2 Water Sector Strategic Development Plan 2017–22 (SDP): Targets for Sanitation and Wastewater in the West Bank

Indicator	Actual 2014	Target 2022
Percentage of households connected to sanitation networks	31%	45%
Percentage of wastewater treated in wastewater treatment plants	13%	24%
Percentage of treated wastewater meeting specifications	0%	100%
Area irrigated with treated wastewater	0	52,300 ha

Source: *Water Sector Strategic Development Plan.*

Table 4.3 Small-scale On-site Wastewater Treatment Projects Implemented in the West Bank

	Number of projects	
Implementing agency	**Black**	**Grey**
Applied Research Institute – Jerusalem (ARIJ)	252	107
Palestinian Hydrology Group (PHG)		156
Union of Agricultural Work Committees (UAWC)		67
FAO		67
Palestinian Wastewater Engineers' Group (PWEG)		81
Palestinian Agricultural Relief Committees (PARC)		80
Total	**252**	**558**

Source: *ARIJ 2016.*

One example of an integrated small-scale plant for a refugee camp will give an idea of the contribution of the NGO sector to decentralized treatment which, in the political and security situation, is often the only option. In 2013, the Applied Research Institute-Jerusalem (ARIJ) started working on providing an integrated system of wastewater treatment and reuse in Sair in Hebron Governorate; with the support of the Spanish Agency for International Cooperation and Development (AECID). This project was designed to deal with the problem of the wastewater stream coming from the al 'Arroub Refugee Camp. The stream passed through Shuyukh Al Arroub and 'Orkan Trad, polluting the environment and exposing the population to health risks. The project offered an integrated treatment solution adapted to local conditions and designed to produce an effluent that could be reused in irrigation. The plant is operational, with an average treatment volume of 1,200 cubic metres per day.[33]

Wastewater reuse: A pilot project at al Bireh[34]

In 2002, the US NGO American Near East Refugee Aid (ANERA) and the Dutch government proposed to carry out a pilot project to demonstrate reuse of the treated effluent from the al Bireh wastewater treatment plant.[35] A farmers' association was formed and agricultural land was identified. It appears, however, that the Dutch dropped out and it took US support to get agreement from the Israelis to allow the necessary pipeline to be constructed. When Israeli approval was finally forthcoming in 2004, USAID financed the pilot project under its *West Bank Water Resources Program.*

Al Bireh Municipality in cooperation with PWA and the Ministry of Agriculture (MoA) ran the demonstration site. Following Israeli and US EPA standards, two effluent qualities were identified for reuse: 'high' and 'very high'. Sub-surface irrigation was used for the high-quality effluent, and a regular drip irrigation system was used for the very-high-quality effluent.

According to reports:

> The objectives of the demonstration project [were]: establishing the initial institutional relationships, raising the profile of wastewater and compost reuse,

> and developing the first stage of on-the-ground experience of reuse. Twenty-five different species of orchard trees, 15 date palms, 500 flowers and shrubs, 300 m^2 of grape stocks [of four different species] and a 600 m^2 nursery for annual cultivation of 80,000 seedlings of indigenous trees and culinary vegetables were planted. Four automatic irrigation head controls were installed, including fertilizer injection points, pressure control and filtration devices.[36]

The programme was completed, although with some hiccups.[37] Reported findings were that 'coordination between stakeholders is a key component', and that really high-quality effluent was essential both for the agricultural production and to protect downstream springs and aquifers. Based on this pilot experience, the EU financed a feasibility study for a larger-scale reuse project. A trunk line would bring the treated wastewater from al Bireh, which is at 700 metres above sea level, all the way down to al Auja in the Jordan Valley 250 metres below sea level. The village of Deir Dibwan, located about halfway along the proposed pipeline, would also be served. The study was completed in 2016 but the project is 'still looking for a donor'.[38]

One issue raised by the experienced French researchers Julie Trottier and Jeanne Perrier in connection with this proposal to bring treated wastewater to al Auja is equity. The PWA has long studied the option of brokering swaps of treated wastewater for fresh water – we have seen the successful experience of both Israelis and Jordanians in this. In fact, one objective of the PWA's 2013 *National Water and Wastewater Strategy*, which targets the reuse of 32 million cubic metres of treated wastewater by 2022 – and 93 million cubic metres by 2032 – is to swap treated wastewater for fresh water, or to compensate farmers who have suffered a decline in groundwater use for irrigation by bringing them treated wastewater.[39] The al Auja proposal appeared to fit the latter case as the major spring there had largely disappeared in recent years probably because of interference from a new Israeli well. Trottier reports that the bananas trees irrigated from the al Auja spring all died for lack of water. However, the drying up of the spring has led to a significant shift in land ownership. Land prices fell and those who had enough capital bought up vacant farms and undertook the massive plantation of date palms. Thus if treated wastewater does finally reach al Auja, it is likely, Trottier argues, to benefit those who bought up the land far more than the original farmers who actually suffered loss of their historic water rights.[40]

Although there is nothing so far on the ground, there are other proposals afoot for wastewater reuse. We saw earlier that the second phase of the Hebron plant is for an irrigation scheme using treated wastewater. There is also a project for reuse of the wastewater produced by the Nablus West plant over different expanses of land located next to the plant. USAID is financing a 12 hectare irrigation scheme south of the plant. KfW, German aid, is financing a 2-hectare pilot northeast of the plant, scheduled for completion in 2021, with plans for future extension to 280 hectares.[41]

* * *

Wastewater has proved to a rare animal in the West Bank scene – one where Palestinians and Israelis have the absolute imperative to cooperate, if only to protect public health

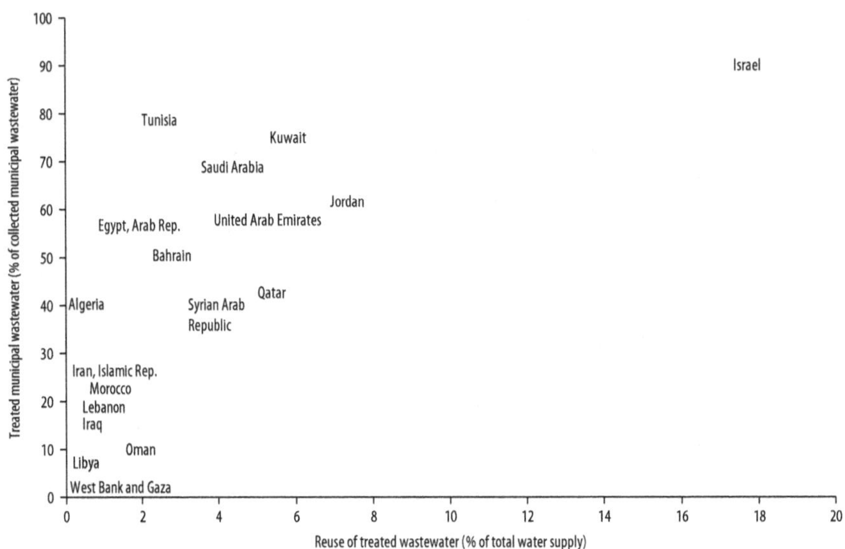

Figure 4.1 Comparing Reuse of Treated Wastewater and Percentage of Wastewater That Undergoes Treatment. *Source*: Beyond Scarcity, World Bank 2019.

and the environment. However, the political and security concerns engendered by the Israeli occupation and by the spread of Israeli settlements have continually blocked development, with consequences that threaten a human and environmental disaster. The same problems have constrained the economic reuse of treated wastewater even while Palestinian agriculture is desperately short of water. The challenge is the more striking and illustrative of a whole theme because Israel leads the world in wastewater treatment and reuse – and Palestinian West Bank and Gaza treat and reuse less of their wastewater than almost any other country – see Figure 4.1. Perhaps it is on these two counts that the divide between the two peoples – who a century ago started from much the same point in the same land – is the most arresting.

Yet wastewater is a topic where citizens' voice has actually had some effect, even amongst the constant Israeli preoccupations with security. The clamour of NGOs, the press and private individuals who supported the environmental clean-up in Israel that we reported on in Chapter 1 has also lent some impetus to change of policy both on cross-border issues like the Hebron Stream and on issues of wastewater treatment and reuse within the West Bank.

Progress, however, has been very slow and the outlook remains uncertain. For West Bank Palestinians to achieve the same levels of amenity, public health and environmental protection as the Israelis, and to be able to add treated wastewater to the agricultural water inventory as Israel has so successfully done, requires a considerable movement on the political front, as well as the rapid economic growth needed to underwrite so high a cost of investment as a sustainable sanitation and wastewater reuse programme. How these challenges may begin to be met is a subject of discussion in Part III of this book.

Chapter 5

SECURITY IN WATER FOR AGRICULTURE AND IRRIGATION IN THE WEST BANK

The source of water for agriculture in the West Bank is the rain and snow that falls on its hills and plains. The moisture that is retained in the soil profile feeds a relatively low-value dryland agriculture. The precipitation that is captured by water harvesting on the ancient terraces that crowd up and down the hillsides supports tree crops, particularly the ubiquitous olive trees which cover more than half the farmed area. Run-off captured behind small dams or in tanks is used for domestic purposes and for small local irrigation and for watering stock. The moisture that seeps beneath the surface into the rock matrix and emerges as springs or is pumped out of wells supports a vigorous market gardening economy of high-value crops, often grown under the protection of plastic.

Agriculture in the West Bank is a varied sector of small farms that have become increasingly commercialized over the last half century. Farming contributes more than 5 per cent to GDP and employs over 100,000 people. There is much further potential – only a fraction of the irrigable land is irrigated, a far smaller share than in Israel or in Jordan. Under the right conditions, the irrigated area could expand fourfold and agriculture could add as much as 10 per cent more to GDP.

But there are three big constraints, all of which stem from the peculiar political status of the West Bank as a fragmentarily autonomous territory where Israel's will penetrates every department of Palestinian lives every day. First and foremost is the constraint of water. The restrictions on water use imposed by Israel under full Occupation in the 1970s first constrained the sector and then propelled it to much greater efficiency and productivity. Those same constraints were essentially frozen by Oslo so that today, with most productivity and efficiency gains already captured, the water constraint simply stifles growth. At the margin, no more land can be irrigated because there is no more water.

With the tight restrictions on developing water and water infrastructure, West Bank farmers cannot develop the storage needed to carry over water, including treated wastewater, to the summer season when they need it most. Lack of storage also denies farmers the tools they need to manage the growing risks from climate change.

Second comes the market opportunity that is the lifeblood of high-value irrigated agriculture. Again the Occupation first opened up markets, particularly the Israeli market, and then restricted it. Today the market shrinks and expands, but mostly shrinks, in rhythm with the politics. Third, of course, is the continuation of the Occupation under the 'temporary' Oslo deal. Almost two thirds of the West Bank remains under Israel's direct control. The fertile lands and water resources of Area C are under Israeli control. Settler agriculture in the West Bank highlands and in the Jordan Valley takes an increasing share of West Bank land and water resources and today comes to rival Palestinian agriculture in extent – and to far exceed it in productivity.

These three constraints illustrate a tragic irony of the West Bank situation. At first the Occupation was a vector of modernization in agriculture, and then its aftermath and all that has happened since Oslo have more often been a brake.

Today the Palestinians are encouraged to emulate Israeli achievements in agriculture. They have done much to achieve that. Irrigated horticulture in the West Bank is not exactly world-beating but it is of a fair standard – fertigation in plastic houses of high-value crops for market, for example. The Palestinians would like to climb to higher levels of efficiency and productivity, but it is hard to see how they can do that without secure access to their lands, without more of the fresh water beneath their feet, without the ability to capture and store run-off, without the freedom to treat, store and reuse the growing volumes of wastewater, and without free access to the input and product markets vital to modern hi-tech agriculture.

* * *

Agriculture in Jenin: All you need is water[1]

In the north of the West Bank, in the great plain of Jenin, we arrive at the Jalama gate in the Separation Wall, on the Green Line between the West Bank and Israel. Here we meet Abdullah, a rangy thirty-something. He is standing by his pallet of *kusa* (squash). Abdullah is an exporter, although only in a small way of business. He sends about a ton of fresh produce into Israel each day. His market is mostly Palestinian Israelis who live in the northern part of Israel, in Nazareth, Acre and Haifa. They like to buy West Bank vegetables for their traditional cuisine, and also as an expression of solidarity with their West Bank cousins.

At the gate there is a truck park and Israeli security and a warehouse. Abdullah has to offload his *kusa* to be checked over and then wait for an Israeli truck to come and pick it up. He says the money is fair but not sensational: a box of *kusa* would have got him NIS 50-60 ($14–17) today in Jenin, and he is expecting NIS 60–70 ($17–19) at the border.

Abdullah reckons about 200 pallets total cross this checkpoint each day, off-loaded, inspected, then loaded onto Israeli trucks. He has a licence to trade. To get the licence he sends a sample to Tel Aviv. When he gets the licence, it is valid for three months. 'Every so often', he says, 'maybe once a year, they send my stuff back. There is some phytosanitary problem or other.' But the worst is when there is a security alert. 'Then they just close the border. But *alhamdulillah* so far this year things have been alright.'

* * *

Like everywhere in the Palestinian West Bank, memories here go years back. Qadoura Mousa, the governor of Jenin, talks of the time when Jenin was one of the richest agricultural areas in Palestine. 'We had a lot of water in those days', he says, sweeping his hand around in a broad gesture, as though conjuring up both the memory and the well-watered land. 'Marj Ibn Amr – 62,000 dunums[2] – it was the best agricultural area in all Greater Syria. But the Israelis have taken all the water from our springs and the springs are dry.'

The governor goes on: 'we have to revive our agriculture as a source of employment.' We hear this everywhere in Jenin. 'In the past, before 2000', Qadoura says, waving his hand in emphasis, 'many of our people worked in Israel.' With the downturn in the Palestinian economy and the return of those who had worked in Israel, he says there is a crying need for water for agriculture to create jobs and incomes.

The livestock economy, too, is in decline because of lack of water and pasture. Jenin is a major area for raising sheep. The head of the Agricultural Union for Jenin Governorate is there with us and he now chips in. 'Sheep numbers are going down all the time. People cannot find the water, and pasture has been lost behind the wall. In Arrabona, there were 2,500 head, but now it's down to just 1,200.'

Yet the potential is there. The Agricultural Union head says that the ten villages of north-east Jenin still have 25,000 dunams (2,500 hectares) of the best agricultural land. 'Less than five per cent of our land is irrigated, largely over by Jalama. The irrigation is 98 per cent intensive plastic house cultivation. We are good at it, just like the Israelis. But the rest of our land we cannot irrigate because there is no water.'

As we drive over the plain, we see that there are indeed many plastic houses. In the ones that we visit, it is clear the standards of management and husbandry are high by any standards. These are small operations. Most irrigated farms have just one or two plastic houses, covering 1–2 dunams, less than one fifth of a hectare. But it seems even a small operation can be profitable. The growers tell us they are getting 6,000–7,000 shekels ($1,800) a year in net income from a single plastic house.

'The problem is not land or knowledge or technology or skilled workers or markets', says Abu Rashid, the mayor of Falamyeh. 'It is water.' One of the farmers, Amjad, whose farm is at Jalama near the gate in the wall, says that they used to have five licenced wells, each producing 70–80 cubic metres per hour. 'But then', says Amjad, 'Israel drilled 600 wells along the Green Line – and all our wells went dry. We apply for permission to deepen them. It takes years. Nobody ever succeeded.'

Another farmer, Salem, says: 'Two years ago, I applied for permission to deepen my well. The PWA passed it on to the Civil Administration. I am still waiting for a reply.'

By now, several other farmers have come up to join our group. One, Jamal, says he had two wells. One went dry seven years ago, another one last year. He too applied to deepen them. He never got any reply. He says that 'one of those NGOs came with a project to rehabilitate wells. But you are not allowed to deepen them, so it was all fruitless.'

* * *

Over by Deir Ghazzali we find one well owner who is still able to irrigate. His well is productive, although on the wane. He irrigates about 100 dunams of his own land (10 hectares) and sells water to his neighbour for a further 150 dunams (15 hectares). He produces fruits, *zatar* (thyme), tomatoes and onions. He doesn't export, at least not directly. He prefers to sell to traders at the farm gate. It is less risky, less hassle. He is contemplating whether he should deepen his well, as it will certainly dry up soon. But he reckons that drilling costs could be as much as $1,000 a metre at that depth, and the whole project could cost him $40,000. He is aware that anyway he will need a licence. He is not confident about getting one, and he is not sure about the water resource either. 'I don't believe that the PWA has the information to help me', he says.

* * *

Clearly agriculture is very short of water. Overall, there is a feeling that farming can be a profitable activity and create considerable employment – but it is deprived of the water it needs to fulfil its potential.

There is a feeling of great unfairness. When we go to the village of Fuqua, a farmer called Khaled tells us that the community has to buy its drinking water by tanker from the Mekorot filling point at Arab al Suweitat almost 20 kilometres away.

Then he takes us up to the top of the village, which stands on a low hill commanding a view of the Separation Wall. Beyond the wall, over in Israeli territory, we see a large ploughed field. It is November and the field lies fallow. But Khaled says, 'In summer you can stand here and watch the farmers on the Israeli side irrigating their potatoes and carrots by sprinkler.'

Khaled is incensed, in the grumbling way of farmers anywhere in the world. 'They are using all our water, and then they send soldiers onto our farms to read the meters on our wells. Fair shares is what is needed.' He means that Palestinians should have access to as much water as the Israeli farmers.

Farmers also feel that they are paying much more for water than the Israelis, placing them at a competitive disadvantage. They say that Israeli farmers pay less than a shekel for their water – 0.6 shekel per cubic metre (about US15 cents), whereas Palestinian farmers are paying between 4 and 12 shekels per cubic metre, between US$1 and US$3.[3]

'All we can do is rainfed agriculture, which is much less profitable. You get maybe a net income of 250 shekels (US$70) a dunum[4] – if the rains are good. But you can get ten, twenty times that from a plastic house with drip irrigation.'

* * *

Usually on these trips, you have to hang about a bit to find out what is really going on. So it is on this occasion. After quite some time we learn that many plastic houses are in fact irrigated by shallow unlicenced wells. The well owner we met over by Deir Ghazzali – he doesn't want to give his name – lets on that 'maybe 95 per cent of plastic houses are irrigated from unlicenced wells, either directly or from tankers.' Indeed, it is a common sight in the area to see a tanker plugged in to the drip system at the back of a plastic house. We also see many plastic houses set up to harvest rainwater from the roof and to collect run-off from the surrounding area. The water flows into ponds lined with black plastic. From there it gets pumped and filtered and then fed into the plastic house.

Local people are of two minds about the explosion of unlicenced agricultural wells. Some see it as the only way to create jobs and income. Others, particularly community representatives on the local Joint Service Council, see it as an individualistic and selfish act 'that only creates problems for others'. This group blames the Palestinian Water Authority for not putting any pressure on the unlicenced well owners. And, of course, for not getting enough water from the Israelis.[5]

* * *

We have a chance to talk separately to the women in one village and they have yet another take on water shortages and agriculture. 'There is a big risk in the food', they say. 'Some farmers irrigate with sewage, so we cannot trust the food. We have had a lot of problems. They get the trucks to come at night so no one can see.' Their children have often been horribly sick. The women describe how they try to make their vegetables safe for eating through washing with carbonates and boiling. 'But with the boiling, we lose the vitamins.'

The women also tell us that water scarcity means high prices – and sometimes going short. In times of greatest water scarcity, they say that the cost of fruit and vegetables, and even the cost of flour, become too expensive, even for a middle-income household. They believe that food prices have steadily increased over recent years, in part because of water shortages and extended drought. 'We are forced to eat less and to change our diets. With water so scarce and expensive, often we cannot grow vegetables for the children in our household garden.'

* * *

Yet, for all the difficult circumstances, people try to be optimistic about farming. Ali from Arrabona says: 'If we solve the agricultural water problem, we solve the unemployment problem. Instead of sitting doing nothing or becoming a thief, do agriculture. Even a garden of half a dunum would be something – tomatoes, vegetables – food security – local markets.' Even markets do not seem such a hurdle to Ali: 'We will send to other areas. All we need is water.'

The lessons from Jenin

So what did we learn from all this outrage and grumbling? Jenin is certainly a rich agricultural area and with potential for more farming that could be a source of much-needed employment and incomes, particularly for intensive irrigated production. Rainfed agriculture is much less profitable. Local farmers have high standards of management and husbandry for irrigated agriculture. Their main problem is that water is very scarce and very expensive.

Farmers feel that water is very unfairly divided. They see abundant sprinkler irrigation on the Israeli side. They believe that the Israelis have exploited groundwater on their side and this has led to a drop in the groundwater table and the drying up of springs, while Palestinian water use is strictly controlled by the Israelis. Wells run dry and cannot be deepened. Short of water, many farmers turn to water from illegal wells to irrigate.

Water shortages also drive up food prices, and there can be health problems when farmers irrigate with wastewater. Yet despite the difficult circumstances, people are positive about farming. Although, as we shall see, there are other constraints, particularly markets and the limitations of the Occupation, the principal problem is that there is just not enough water for the prosperous agriculture of which the West Bank is capable.

The West Bank agriculture sector

The land

From the point of view of geography and natural resources, the West Bank forms a fairly discrete entity – a hilly area between the Mediterranean and the Jordan Valley where rainfall is much higher than in the surrounding plains. So although the West Bank was never in history a political or economic or social entity separate from the rest of the Palestinian lands, it can be described succinctly.

About one quarter of the land in the West Bank, 1.7 million dunams (170,000 hectares), is cultivated – see Table 5.1. Less than one tenth of that area is irrigated. Although there is fair rainfall in winter, this is generally quite a dry land, with hot weather and hot drying winds in summer which quickly evaporate any moisture remaining in the soil from the winter rains. This high rate of evaporation leads to a build-up of salts in the soil as the water quickly dries away from the top few inches and leaves the salt behind. Soils are relatively rich in potassium but low in organic matter and so lack the nitrogen needed for plants to grow.

Many soils in the centre and south of the West Bank are hard to work when wet because there is a predominance of clay. They also tend to crack when they are dry.

Table 5.1 Rainfed and Irrigated Areas in the West Bank (hectares)

	Fruit trees	Field crops	Vegetables	Total
Rainfed	106,900	43,400	4,000	154,300
Irrigated	2,100	1,500	8,600	12,200
Total	**109,000**	**44,900**	**12,600**	**166,500**

Source: PCBS (2006).

Further north, in the higher rainfall areas, around Jenin for example, the soils are typically of a more generous composition, eroded limestone and marl that hold moisture well and are favourable to crop growth. In these areas, moisture remains in the soil profile well after the end of the rains. Winter cereals can be grown here right up to mid-summer with little or no extra irrigation water added.

In the hilly areas which characterize much of the West Bank, there are considerable outcrops of rock but the hand of man has long developed artful and carefully crafted terraces where rich soils have built up over the generations. These terraces allow cultivation on otherwise barren hillsides.

The eastern slopes of the mountains that run down towards the Jordan River are generally steep and rocky. On these slopes, cultivation is possible only in some of the deep valley bottoms where there is flatter land and productive soils have built up.

Some of the best lands are in the foothills of the escarpment and along the western bank of the Jordan where there are deep alluvial soils. However, all this ancient valley is affected by salts which have washed down from saline springs over millennia. Salt-tolerant crops like date palms can withstand the salinity but for these soils to be truly productive they need a leaching dose of fresh water large enough to flush the salts down below the root zone of plants. The climate in the valley is exceptionally dry and hot but where there is ample fresh water, as around Jericho, or where water is diverted from the river, agriculture can be highly productive. In the river plain itself, extensive irrigated agriculture can be practiced – on the Jordanian East Bank side there are 30,000 hectares of intensively irrigated, hi-tech commercial agriculture.

Farming

About two fifths of West Bank households are farming households. Farms are on the whole quite small – the average West Bank farm is 30–50 dunams (3–5 hectares), with the vast majority of farms (94 per cent) smaller than 40 dunams (4 hectares) and very few farms as large as 200 dunams (20 hectares). Holdings are often fragmented into several parcels.

Most farming is 'dry farming', simply dependent on whatever rain falls and is retained in the soil profile. Field crops, which cover about a quarter of the farmed area (27 per cent) – see Table 5.1 – are predominantly rainfed winter cereals – barley in the drier areas, wheat where there is more rain.

The terraces on the rocky hill slopes capture and retain enough water for the cultivation of olive trees, which need moisture year-round. Olives are the leading crop, estimated to cover more than half (54 per cent) of the total area cultivated. Other fruit trees are planted on most farms and they account for a further tenth (10 per cent) of the production area. About one third of farms grow some vegetables, both for market and for home consumption, and some specialize in commercial horticulture solely for market. Vegetables account for a further one twelfth (8 per cent) of the farmed area.

About a quarter of the farmed area produces two crops a year. This is usually a cereal in winter and, if irrigation water is available, a high-value crop in summer – tomatoes, melons or perhaps maize. Fallowing is practiced to rest the land and restore fertility. About a third of the land lies fallow each winter, and half or more in summer when water is scarce. Either animal manure or chemical fertilizers are added to correct the nitrogen deficiencies. Rates of fertilizer application are low – 40 per cent of levels in Jordan and just one fifth (20 per cent) of Israeli levels.

Agriculture in the Palestinian economy today

Fifty years ago, before the Six-Day War, agriculture was the most important sector of the Palestinian economy, accounting for one third of GDP, over 40 per cent of employment, and 20 per cent of exports. The period of the Occupation, from 1967 up to the time of Oslo, saw growth, although with some ups and downs due to the changing nature of the Occupation, shifts in Israeli policies and, at the end of the period, the impact of the first *intifada*. Over this period, the structure of the sector changed considerably, with more commercial horticulture – much of it hi-tech irrigated production – and with livestock and vegetable production growing in both relative and absolute terms. Over the period, agricultural GDP in the West Bank went up by more than three times (in constant 1986 terms) from just under $200 million equivalent in 1968 to $700 million in 1990.

At the time of Oslo, agriculture represented about 12 per cent of total West Bank GDP, a smaller share of a larger economy than in 1967. Recent years have seen a further decline in this share – for the last decade, agriculture's share has been around 6 per cent. Real value added has also fallen considerably from its 1999 peak. The *al Aqsa intifada* years showed particularly poor results, with agricultural value added seeing significant variations that reflected both the political situation and the weather. More recently, value added has recovered, although remaining below the level of the 1990s. Overall, agriculture's declining share in the economy has been more due to the growth of overall GDP than to the admittedly lacklustre performance of agriculture.

One fact not captured by these statistics is the extent of non-monetized home consumption. The 2010–11 agricultural census showed that nearly three quarters (71 per cent) of all Palestinian agricultural holdings used *all* their produce for family consumption. In fact there is a high degree of self-sufficiency overall. Including Gaza, the Palestinian territories are self-sufficient in vegetables, grapes, figs, olive oil, poultry meat, eggs and honey. There is nonetheless a high rate of food insecurity – 34 per cent in 2012 – but this is more a function of income than of food availability.

The agricultural sector is an important employer, with the sector absorbing labour at a rate faster than the growth in sector value added, although more slowly than the rate of growth in total employment. For both West Bank and Gaza together, agricultural employment in 2009–12 was 84,000, about 12 per cent of total employment, compared to fifteen years earlier when employment was lower at 48,000 but a slightly larger share of the total workforce (13 per cent). In addition a large workforce of family labour contributes to agricultural production, but their input is not monetized. The consequence of the influx of labour to a sluggish sector has been reduced labour productivity[6] and lower wages in agriculture than in other sectors.

Today the overall economic outlook for farming is poor. Quite apart from the dominant problem of water shortage, other factors – the decline in the internal West Bank economy, the closures, the Separation Barrier, the movement and access restrictions, and the brake on export markets – have a particularly depressing effect on agriculture. The general constraints faced by the economy have eroded incentives and reduced potential in agriculture. Although some exports still get through, produce markets are largely restricted to within the West Bank. The domestic market is, in any case, small and purchasing power in that market is low, which depresses prices further. Yet at the same time, farmers' costs are high, with prices of inputs steep in relation to border prices. The results of these constraints have been weak or no growth, a brake on agricultural investment and intensification, and declining labour productivity and earnings.

The case of declining olive oil production

The olive oil sector illustrates some of the problems West Bank Palestinian farmers face. The olive is a famous traditional West Bank product and the oil has long been prized as a Palestinian speciality much favoured in household diets. As we have seen, olive trees cover a good half of the cultivated area in the West Bank and the revenue of olive oil sales has long been a mainstay of farmer income. Olive trees are an excellent response to water scarcity, as they require little more than residual soil moisture once established. They can be grown on slopes and other marginal lands where forms of water harvesting like terraces or half-moon cuvettes can keep the plant roots adequately moistened.

By virtue of their long economic, social and cultural associations with Palestinian life, olive trees are also emblematic of Palestinian identity. In 2014. UNESCO designated a Palestinian village near Jerusalem, Battir, as a World Heritage site because 'its olive production characterizes the landscape through extensive agricultural terraces, water springs, ancient irrigation systems, human settlement remains, olive presses, and an historic core'.[7] The 9 million or so olive trees planted across the West Bank are at once a symbol of Palestinian aspirations to nationhood and an assertion of Palestinian claims over the land. Many farmers

Figure 5.1 West Bank Olive Harvest, Wikimedia Commons.

have planted olives to ensure that their claim to land is well established and, they hope, proof against Israeli seizure.[8]

Production of olive fruits dropped sharply over the decade 2001–10, from an average of 114,000 tons in 2001–4 to 76,000 tons in 2010–11. Production of olive oil also declined, from an average of 23,000 tons a year in 2000–4 to an annual average of 14,000 tons in 2007–10, although picking up again to 21,000 tons in 2014. In part, these variations were due to the natural cycle of the olive tree but the real problem has been the shrinking of the major market, Israel. For many years, imports from the Palestinian market accounted for about two thirds of Israel's olive oil imports, on average 4,000 tons of olive oil each year. Israel's imports began to decline at the turn of the century with the start of the *al Aqsa intifada*. Although Israel remained the largest market for Palestinian olive oil for another decade, by 2008 Israel was importing less than 1,000 tons (890 tons in 2007 and 2008). In 2009 and 2010, olive oil exports to Israel had dwindled to just 23 tons.

The prospects – and the need – for a thriving agriculture

Despite all the challenges, agriculture inevitably plays a key economic, social and political role in all plans for building up the West Bank economy. In fact, agriculture plays a far more important role in the small Palestinian economy than it does in the large, fast-growing Israeli economy. Where agriculture is 6 per cent of the Palestinian economy, it is less than 2 per cent of the Israeli economy – and Palestinian agriculture has potential to provide a still larger share than it does today. Agriculture can create incomes and jobs. It can provide independent food security. It contributes to poverty reduction, particularly to reduction of rural poverty. A lively, profitable agriculture can also play a role in avoiding a rush to the cities and in maintaining Palestinian physical presence in rural areas. These effects are palpable. Despite the constraints, the *intifada* and closures have brought many of the unemployed back to farming.

The sector has value even beyond economics and livelihoods. Just as land and water and toil in agriculture were at the heart of the Zionist enterprise, so possessing land and water and working them hard can create values for Palestinians of hope and pride of ownership, of feelings of identity.[9] With almost two thirds of the West Bank under settlements or in the grip of the tight restrictions on Area C, simply staying on the land and continuing to use it is, just in itself, an assertion of liberty for all Palestinians.

Irrigated agriculture

Irrigated agriculture covers only a fraction – about 7 per cent – of the cultivated land in the West Bank – some 12,000 hectares out of a total cultivated area of 165,000 hectares (see Table 5.1). This level of irrigation is only one half of that in neighbouring Jordan, where 15 per cent of arable land is irrigated. It is only one sixth of the 44 per cent share of cultivated land which is irrigated in Israel.[10] Nonetheless, irrigated agriculture produces half of the West Bank's agricultural value added. For this, it uses the lion's share of the West Bank's water resources that are available to Palestinians.

Although irrigation potential is high, the overriding constraint is lack of water. Every West Bank farmer would like to expand irrigation, particularly to grow high-value crops in plastic houses – protected agriculture – which even under present conditions is profitable. But there is no more water. No new agricultural well has been licensed since 1967. Many of the old wells and springs have been progressively drying up – we discuss this further in this chapter.

Current agricultural water use in the West Bank is about 62 million cubic metres, almost two thirds (60 per cent) of internal freshwater resources – see Table 2.4 in Chapter 2. Of this, about 28 million cubic metres is from agricultural wells and 39 million cubic metres is from springs.[11] It is roughly one tenth of the water that the Israelis use for their agriculture. Of course, the population of Israel is much bigger, some three times larger, but even so per head of the population, agricultural water availability for West Bank Palestinians is just a fraction of that of Israel – less than 40 cubic metres per head for Palestinians, while Israelis have well over 100 cubic metres.

Water for Palestinian agriculture is likely to decrease further as demand rises from other sectors, because there are incentives to transfer water out of agriculture to domestic use. Already in 2007, about 3 million cubic metres was supplied to municipal and industrial uses from agricultural wells. Although there are structural and socio-economic constraints to inter-sectoral water transfer – see Chapter 4 – there are active local water markets where farmers sell spring and well water to tankers for domestic water supply.[12]

Water shortage has driven up costs. Even when farmers can get it, water is very expensive. As we saw in Jenin, farmers were paying up to NIS 12 per cubic metre ($3.50) for water to irrigate plastic houses – and some are mining the aquifer in competition with each other just in order to earn a basic living.[13] The causes of these high prices are the dwindling availability of agricultural water and the high transaction costs for water transport. These prices are higher by several multiples than those paid by competing Israeli farmers, who pay between NIS 1.650 ($0.49) and 2,411 ($0.70) for fresh water for irrigation – and about half that for treated wastewater (2010 prices).

The Palestinian view is that irrigated agriculture has enormous potential to drive growth in the West Bank economy. The most binding constraint is the lack of water which they see as imposed and enforced by the Israelis in the meagre allocations of Article 40 and made worse by the 'resource consuming settlement project'.[14]

The changing pattern of irrigated agriculture

In the West Bank, production of high-value crops, particularly in the warm but dry summer months, depends on the availability of irrigation water, which is also used to provide supplementary irrigation to largely rainfed crops. Irrigation has been practiced in the West Bank since time immemorial, using water from springs, wells and the Jordan River. The quality of water is good although, as we said earlier, salinity affects some sources in the Jordan Valley. The big problem is that water is in short supply, limiting the area which can actually be irrigated, and its cost is high, limiting profitability.

In 1967, West Bank irrigation was largely traditional, fed by springs, water harvesting and wells. Farmers conveyed water, often over considerable distances, by small canals to their fields. Irrigation water was often shared and traditional institutions of collaboration divided and managed water in agreed ways and also provided for operation and maintenance of systems and for resolving disputes.[15]

Traditionally, farmers applied irrigation water on their farms either by flooding bunded basins or by running the water down furrows. In the late 1960s, new and more efficient technology came in and, as markets for higher-value crops opened up, farmers progressively adopted pressurized irrigation, initially sprinkler, then drip irrigation systems. Farmers began to store their water allocation in reservoirs and then pumped it under pressure to the field when the crop needed it. The restrictions on water for agriculture imposed by the Israelis gave an added impetus to getting the maximum crop per drop through efficient water use.

It is a historical irony that it was the Israeli occupation which stimulated West Bank irrigated agriculture to modernize in the way that it did. This is not to say that modernization would not have come anyway – after all, neighbouring Jordan accomplished a very successful modernization of its agriculture in the same period. But the Israeli occupation brought very specific changes that made irrigated agriculture in the West Bank for a time a junior partner in Israel's own agricultural modernization. The greatest change was not in the irrigated area but

Figure 5.2 Traditional West Bank Irrigation Canal, with permission from Nora Stel.

in water use efficiency and productivity. West Bank farmers adopted efficient pressurized irrigation and plastic house technology that allowed them to improve yields while using less water.

The irony is that a principal spur to greater irrigation efficiency was the restriction on water use imposed by the Israelis. The Civil Administration managed a permit system for well drilling, rehabilitation and cleaning. Quotas were set on all irrigation wells,[16] and meters recorded how much water was pumped out. Enforcement was strict and well owners who exceeded their quota were heavily fined. Public, private and non-governmental organizations assisted farmers in improving water use efficiency, and some on-farm research on irrigation was conducted.

Water use in irrigation and the cost of irrigation water

Total water used for irrigated agriculture has changed little since before 1967, averaging around 60 million cubic metres a year. What changed during the

Figure 5.3 Restrictions on storage impede irrigation: Israeli soldiers watch as machinery destroys a Palestinian cistern, with permission from Palestine Portal.

Occupation was the specific water use per dunam, as West Bank irrigators achieved substantial water savings, particularly in protected agriculture. Traditional irrigated crop husbandry systems in the 1960s used a lot of water – an average of 1,600 cubic metres per dunam in the West Bank – a massive and wasteful 16,000 cubic metres a hectare. The switch to modern pressurized irrigation cut that water ration by two thirds – by 1990, average water use in West Bank irrigation was no more than 570 cubic metres per dunam, a modest 6,000 cubic metres per hectare, on a par with water use in Israel – see the section 'Water for agriculture' in Chapter 1. These very large water economies were achieved particularly when crops were grown under protection, for example, under plastic cloches or in the plastic green houses that today dot the landscape. The high price of water that we noted earlier has also given incentives to save water and to use it efficiently. This, combined with the restrictions on water use which continue to this day under the provisions of Article 40, has created incentives for farmers to use what water they can get more sparingly and efficiently, to get the maximum '$ per drop'.

Productivity

In irrigated areas, a modern, water-efficient, protected and open cultivation system has come to predominate, notably for vegetables. Although productivity levels are typically well below those in Israel and most developed countries, they are comparable to or exceed those in other Arab countries, with Palestinian agriculture yielding about $7 per cubic metre of water used compared to $5 in Algeria, or less than $1 in Egypt, Morocco or Lebanon – see Figure 5.4. The higher productivity levels in neighbouring Jordan which has similar agro-climatic conditions and resource constraints – $11 per cubic metre compared to the $7 per cubic metre in the Palestinian territories – show that there remains extra potential in Palestinian irrigated horticulture. For a number of crops, there is scope to raise

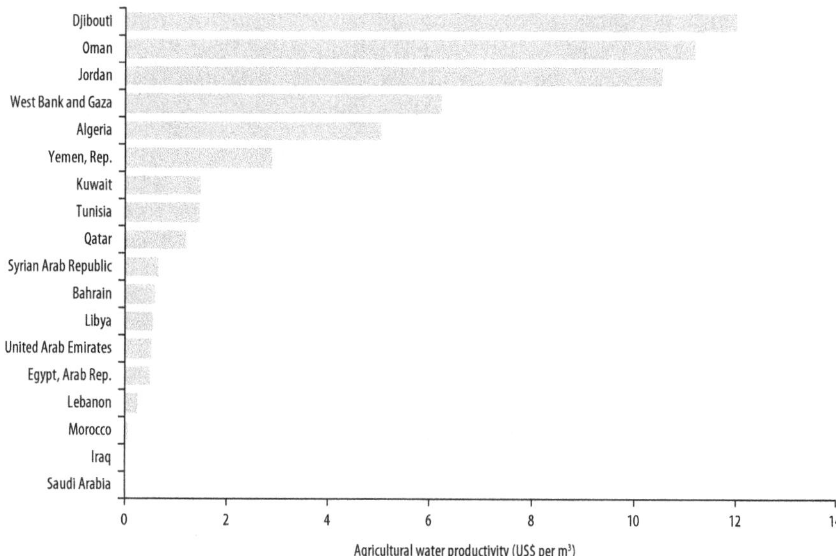

Figure 5.4 Agricultural Water Productivity. *Source*: *Beyond Scarcity, World Bank 2019.*

yield levels substantially by introducing improved varieties, better husbandry and better input use. There is also scope to increase value added by improving quality through better post-harvest handling and packing. In contrast to the irrigation sector, there has been little change in the traditionally low productivity levels in the rainfed agriculture that dominates the West Bank. Because of the uncertain precipitation, traditional, low-risk, low-input technology continues in use.

The commercialization of West Bank agriculture

The development of markets for agricultural produce

Self-sufficiency, trade and consumption Historically, the West Bank was largely self-sufficient in food. After 1967, with the growth of population, rising incomes and the increase in production of higher-value exportable produce, local demand strengthened, trade in agricultural products grew and self-sufficiency declined (although remaining high for traditional foods and fresh produce – see the section 'Agriculture in the Palestinian economy today' earlier). By 1986 it was estimated that the value of local consumption exceeded the value of local production by 18 per cent.[17]

Food was thus imported, but at the same time between a quarter and a half of local production of fruits and vegetables was exported. In a water-scarce agricultural economy, this was a practical 'virtual water' strategy, buying lower-value food imports with the earnings of high-value exports that paid high returns to water, the scarcest factor of production. With rising incomes and the availability of food, dietary standards improved considerably in the period from 1967 up to Oslo, by about 20 per cent. By 1993, consumption in the West Bank was not far off Israeli levels – 2,931 calories per person daily for Palestinians against 3,059 for Israelis. Only in animal protein and fat did Palestinians lag behind Israeli consumption levels.[18]

The growth of commercial agriculture With technological improvements and the opening of new outside markets, West Bank horticulture exports began to do well during the Occupation. The boom lasted throughout the early period of Dayan's 'Open Bridges' policy[19] and well into the 1970s. At one time, the West Bank was exporting close to half of its total production. The main markets for Palestinian fruits and vegetables were Jordan, other Arab countries and Eastern Europe. Olive oil products were particularly popular in the region. Palestinian pickled olives, olive oil and olive oil-based soap, which were exported to Jordan and the Arab world beyond, made up nearly 90 per cent of Palestinian industrial exports in the period.[20]

The local market for agricultural produce also grew quite substantially during this period. Population and income growth expanded the customer base, and rising incomes led to higher demand for vegetables, fruit, meat and dairy products. The 'Buy Palestinian' preference of the population for locally produced products also swelled demand, and this was later strengthened by political will at the time of the *intifada*. For some produce, more efficient production and marketing and the influence of competing products imported from Israel drove down prices and made the sector more competitive. The resulting lower product prices also helped fuel demand.

The Israeli market These achievements were the more remarkable, given that West Bank production for both local and export markets was affected by numerous regulatory, administrative and security requirements. The trade regime between the Occupied Territories and Israel had an asymmetrical character which certainly constrained growth and squeezed margins below what a more equal regime would have allowed. While Palestinian exports to Israel were increasingly subject to controls and quotas, Israeli products entered the Occupied Territories without limitation, with the result that by the end of the 1980s, Israeli produce dominated many West Bank markets. Israel's market share of the West Bank market for dairy, beef and cereals reached 50–80 per cent.[21]

Trade beyond Israel In the early years after 1967, regional markets were largely deficit in horticultural produce and the West Bank emerged as a successful exporter to those markets. Middle Eastern and East European countries were keen to import and they welcomed Palestinian fresh fruit and vegetables. In 1978–9, close to 200,000 tons of Palestinian citrus and 100,000 tons of Palestinian vegetables crossed the bridges into Jordan, headed for the Jordanian market and beyond. In 1984 total exports still exceeded 220,000 tons.[22] Adoption of modern irrigation and plastic house technology gave Palestinian exporters a clear competitive edge.

However, in the 1980s, the situation began to change. Jordan by this time was expanding its production of fruit and vegetables with which Palestinian produce was competing. The Jordanians themselves were now adopting the new technologies both in the highlands and particularly in the protected and highly productive fields of the new Jordan Valley irrigation schemes, where water was priced very low and the production conditions were highly favourable year-round.

Then came the outbreak of the Iraq–Iran war in 1979 which severely restricted citrus and vegetable exports. Jordan itself was badly affected by a declining market share and heavy competition in its traditional markets in the Gulf. Politics also came into it when in 1988 Jordan finally abandoned its claim to the West Bank and pursued a policy of disengagement. The West Bank was now considered a third-party entity. Jordan introduced annually negotiated import quotas and marketing windows and increasingly restricted the issue of import licences. Import quotas and time limitations had to be negotiated annually. The overall impact was to severely limit the amount of West Bank farm produce that could enter Jordan. Citrus from Gaza was allowed on the understanding that it would transit to other markets.

The process was further complicated by a ban on anything originating in Israel. No Israeli product was permitted entry across the bridges. This required certification by West Bank authorities of the local origin of produce of individual Palestinian farmers. The task was handled by local authorized liaison officers, who consulted with the marketing authorities in Jordan. At the same time, Israel restricted imports of Jordanian products into the West Bank.

The Iraq–Iran war also limited the Iraqi market and closed the market of Iran itself, which at one time had been the destination for half of Palestinian citrus exports. Other countries in the region – Turkey, Syria, Egypt, Saudi Arabia, the Gulf countries – were also eagerly adopting the new horticultural technologies and developing both internal and export trades. With economic adjustments in Eastern Europe in the twilight of the Soviet Union, markets there also declined or were lost altogether. And then, in the early 1990s, the Gulf War closed most regional markets completely.[23]

Although Palestinian produce continued to have access in some markets, by the time of Oslo, West Bank products were facing considerable constraints. Trade with Jordan and beyond was subject to quotas imposed by Jordan and by Israeli security regulations which increased costs and led to delays, which could be mortal for perishables. The effect was noticeably hard on exports to Jordan of grapes, tomatoes, eggplant and melons.[24]

By that time, in any case, relatively high production and marketing costs in the West Bank, quality concerns, quota restrictions – all were affecting export potential. Changing requirements and increased competition in external markets and the increased restrictions imposed by the Israelis and by the authorities in the importing countries reduced exports by 1993 to a fraction of past levels.

In addition, the terms of trade moved against Palestinian produce. During the twenty years in the period 1967–87, the cost of inputs rose steeply (by five to eighteen times depending on the product) while the price of output produce rose only by a multiple of two or three.[25] Palestinians saw unequal competition in the price of irrigation water. In the more water-scarce areas, irrigation water cost West Bank farmers up to five times what Israeli farmers paid and up to thirty times as much as farmers paid on Jordan's irrigation schemes on the East Bank of the river.[26]

The effect of Israeli regulations From the outset, the Israelis imposed numerous regulations that cost the Palestinians dear in both time and money, and with the *intifada* came a new clamp down from the Israeli side. By the early 1990s, transport of products to and from the West Bank and Gaza required at least five permits: personal clearances from the offices of VAT, income tax and the police; a vehicle pass which was also contingent upon the truck owner having obtained clearances concerning VAT, income tax, real estate tax, local municipality and police; a magnetic card for the driver; a produce permit and a departure of product permit (to be obtained twenty-four hours prior to transport).

Once all this had been sorted out, the shipment could be loaded and the driver could set off. If the driver was travelling between West Bank and Gaza, he was required to use specified roads linking Gaza to the edge of Hebron District. On that road – or any road – there might be security-related curfews, or simply bans on Palestinians entering Israel.

Everything had to be inspected minutely. Each vehicle in the West Bank's ancient truck fleet, which was largely of pre-1967 vintage, was completely stripped down to bare essentials to facilitate security inspections. Arriving at the Allenby Bridge, the principal entry point to Jordan, all produce was subjected to a 100 per cent search. Sometimes this damaged the produce. Other times, it just took forever. Trucks needed to line up the previous day to try to get to Amman and back the following day. This further added to costs and to the risks to product quality.

Sometimes the security checks were 'regular', a relatively quick once-over. The truck could then travel on to Amman and get back over the bridge to the West Bank the same day. But if the driver fell afoul of a 'special' security check, his vehicle could be completely disassembled. This might take the truck out of circulation for up to five days.

Trade restrictions such as these inevitably drive up costs, and so it proved. For a typical load of fruit or vegetables, extra transport costs typically added up to 15 per cent of shipment value or more. The costs for a single 8–10-ton truck shipment for less than a hundred kilometres across the bridges to Amman was estimated in 1993 at $500–900 per truck, on the basis that the truck would be back within twenty-four hours. If the trip took five days, the cost would be much higher. With so much uncertainty, most truckers were reckoning on just four trips a month – and they required payment in advance.[27]

Market access today

Were the questions of water and land to be by some legerdemain resolved, the biggest constraint to agricultural growth would be access to markets, particularly to the high-value markets that Israel so successfully serves. Market access for Palestinian produce remains subject to multiple constraints and barriers. As has been well documented, access restrictions and closures across the West Bank and at its borders have a large impact on both economic activity and quality of life. Unpredictable closures are hard to factor into any planning, as closure is a military action, usually decided locally. Nowhere are the impacts felt more severely than in irrigated agriculture, which depends for its viability on efficient transport to ready markets. Trade in high-value irrigated products is particularly constrained. In fact, since Oslo, Palestinian agricultural exports have only declined.

The constraints are physical as well as economic and institutional. The erection of the Separation Barrier has cut off the West Bank farmers from their markets in Israel. Physical access restrictions and closures further limit markets within the West Bank and increase transaction costs. As produce moves with difficulty through the 640 checkpoints that control movement from one district to another, costs are then passed on to the consumers. At Baka al Sharqiyeh (West Bank), where fresh produce was traded with Israel before the construction of the Separation Barrier, the market place has since been destroyed. As a result, there has been a dramatic downturn in the local economy. As one donor told us: 'Decisions about closure are decentralized. The officer at Bardala may decide suddenly to close the agricultural gate, so that farmers have at a moment's notice to go an extra 70 kilometres round to the next gate.'[28]

At the same time, the West Bank has been a captive market for Israeli produce, which often arrives at times of peak production in the West Bank, depressing prices and leading to allegation of dumping. UNCTAD concluded in 2015 that the chronic Palestinian trade deficit, particularly that with Israel, was caused not by policy or lack of economic potential but by 'political and economic constraints' and by 'pervasive restrictions imposed by Israel on Palestinian trade'.[29]

Restrictions on agricultural imports to the West Bank have also dulled productivity and increased costs. For many years Israel has controlled the import of 'dual use' goods and equipment to the West Bank. The list of items that might be put to other uses than agricultural production has grown long. The most constraining restriction is that on most fertilizers. The result has been that fertilizer use is much lower than optimal – 40 per cent of levels of use in Jordan, for example. The production foregone has been estimated to be in the range of 20–33 per cent.[30]

Costs to the West Bank economy of lost opportunities in agriculture

Plainly irrigated agriculture could be a driver of growth and livelihoods in the West Bank, but it is performing well below its potential. A 2009 assessment[31] estimated the annual 'losses' – or value foregone – to the West Bank economy as

Table 5.2 Estimated Costs to the Palestinian Economy of Foregone Opportunity in Irrigated Agriculture

	Loss of gross margin ($m)	Agricultural jobs foregone
Land closures in the Jordan Valley	58.9	12,500
Loss of land to the construction of the Separation Barrier	7.9	1,850
Loss of land beyond the Separation Barrier	2.4	530
Loss due to non-development of irrigated agriculture	410.7	96,000
Total	**$479.9 million**	**110,800 jobs**

Source: MAS (2009).

a result of movement and access restrictions and other Occupation constraints. The study took account of land closures affecting 60,000 dunams (6,000 hectares) in the Jordan Valley, as well as the nearly 9,000 dunams (nearly 1,000 hectares) of irrigated land destroyed to build the Separation Barrier, and of the irrigated land isolated on the other side of the Separation Barrier. The assessment also attempted to calculate the cost of the lost opportunity in irrigated agriculture due to lack of access to water resources.

In aggregate, the assessment concluded that the 'losses' were nearly half a billion dollars each year (equivalent to about 10 per cent of GDP) and that more than 100,000 jobs were 'lost'. This assessment is only indicative but is useful to illustrate foregone opportunities. It is the scarcity of water which accounts for the lion's share of this – $411 million out of the total $480 million (see Table 5.2).

A later study (2013) by the World Bank came to the conclusion that irrigating the more than 325,000 dunams (more than 30,000 hectares) of arable land in Area C that was not already occupied by settlers would require some 189 million cubic metres of water per year and 'irrigating [the] unexploited area as well as accessing additional range and forest land could deliver an additional $700 million in value added to the Palestinian economy – equivalent to 7 per cent of 2011 GDP'.[32]

Constraints and risks: What stops Palestinian agriculture in the West Bank from matching Israeli achievements?

Water use in agriculture: efficiency and productivity

Water availability is one thing, the way water is used is another. We have to say – and Palestinians agree – that water resources could be used more efficiently than they are at present in the West Bank. Some of this very scarce resource is being wasted. This is true, as we have seen in Chapter 2, in water supply where more than two fifths (44 per cent) of the precious and costly resource is lost in conveyance and network supply systems or otherwise unaccounted for. And this is also true in irrigation.

Even if a farmer has little water, there are many ways to eke it out both in technology and in crop husbandry. Chapter 1 demonstrated how brilliantly the

Israelis have developed and applied these measures. These include improving water use efficiency, minimizing losses between the water source and the plant root, and making sure that the right amount of water reaches the plant roots at the right time. Making these improvements involves technical fixes like piping water instead of flowing it through leaky open channels, and using micro-irrigation that drips water in exactly the right quantities down to the plant roots.

In addition, there are many ways to improve water productivity, the value that each drop of water returns. In the West Bank, water is the scarcest factor – rather than land or labour or capital – and so farmers need to focus on maximizing returns to that factor. This means choosing crops which are more water efficient, that pay the most shekels for every drop. It also means managing the whole production, harvesting and marketing cycle to minimize water use and maximize yields and value.

Learning from Israeli agriculture

The Israelis, of course, are adept at all this. In fact they even devised some of the technology and have spread it worldwide. This has allowed them to make notable strides in water conservation, reducing water use in agriculture from 8,700 cubic metres per hectare in 1975 to around 6,000 cubic metres per hectare today,[33] while increasing the value of agricultural output twelve fold.

Siegel points out that the advances that Israel has pioneered are also technically possible for Palestinians: drip irrigation that not only saves 50–60 per cent of water but increases yields; fertigation and nutrigation; sensors that deliver the exact quantity of water needed at precisely the right time direct to the plant roots and so on. And the agronomic changes that Israel has pioneered could be possible for the Palestinians too – the high-value export crops, the new seeds and varieties, the melons, peppers, tomatoes and eggplants that grow on diluted brackish water and taste the better for it. Siegel says that with improved technology and agronomic changes, Palestinians could make the desert bloom as the Israelis have. He says that with improved seeds and drip 'the desert is the best place to grow crops'.[34]

All this is true. The Palestinians probably have roughly the same human endowments and aptitudes and the same desire to make a decent living for their families as the Israelis, and they should certainly set to work to learn from Israel and do the same as their neighbours. Some of this did actually happen. The pace of change in Palestinian agriculture over the last fifty years has been fast and when markets were open, at times during the Occupation and especially in the brief honeymoon after Oslo, Palestinian farmers were doing well, with the advantage of cheaper and more abundant labour. But today, Palestinian agriculture is depressed, output is stagnant and yields are on average only half of those in Israel. So what is wrong? Are there binding economic, technical and physical constraints? Do Palestinian farmers have the means of managing the multiple risks presented not only by the perennial hazards of the climate and by the new hazard of climate change but also by the peculiar hazards created by the ABC mosaic, movement and access restrictions, the constraints of Article 40 and the continued occupation of most of the West Bank?

We look at the litany of problems in turn.

Managing water risks and constraints

The first and foremost risk and constraint is, unavoidably, lack of water because '*land without water in the Middle East is a meaningless abstraction*.'[35] The difficulty that West Bank Palestinians have in accessing safe and economic water sources is the biggest brake on their agricultural economy.

In the rainfed farming which predominates in the West Bank, the source of water is rainfall and in particular the part of rainfall which is retained in the soil profile and can be taken up by plant roots. Much of the West Bank receives rain adequate to grow annual crops as well as trees like the olive which are adapted to the agro-climatic conditions. Rainfed farming, however, is constrained by multiple restrictions and controls – see further in this chapter on this – but is also prey to the increasing vagaries of the climate. Rainfall variability within seasons and between years has increased and the incidence of droughts and heat waves has grown alarmingly. Altogether rainfed farmers experience a hotter, drier, more uncertain climate which affects farming systems and yields. The result is growing risk aversion and a recession of rainfed farming.

The favoured tool to manage these increasing risks is irrigation, if only supplementary irrigation to give a just-in-time watering to wilting crops. Here the greatest constraint to growth and risk management in West Bank agriculture kicks in – lack of water available when it is needed. This lack has several components. First, obviously, come the limitations placed under Article 40 on farmers' ability to develop and use the groundwater that lies beneath their feet. At Jayyous, for example, the five agricultural wells are located in the closed area. These wells are monitored by Mekorot, and withdrawal from the wells is strictly controlled. Yield from these wells is not enough to irrigate the surrounding 8,000 dunams (800 hectares), so the farmers have turned to a less economic source of water, paying high fees to pump water from the Azzun well 3 kilometres away. The water quality from this more distant well is very poor, local farmers report, because of its proximity to a garbage dump.[36]

The second constraint and risk is that even existing wells and springs are drying up. A traditional source of water for agriculture in the West Bank has been the numerous springs that rise in the limestone hills. Many of these springs have dwindled or dried up in recent years: the causes include drought and overpumping from the Mountain Aquifer. In 2004, there were some 400 springs discharging over 50 million cubic metres a year. A decade later, there had been a considerable decline in yield. The PWA reported total spring discharge in the West Bank as 39.5 million cubic metres (see Table 2.4 in Chapter 2). The Palestinian Central Bureau of Statistics reported a steeper decline for 2011, with the effective discharge that year little more than 21 million cubic metres (see Figure 5.5). Thus, even if all the

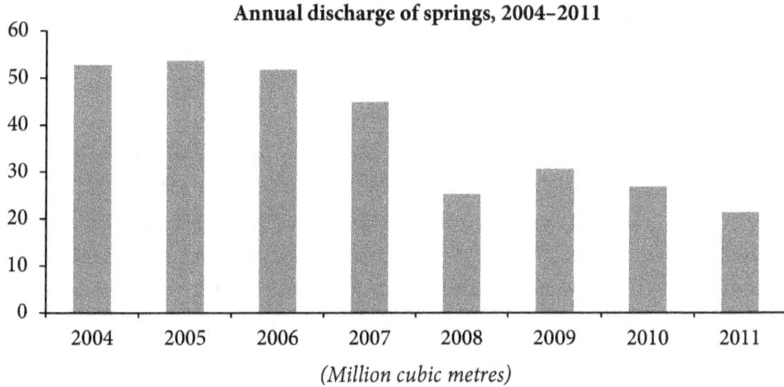

Figure 5.5 Annual discharge of springs, 2004–11. *Source*: UNCTAD 27 from Palestinian Central Bureau of Statistics.

different figures do not always agree with each other, it is clear that the slope is downward.

The third constraint and risk is the high cost of water. Palestinian farmers who do not have a right to a water source are paying market rates for water. Water is the vital input, but scarcity and regulation have driven market rates sky-high. Yet water is under everybody's feet, ample water, many millions of cubic metres, liberally refreshed by the rains each winter. The rain that rains on the West Bank mostly infiltrates into aquifers which lie beneath the very land on which Palestinians tread. Why they cannot drill down and extract this water, and why the Israelis permit themselves to take whatever they like of it – which is far and away the biggest share – is incomprehensible to the water-short West Bank farmer. The temptation simply to help themselves is great, and their anger when their own Water Authority tries to stop them – or, worse, when they are arrested and carted off to prison by Israeli soldiers – is equally great (see Figure 5.9).

Palestinians consider this lack of water a gross injustice, and this is not only when they compare their ration to that of Israeli farmers. They look, in particular, at the Jordan River which flows past their territory. They refer back to the Johnston Plan of 1955 which allocated 100–150 million cubic metres annual share of Jordan water for West Bank Palestinians. They also look back to the 150 pumps that they had in the river before 1967 which pumped out 30 million cubic metres annually, far short of their claim under Johnston but enough to irrigate a thriving agriculture on the fertile platform above the river.[37] Access to that 30 million cubic metres would add half as much again to current water for Palestinian irrigation in the West Bank (about 62 million cubic metres). If they had the Johnston Plan allocation of 100 million cubic metres, that would more than double the current water available for agriculture – to 160 million cubic metres. Today the western side of the river and most of the escarpment above have been effectively confiscated, either to become military zones (between Israel and Jordan, a country with which Israel has had a peace treaty for more than twenty years) or to be turned over to settlements and settler agriculture. One estimate (UNCTAD 2015: 26) was that if an extra 100 million cubic metres of Jordan water were to be made available to Palestinian agriculture, it could irrigate 120,000 dunams (12,000 hectares), creating 120,000 jobs and boosting GDP by $400 million annually.

The final constraint in water is that not only are West Bank Palestinians prevented from developing water resources but they cannot develop the means to store water for agriculture either. Yet the capacity to store water until it is needed is the most important risk management tool in farming in the West Bank. The Palestinians would like to supplement their agricultural water resource by further water harvesting, but this too has been denied them. Hill dams, sub-surface and check dams, infiltration basins and the like would capture run-off, increase groundwater infiltration and help to store water upstream – there is at present very limited surface water storage available for Palestinians to carry water over from season to season. Only village tanks keep enough water into the summer to serve household needs and to water stock. Water harvesting and surface storage technologies are widely practiced throughout the region, and very much so in Israel (see Chapter 1). However, approval of these structures in the West Bank falls within the remit of the JWC, and they have not been permitted – indeed, 'unauthorized structures' are routinely destroyed (Figure 5.3 and 5.6).[38]

Nor has development of the Ein al Fashka springs been authorized by the Israelis[39] – these springs deliver some 100 million cubic metres of brackish water annually to the Dead Sea. Palestinians wish to follow Israel's example and invest in desalination of this water for agriculture, but this request has been denied. The Palestinians consider that access to these extra resources would allow them to vastly expand their irrigation and to rival Israel's prowess in high-productivity agriculture.

Figure 5.6 Palestinian boy drinking from tanker, Image courtesy of IMEMC.

Loss of land and settlement agriculture

Second only to lack of water amongst constraints is loss of land. Here the ABC of Oslo is the first problem. Nearly two thirds of West Bank agricultural land (63 per cent) is located in Area C where tight restrictions are practiced by Israel. Nearly three quarters of Area C, some 43 per cent of the entire West Bank area, has been allocated to settlement local and regional councils.[40]

These Israeli settlements are progressively encroaching on agricultural land. But the most flagrant abuse in Palestinian eyes is settler irrigation, which covers an area almost as great as Palestinian irrigation in the West Bank and is better watered and more productive. Exact details are hard to come by. One source asserts that as early as 1987 'Israel has allowed its settlers in the West Bank and Gaza to irrigate 47,000 dunums (nearly 5,000 hectares) of confiscated land with water allocations per unit area nearly double that on Palestinian land.'[41] Certainly the process appears to have begun as early as the late 1970s with settlements near Bethlehem, where a thriving settler agriculture of vineyards, olive groves and fruit trees grew up.[42] Since 2001 settler agriculture has grown apace in the highlands, notably within the exclusion zones originally established for security reasons around settlements.

A similar itinerary was followed in the Jordan Valley, where military outposts have been converted to civilian settlements and irrigated agriculture has developed for dates, protected horticulture and field crops. Irrigation infrastructure is in place, including for the reuse of treated wastewater and over 65,000 dunams (6,500 hectares) are farmed. The wastewater originates from the sewage of East Jerusalem and is channelled to the recently constructed Nebi Musa Sewage Treatment Facility and then to the settlements in the Jordan Valley. Other water infrastructure for setter agriculture includes the Tirza Reservoirs, which were established between 1995 and 2001 in the Tirza Valley, inside of the border area closed by Military Order 151 east of al-Jiftlik, and the Og Reservoir in the northern Dead Sea area, which has also stored treated wastewater from in and around East Jerusalem since 2008.[43]

Research by Kerem Navot and the World Bank suggests that in 2012, settlement agriculture in the West Bank highlands and in the Jordan Valley covered 93,000 dunams, over 9,000 hectares, of which half lay within settlement boundaries, and half beyond.[44] This is equivalent to three quarters (73 per cent) of the entire area in the West Bank irrigated by Palestinians (12,200 hectares). Cropping patterns in settler agriculture are typically high value. In 2013, the World Bank estimated that settlements provided most of the pomegranates that Israel exported to Europe as well as 22 per cent of Israel's export of almonds, 13 per cent of the olives and 40 per cent of the dates.

With settler agriculture juxtaposed to Palestinian agriculture and in some locations replacing it, friction has been common. Palestinians have protested, to little effect other than on their own safety and liberty. Sadly it is often reported that settlers have harassed Palestinian farmers and damaged their crops and infrastructure, and that these actions have gone unpunished by the authorities (Figures 5.7 and 5.8).

Figure 5.7 Settler agriculture in the Jordan Valley, with permission from Kiva.

Figure 5.8 Palestinian crops in the Jordan Valley destroyed by Israeli army, with permission from Amnesty International.

Restrictions in Area C

The complex array of restrictions on movement and access places a great constraint on economic development and growth in the West Bank, imposing physical, institutional and administrative impediments to the movement of people and goods within and in and out of the West Bank.

In 2017, we went deep into Area C to the southeast of Bethlehem, into the beautiful, desolate lands that lie between Hebron and the Dead Sea. For part of the way there was an old pipe that lay alongside the track. At the end of the track was a desert camp of Bedouin herders, a vast tent, carpets, a television powered by a car battery, a goat pen, the warmest of welcomes that tradition and good nature could provide. The abandoned pipe, our hosts said, urging bitter coffee on us, was an old NGO project to bring them drinking water, long since put a stop to by the Israelis. Today they buy water by the bowser in town from an Italian NGO and tug it out to their encampment. They show us, too, the remains of a water harvesting scheme, stones and dug channels to direct run-off into a lined chamber. We all show interest in the technology but sadly there is no water. It is a very hard life. These desert dwellers in Area C are used to it but we just wish improvers were here to tell them about improved seeds and drip irrigation and desert agriculture. However, the truth is that these Palestinian Bedouin are not welcome to the Occupier, who would plainly like them to go away.[45]

Area C occupies almost two thirds of the West Bank (61 per cent) and is home to about 180,000 Palestinians, about 7 per cent of the Palestinian West Bank population. The area is richly endowed with minerals and fertile land. It contains 90 per cent of the forested area of the West Bank, half of the water wells, and more than one third of the natural springs. It is also a contiguous area, in sharp contrast to the 'territorial islands' of Areas A and B.[46] Despite the provisions of the 1995 Interim Agreement that Area C 'will be gradually transferred to Palestinian jurisdiction', to date only 2 per cent of Area C has been transferred to Area B status.[47] For now Palestinians are simply excluded from vast swathes of their own territory (Table 5.3).

The way in which Area C is administered essentially precludes Palestinian businesses from investing there, and conditions for existing residents and economic activity are highly restrictive. Less than 1 per cent of Area C is designated by the Israeli authorities for Palestinian use. This 1 per cent is essentially just the small built-up areas where Palestinians live. The vast bulk of Area C is heavily restricted or off limits altogether to Palestinians: 68 per cent is reserved for settlements, 21 per cent is closed military zones and 9 per cent is allocated to nature reserves.

Table 5.3 The Share of West Bank Natural Resources Located in Area C

Natural resource	In Area A	In Area B	In Area C	Total	Natural resource in Area C as a percentage of total in West Bank
Nature reserves (dunams)	52,300	42,600	607,730	702,630	86
Forests (dunams)	7,000	9,000	59,016	75,016	91
Wells	223	87	287	597	48
Springs	70	122	112	304	37

Source: Applied Research Institute in Jerusalem (ARIJ), 2013.

Palestinians are denied construction permits for residential or economic purposes even in the villages that lie within the 1 per cent of area C where they still have a toehold. Nor are Palestinians allowed to exploit the mineral resources or to develop public infrastructure in Area C.[48]

Area C includes much of the land of the West Bank suitable for agricultural production. This is inherent in the zoning system under which Area C comprises the territories beyond Palestinian urban and peri-urban areas. The Land Research Centre (LRC) has estimated that almost half a million dunams of land (50,000 hectares) suitable for agriculture in Area C are not cultivated by Palestinians, either because of restricted access, or because the land is amongst the 187,000 dunams (nearly 19,000 hectares) being cultivated or occupied by Israeli settlements, or because of lack of water. In addition, another 1 million dunams (100,000 hectares) could be used for rangeland or forestry, were current restrictions lifted.[49]

The Separation Barrier

For those who live near or beyond it, the Separation Barrier is a big problem. It occupies considerable Palestinian land. – see the section 'Costs to the West Bank economy'. It has also cut off productive agricultural areas and wells from the farmers who own them. Ten per cent of West Bank land now sits in the area located between the Green Line and the Barrier. Ten thousand Palestinian people live in this 'closed area', and thousands more own land there.

Farmers who live on the Palestinian side of the Separation Barrier but have land beyond it must obtain permits from the Civil Administration if they need to go through. When we were in the Jayyous area in 2008, 452 local farmers with land beyond the wall had put in applications to farm their land, but only a quarter of them – 110 in all – had been granted permits.

So at half past six in the cold of one November morning that year, we went down to the gate at Jayyous to have a word with the farmers waiting to go through. They, of course, were the lucky one in four who had actually obtained the permits to cross to the closed area beyond the Barrier, which here is a high double-chain-link fence. They have with them the equipment and materials they need – the hoes and spades and fertilizer which have to be taken through and back each day.

For a long time, nothing happens. Everyone stamps their feet and rubs their hands together. It feels like it is freezing on these early mornings in the highlands at the start of winter. Official opening hours are from 6.30 am in the morning to 5.30 pm in the evening but the farmers tell us the operating times can be quite random. They say the gate often does not open for days at a time. There is a notice stuck to the high fence saying, '*In case of problem, call the Hotline*'. The phone number is the Civil Administration, the Occupation authority. We nod towards the notice but the farmers hunch their shoulders and turn their backs.

They hate the permit system, quite apart from the constant humiliation that is the daily bread of the Occupation. One man says he lost his crops: 'I had three dunums of cucumbers. My permit expired, and I lost my entire crop because I could not get there to harvest in time.' Another was denied access to his damaged plastic house for four critical days and he lost all his seedlings.

One farmer is being talked about even though he is not actually present. He is the one who was invited by an NGO to a conference in Europe to talk about the effect the closure has had on his livelihood and on his family. When he got back, his application for permit renewal was denied and he has never yet got another one.

We wait and chat. They talk about how settlers have just attacked some nearby Palestinian farms, destroying a new irrigation system a French NGO had just put in. They called the IDF but nobody came.

The early morning mist clears and from our high vantage point we are amazed to see the sea, like a silver blade along the horizon. It looks not far off and it really is not so very far, about ten or fifteen miles. Stupidly, we ask how long it takes to get there. We are thinking, like children, of beaches and sand and sun. At first nobody bothers to reply until finally one wag says 'Sixty years and counting'.

The gate opens. The farmers bid us farewell and set off through, carrying their tools and trundling the sacks of fertilizer in wheelbarrows.

Before the *al Aqsa intifada*, produce from this fertile region was sold all across Israel and the West Bank. Nowadays it is restricted largely to the West Bank – and then only to areas that are not 'closed' for security reasons. Nablus, for example, is nearby and traditionally the biggest market for produce from Jayyous. But these days it has become increasingly difficult and costly to access because of the closure regime. Costs have soared and wholesale prices are down 50 per cent.

Mohamed Jabber, the mayor of Jayyous, says: 'Unemployment here is 75 per cent because of the Separation Barrier. People cannot get to their land and they cannot get permits to do their work. Before, with our rich agriculture, we were quite well off. But then came the restrictions' – he means the closures and all the movement and access array of controls – 'so now, half we Jayyousis live below the poverty line. And yet this is a wealthy area, because of what we can do in agriculture.'[50]

The potential for wastewater reuse in Palestinian agriculture

Amidst all the constraints is an opportunity – the potential for wastewater reuse. As we have seen in Chapter 1, Israeli agriculture has been using wastewater for many years, and many Israelis would like to press the Palestinians to follow suit. The absence of reuse is often mentioned by Israelis as a failing of the Palestinians and a shameful waste of water. But what are the possibilities that wastewater reuse can be a handy extra resource in the West Bank as it is in Israel?

The advantages of using treated wastewater in agriculture are several: it is available for 365 days a year, it comes in reliable and predictable quantities that are not affected by drought, and, because it is a by-product, it can be priced in line with policy rather than on a commercial or full-cost recovery basis. In the West Bank context, it would add to quantities agreed under Article 40. Up to half the quantity of municipal and industrial supply could theoretically be reused. This might provide up to 40–50 million cubic metres of extra water to agriculture, almost doubling the agricultural water budget. The West Bank could, in principle, emulate Israel where agriculture now uses more wastewater than fresh water. It would, however, require ample storage because wastewater is produced every day but peak demand for irrigation water is concentrated in the dry, hot summer months.

However, although it is Palestinian policy to promote reuse, attempts so far have not got very far. In Chapter 4 we mentioned the wastewater reuse pilot programme prepared as part of the al Bireh Wastewater Treatment Project. Larger-scale projects are now proposed both for the al Bireh effluent and for that from the Nablus West plant. As we have seen in Chapter 4, the Palestinian Water Authority has very ambitious plans for wastewater reuse, targeting reuse on more than 50,000 hectares by 2022.

While at the limit some of this may be technically feasible, it would require a coherent programme of investment and institutional and behavioural change. First, it would require the treatment capacity to be in place, and, as we have seen, this remains limited. Second, it would require the infrastructure to store the treated wastewater and then to convey it to the point of use when it is required. Palestinians would have to develop the kind of large-scale water storage capability – ponds, tanks, reservoirs, underground storage in aquifers – that the Israelis have built up, together with a network of pipes to convey the treated wastewater to the storage facilities and then on to farmers' fields.

Third, it would need a major programme of regulation, incentives and education to promote farmer uptake. A regulatory and incentive framework would need to be developed, along with a campaign to sell the product to farmers. All of this would require inventive design, considerable financing and forceful execution. But most importantly, under the constraints of Article 40, the ABC mosaic and movement and access restrictions, it would require the consent and the active cooperation of the Israelis.

Cultural attitudes have been said to be an impediment. When we asked the then head of the Israel Water Authority in 2008 about solutions to the Palestinian water problem, he said: 'The main problem is the non-use of treated wastewater. The sewage poisons the groundwater – and it's a waste. They need to shift, but it is not allowed by religion. We overcame this in Israel.' Palestinian observers tend to downplay this and certainly it seems a surmountable problem. One Palestinian specialist told us: 'There is no problem in Islam.' In fact Palestinian farmers already sometimes do use sewage, even untreated – see the discussion we had with the village women that is described at the start of this chapter.

A step-by-step collaborative approach is required. Clearly, wastewater reuse has to become an increasing resource for Palestinian farmers, as it is in Israel. There needs to be cooperation between Palestinian agencies: the Ministry of Agriculture, civil society, NGOs and the PWA.

But to be frank, the problem does not lie in Palestinian reticence at all. The problem lies in the Occupation, and particularly in the restrictive practices of Israel to the development of Palestinian wastewater treatment plants and to Palestinian reuse of treated wastewater in Area C. Unless Palestinians can build wastewater treatment plants and develop the infrastructure, especially storage and pipelines all across Area C, and unless Palestinians can freely access and develop their farms in Area C, there is no scope for wastewater reuse on other than on a pitifully small scale. The best hope is at al Bireh and at Nablus West, and later on at Hebron where, as we saw in Chapter 4, a large reuse project is planned once the treatment plant is up and running. But moving from planning to action on this will require the Israelis to ease the tight restrictions they impose on such developments.

* * *

Agriculture is one economic sector where the West Bank has real potential to create incomes, employment and fiscal revenue. Yet it is a highly constrained and dwindling sector, beset by lack of water, prey to the risks of climatic variability and growing aridity, and held back by lack of market access and by the multiple and pervasive constraints of a persistent Occupation. Encouragement to emulate the stellar success of Israeli agriculture sounds hollow indeed when water is so limited, the reuse of wastewater is made virtually impossible and access to outside markets is so constrained. Most galling is the successful settler agriculture, particularly that in the natural greenhouse of the Jordan Valley where West Bank Palestinians might have rivalled the achievements of their East Bank neighbours in Jordan.

Half a billion dollars and 100,000 jobs is the potential of a less constrained agriculture. Even if the Johnston allocation of Jordan water to the West Bank is not to be, freedom to treat and reuse wastewater in the highlands and in the alluvial plain alongside the Jordan would have a transformational effect on Palestinian society and its economy.

Figure 5.9 Palestinian farmer arrested for water theft, Photograph by courtesy of +972.

Chapter 6

WATER SECURITY IN THE GAZA STRIP

Eyeless in Gaza, at the mill, with slaves

John Milton[1]

In the troubled history of the lands that remained to the Palestinians after 1948, the Gaza Strip stands out as the most vexed. Its population today of nearly 2 million, crammed into an area half the size of tiny Singapore, is made up largely of descendants of refugees from the rural south of Mandate Palestine, who are relegated to looking out through the security barrier towards their former family homes and fields.

Living conditions in the Strip are dire. For twenty years or more the economy has been described as 'collapsing'. The seven young people in every ten who are out of work may slip easily into hopelessness. IDF general Eyal Ben-Reuven said 'the humanitarian crisis lays the groundwork for hatred'.[2]

Agriculture is the mainstay of the productive economy and after the Israeli pull-out in 2005, bold investors put $14 million into greenhouse agriculture. Former World Bank president Jim Wolfensohn planned for 400 truckloads of fresh produce leaving the Strip for high-value export markets every day. But in the event, daily shipments averaged just twelve trucks and in a year the venture folded, haemorrhaging more than half a million dollars a day. With scant access to markets, agriculture has sunk to an all-time low.

Water resources are scant and, in the absence of decent public supply, people have helped themselves, digging a myriad unlicensed wells. As a result, the groundwater resource is heavily overdrawn and seawater is flowing into the aquifer. Today well water is so salty that it is undrinkable and households depend on costly desalinated water from the active private vendors.

Frequent hostilities and constant restrictions on movement and access make coherent development of infrastructure a near impossibility. All is Band-Aids, emergency projects and botched jobs. One signal but sadly not solitary case is the North Gaza Emergency Sewage Treatment Project – NGEST. Begun on an emergency basis in 2004 to resolve the drastic sewage crisis, this project was completed and operations began only in 2018, fifteen years later.

But the NGEST plant solves little of the problem. Full treatment of all sewage in the Strip has been planned since Oslo but the plants have never been built. Even those that have been set up work at half capacity as lack of spares and materials and the constant power outages restrict their operation. Every day, some 80,000 tons of raw or partially treated sewage discharge to open ponds or course into the Mediterranean and drift up the coast. Israelis complain that their beaches are closed (most of Gaza's beaches were long since condemned) and desalination at Israel's Ashkelon plant has been several times suspended. Ariel Sharon complained that this was a 'sewage *intifada*', which implies an intentionality that is quite absent.

The great hope for drinking water supply is large-scale desalination and, for agricultural water, the reuse of treated wastewater. Israel provides world-class models of both technologies, efficient and low cost. Plans are well advanced for a major desalination plant in the Strip and for further sewage treatment capacity. Donors are lined up ready. But these plans face big risks in implementation and in operation, both from hostilities and from the persistent restrictions on imports of equipment, materials and energy. The experience with NGEST suggests that only with a political resolution can infrastructure solutions alleviate the desperate shortage of drinking water or stem the flow of sewage to the sea. In the meantime, small-scale desalination provides a modicum of high-cost drinking water, and sewage is still pumped into lakes and the Mediterranean.

* * *

We first knew Gaza as myth and history. Milton's rolling periods and God-gifted organ voice in Samson Agonistes. The struggle with the Philistines, Delilah giving her lover a short bob and Samson pulling down the columns on himself and on the throng. Gaza as an ancient trading port within the small Philistine empire between the deserts and the Mediterranean Sea. Philip the Evangelist sent on the road to Gaza to baptize the Ethiopian convert. Gaza as the only point in Palestine that never yielded to the Crusaders.

When we came first to Gaza in 2008 it was in the wreckage of hope. We entered through the long security structure without a human face, an apparatus as gigantic as a New York department store, security on the scale of a major industry, built for thousands. It was put up in another time, after Oslo, when for a brief period the people of Gaza could travel freely back and forth into Israel. Many went for work. Elderly people went to visit their old homes up the coast, in the old Philistine settlements of Ashdod and Ashkelon and right up to beautiful Jaffa, the Pearl of the Mediterranean.

Today this monstrous carbuncle is working just for us, and for a morose young Palestinian dejectedly swaddling his sick baby that he is bringing back from an Israeli hospital. Our bags whisk away to security on a moving belt, and then you go through chamber after chamber, standing in a Perspex tube and putting up your hands. Machines whirl around you, probing, a voice mumbles something and then repeats testily *Go ahead*! Lights turn from red to green, and then you're almost through.

Not quite because a voice says from behind a screen. The book, what is the book? We think, yes, we are all people of the book after all, *ahl ul kitab*. But it's not that, it is my bedtime read: *France The Dark Years 1940-1944*. Yes, what is the subject? I say *An oppressed people struggle against an unjust occupation. OK*, the voice says, *move on*. I wonder what would have been the wrong answer.

In the end, when the final barked command comes from the Tannoy and we are released into the dazzling December sunshine, there are our bags, looking somehow more the worse for wear than ever.

There is a long trudge to the rough hut where the Palestinian border guard sits in the shade at a rude wooden table. On the right, just visible beyond some considerable wreckage, is the Mediterranean, adding a dab of gloss amongst the shattered concrete and steel bars poking up. This is the Gaza Industrial Area, set up after Oslo and quite destroyed during the *al Aqsa intifada*. The Palestinian passport officer copies our names in biro into a dog-eared ledger which looks like an old-fashioned register in a shabby hotel. And we enter the Gaza Strip.

* * *

On our visit in 2008, the engineer from the Palestinian Water Authority, greets us. Going into town we cross a wadi. It is choked with sewage. The stench is terrible. Our guide looks indifferent.

'80,000 cubic metres every day', he says in a matter of fact way. '80,000 tons of raw sewage on a daily basis. The treatment plants barely work, so we just dump it into the Med.'

'Sounds drastic.'

'I can't take my kids to the beach any more. Even the Israelis are complaining. The stuff floats up the coast and gets into their nice new desalination plant at Ashkelon.'

The problem is that everything has to come through Israel – and almost every item seems to be a security problem. Even PVC pipes are somehow suspect. Our guide says,

'At Khan Younis, we started work on the sewage line. Italian financing paid the whole contract sum. But then we couldn't complete the last three kilometres. They wouldn't let the pipes in. And in the end there was no cement either. . .'

All this sewage is having a bad effect on people's health across the Strip. Nitrates are contaminating the water supply, and this is causing 'blue-baby syndrome' amongst infants. Faecal coliform bacteria cluster around the outfalls. Fish are infected. The whole coastline is contaminated.

'Some time back', our guide says, 'the holding pond at Beit Lahiya burst its banks. There was a sewage tsunami. Five people died in the surge. That did convince the Israelis to let us carry on with the plant. And your Tony Blair helped. He was practically riding shotgun on every lorry load of materials.'[3]

'So at least one plant is working?'

Our guide gives a short, dry laugh.

'Sadly no. There were still some instruments and other things we couldn't bring in. . .'

We arrive in Gaza City. There is a strike and a march of angry protesters in the square. They are health workers who have not been paid for four months. But apart from this noisy parade, it is an ordinary day, people lounging and queuing. Unemployment is 50 per cent, so strikes make little difference. The main work is in the private sector, in the tunnels.

Yet people are not quite despairing. In the evening, we have a sensational sea food dinner, 'Best ever', Sandy says. Then at the rather good hotel on the front, the saloon is packed. *Le tout Gaza* is there, sipping juice and looking out dreamily to sea. Whole families, children tumbling everywhere, grannies laughing with the little ones.

Our guide, the young engineer, says, 'I came back from the Gulf to see my mother ten years ago, and then the border closed and I haven't been let out since. But we cannot despair when we have our families. This is what we live for. This is what we hope for.'

The Gaza Strip and its water resources

For thousands of years, Gaza has been the gateway between the Sinai desert and the fertile lands of Canaan. Its climate is on the hinge between the arid desert to the south and the better watered coastline to the north. The weather is hot and dry for most of the year. Rainfall averages under 200 millimetres annually, somewhat less in the south of the 25-mile (41 kilometres) length of the Strip, slightly more in the north, where the city of Gaza is located. Just beyond the city is the seasonal watercourse of Wadi Gaza, where in the past spate flows rushed down in winter from the Palestinian highlands around Hebron. Although heavily polluted, it is still a wetland and host to a rich variety of flora and fauna and a haven for migrating birds.

In 1948, Gaza had just 50,000 inhabitants, largely living off fishing, trade and about 6,000 dunams (600 hectares) of citrus groves. Then refugees flooded in, largely from the rural areas in the south of Mandate Palestine. The population shot up to 250,000 and, largely by natural increase, reached nearly half a million by 1966.[4] Economic opportunities were scant and as most of the refugees were from a farming background, agriculture quickly developed, particularly production of vegetables for local consumption and citrus for export.

Today, the Gaza Strip is a tiny, heavily populated enclave, with a population of nearly two million crammed into its 140 square miles (360 square kilometres). In an area slightly over 1 per cent of the total land area of Mandate Palestine, it accommodates a population that is almost as great as the entire population of Palestine in 1947.[5] It is said to be the third most densely populated territory in the world and is often considered to be 'unliveable', not just because of over-crowding but also because of the widespread poverty and the status of human services like health, education, energy, water and sanitation.

Water resources and the history of their management

A certain amount of rainfall is captured through rainwater harvesting, and there is still some occasional seasonal flow in the wadis that cross the Strip (although greatly reduced – see discussion in this chapter). However, the main freshwater resource of Gaza is groundwater. Two aquifers lie beneath the Gaza Strip. An upper freshwater aquifer slopes from the east at 30 metres below sea level to the west at 110 metres below sea level. This aquifer forms part of the much larger Coastal Aquifer, which has vast storage capacity and runs in the narrow strip of quaternary sands that extend for over 150 kilometres north from Gaza along the coast of Israel.[6]

With normal flows, the current sustainable yield of the segment of the Coastal Aquifer underlying Gaza is estimated at about 57 million cubic metres, around 15 per cent of the total yield of the shared aquifer, which is estimated at 360–420 million cubic metres. Despite the rapid increase in production of recycled and desalinated water in Israel and the building of the country's freshwater inventory over the years – see Chapter 1 – the Coastal Aquifer remains a vital part of that country's water resources, today providing one fifth of its total renewable freshwater resources. In the past, Israel heavily overdrew on this aquifer with risks to the resource, but availability of new sources and the integrated resource management practiced have corrected this. In the Gaza Strip, by contrast, abstractions have for years been running well above any estimate of sustainable yield. Contrary to the West Bank situation where Palestinians are the upstream riparians, Palestinian Gaza is downstream of the portion of the aquifer that underlies Israel, with flows coming from Israel into the Gaza part of the aquifer.

Because the freshwater aquifer lies below sea level, there is a perpetual risk of seawater intruding or of the fresh and saline waters mingling. When this shallow aquifer is overdrawn, seawater is pulled in to fill the voided space in the rock matrix.[7] Deep beneath this freshwater aquifer, at about 400 metres below sea level, lies a lower saline aquifer containing large quantities of brackish water[8] within old sedimentary rocks.

Water under the Occupation In 1967, at the time of the Six-Day War, Israel occupied the Gaza Strip. As in the West Bank, so in Gaza, water was declared state property[9] and, in 1977, well licencing, metering and water quotas were introduced.[10] Private water development was banned, although the drilling of some new wells for potable supply was allowed under permit.

Israeli management and use of Gaza's groundwater was controversial. Israeli settlers came in and soon Gazans began to see a huge disparity between the water to which they had access and that allocated to the settlers. Although there is no certainty, Palestinians assert that in 1984, 'just 2,110 settlers were using 30-60 million m^3' of local water, while more than half a million Gazans had to make do with just 100 million cubic metres. If correct, this would be equivalent to 15,000–20,000 cubic metres a head for settlers, and just 200 cubic metres a head for Palestinians. The settlers would have benefitted from between 75 and 150 times as much water per head as the Palestinians – and would have been making a substantial contribution towards the depletion and ruin of the aquifer.[11]

Palestinians comment unfavourably on Israel's stewardship of Gaza's water resources during the Occupation. They point out that 'given the scarcity and vulnerability of water in the Coastal Aquifer of the Gaza Strip, effective management of water resources appears limited, particularly in contrast to the careful management of Israel's portion of the Coastal Aquifer'.[12] The Civil Administration did maintain a hydro-meteorological network and monitored groundwater levels and water quality, but data from these networks were not generally available and do not appear to have supported sustainable water management.

During this period, a gap between demand for water and stable supply first opened up. Mekorot brought 5 million cubic metres a year to the central part of the Gaza Strip where groundwater quality was worst, and a reverse osmosis desalination plant was piloted. Mekorot also developed water in the good-quality part of the aquifer near Deir el Baalah, linking the wells to Israel's National Water Carrier (the NWC)[13] and supplying water to the Israeli settlements and to the Gazan population. The Gazans also claimed that Mekorot drilled twenty wells of 20-inch bore along the Green Line around the Strip, each well capable of pumping out 200 cubic metres an hour. But most of the excess demand was met by overpumping of the aquifer within the Strip, which led inevitably to saline intrusion and the decline of water quality.

The Gazans also asserted that at this time Israel built check and diversion dams along Wadi Gaza in its middle reaches, where it traverses Israel between the Hebron mountains and the Strip. As a result, they claim, the wadi no longer flowed within the Strip even in the rainy winter season, and the recharge to the Coastal Aquifer that could have been expected was lost, at least in part.

Whatever the truth of these varying plaints, it is clear that overall during the Occupation the kind of effective water management that the Israelis brought to their own water crisis during these years – strong institutions, economic and regulatory instruments, political backing, investment, technological innovation and public awareness and cooperation – these were not brought to bear on the water shortages of Occupied Gaza by the responsible authorities. Despite the regulation the Israelis sought to impose, the number of boreholes proliferated during the Occupation. In 1986 there were 2,195 wells, of which only 40 were for domestic use and 2,150 for agriculture. By the end of the Occupation, twenty years later, this had skyrocketed to more than 12,000 wells. Of these only 2,500 had permits. The aquifer was placed under intolerable strain and by the end of the Occupation in 2005, it was in crisis.[14]

It appears that this pattern of poor stewardship became more pronounced once Likud came to power in the late 1970s. One former Israeli water commissioner considered that this was because Gaza's aquifer was downstream of Israel's water system, so damage to the Gaza aquifer would harm the Gazans, but not the Israelis. It is striking that the management of Gaza's water resources did not form part of Article 40 of the Oslo Accords. The Palestinian view is that Article 40 neglected water in Gaza because it was immaterial to Israel's interests.[15]

After the Israeli withdrawal Once the al Aqsa *intifada* broke out, Israel adopted a new approach to the Gaza Strip – withdrawal and containment. The settlements were closed down in 2005 and Israel withdrew its administration and security forces. A series of small wars broke out in which much of Gaza's production capacity and infrastructure were damaged. In June 2006, the Israeli Air Force destroyed Gaza's sole electrical plant, with a serious impact on water production and distribution and on sewage treatment and disposal. Following the Hamas takeover of 2007, hostilities intensified. In December 2008, massive air strikes destroyed much infrastructure including, it was reported, some 800 water wells and leaving 500,000 people without running water. A ground incursion by the IDF followed. Over the subsequent decade, this pattern of hostilities, lulls and then renewed hostilities has persisted, with a continued cycle of destruction and reconstruction of water infrastructure.[16]

Water resources and their management in Gaza today

The Palestinian Water Authority – and its double In the Gaza Strip as in the West Bank, the statutory body for water resources management is the Palestinian Water Authority (PWA) – see Chapter 2. Effectively the PWA is the Palestinian water ministry and it reports to the Palestinian Authority in Ramallah. Up to the time of the Hamas takeover of Gaza, PWA had developed a relatively strong presence in Gaza. There was a well-staffed PWA branch with good capacity under a PWA deputy chairman. However, the effectiveness of this office began to deteriorate after Hamas took power, in tandem with the deterioration of relations between Hamas and Fatah. In June 2008, Hamas occupied the PWA offices in Gaza City and installed a 'PWA' of its own creation. The 'official' PWA lingered on enfeebled in makeshift offices.

Up to the time of the takeover, PWA had been progressively implementing a regulatory programme for Gaza wells. Over a three- to four-year period, the PWA had fixed 700–800 metres to wells, reading them annually. However, once Hamas had taken over the PWA offices and installed its own mimic PWA, the 'official' PWA's regulatory function fell into abeyance. There was a mushrooming of wells drilled by citizens without licence. Essentially, as crises with Israel recurred, households were anxious to secure their own supply.

The political situation steadily reduced the effective linkages with Ramallah. Despite enormous effort within the 'official' PWA to maintain contacts with its Gaza branch and to integrate its plans and investments within the larger framework, the water sector in Gaza became progressively detached from the preoccupations of the Palestinian Authority. The few remaining PWA staff in Gaza complained on every occasion that Gaza was ignored.

Investment planning became ever more complex as the financing agencies were working with a disconnected institutional set-up. With a general international aversion to treating with Hamas, aid agencies had to rely on the 'official' PWA, working from Ramallah under Fatah, for investment identification and approval, and for implementation support. Aid partners were in the invidious position of financing investments in a territory where they could not talk to the de facto government.

The Coastal Municipalities Water Utility (CMWU) At the time of Oslo in 1993–5, Gaza water supply was fragmented, with twenty-five separate municipalities providing water services to their residents through local area networks supplied from local wells. Post-Oslo, plans for Gaza water supply were to establish a single autonomous utility, the Coastal Municipalities Water Utility (CMWU), to take responsibility for service delivery, both bulk and retail, in all twenty-five municipalities and to invest in a central desalination plant and a bulk carrier that would distribute desalinated water throughout the Strip.

In 1996 the CMWU was set up and staffed. The plan was for a step-by-step consolidation of water supply. Initially, the existing twenty-five municipal water departments were to receive technical support from the CMWU to improve their operations. It was then expected that they would progressively transfer their staff and assets to CMWU. Financed by a US$25 million World Bank credit, an international operator was brought in to help develop capacity and procedures. A four-year management contract was awarded to a joint venture of Lyonnaise des Eaux and Khatib & Alami in 1996. When the contract ended in 2000, it was renewed twice for one year each time until 2002. The programme did in fact have some success, with reduction in non-revenue water to 25 per cent, and an increase in the bill collection rate to 85 per cent. However, actual responsibility for service provision remained with municipalities and during this time illegal connections proliferated – more than 16,000 by 2002. In the end, the conditions created by the *al Aqsa intifada* led to a force majeure situation that resulted in the termination of the contract.[17]

Subsequently, reticence emerged about the plan to fuse the municipal water departments into a single utility. In the turbulent circumstances that have prevailed in Gaza over the last decade, some municipalities, particularly Gaza City, raised objections about losing control and becoming dependent on a single source. It was not a negligible factor in this reluctance that the pipeline would, at least initially, be bringing them desalinated water from Israel, which created both political and security concerns. The preoccupations of other municipalities were more mundane – they simply wanted to keep the cash generated by the water supply operation. Like many of their counterparts in the West Bank, Gaza municipalities were not paying their bulk water bills, so that even though collection rates were very low they could still generate a 'surplus'.[18] In some municipalities, there were mayors installed by Hamas and these were not acceptable to the donors who were supporting the CMWU project.

When we were in Gaza in 2017, we met the CMWU chief executive Monther Issa Shoblaq, a charming, courteous man and a very effective manager. He told us that the CMWU has about 850 staff and is providing bulk water throughout the Strip. The utility runs twenty brackish water desalination plants and a small seawater desalination plant which produces 2,600 cubic metres daily. He said, too, that the CMWU is handling a massive investment portfolio of roughly $1.6 billion. This includes construction of two central wastewater treatment plants; one in the Middle Governorate and the other in the Southern Governorate, at a total cost of around $130 million.[19]

However, for all the effort and the progress made, Dr Shoblaq believes that the CMWU has not yet matured into a full-service utility. Only four of the twenty-five municipalities have so far ceded their staff and assets to the CMWU, so only in these locations is CMWU providing a retail service. Inevitably, the biggest challenge has been keeping operations going in the face of the regular hostilities and seemingly almost permanent closures. Considerable damage has been caused by Israeli raids. Ever since the 2006 destruction of Gaza's only power plant, electricity is in constant short supply and power outages are a daily occurrence. Like everything else in the Strip, providing water services is an uphill struggle. In Dr Shoblaq's view, only a political settlement can really bring water security to the long-suffering population.

Total water availability Total water availability in the Gaza Strip in 2014 was 179 million cubic metres – see Table 6.1. The lion's share of this – about 171 million cubic metres – came from the local aquifer. However, only one third of that 171 million cubic metres was sustainable groundwater yield and the rest was overdraft, further depleting the aquifer storage and increasing the rate of seawater intrusion. About 5 per cent of the total availability – 8.2 million cubic metres – was potable water from other sources: 5 million cubic metres was locally desalinated water used directly for drinking, and a further 3.5 million cubic metres was drinking water purchased from Mekorot under the Oslo Accords.[20] Of the 179 million cubic metres, about 93 million cubic metres was allocated to municipal and industrial (M&I) uses and the balance (86 million cubic metres) went to agriculture.

On a per capita basis, total supply was equivalent to 270 litres per person per day, and domestic supply amounted to about 145 litres. This availability at household level is not ungenerous – it compares with availability at the tap in the West Bank of 65 litres.[21] However, most household supply is water mined from the aquifer at the expense of the sustainability of the resource, and this supply is in any case undrinkable and could only be used for household chores. Taking household, industrial and agricultural uses combined, about 2 litres out of every 3 used in Gaza are irreplaceable groundwater that not only deplete the aquifer but contribute to the drawing in of seawater and the continued destruction of the aquifer structure and water quality.

Unsustainable extraction Clearly, groundwater abstraction in Gaza is out of control. Gaza's only internal renewable water resource, the Coastal Aquifer, which until a few years ago provided abundant fresh water to the population, has for years now suffered extreme unregulated overuse. In 2014 more than 170 million cubic

Table 6.1 Total Water Availability in the Gaza Strip in 2014, in million m^3

Source	Total volume	Agriculture	Municipal and industrial
Pumped from wells	170.7	85.7	85.0
Desalinated water	4.7	0	4.7
Purchased from Mekorot	3.5	0	3.5
Total	178.9	85.7	93.2

Source: PWA Water Tables 2014, Tables 2 and 3.

metres was pumped out, almost three times the sustainable yield of 57 million cubic metres. This overdraft has been going on for decades with a consequent continual decline in the static water level.[22] Part of the problem is that the population has responded to water scarcity by expanding the drilling of private wells. As we have seen, more than 10,000 unlicensed wells were drilled during the Occupation. After Oslo, unlicenced drilling and extraction continued, despite the PWA's attempts at regulation. PWA also seeks to fault Israel, pointing to the very many wells it claims Israel drilled close to the Gaza border (see discussion earlier) which 'have a negative impact by minimizing the lateral flow toward the Gaza Strip'.[23]

Undrinkable quality Salinization and contamination of the Gaza aquifer have increased dramatically, and today most groundwater in Gaza is no longer drinkable. The major parts of the aquifer have chloride concentrations of 500–1,500 millgrams per litre, while along the coastline the concentration of chloride exceeds 2,000 milligrams per litre. These levels compare with US EPA standards of a maximum concentration of 250 milligrams per litre for chloride ions. The aquifer today also contains high proportions of nitrates, well above international guidelines for potable water resources.[24] Almost all the 260 municipal drinking water wells have these high salt and nitrate levels – their water is unfit for human consumption.[25] Overall, the aquifer is now so degraded that 97 per cent of the groundwater in it is no longer considered potable.[26] In fact the water is so salty that it is approaching the point where many crops will not tolerate it either.[27]

This deterioration in quality has been largely caused by seawater intrusion. As we saw earlier, where pumping depletes the aquifer, seawater is drawn in to take the place of the disappearing fresh water. Sewage contamination is also worsening groundwater quality. With almost all Gaza sewage untreated and most sewage captured either in cess pits or in huge sewage lagoons, contaminants are infiltrating into the groundwater. Nitrates also filter down from agriculture.

Outlook for the aquifer The continuing overdraft further depletes an aquifer already in a ruinous condition, continually reducing the yield and compromising quality. At some point in the near future, the quantity available will be so diminished and the water will have become so saline and polluted that all needs of the Strip, both human and economic, will have to be met by desalination or by water imports.

So where does Gaza get its water from? Desalination and water purchase currently provide drinking water. Total annual supply to households through the network is currently about 95 million cubic metres, but most of this is undrinkable aquifer water that is used for household purposes like washing.[28] Drinking water is largely supplied by private reverse osmosis plants, which provide more than 4 million cubic metres to Gaza households. Purchases from Mekorot are also on the rise. Purchases in 2016 were about 8 million cubic metres, compared to the 3 million cubic metres purchased in 2014.

The bulk water question

Possible new sources of bulk water for Gaza have long been considered. After Oslo, in the brief time of hope, water imports from Turkey were considered. The water might have come from Turkey's 'water port' on the Manavgat River, by tanker or Medusa bag or even by pipeline. Water transfer from the West Bank aquifers was also mooted, which now seems ironic given the tight controls on quantity under Oslo and the West Bank's own current chronic water shortages.

Is it possible to recover the aquifer?

One possibility that is considered is recovery of the aquifer. Even though the aquifer is very far gone, it might not be impossible technically to nurse at least parts of it back to health. This would require careful assessment, monitoring and regulation, reducing pumping and protecting water quality against both saline intrusion and contamination from sewage and agricultural chemicals. The programme would need to be managed in conjunction with surface and groundwater management in Israel. It would mean much less water could be pumped not just during the recovery period but ever afterwards.

A recovery programme of this nature is certainly technically feasible for the parts of the aquifer where saline intrusion has not yet reached tipping point. Twenty years ago, Israel achieved much this result by vigorous state action with the stretch of the Coastal Aquifer that lies beneath its own coastal plain. But the factors that aided Israel – strong governance, capital, relatively abundant alternative sources, the ability to recharge aquifers with fresh water from the Mountain Aquifer or Tiberias or with treated wastewater, the option of desalination to compensate for lower groundwater availability, and above all the security and prosperity to undertake so challenging an endeavour – none of these factors exists in Gaza today.[29]

In practice, conditions in Gaza suggest there is scant prospect of recovering control over the aquifer. Recovery is not only demanding technically but also in terms of the required governance conditions. Even in high-governance territories, recovering control over groundwater once it has been lost has proved an uphill struggle[30] – and governance is not a forte in the Gaza Strip. It is doubtful that there is the political will to get tough on unlicensed abstractions and there is neither the legal framework nor the institutional capacity to regulate well drilling and groundwater pumping in such a way that abstraction could be reduced.

In reality there is little prospect of nursing those segments that are technically recoverable back to potable quality. Although aquifer water can continue at least for some years to provide a source of low-quality network water and feedstock for brackish water desalination, alternative sources are needed for drinking water.

Could Gaza simply import more water from Israel via the Israeli National Water Carrier?

Mekorot purchases have varied over the years. Under Article 40 of the Oslo Accords, Israel agreed to supply 5 million cubic metres a year, which was the then capacity of the Mekorot pipeline that connected the Israeli settlements in the southern Gaza Strip. After the Israeli withdrawal from Gaza in 2005, deliveries hovered around the 5 million cubic metres mark until 2012 when they dropped to 4.1 million cubic metres. In 2014, the year of Operation Protective Edge, which caused severe damage to civilian infrastructure, Israel supplied only 3.5 million cubic metres (see Table 6.1). Supplies increased again thereafter, and a new pipeline was completed in late 2013. Located in the area of Nahal Oz, it is designed to supply an additional 5 million cubic metres of Mekorot water each year, increasing total capacity to 10 million cubic metres. In 2015, purchases were about 8 million cubic metres.[31]

Pipeline capacity thus gives Gaza the ability to import the equivalent of about 15 litres per person of high-quality drinking water each day – about one sixth or so of the minimum demand for domestic water. Further purchases from Israel would require additional infrastructure as well as some kind of political entente. Of course, increasing purchases would further erode Gaza's flimsy autonomy in water resources and would be seen by the population as diminishing what little water security the territory currently has.

Decisions on means of supplying further drinking water are essential

For almost two decades, Gaza has been wrestling with the problem of sourcing new water. The *Coastal Aquifer Management Plan* (2001) concluded that the quantity and above all the quality of aquifer water meant that Gaza was incapable of supplying itself adequately but must find new or alternative sources of water. After the ideas of imports from Turkey or from the West Bank had been put aside, the sources considered were bulk importation from Israel, desalination within Gaza and wastewater reuse. Both a new pipeline from Israel and a large Gaza desalination plant were envisaged at the time. Part of this plan has been carried out – as we noted earlier, the new pipeline is in place. The desalination plant, which long languished on the drawing board, is at the time of writing (2020) an active project (see discussion herein).

There are other, more imaginative options for Gaza.[32] These options are discussed in Part III of this book, where we explore how cooperation between Israel and the Palestinians might be reset in order to achieve water security for both peoples. Some of these options would require Israel to play a full partnership role. They include: (i) building a large desalination plant in the Strip – but with Israeli help, so bringing the benefits of Israel's world-beating expertise and making market-based delivery options and financing a possibility; (ii) swapping Israeli desalinated water supplied to Gaza with water rights in the West Bank; and (iii) perhaps the most practical, trading Gaza wastewater to Israel in exchange for desalinated water.

For the moment, however, the leading possibility remains desalination within Gaza. It is to the current practices of desalination and the prospects for its development that we now turn.

Practices and prospects for desalination

Demand for water, already outstripping supply, is expected to continue to rise. In 2015, total M&I demand was estimated to be 103 million cubic metres, against supply of only 93 million cubic metres, and most of the water actually supplied was not of potable quality. Based on a projected growth rate of 3.2 per cent of the Gazan population, demand for M&I water in 2035 is expected to exceed 140 million cubic metres. Of this, current demand for domestic potable water is estimated at 55 million cubic metres, projected to rise to 100 million cubic metres by 2035.[33] In its strategy to close the supply/demand gap and to meet future demand for both domestic water and agricultural water, the PWA's current planning includes improvements to the water distribution system to reduce losses; water conservation in agriculture; development of wastewater treatment and reuse; and increased supply of bulk water resources through a central desalination plant and bulk carrier.

But is a single large desalination plant the best option? Is it even feasible? Are there alternatives that might have a better risk/reward profile? Here we look at the current and potential role of private desalination and supply, at the option of larger-scale desalination, and at the pros and cons of importing desalinated water from Israel.

Private desalination today

Currently, more than 90 per cent of Gaza's inhabitants access water from two sources: network water supplied by the municipality and desalinated truck water provided largely by private suppliers. Almost all Gaza residents find the municipal water too salty and impure for human consumption and use it only for bathing, cleaning and gardening. By contrast, desalinated water is appreciated for its taste and quality and is used by almost everyone for drinking and cooking. It is estimated that desalinated truck water represents 97 per cent of the water used for drinking and two thirds (67 per cent) of the water used for cooking. A rising number of consumers say they also use desalinated water for bathing and *'udud* (ablutions). The typical household spends about the same amount on each source: NIS 60 ($15) every month on each of network water and desalinated water from tankers.

Small-scale desalination and the truck market The small-scale desalination and truck water market in the Gaza Strip comprises more than 250 small-scale providers and is growing fast – in 2010 there were only about 20 providers in the business. Providers fall into three categories: private businesses running one or several small reverse osmosis (RO) plants and a fleet of trucks; private businesses comprising only trucks or a single truck and purchasing bulk desalinated water from the RO plants; and public bodies, non-governmental organizations, educational institutions and aid agencies such as UNICEF running their own small- or medium-scale RO plants.

Small-scale desalination in Gaza had its origins some two decades ago as the quality of network water started to become unacceptable. In 1998, a UK company, Acqua, launched a pilot project with a small desalination plant of 200 cubic metres per day to provide potable water to Shejaia, a governorate east of Gaza City. The price for a jerry can (20 litres) was 3 NIS ($0.80), equivalent to NIS 150 per cubic metres (over $40 per cubic metres). Poor households reportedly were unable to afford such prices. In 2000, a NGO project in a refugee camp, 'Beach Camp', provided desalinated water for poor households at one third of the price – 1 NIS (about $0.30) per jerry can. Several small private investors also supported this project on a micro-finance basis.

Over time, desalination took off and by 2015, 154 small RO plants were reported in Gaza, and there were 106 associated businesses distributing water through trucks. Of the 154 plants, 45 per cent were private, 29 per cent were non-governmental organizations, 19 per cent were public and 13 per cent were run by educational institutions. Two thirds (68 per cent) of the plants were not licenced and 40 per cent were using water from unlicenced wells as their source.

The daily production of all RO plants in Gaza in 2015 was 13,000 cubic metres in summer and 9,000 cubic metres in winter. This is equivalent to 4 million m^3 annually (source: PWA 2015).[34] Desalination and water supply have in fact become an important part of the Gaza economy – sales in 2015 were about NIS 130 million ($35 million). Employment in the plants and trucks is estimated at about 1,500–2,000 full-time jobs.

Private water production and transport is based on a simple business model: extraction of brackish water from deep wells, largely private wells located within the operation's site; desalination of this brackish water with small RO plants imported from Israel and distribution of the desalinated water within a 2–5-kilometre radius around the plant through water trucks, each carrying 5–10 cubic metres. A small number of standpipes also supply desalinated water. The investment costs of one of these small plants range between US$ 20,000 and US$ 40,000.

Customers (mainly households) typically buy 250–500 litres of water from a tanker once a week, and store it inside the house. Some poorer customers buy drinking water from supermarkets in 20-litre jerry cans. Truck customers are ready to pay a relatively high tariff for this service (NIS 30–35 per cubic metres, $7–9 per cubic metres), fifteen times or more higher than the tariff for municipal water, which averages NIS 1.90 per cubic metres (US$ 0.50) – but then municipal water is undrinkable. Those buying jerry cans pay considerably more on a per cubic metre basis.

Most of the wells used by private water producers are connected to the national power grid. However, because the power supply is unreliable, most producers also have a standby generator. Few suppliers chlorinate their water. One study found that although most plants are monitored (59 per cent by the Ministry of Health), 'nearly half the RO plants produce water contaminated by coliform'.[35] Tankers and storage tanks in supermarkets and domestic dwellings are rarely properly cleaned.

Nonetheless, Gaza customers are satisfied overall with the private service and are ready to pay for it, stressing water quality and ease of access. A 2016 study concluded that 'whatsoever the evolution of the political and institutional context in the Gaza strip, the private desalination and truck delivery business will continue to grow into the medium term'.[36]

PWA accepts that this coping strategy is the only practical solution for the time being, and that it provides water security at the household level. However, only about 30 per cent of these plants are registered with PWA and the Ministry of Planning and only the registered plants are in compliance with regulation, inspection and water-quality standards. Consumers rate water quality as generally high and attribute this to the strong competition in the market. Given the findings on coliform contamination, PWA has concerns and recommends that the water be chlorinated at both the plant and household levels.[37]

Household-level desalination Household-level desalination also became popular in recent years. Over half of Gaza households have installed small reverse osmosis (RO) desalination units in their kitchens – each unit costs about US$300–400. Production capacity is about 100–200 litres a day, and water quality is high, reaching TDS levels of below 100, and filtering out the nitrates, which are frequently present at dangerously high levels in Gaza's groundwater. It is estimated that the Gaza private sector has supplied about 100,000 of these small RO units over the years.

Access by the poor Poor households are unable to afford a domestic RO installation and, as we have seen, would typically have to purchase jerry cans at a relatively high price. There are, however, low-cost alternatives available for poor households. One is 200-litre polyethylene tanks, which are filled by a tanker once a week at a price of 10 NIS (US$3.25). The tanks themselves have often been given free, as the household enters into a contract with the private provider.

Risks Although private sector desalination is generally affordable, self-sufficient and sustainable, it is very energy intensive, with electricity accounting for almost two thirds (60 per cent) of total operating costs. For a household, the installation of an RO desalination unit can increase monthly electricity expenses by up to 25 per cent. In addition, production from all types of plant is subject to interruption from the frequent power cuts.[38] Restrictions on movement and access and frequent closures of checkpoints limit the import of spare parts and of essential chemicals, including chlorine for disinfection and the sodium hydroxide needed to restore the pH balance of desalinated water.

The possible future role of small- and medium-scale desalination options Despite the huge economies of scale of larger desalination plants and piped network supply, the combination of smaller-scale desalination and tanker/supermarket delivery is in many ways a lower-risk option. The capital cost of a small plant is within the reach of the Gazan private sector, and small plants are technically easier to put up and run. Small-scale production is very flexible and responsive to demand, and this is a vibrant area for entrepreneurship and for public-private partnerships, provided that questions of regulation and water-quality control can be resolved. The main problem is the cost to the consumer – as we have seen, current prices are of the order of NIS 30–35 per cubic metres, about $7–9 per cubic metres – which may be affordable for small quantities of drinking water but not for all domestic supplies.

Medium-scale plants may also be a viable option. An example of this approach is the recently constructed UNICEF plant which opened in 2017 in the southern part of the Gaza Strip. The plant, which cost 10 million euros ($11.3 million) and was financed by the EU, is in fact the largest desalination plant in the Strip at present. With a capacity of 6,000 cubic metres a day or 2 million cubic metres a year, the plant is designed to supply 80 litres of potable water each day to 75,000 people in the towns of Khan Younis and Rafah. UNICEF has already started work to triple the capacity of the plant.

USAID has also supported medium-scale desalination, although encountering considerable implementation hitches. The Middle Area Desalination Plant was expanded in 2017–18 under a USAID contract to a capacity of 4,500 cubic metres a day, about 1.7 million cubic metres a year. According to USAID, 'the twenty-four-month project was not without challenges in this volatile area.' These 'challenges' included negotiating the entry of each container-load of equipment one by one with the Israeli Ministry of Defence.[39] However, USAID reported as of 31 January 2019 that the plant had been successfully commissioned and handed over to the PWA.

There are advantages to medium-scale plants. One is that management requirements and risks are lower than for large-scale plants – medium-scale plants could be run either by non-governmental organizations, by public organizations or by the private sector. On the other hand, there are challenges and risks, notably the dependence on imported energy and spares. Already in January 2019 it was reported that, with only four to five hours of electricity available daily in Gaza, the

Figure 6.1 Children fetching water from a temporary tank in the Gaza Strip, with the ruins of the Khuza'a water tower in the background, Photograph by courtesy of CMWU.

UNICEF plant was producing well below capacity. A solar energy field was being built to even out energy supplies.[40]

A hybrid option A hybrid option might be to associate medium- or smaller-scale desalination with local area networks. Brackish aquifer water would continue to be supplied through the current network and desalinated water would be distributed through a separate network only for potable purposes. The logic is essentially both cost and feasibility. If a ration of 20 litres of drinking water per day is taken, just five or six medium-scale plants would suffice to provide potable water to the entire population. The idea then would be to bypass the major cost incurred in distributing potable water by tanker by constructing a separate piped supply system dedicated to the potable desalinated water.

This parallel system would deliver relatively small quantities of drinking water to households (or to standpipes or neighbourhood centres or shops). The current supply of brackish water through the old network would continue, providing water for non-potable domestic uses. This approach of a separate system for potable water is already practiced in Gaza on a small scale with some standpipes and public fountains. Such dual systems are not unknown around the world – some towns in Florida and Arizona already use dual network supply systems like this. The advantages are that potable water would come to households out of the tap at a lower cost than if desalinated water were mixed with saline groundwater in a single network. The disadvantages are the cost of duplicating the network and the continued drain on the aquifer.

Larger-scale desalination within Gaza[41]

As we have seen, larger-scale desalination has long been on the table as the solution to Gaza's drinking water problems. The option of a major desalination plant within the Strip and use of desalinated water as the principal source of network supply was first mooted in a big way soon after Oslo, and USAID went a long way towards completing the studies for the plant. However, the project fell afoul of politics after Hamas took over Gaza. It has now been revived, with different backers. Plans for the construction of a single large-scale central plant together with supply and distribution infrastructure are now being supported by donors led by the European Commission, the European Investment Bank, the Islamic Development Bank and the World Bank. In March 2018, donors committed 456 million euros ($560 million) to build the plant.

The project is for a seawater reverse osmosis (SWRO) plant with an initial capacity of 55 million cubic metres and a final objective of an overall capacity of 100 million cubic metres. The initial capacity would be adequate to supply 85 litres a day of potable water to each resident throughout the Gaza Strip.[42] Power will be initially provided by an on-site plant. Extra electricity will be provided by a photovoltaic plant installed on the roofs of the SWRO buildings, together with off-site photovoltaic capacity on ground structures, and two wind turbines. Longer term, power is to be supplied from the grid (see discussion herein).

Alongside the project for the plant itself an 'associated works' programme will include construction of a North–South carrier which will allow the distribution of the desalinated water throughout the Gaza Strip. The works will also include reservoirs for storing desalinated water and for blending it with water from other sources, primarily groundwater. In order to save as much of this precious and expensive desalinated water as possible, the current high rate of system leakages will be reduced. A non-revenue water reduction plan will be designed to reduce non-revenue losses within the distribution system from the current average 38 per cent to about 20 per cent by the year 2030. The plan is also to provide for action to increase revenue collection efficiency from the current 38 per cent to 80 per cent and above.[43]

Inevitably in the Gaza context, the risks are considerable during both construction and operation. The main risks during construction are hostilities and Israeli movement and access controls, particularly on hardware. The problems are well illustrated by the experiences with the USAID-financed Middle Area Desalination Plant described earlier. The main risk during operations, apart from the ever-present risk of hostilities breaking out, is energy supply which is critical to the desalination process. The plan is to provide some resilience by covering up to 15 per cent of the energy needs from the renewable solar and wind facilities described earlier. However, at present the main source of energy is likely to be the Israeli grid, and the plan requires cooperation with Israel for major power supply through a new transmission line.[44]

Within the first two years of operation, the power supply will be covered by the on-site plant using reciprocating engines fired with diesel fuel. Once the grid connection is in place, the reciprocating engines will serve as backup only, to mitigate the risk of interruption of the power supply. If Gaza by then has access to natural gas, the engines will be switched from diesel fuel to natural gas firing. This will depend on progress of the Gas for Gaza programme, for which planning procedures have already begun on Israeli territory.

This is a costly programme and water production costs will be high. Overall, the total capital cost is estimated at about 515 million euros (about $580 million). Annual operating costs are expected to be in the range 65–110 million euros ($75–125 million), depending largely on energy supply options. This translates into average water tariffs to cover supply costs of euros 0.70 to 1.20 per cubic metre ($0.80–1.40), with the difference mainly depending on availability of grid connection and natural gas. Because these costs are well above current tariff levels (average NIS 1.90 per cubic metres, $ 0.50) and are high for the relatively poor Gaza population, the sponsors are proposing a fund of 46 million euros ($52 million) as an operational subsidy to reduce water bills for low-income households. Key to the feasibility of this scheme will be the cooperation of Israel, which is said to have 'agreed in principle on the regime to apply for entry of materials and on important developments with the *Gas for Gaza* pipeline'.

In summary, there are many pros but also significant cons to this desalination option. The advantages of this option are that the source is within Gaza, so it brings some measure of autonomy, and there is limitless raw material. The disadvantages are the high capital cost of both the plant and the main and distribution networks (the 'associated works');[45] the difficulty of doing big infrastructure projects in Gaza; the high-energy requirement, hence high cost and dependency on Israel; and the high cost of the desalinated water to be supplied to the consumer. Beyond that is the military, strategic and geopolitical risk of a project and operating arrangements that inevitably require continual cooperation between Israel and the Gaza authorities. Finally, as with Israel's desalination projects, the carbon footprint will be high unless more power can be provided from renewable sources.

At the time of writing (2020), the World Bank and partners had approved $117 million for a first phase of the associated works which would finance the construction of the southern part of a Gaza water carrier and the distribution infrastructure to bring 30 million cubic metres of water annually to 870,000 people in 16 municipalities in the southern and middle governorates. Although presented as part of the larger declination project, these works essentially comprise the infrastructure that could just as well convey and distribute imported water.[46]

Purchasing desalinated water from Israel

Israel is currently in a position of water surplus, or at least of potential water surplus, and hence there could be extra availability for supply to Gaza. Desalinated water is potentially available from the desalination plants along the coast of Israel (see Chapter 1) – these plants are reported to be working at only 75 per cent of their total capacity of 585 million cubic metres, and to be looking for commercial sales. Further Israeli desalination capacity of an extra 300 million cubic metres is expected to come on stream by 2023 from a second plant at Sorek and from one in Western Galilee (Chapter 1). A purchase under the guise of a commercial transaction could to some extent depoliticize the issue of water imports. Diplomatically, the first purchases could be implemented under the possible Red–Dead agreement where Israel commits to supplying an extra 34 million cubic metres to the Palestinians annually, including 10 million m^3 for Gaza.

The advantages of purchasing from Israel are that it is technically simple and the initial quantities of water are readily available from two plants not far distant, at Ashdod and Ashkelon. Meeting the current demand[47] for domestic potable water (55 million cubic metres annually) and projected demand by 2035 (100 million cubic metres) would represent from 10 per cent to 17 per cent of Israel's current production capacity – and, as we have seen, Israel is planning further capacity. Sales could be on a turnkey commercial basis from the delivery points already available along the border. Increasing levels of purchases would, nonetheless, require new infrastructure not only within Israel but also on the Palestinian side – essentially the water carrier the length of the Gaza Strip included in the associated works mentioned earlier, which are being designed to serve either the large-scale Gaza desalination option or deliveries from Israel.

Further water purchase from Israel is thus a feasible option, but the prospect would inevitably raise questions of politics on both sides. For the Palestinians it would be a politically unpalatable solution and would be seen as increasing strategic vulnerability. The increased dependence on Israel would inevitably be seen as diminishing Gaza's water security – or at least its 'water autonomy' – and it would create apparently economic ties that risked getting tangled in politics. In addition, it would be a relatively high-cost option, given the high unit cost of water purchased and the high cost of the associated works. Cost, which would depend on negotiation with Israel, could, however, be lower than for desalinated water produced within Gaza – the marginal ex-factory cost of Israel's desalinated water is as little as $0.54 per cubic metres (see Chapter 1), which compares with the likely ex-factory cost of the Gaza plant of $0.80 per cubic metres or more.

Water supply services

Deterioration and resilience

When we were in Gaza in 2008 we found high rates of network coverage, but border closures and conflict had led to severe deterioration of water supply reliability. Water supply coverage and water availability were in fact better on paper than in the West Bank, and theoretical water availability had risen by 50 per cent between 2000 and 2005, from 52 million cubic metres to about 76 million cubic metres. The rate of connections was high, covering all forty Gaza communities and 98 per cent of the then population (1.36 million out of 1.39 million). Per capita supply was higher than in the West Bank, and had been going up, with average daily supply (before losses) of 152 litres per person in 2005, compared with 97 litres (before losses) in the West Bank. However, water quality was already appalling, and very few people actually drank from the tap or used network water for cooking.[48]

In addition to the undrinkable quality of supplies, efficiency was already in steep decline. Average consumption was only 60 per cent of supply levels, due to network losses. For the same reason, although total municipal supply had increased by 24 million m^3 2000-2008, actual availability after losses increased only by 10 million m^3, from 35 million m^3 to 45 million m^3, over the same period. Some 15 million cubic metres, two thirds of the increased supply, was simply lost to leakages and illegal connections.

Our 2008 visit to the Strip coincided with a period of crisis in water supply. As the movement and access restrictions began to bite, it had become increasingly difficult to maintain services. From around 2005, water supply had started to become very intermittent, and, when we were there, it had fallen to crisis levels as the deteriorating political and security situation curtailed access to power, fuel and spare parts. In November 2008, most water wells had stopped because of lack of spares, others were working at half capacity. Electricity cuts and lack of diesel for generators had affected water distribution through the network as well as the ability to pump water up to household rooftop reservoirs. The utility had run out of chlorine, the chemical indispensable to ensuring water disinfection. There was also a lack of related chemicals such as anti-scalants and of all manner of spare parts. Small items such as membranes and dosing pumps were available 'through the tunnels' – at twice the price. As a result, at the time, more than 50 per cent of households did not have access to network water at all, and many of those that did had not had water for more than ten days.

The private sector and households had their recourses. As we have seen, they were coping through unlicenced wells and small-scale desalination, but the utility revenue base had collapsed and the collection rate had fallen to 20 per cent. The public water suppliers were collecting only 20 cents on the dollar.

The December 2008/January 2009 military offensive that occurred just after our November 2008 visit caused severe damage to the networks, creating yet worse supply conditions and requiring substantial rehabilitation efforts. In late February 2009, 150,000 people were still cut off from network supply, and in three areas (Sheja'yaa, Zaitoun and Tal Elhawa) damaged infrastructure had led to contamination of drinking water supply by sewage.[49] The continued closures were preventing the import of pipes and other materials needed to rehabilitate destroyed water supply and sanitation systems, worsening negative impacts on Gaza's population and water institutions. Some items were held up for more than eighteen months before they were cleared by Israel. Some items were never cleared.

Water supply today

The performance of Gaza's water suppliers We came back to Gaza almost a decade later, in a relatively quiet period in late 2017. When we took a close look at service provider performance, we found a very mixed picture. Connection rates were still high, but they had not kept pace with the expansion of the number of people and households (see Table 6.2). The reported connection rates of around 93 per cent were down from the 98 per cent recorded ten years earlier. Average quantities (before losses) being delivered through the network were 92 litres per person per day, slightly higher than in the West Bank (average 80 litres in 2014, see Chapter 3), but low by global standards.[50] These average figures masked wide variations amongst service providers, ranging from 74 litres a day to 114 litres. Variations were, however, much less dramatic than in West Bank, where the range was from 26 litres a day right up to 242 litres.

Most service providers were delivering water only intermittently. Only 30 per cent of households in Gaza had daily network water supply, compared to 50 per cent in the West Bank. Supply in Gaza was also still being affected by the security situation. During the conflict in the summer of 2014, for example, most of the population received no network water for several weeks.[51] However, the key problem of Gaza water supply was simply that with the extremely high levels of salt, almost none of the water delivered through the network was drinkable. In addition, quality with respect to coliform and nitrates was poor – see the performance indicators in Table 6.2.

Network (piped) water is affordable and costs little in relation to incomes, even for the quite poor population of the Strip. Water bills come to no more

Table 6.2 Water Service Key Performance Indicators for the Gaza Strip (KPIs), 2014

Purpose of KPI	Definition of KPI	Gaza: Average	Gaza: Range	IBNET global median[a]
Measuring access	Percentage of households connected to the network[b]	93%	n.a.	89%[c]
Measuring quantity	Quantity of water provided each day to households	92 litres per capita	74–114 litres	162 lcd (119–221 lcd)
Measuring quality	Percentage of samples at source free from total coliform	86%	64–100%	WSRC benchmark for 'good' performance: >95%
Measuring affordability	Selling price	NIS 1.90/m^3	NIS 0.97–5.20	n.a.
	Water cost as share of GNI per capita	0.60%	n.a.	0.55%[d]

Source: WSRC, except 'households connected', which is from the PWA Strategic Development Plan (SDP), 49, and IBNET data, which are from IBNET Blue Book 2014.

Note: IBNET = International Benchmarking Network for Water and Sanitation Utilities; GNI = gross national income; KPI = key performance indicators; WSRC = Water Sector Regulatory Council; n.a. = not applicable.

[a] Based on data for over 1,000 utilities worldwide.

[b] These data on access from the supply side are close to the demand side data from the MICS and LGPA.

[c] IBNET Blue Book Table 1.1.

[d] IBNET Blue Book Table 1.14.

than about 0.6 per cent of median per capita income, about equal to the global median, although the cost varies widely amongst the twenty-five providers, with one municipality charging NIS 5.20 per cubic metres, the equivalent of more than $1.50.[52] However, as we have seen, almost all Gaza households depend on more costly tanker water for drinking, and the biggest household water cost is tanker water at much higher prices.

The efficiency of Gaza's water suppliers

Levels of water lost from the system before it reaches the customer represent a dramatic loss for a very water-scarce economy.[53] Almost two fifths of water supplied in the Strip is being lost before it reaches consumers – non-revenue water averages 38 per cent, and as much as 53 per cent in one governorate (North) – see Table 6.3 *Efficiency and Financial Viability.* These losses amounted to 600 litres per day *for every connection in the Strip*, enough to almost double water supply to each household.

Suppliers were recovering only a small fraction of what it cost to supply the water. Average costs in fact were relatively moderate – only half West Bank levels and equivalent to the global average, although the range is very wide, from NIS 0.88 to 6.89 per cubic metres ($0.23–1.97). However, tariff rates were low. With a working ratio averaging 1.50, on average, the typical supplier was billing customers only 67 cents for every dollar of cost. Worse, with a collection efficiency of 37 per cent, only one person in three paid for their network water anyway. The highest

Table 6.3 Efficiency and Financial Viability Key Performance Indicators for the Gaza Strip (KPIs), 2014

		Gaza		IBNET global median
Purpose of KPI	**Definition of KPI**	**Average**	**Range**	
Measuring efficiency	Percentage of non-revenue water WSRC benchmark for 'good' performance: <28%	38%	25–53%	27%[a]
	Operating costs per m³ of water sold	NIS 2.71	NIS 0.88–6.89	NIS 2.68[b]
Measuring financial viability	Working ratio (operating costs/ sales – > 1 = deficit) WSRC benchmark for 'good' performance: between 1 and 0.95	1.50	0.75–5.75	0.92[c]
	Collection efficiency WSRC benchmark for 'good' performance: >95%	37%	5–56%	n.a.

Source: WSRC.

Note: IBNET = International Benchmarking Network for Water and Sanitation Utilities; KPI = key performance indicators; WSRC = Water Sector Regulatory Council.

[a] IBNET Blue Book, Table 1.3

[b] IBNET Blue Book, Table 1.9. Median \$0.70/m³ = NIS 2.68/m³; highest quartile, \$0.40/m³ = NIS 1.53/m³; lowest quartile, \$1.12/m³ = NIS 4.29/m³.

[c] IBNET Blue Book, Table 1.8. The median operating cost coverage was 1.09 = working ratio of 0.92; the highest quartile operating cost coverage was 1.38 = working ratio of 0.72; and the lowest quartile operating cost coverage was 0.83 = working ratio of 1.20.

collection rate amongst all twenty-five service providers was only 56 cents on the dollar. One provider collected just 5 cents on the dollar.

It is no surprise, therefore, that the financial performance of Gaza service providers was amongst the worst in the world. The high level of non-revenue water, the low selling price and very low collection efficiency mean that the average service provider was covering less than one quarter (24 per cent) of its costs. This dramatically low viability leaves service providers dependent on subsidies for both operations and investment, with little room for improving services and with no prospect of attracting private finance. As in the West Bank, service providers finance their operations simply by not paying their bills.

Sanitation and wastewater

When we were in Gaza in 2008, we found sanitation services in crisis. In only one way was the situation better than in the West Bank – almost two thirds (60 per cent) of Gaza households were connected to a sewerage network, compared to only 30 per cent in the West Bank. However, some municipalities in the Strip, Rafah for example with just 2 per cent of households connected, had virtually no network sewerage at all. But the big problem was in what happened to the sewage that entered the system, and in what happened when it came out.

Sewage treatment was vestigial. The three existing wastewater treatment plants were functioning only intermittently, so little sewage was being treated. Most was simply being discharged raw to lagoons, wadis and the sea. We saw huge sewage lakes, turgid, brown, disgusting, right next door to where people were living. The largest of the three plants – the Gaza City treatment plant – had been overloaded way beyond capacity. At the time of our visit, the WHO told us the plant had 'not been functioning for more than a year'.[54]

Coping strategies at Khan Younis

The two households in five which were not connected to a sewerage network were using cess pits and in the prevailing economic climate they were not being properly emptied. At Khan Younis, for example, cess pits were releasing foul water into the aquifer, and we saw it flooding on the roads. Typically, most of the emptying of cess pits was by municipal trucks, and there were some discharge points where the trucks could empty into the sewer system. However, people were poor and most households found paying for emptying by truck too expensive. They would have had to have paid out NIS 20–30 each time (about $7–10). In any case, the treatment plants were not capable of dealing with the extra load.

At Khan Younis, a new wastewater treatment plant was still only on the drawing board, so all the sewage collected by the trucks was being dumped into storm water drains and into the lagoon. In fact, this Khan Younis treatment plant project had long been in Palestinian plans. Money for a sewage network, pumping station and treatment plant had originally been committed by Japan as far back as 2000. However, once the *al Aqsa intifada* got underway, the Japanese withdrew. Then $13 million was provided by Italy for the network and pump station, but after Hamas took over in Gaza, the Italian contribution too was frozen.

In the meantime, residents had to make do and mend. Most people connected their sewer outlets to the storm drainage system. When we were there, raw sewage was flowing into the stormwater lagoon at Hay al Aml. The stormwater box culvert in the lagoon had blocked up with solid matter, so the sewage was being pumped out to four further temporary lagoons. The local authorities said that these lagoons too were rapidly filling up, and soon the sewage would have to be pumped raw to the sea. The sanitary engineer on site threw up his hands and said, 'This is not a solution. This should not be done. Now they will pollute the sea, and Gaza's last clean beach. Where will I take my kids at the weekend?' When we taxed the PWA people with this, all they could say was 'Any of this, all of this – the lagoons, the pumping, the beaches, everything – it's all for emergency. It's not a project. We never planned for this.'[55]

Beit Lahiya

In 2008, we also went to Beit Lahiya to see the North Gaza Emergency Sewage Treatment (NGEST) project. This World Bank–financed project was under construction. In fact during our visit we were confidently told that the plant was 'almost complete'. Its bold aim was secondary treatment and ultimately to recharge the aquifer with treated wastewater, using the techniques the Israelis had mastered (see Chapter 1). In the meantime, wastewater was being stored in the notorious Beit Lahiya sewage lake. 'Notorious' because it was at Beit Lahiya that in March 2007 an emergency lagoon embankment had failed, causing a deadly tide of sewage to flood the village of Um Al Nasser. Five people died, drowned in filth, and 2,000 lost their homes.

This disgusting incident made people sit up. The NGEST project was approved by the World Bank board on an emergency basis and then began the arduous business of implementation under the ever-tighter security controls. Tony Blair, who was at the time the Quartet Special Representative, took on the role of fixer with the support of his team, encouraged by the international community and by environmental and humanitarian lobbies in Israel. As a result, the project, the first major infrastructure investment to be implemented in Gaza in eight years, was treated as an 'exception' by the Israeli Defense Forces (IDF). The IDF had agreed to this on the proviso that the World Bank should act as an impartial third party to oversee logistics, particularly the movement of goods and parts. Every two weeks, meetings were held to review the movement of all goods, item by item. Every three months a larger group, including the Israeli Ministry of Defence, discussed higher-level issues, such as design problems and the movement of workers. On occasion USAID, because of its clout with the parties and in the sector, would participate.

Despite all this, each truck had to be individually cleared by the Israeli Ministry of Defence, the Civil Administration, Shin Bet (Israeli intelligence agency) and the IDF. In addition, border crossings into Gaza were frequently closed, causing additional delays. Delays were also experienced as design specifications had to be modified, changing steel pipes for PVC in some parts of the plan, where feasible. Even getting workers on- and off-site every day was difficult as the construction site was 200 metres from the security barrier around Gaza. The movement of each worker had to be cleared every day by the IDF.[56]

At the time, there were differing takes on the Beit Lahiya experience. An engineer on the project told us, 'It took five deaths in a flood of sewage for the Israelis to relent. Tony Blair had to call Ehud Barak personally to get the last few truckloads of materials through.' A member of the Israeli Water Authority commented: 'We helped a lot with Beit Lahiya. The army said "No", but we persuaded them. And Palestinians did use the pipes for *qissam*! (steel rockets).' However, this official did not think the Beit Lahiya approach was a real solution: 'My ability to help as long as they are shooting at civilians is small – the media will kill us. Chlorine is alright, they can claim it is an epidemic.' Another senior Israeli official saw progress on NGEST implementation as a demonstration of Israeli good faith – and Palestinian bad faith: 'We helped them despite the security considerations. It shows that if they have a good reason, they can implement. But they don't want.'

Until the new plant was ready, the sewage had to be stored. So, soon after the 2007 flood, two more temporary lagoons had been built to hold the sewage. When we were there, with the treatment plant not yet ready, the stopgap lagoons were still in use. However, the effluent level in the lagoons was rising and the management said there was not enough power to pump the sewage out. One of the temporary lagoons did actually collapse during our visit, mercifully without loss of life. But then came the intense hostilities of December 2008 and January 2009, On 7 January 2009, at the height of hostilities, the normally reticent World Bank put out a press release:

WORLD BANK NEWS RELEASE, JANUARY 7, 2009, DISSEMINATED DURING THE ISRAELI OFFENSIVE ON GAZA: BEIT LAHIYA SEWAGE LAKE

Lake structure requires constant and vigilant maintenance under normal conditions. Pumps transferring sewage from the lake to infiltration basins, critical to the relief of pressure on structure, are not in operation due to lack of electricity and fuel. The integrity of the lake structure is endangered by the potential impact of nearby explosions and sonic booms and possible heavy rain. Failure of the lake structure would put about 10,000 residents of the surrounding area in danger of drowning and spark a wider environmental and public health disaster.

The Government of Israel should immediately facilitate entry of and safe transport of fuel, spare parts and PWA maintenance staff to the lake site. In addition to refraining from deliberately targeting the structure itself, a wide no-fire zone should be secured around the lake.

When we went back to the Strip nearly ten years on, in 2017, we were eager to see NGEST at work. But incredibly, they told us that the project was still 'nearing completion' – more than a decade after the emergency operation was initiated and eight years after we had been told that the plant construction was almost complete. The World Bank reported soberly : 'The project faced numerous challenges, including years of blockade, restrictions on the entry of critical materials and equipment, damages from war and conflict to existing infrastructure, and suspension of works due to hostilities.'

In the meantime, as the Bank also laconically reported 'raw wastewater has no border' and every day of the years between our two visits to Beit Lahiya tens of thousands of tons of raw sewage had been seeping into the groundwater or flowing straight into the Mediterranean Sea. Not only had Gaza's entire coast been polluted but sewage was reaching Israeli beaches and threatening to clog the intakes of the desalination plants at Ashdod and Ashkelon – the Ashkelon plant, which supplies about 15 per cent of Israel's drinking water, had been closed several times. Sewage was also flowing over the land border, 'flowing through Nahal Hanun [and collecting] in the sands of Moshav Netiv Ha'asara, polluting the area and the groundwater. Once every few days, Israeli trucks come and draw the sewage.' In 2017, the IWA ordered construction of a sewage pipe at the Erez Crossing to take the wastewater to treatment plants in Sha'ar Hanegev and Sderot.[57]

Eventually, in March 2018, the Beit Lahiya plant was commissioned, complete with a pressure pipeline, a new terminal pumping station and nine infiltration basins. However, the problems did not end there. The treatment facility requires sufficient power to operate, which is not always available due to the persistent Gaza electricity crisis. The Palestinians and the Israelis made some temporary power arrangements specifically for the plant, but what was really needed to make sure the facility worked properly all the time was a dedicated electricity line built from Israel straight to the plant. We were told that Israel had actually approved the request after long delays – but nothing had so far happened on the ground.[58]

The sanitation situation today

On our return visit to Gaza in 2017 we found that the intervening decade had seen considerable investment in wastewater and that this was beginning to make some difference on the ground. In fact, Gaza wastewater was much the biggest recipient of investment in the Palestinian water sector over the period. Even though investment effectiveness had continued to be restricted by hostilities, incursions and movement and access restrictions and other constraints, improvements had resulted. Levels of wastewater collection and treatment were higher than in the West Bank. According to a 2016–17 survey, the *Local Government Performance Assessment* (LGPA), virtually the entire population (99 per cent) of Gaza had access to 'improved unshared sanitation', with 78 per cent now connected to sewage networks.[59]

By 2017, about 48 million cubic metres of wastewater was being collected each year, half of the total water supply to M&I uses. Over 90 per cent of this collected wastewater was being at least partially treated. However, plants were still overloaded and functioning poorly, partly as a result of underfunding and partly as a result of Israel's restrictions on movement and access of people and goods. Partially treated wastewater (25 million cubic metres a year) and raw sewage (7 million cubic metres a year) – over 80,000 tons a day – were still being discharged to ponds and to the sea.

Even treated effluent was often of poor quality and there was little or no reuse. Households not connected to the sewer network – nearly one quarter (22 per cent) of all households – still had recourse to cess pits. Emptying and disposal of sewage from these pits remained a problem, especially for the poor. According to the LGPA, more than a third (35 per cent) of Gaza households in the poorest quintile had experienced a sewage overflow in the previous twelve months.[60]

Health and environmental impacts

With such poor water supply and sanitation conditions, health impacts are predictably severe. When we were in Gaza in 2008, the WHO told us 'a quarter of all disease in Gaza is water related'. They reported that the proportion of contaminants in the samples they collected from wells was growing fast.[61] A WHO study had found a high concentration of nitrates in the water supply from wells in different localities within the Strip, and this nitrate contamination was found to be the cause of the incidence of 'blue-baby syndrome' amongst infants. While this disease primarily affects young children, nitrate contamination can also affect pregnant women and can increase the risk of certain types of cancer.[62]

In the summer of 2017, a five-year-old boy died in Gaza after swimming in a pool of polluted water. According to Professor Nadav Davidovitch, chairman of the Public Health Doctors Organization in Israel and head of the Public Health School at Ben-Gurion University: 'People in Gaza live below the red line and are at high risk of respiratory and intestinal diseases. At the moment there is no cholera in Gaza, but it is enough for someone who is sick to arrive to Gaza for the disease to spread. The conditions on the ground will cause the disease to spread like wildfire.'[63]

The impact on the environment is dramatic. In 2009, Wadi Gaza was choked with sewage and it was no better when we were there in 2017. Palestinian attempts to obtain UNESCO World Heritage status for the Wadi Gaza coastal wetlands, a vital staging post for birds between Europe, Asia and Africa, were on hold because the wadi was full of sewage and stinking to high heaven.[64] The effect on the coastline is dire. Along the length of the Strip, sixteen sewage outfalls go direct to the coast, releasing 70,000–80,000 cubic metres of wastewater every day into the sea. This is more than half of all Gaza's sewage, 70,000–80,000 tons of foul untreated or partially treated sewage pouring out day after day into the Mediterranean. Faecal coliform bacteria cluster around the outfalls where the raw sewage flows out. Fish are infected, and the beaches are fouled. One of the few amenities of life for families in Gaza is ruined. The livelihoods of those who depend on the sea for their income are under threat.

Due to coastal zone mixing and currents, Gaza's sewage discharges can affect water quality at the intake of the Israeli desalination plant at Ashkelon. Israeli estimates of the quantities discharged are higher – 'approximately 100,000 cubic meters of untreated sewage flow daily from the Gaza Strip into the Mediterranean Sea and the coast of Israel'. Israel's beaches are forced to close and, as we have seen, the Israeli government has approved a plan to pipe at least some of Gaza's sewage away and to treat it within Israel.[65]

The emerging health and environmental catastrophe is contributing to Israeli rethinking about Gaza. Israeli outrage is driven not only by humanitarian concern but by concerns for their own environment and economy. Israelis may even see these sewage flows as a continuation of what, as we saw, Ariel Sharon dubbed a 'sewage *intifada*'. Rotem Caro Weizman from Israeli EcoPeace told the 2018 Sderot Conference on the Gaza water and sanitation crisis that 'Gaza's sewage managed to do what Hamas missiles failed to do – paralyze an Israeli strategic infrastructure. The crisis in Gaza will not remain in Gaza alone but will threaten and harm Israel and regional stability – it is one of not just health and environmental factors but of national security.'[66]

This view is shared by segments of the Israeli military establishment who consider that the humanitarian crisis is worsening the political and security environment. At the 2018 Sderot Conference, a senior officer, Eyal Ben-Reuven, noted that it is 'impossible and incorrect to separate the military-security reality from the humanitarian one . . . regional efforts should be sought to solve the humanitarian crisis and Israel should lead these efforts. We are much closer to fire and war than to reconciliation.'[67]

> 'Gaza is a ticking time bomb,' General Ben-Reuven went on to say. 'In the winter and summer there are 6-8 hours of electricity a day and this is a terrible situation for the general population, especially the children. This impasse lays the groundwork for hatred and terror among these children – the evils we wish to eradicate. In Israel, when we talk about Gaza, we only talk about the security situation and we do not talk about the humanitarian issue – it's not published in the media. Israel has a deep interest in forming and leading an international humanitarian campaign on this issue – to connect the regional and international components that are willing to take part in this effort.'

Water for agriculture

A desert of greenhouses

When we went to Gaza in 2008, we were hoping to see prosperous agriculture. Farming uses half the scarce water and is the mainstay of Gaza's productive economy. Some 80 per cent of residents who were refugees from what is now Israel, or their descendants, hailed from displaced farming families. Agriculture was their natural vocation and before 1967 agriculture was the most important productive sector. In 1966, on the eve of the Occupation, one third of employment was in agriculture, and agriculture and fisheries combined contributed over one quarter of Gaza's GDP (26 per cent). Financed largely by remittances, citrus groves had expanded greatly, up from 16,000 dunams (1,600 hectares) in 1960 to 68,000 dunams (nearly 7,000 hectares) in 1966. As a result, citrus production was booming, with output reaching 250,000 tons and bringing in $20 million a year in export earnings.[68]

The Occupation brought structural change. By 1986, nearly half the Gaza workforce (45 per cent, 45,000 people) were working in Israel. This dependence on Israeli employment was reflected in the agriculture sector within Gaza, which by 1986 was employing only 7,800 people. In fact, a slightly higher number of Gaza Palestinians were employed in Israeli agriculture (7,900) than in their own agriculture back home. What was prospering in agriculture in the Strip was horticulture practiced by the Israeli settlers there. In 1986, settlers had 3,000 dunams (300 hectares) of greenhouses in the Strip, outstripping by far Palestinian greenhouses which occupied only 570 dunams (less than 60 hectares). The settler operation was hi-tech, high-value, drip-irrigated and fertigated horticulture for export to Israel and beyond, with revenues of up to $100 million a year.

Then the *al Aqsa intifada* broke out and hostilities and reprisals wrought terrible damage on Palestinian infrastructure. It was reported that some 370 agricultural wells were destroyed by the IDF during the troubles.[69] At length, in 2005, came the Israeli pull-out and, with the withdrawal of the settlers, hope returned for a while. There was, in fact, a 'withdrawal dividend' for agriculture – in September 2005, control of some 4,000 dunams (400 hectares) of land which had been farmed by settlers was handed over to the Palestinians. With international support, including from James Wolfensohn, the former head of the World Bank who was then heading up the Quartet, management of the site was taken over by PADICO, a Palestinian company established and owned by the PA. The key asset here was not the land or even the wells. It was the vast area of greenhouses the Israelis had built for high-value horticulture.

Wolfensohn raised $14 million from US philanthropists, putting in $1 million of his own money and getting $10 million from Bill and Melinda Gates. During 2005 and into 2006 the greenhouses were rebuilt and operations were launched. Some 4,500 workers were recruited, with 300 supervisors. Subcontractors were brought in to repair and manage the wells and the irrigation systems. A first crop was planted, mainly tomatoes, strawberries, peppers and herbs. In November 2005, this first crop was harvested and workers began planting a second crop.

Meanwhile, Wolfensohn put all his political capital on the table and got the Americans to induce the Israelis to sign an agreement that would allow export of all agricultural produce from Gaza. Convoys of up to 400 trucks a day to the West Bank were envisaged. But then there was the Netanya suicide bombing of December 2005.Hamas fired some rockets into Israel, Israel responded with military reprisals and a downward spiral began. In 2006, an average of just twelve trucks a day left Gaza, and the tighter the restrictions became, the higher the bribes truckers had to pay at the border to get their consignments through.

With the intermittent hostilities and almost continual border closures, the vast majority of the valuable produce could not leave Gaza for its intended markets. Fruits piled up, rotting, and by 2007 losses had reached an astronomical US$600,000 a day. The operation had to close. When we were there in 2008, the area made a dramatically sad sight, gaunt steel frames stretching as far as the eye could see, all glass shattered, plastic flapping in the wind.[70]

Contemporary Gaza agriculture

Today, although the ambitions of 2005 have long since evaporated, Gaza still has a vital and potentially profitable irrigated agriculture sector. The sector constitutes a relatively small part of the overall economy – 7–8 per cent – but despite all the constraints, agricultural products still account for the lion's share of export earnings – 85 per cent. At least 30,000 Gazans formally work in agriculture, in addition to many informal workers and day labourers. This employment is a vital factor in a territory where unemployment is touching 50 per cent, four fifths of the population are on some kind of social assistance, and nearly 40 per cent live below the poverty line.[71]

Farms are typically small to very small. With more than 20,000 holdings in the Strip, the average farm size is no more than five dunams (half a hectare). More than three quarters of the cropped area (77 per cent) is irrigated, using about 80–90 million cubic metres of water annually. The irrigated area is about 82,000 dunams (8,200 hectares), and the main crops are vegetables (32 per cent of the area), olives (24 per cent), field crops (23 per cent) and fruits (21 per cent). The Palestinian Ministry of Agriculture reports, however, that Palestinian farmers are excluded from areas along the Separation Barrier for up to 1 kilometre and that 'up to 40 per cent of Gaza's cultivable area is inaccessible for this reason'. There is some irrigation with brackish water. Efficiency is high, with average water use of 400–500 cubic metres per dunam (4,000–5,000 cubic metres per hectare), low for such a warm climate and intensive production system. Protected agriculture is the norm. Agriculture can in fact be very profitable, if only outside markets are available. [72]

However, activity has been reduced to low levels. On the production side, the main problem is the decline in water quality. The increasing levels of salt in the water affect yields and farmers are turning to more salt-tolerant crops. Water availability is an issue too. Imad Kamhawi, the head of a USAID agricultural project,[73] told the *Times of Israel* in 2016: 'The issue is there is only eight hours a day of electricity [for pumping water], but you never know when those eight hours are going to come.' Another issue is the difficulty in importing fertilizer which has to come through Israel. Fertilizer is hard to get because it is considered 'dual use' by the Israelis – it can also be used in preparation of explosives.[74]

But the biggest problems are the controls and closures that impede the flow of goods and access to markets. Gazan farmers are competent and experienced. Many of them hail from a centuries-old farming background further up the coast and in the highlands and have agriculture in their blood. They have access to agricultural education at the Beit Hanoun Agricultural School as well as extension services and two agricultural research stations. They have demonstrated that they can adapt to the hi-tech, intensive cultivation technologies which came in during the Israeli Occupation and which they saw the settlers using, and they have access to the capital needed to invest in production systems every bit as advanced as those beyond their borders. But the problem is markets. Production of fresh fruit and vegetables for export requires efficient facilities and management of the whole length of the value chain 'from farm to fork'. The higher-value markets in Europe require not only a perfect product but perfect timing – this quantity, this quality, this size, this standard on each day of, say, a twenty-day window for strawberries in a contract with Marks & Spencer. In this market, an industry in Gaza that may be faced with closure at any hour or on any day is dead in the water.[75]

Getting the produce out of the Strip is the biggest challenge – the riskiest and the most costly. In 2014, Gaza produce was allowed into Israel for the first time since 2007. The move was negotiated as part of the agreement between Israel and Hamas that summer to cease hostilities.[76] However, that did not open a floodgate for exports. Intermittent closures persisted, making it virtually impossible to plan an export campaign and leading to immense waste and loss of earnings. See, for example, this news report from 2018:

> *Israel reopens Gaza commercial crossing after month-long closure.* The crucial Karam Abu Salem border crossing (Kerem Shalom crossing) reopens, allowing the vital transfer of goods into besieged Gaza. Israel sealed off the border last month, saying it was in retaliation over Palestinians setting fire to Israeli land. After partially lifting the closure, Israel blocked the supply of fuel into Gaza two weeks ago.[77]

Even when the border is open, the Israelis still require stringent searches of all Gazan produce. Everything must leave via Israel through the Karam Abu Salem crossing, where it has to go through three separate security areas, and each time the fresh produce must be unloaded and reloaded into separate trucks. This process can take two to four hours. All that time, the fruit and vegetables are in the sun as there are no proper facilities for keeping items cold. Workers have to be paid for each unloading and reloading, which adds to costs.[78]

Strawberry farmer Ahmed Shafai, seventy-nine, told the *Times of Israel* in 2016 that it could cost NIS 4,000 ($1,050) per truck in fees to get it through the border crossing. Produce destined for the West Bank must then go through another similar security check on its way into the West Bank. 'It's actually cheaper to export strawberries to Europe than to Ramallah', Shafai said. He estimated his extra costs due to the security requirements are about NIS 2.9 ($0.90) per kilo, a significant amount when the wholesale price of strawberries is only NIS 11-13 ($3-$4) a kilo.

A telling incident was on 9 May 2016 when the US consul general in Jerusalem wanted to put on a reception with Palestinian *mezze* and juices, with shrimp and sardines caught off the coast of Gaza as well as traditional desserts. First, he had to get special permission to bring in produce from Gaza, and then at the reception he told his wondering and doubtful guests: 'All of the produce and seafood you see before you, that you are eating right now, the fruit in the specialty juices – all of it was produced in Gaza. *I don't think anyone in Jerusalem has been able to say that for the last ten years.*'

A number of international aid organizations are working to improve Gazan agriculture, but these are more coping strategies than economic ventures. The Netherlands has a programme called the *High Value Crops Export Programme* for the production of fresh produce for the European market. A dispatch from the website in 2013 records 'six truckloads of strawberries, spices and carnations were transferred from Gaza on 3 December . . . en route to markets in Europe'.[79] Expectations for the 2013–14 season were over 3,000 tons of vegetables, spices and strawberries as well as 2.5 million stems of flowers. The programme supports quality production but also has an essential 'diplomatic' component. The website contains an appeal from the Dutch government to the Israeli authorities 'to allow the transfer of such crops, and other agricultural products, from Gaza to the West Bank'.

Another initiative, by the FAO, is promoting rooftop gardens in Gaza City, including aquaponics and hydroponics training – enabling families to grow all of their own vegetables using a special blend of water and fertilizers that do not need soil. Aquaponics also allows families to raise their own fish for consumption, since the fish droppings provide fertilizer for the plants in a closed water system.[80]

Planning and investment for water supply and sanitation in Gaza

The struggle to build water systems

The Palestinians have long planned for the improvements they would make to their water systems. Just as for the West Bank, the Palestinian Authority conceived ambitious plans for the Gaza Strip following the Oslo Accords. The 2001 *Master Plan for Water Supply and Sanitation* provided for investment in an integrated water production and conveyance system, inspired by the Israeli model. The system was to include increased supply from local aquifers together with desalination as the two supply sources, construction of a water carrier from the West Bank and the creation of a regional utility and an integrated bulk water system within Gaza. The master plan also proposed a very large expansion of wastewater treatment capacity, including rehabilitation and extension of the three existing plants at Gaza, Beit Lahiya and Rafah, and construction of three new regional treatment plants by 2005, to serve the northern, Gaza City and southern areas.

When we were in Gaza in 2008, four years after the planned investments should have been completed, virtually nothing had been done on the ground. In fact, it had proved impossible to implement the plan under the conditions of intermittent hostilities and constant emergency closures and restrictions. Virtually everything was classified as 'dual use', meaning that the Israelis considered it could be weaponized. Whatever implementation had started had been frustrated by the effect of the continual closures and incursions. PWA and CMWU staff told us: 'We tried with emergency funds to implement the main investments, to do at least the main carrier, replacement of the leaky old network, and to set up brackish water desalination plants. But since 2002, there have been only band-aids.'[81]

In fact, such had been the deterioration in the political and security situation, only emergency projects were being implemented. There were supposed to be fifty-four water and sanitation projects underway in the Strip, but almost all were being held up by delayed approvals and closures. Of the thirteen planned projects of value over $1 million, only three had been completed, and they were the smallest with a combined value of $4.4 million out of a total book value of all the large projects of nearly 100 times as much ($386.9 million). Two of the three completed projects – emergency works at Beit Lahiya and Khan Younis wastewater plants – were stopgap humanitarian projects in response to life-threatening wastewater problems. Of the ongoing projects, only one emergency works project was making much progress – at Beit Lahiya under the North Gaza Emergency

Sewage Treatment Project (NGEST). This was only due to the emergency nature of the problem and to high-level political intervention and intensive managerial effort – but, as we have seen, it was to be a full ten years before this project was completed and actually became operational. Other projects had either not started or they were held up because of lack of materials or other constraints related to the closures.

UN agencies reported in November 2008 that even work on smaller 'relief' projects was impossible. These agencies had a very large number of such projects – bite-sized interventions to relieve some pressing problem – but almost all of these small projects were suspended at the time of our visit. Contracts were being cancelled and engineers laid off. Only one or two projects were going ahead, where the agencies were prepared to take the risk of paying the contractor extra to get material into Gaza.

Going round to talk to these agencies and to see their half-built projects was a depressing experience. UNICEF told us, 'we have hundreds of examples of suspended and cancelled projects.' They said they were 'only doing emergency projects'. They said 'political divisions are undermining the effort . . . and what can you do when there has been no electricity for three weeks?' UNDP said they had been obliged to fire fifty engineers, as no projects were going forward. One $5 million UNDP water project had got started in Rafah but after a year, the agency had been obliged to terminate the contract, which was less than 10 per cent completed, and to pay the contractor compensation. They told us there were '17 cases of contract termination currently . . . three contracts have been launched but are pending . . . the UN Special Representative is trying negotiations with Israel . . . but so far to no avail'.

UNRWA reported fifty contracts suspended or terminated at the time. They had just fired 130 engineers. Only two projects were going ahead – water wells in al Aml at Khan Younis needed to supply a health centre and three schools. But the contractor had asked for more money, an extra $50,000 to complete the job. The UNRWA staff breathed the great *non-dit* – that the extra cost was for 'materials smuggled through the tunnels'.[82]

Pipes had become a virtual impossibility to obtain, and many projects had been left incomplete. In normal times, contractors had to buy their pipes from Israeli factories, which sent them to the border. But by the time of our visit in November 2008, it had become virtually impossible to import pipes at all due to Israeli restrictions on movement and access and security concerns that pipes could be used to make rockets. Even PVC pipes were somehow suspect. Representatives of Khan Younis municipality tried to explain what might seem inexplicable:

> Through UNRWA, we tried to replace 12 inch PVC pipes with 24-inch . . . but this was refused. At Khan Younis, work started in February 2007 to implement the sewage line. Italian financing paid the whole contract sum, but 2,800 metres were left incomplete, so the whole line was unusable. The contractor told us: 'There is no cement either . . . construction materials for three plants have been denied.'[83]

Purchasing materials for water programmes was a challenge at the best of times. Because everything legal had to come through Israel, it took time and costs were high. A private company in Gaza wishing to purchase materials had to apply through the PA in Ramallah, then arrange to purchase from an Israeli middleman, then meet the middleman at the border to clear and receive the goods. International companies had despaired of working in Gaza. An international tender issued in 2007 for the North Gaza wastewater treatment plant was cancelled when no interest from international contractors was found. With each renewed round of fighting, things were growing tighter. Soon after our November 2008 visit, the December 2008 and January 2009 military offensive happened and all conditions promptly worsened. Few of the materials needed even for emergency maintenance were cleared by the Israeli military. Photographic evidence of installation of one consignment was required before a further consignment was authorized.

Another problem was donor politics. Each donor had their own approach, and their own reaction to the political situation. The most sensitive to local conditions was USAID, which had initially agreed to finance the carrier and desalination plant but withdrew after the Hamas takeover of the Strip. Our conclusion in 2008–9 was that fundamental change in the political and security situation was needed to create an environment for renewed investment.

Planning and investment today

Coming back in 2018, we had a look at the official plans put out by the Palestinian Water Authority in Ramallah – the *Water Sector Strategic Development Plan* (SDP) 2017–22 and the *Water Sector Investment Plan* 2017–22 (see Chapter 3). The first thing to say about the proposals for Gaza in these two documents is that there is an air of unreality about them, even stronger than when we looked at the same documents with respect to the West Bank. The unreality flows from a rule of Palestinian planning – that plans should be based on the assumption that Palestinian rights will be restored. The West Bank plans had basically assumed that the Occupation would end and that the shackles of Article 40 would fly off. The Gaza plans assume that implementation of the plans will be unconstrained by any of the restrictions that Israel has maintained on the territory for the best part of two decades.

The second thing to say in the case of Gaza is that the unreality is made denser by the fact that the plans are prepared by a PWA that the Hamas administration does not recognize, to be financed by donors who do not recognize the Hamas administration, and to be facilitated by an Israel that will not treat with the Hamas administration, will do much to frustrate it and will probably continue to act violently towards it and the people it seeks to govern.

The plans for mobilizing extra water resources rely principally on desalination (see Table 6.4). In fact, Gaza dominates the combined Palestinian proposals for water resources development, accounting for nearly nine tenths (88 per cent) of the combined total cost. Desalination in Gaza accounts for nearly half of the very large (160 million cubic metres) increase in supply proposed for both the West

Table 6.4 Water Resources Investment Plan for Gaza 2017–22 – Development of New Water Resources

	Gaza	
Component	**Million m³**	**US$ million**
New wells	15	3.0
Rehabilitation of wells and springs	-	0.6
Desalination plants	68	280.0
Reuse	20	46.0
Total	**103**	**326.0**
Percentage of total for West Bank and Gaza	***65%***	***88%***

Source: SDP.

Bank and Gaza – and three quarters of the total budget. Almost all the proposed increase in desalination capacity (68 million cubic metres) is for Gaza, where one large project and three smaller ones are planned, taking up $280 million (76 per cent of the total budget for water resources) during the five-year period. The one large project is budgeted at US$230 million, and three smaller ones together at $50 million. In fact, subsequent project preparation has shown that these estimates are too low – as we saw in the section *Practices and prospects for desalination*, the current estimated capital cost for the central desalination plant alone is the equivalent of $580 million.

A further one fifth of new supply proposed for Gaza would be reuse of treated wastewater in agriculture. The plan provides for an increase in the share of wastewater treated to about one half of all wastewater produced and for an increase in the reuse of wastewater in agriculture from the current very low levels to 20 million cubic metres, nearly one quarter of the Gaza agricultural water budget (currently 85 million cubic metres). This is intended to drive a rapid increase in the area irrigated with treated wastewater from the current 1,700 dunams (170 hectares) to 24,700 dunams (a little less than 2,500 hectares), more than one quarter of the total area irrigated in the Strip. The question has to be how far this proposal is realistic in terms of treatment capacity and quality, and in terms of farmer uptake.

A further 15 per cent of new supply for Gaza (15 million cubic metres) is slated to come from already overstretched groundwater resources. In the context of the current more than 100 per cent overdraft, it is hard to see how the extra abstractions would not simply contribute to the ongoing galloping depletion and saline intrusion.

The plan also proposes a massive investment in sanitation and wastewater. Investment is proposed in expanding connections to network sewerage, in increasing wastewater treatment capacity and in boosting the share of treated wastewater reused in agriculture (Table 6.5).

As these plans are likely to be realized only in very small part, it is idle to overload them with criticism. Key to the resolution of Gaza's drinking water problem is to determine an economic source of supply that is feasible under current restrictions.

Table 6.5 Gaza Sanitation and Wastewater Targets in the SDP 2017–22

Indicator	Actual 2014	Target 2022
Percentage of households connected to safe sanitation (network or septic tank)	72%	80%
Percentage of wastewater treated in plants	25%	50%
Percentage of treated wastewater meeting specs	n.a.	100%
Area irrigated with treated wastewater	1,700 ha	24,700 ha

We should say that although a central desalination unit is the favoured option, it is a very expensive project – and it may encounter considerable constraints unless political conditions improve. Also, the cost of water will be high in a very poor community. This inevitably raises the question of whether there are no other ways of meeting needs than massive desalination. Some are explored earlier in this chapter – smaller-scale desalination combined with tanker and supermarket delivery, promotion of medium-scale plants, smaller-scale desalination combined with a dual system of local area networks. Here we might question the planning process. It might have served Gaza better to lay out and cost a range of options and assess their feasibility, and then to engage in debate with all stakeholders on the best approach.

The realism of the proposed increase in treated wastewater reuse can also be questioned regarding treatment capacity, water quality, conveyance network and farmer uptake. Regarding the proposals for further groundwater abstraction, it is hard to see how such a Gaza groundwater programme could be made sustainable.

* * *

More than a decade after the Israeli withdrawal from Gaza, conditions under which the population live have only worsened. The water is undrinkable, untreated sewage threatens health and pollutes the environment. Agriculture is in continual decline. Investment proceeds in so faltering a fashion that projects may take a decade or more to produce any benefit, and nothing of the grand vision for water security conceived after Oslo has been realized. There is no central desalination plant, no national carrier the length of the Strip, no universal wastewater collection, treatment and reuse. The level of risk is extraordinarily high. In effect, water security has been in constant recession in the Gaza Strip for more than two decades.

The conclusion has to be that which we made as long ago as 2009, after our first visit to the Strip. There are some solutions which are emerging, particularly ways to increase potable water supply through desalination and an efficient water conveyance and distribution system. But only a fundamental change in the political and security situation can bring to the Palestinians of Gaza water security and all that comes with it in terms of health, welfare, amenity, environmental protection and peace of mind.

WHY ARE THE PALESTINIANS SO WATER INSECURE?

In the conclusion to the assessment of Israeli water security in Part I of this book (Chapter 1), we assessed the factors that have contributed to Israel's world-beating performance under three headings: *integration*, *institutions* and *investment*. To understand the reasons for the palpable water insecurity of the Palestinians, we now use the same three yardsticks.

Integration

How integrated is the Palestinian water system?

The first set of factors we examined in the case of Israel was the remarkably integrated nature of the Israeli water system. The principal features of this are national ownership of the entire water resource, the ample systems of storage and the integrated water network based on the physical national grid that conveys fresh water and desalinated water the length and breadth of the country, connecting all potable sources with all points of use. New sources can be readily plugged in and new centres of demand can be supplied with minimal extra investment. This integrated system has allowed Israel to allocate and reallocate water in line with policy and to balance supply with managed demand, both in normal years and in years of exceptionally low or high rainfall.

As we have seen in Chapter 2, water ownership for West Bank Palestinians is split amongst resources controlled by the West Bank Water Department, resources controlled by municipalities and utilities, and private wells largely controlled by farmers and rural communities. The Palestinians have at best only local area networks or point connections to Mekorot supply and have been unable to develop even regional networks for water transfer. As a result, there are areas with abundant water and others with almost none. Under Article 40, the only new source available is Mekorot water. Whenever a new quantum is agreed, the Palestinians must invest in the infrastructure to carry the water from the point of purchase to the point of demand. Overall, rational planning and development of a bulk water conveyance network are not possible, and there is no certainty of future supplies that would allow rational planning to balance supply and demand.

In the case of Gaza, a carrier is being developed that could convey water either from Israel or from desalination plants within the Strip, so here the problem will be less physical connectivity than sourcing the bulk water – and the willingness of municipalities to link into the integrated network.

Can desalination solve water shortages for Palestinians?

Integrated into Israel's potable water networks is the fast-growing desalination capacity, where Israel leads the world in cutting-edge and cost-efficient technology and business models based on economies of scale and efficient public-private partnerships. Desalination is ideally suited to serving Israel's population which is well-off and mostly concentrated along the coast near to the desalination plants.

On the Palestinian side, the West Bank lacks access to the sea and even to most of the brackish and saline sources within the West Bank. In any case, desalination makes economic sense only to meet demand close to the point of production or at least close to sea level – the economics of desalination and pumping to high elevations prohibit it as a solution for all but the most prosperous of upland communities. However, while desalination should be the solution strictly of last resort for the Palestinian West Bank, it is plainly the solution for Gaza, which is on the coast and has all its centres of population nearby and close to sea level. Nonetheless, although desalination is a must for Gaza, there are high political and financial hurdles to be overcome. Private sector investment is unlikely and the high cost of the product is ill-suited to the poor population the plant would have to serve.

Can Palestinians emulate Israel's record on collecting, treating and reusing wastewater?

Alongside Israel's integrated potable water network is the parallel wastewater system which collects and treats almost all effluent and has the capacity to store and recycle it for economic reuse in agriculture. For the reasons explored in depth in Chapters 4 and 5, Palestinians have only limited capacity to collect and treat wastewater and almost no capacity to reuse it.

Institutions

Do Palestinian institutions have the capacity and the popular support needed to run an efficient water system?

Institutional capacity in Israel is of a high order. Governance is excellent, with strong political oversight and accountability of service providers. The IWA is highly competent. Service providers under the 'stick-and-carrot approach' – see Chapter 1 – have become efficient. Although water prices are high, there is by and large popular consent and cooperation borne of a general satisfaction that the system is delivering efficiently, helped perhaps by a sense of national solidarity in the effort to ensure the nation's water security.

By contrast, Palestinian institutions are relatively weak and work in a widely disabling environment of water shortages and imposed regulatory controls. The PWA has limited staff and service providers struggle to provide decent levels of service.

Public trust is low. The blame is largely laid at Israel's door, with Article 40 seen as an 'occupier's charter' and the whole water sector regarded almost as emblematic of Palestinian subjugation and loss. Nonetheless, the manifold failures in water services contribute to a general disillusion with public agencies and to a feeling that neither the PWA nor the service providers are delivering as they should. Inevitably, water shortages create a bloody-minded disdain amongst the population.

Are Palestinian institutions enabled to plan and manage the system to balance supply and demand?

The quality of Israel's water management is amongst the finest in the world. Planning is far-sighted and practical. Investment and management of supply and demand are well thought through.

We have seen in Chapters 2 and 3 – and, for Gaza, in Chapter 6 – the often unrealistic nature of Palestinian planning, built on dreams. In reality, the context creates a planner's nightmare: a strong political impulse to assume away the Occupation in planning; political exclusion of some optimal infrastructure solutions; no physical control over the water resource; structural shortages of water and limited knowledge of where extra water may come from; no storage or leeway to manage shortages; scant ability to avoid environmental harms poorly maintained infrastructure that makes a lot of planning simply 'running to stand still'; legal and regulatory controls by Israel on investment; and strong donor intervention in choices.

. . . and do they have the knowledge needed?

Israel's water planning and management are knowledge-based, with accurate weather forecasting and climate predictions. Aquifer and lake levels are continually monitored. Demand forecasts range from the daily to the thirty-year horizon.

The Palestinians, by contrast, have almost no knowledge of what is happening to the resource. They know what they themselves pump out of the Mountain Aquifers, but this is only one fifth of the total. What Israel or the settlers are pumping out or what is happening to the water table they have no idea. In any case, they have no ability to affect the behaviours of the Israelis or the settlers.

Does the organization of the Palestinian water sector effectively separate the functions of policy and regulation from service delivery?

Israel has established the IWA as both planner and regulator. The IWA allocates water to meet demand and oversees the service providers which have become efficient, self-financing entities able to raise finance in the bond market. Well-devised partnership arrangements have attracted private finance into the desalination business.

We saw in Chapter 3 the concerted effort of the Palestinians to overhaul their water sector on the Israeli model, to set up an independent regulator, to establish a National Water Company on the lines of Mekorot, and to consolidate service providers into larger self-financing utilities. It has to be said that even in Israel, an advanced and advantaged country, this process took a long time. For the Palestinians, on the current showing, it could take a very long time indeed. In the meantime, there is no effective regulation and most of the service providers are simply not viable. Even in Gaza, where the reforms started two decades ago, only four of the twenty-five municipalities have integrated their operations into the utility.

Can Palestinian water services match the financial autonomy and ability to attract private investment that mark Israel's services?

Thanks to past planning and high levels of past investment in the system, Israel is able to deliver good water services at costs that are affordable by the relatively prosperous population and the vibrant economy. This has allowed the country to follow the economic approach of the 'user pays' and to practice full-cost recovery for most services. This business model has also had the knock-on effect of promoting innovation and entrepreneurship.

As for the Palestinians, the woeful financial status of many service providers is amply described in Chapter 3. Costs are quite high and continue to climb as all incremental water entering the system is priced at the cost of desalinated water pumped up from the coast. Despite significant donor aid in recent years, huge investment is still required. Although Palestinian ingenuity is legendary, innovation and entrepreneurship are off the table as engineers and management simply struggle to provide a basic service.

Investment

Is there adequate investment in the Palestinian water sector?

Israel has perhaps the most complete water infrastructure in the world. This has resulted from far-sighted policy and planning, from sacrifices made by the nation, and from generously high levels of external support. More recently, political and economic stability and inventive partnership arrangements have brought in private capital. The windfall of accessible gas reserves has reduced the energy costs of what is a high-energy system.

By contrast, despite ambitious investment programmes, the Palestinians invest comparatively little and local conditions often make investment efficiency quite low, particularly in Gaza. Private sector participation has been limited and Palestinians have no energy source of their own.

Seeking solutions

Overall, it is clear that the water insecurity of Palestinians stems from a combination of contingent rather than structural factors. Based on the natural resource, Israel has developed an integrated water system and the institutions and investment needed to optimize it and so achieve national water security. It is essentially contingent political factors that have prevented Palestinians from matching Israel's achievement.

Political factors have prevented Palestinians from controlling a fair or even an adequate proportion of shared natural water resources and from closing the loop by recycling their wastewater. Despite good ideas and intentions, the Palestinian institutional structure is caught in the double bind of unavoidably poor performance and of imposed limits on knowledge and planning. With scant water and poor service delivery, the sector struggles to win consumer acceptance and to make ends meet. Again, imposed constraints limit the scope for investment to improve services.

The resolution thus has to come from the same source as the constraints – the political arena. Palestinians need more water and need to be enabled to invest in the institutions and infrastructure that can bring their citizens the same levels of water security that Israelis enjoy.

WHAT ARE THE LESSONS FOR STRENGTHENING PALESTINIAN WATER SECURITY?

This book has so far presented an exhaustive assessment of the water security of Israel – and of the water insecurity of the Palestinians. This assessment enables us to sketch out the components that would contribute to Palestinian water security. These components are primarily those that have made Israel so water secure. They start with maximizing the water inventory and establishing as much water autonomy as possible, together with optimizing water and sanitation services and promoting wastewater treatment and reuse. Environmental protection must be built in and water security requires that there are measures for managing risks, particularly the risks from climatic changes. Finally, sound institutional frameworks are needed, both for equitable cooperative management of shared water resources and for efficient and sustainable management of water resources and water service delivery.

Water security for Palestinians in the West Bank

Water resources, water autonomy and a new cooperative framework

First and foremost, the West Bank Palestinians need more water – and that water needs to be under their control. However, at present the only water to which the Palestinians have access within their own territory is the shared water of the Mountain Aquifers. Therefore, any enlargement of the Palestinian water inventory and any chance of 'water autonomy' has to be underwritten by a cooperative agreement over this shared resource, an agreement in which both peoples support the other's water security. Essentially what is indicated is to reset management of shared water resources on the basis of cooperation between equals and the pursuit of water security for both peoples.

The ideal is for Israelis and Palestinians to agree to fair shares and responsible and sustainable management of the Mountain Aquifers within a cooperative agreement, and to allow Palestinian development and management of water and sanitation infrastructure across the West Bank. Israel would have to progressively give up some of its present use of the aquifers if Palestinian needs are to be met. Obligations have to be reciprocal, bringing Palestinian recognition of Israel's needs in water security and respect of cooperative arrangements for management of shared resources.

Water supply and sanitation services

Water security also requires the development of efficient, affordable water and sanitation services for the entire West Bank Palestinian population and their economy. Municipal and industrial supply needs to be by efficient utilities, and supplies to an efficient and prosperous agriculture sector need to be assured. Levels of water supply should depend on managed demand rather than on constraints in bulk water availability. Demand would be managed by efficiency measures – low-flush toilets, industrial wastewater recovery – and by economic measures such as full-cost recovery with step tariffs to give incentives to conservation and to protect the poor. The needs of an expanding, hi-tech agriculture, currently met largely by private supply, would need to be met rationally and efficiently. Israel again provides the model, an integrated network across the entire territory, able to meet agricultural needs from both fresh water and treated wastewater.

Wastewater treatment and reuse

As water supply levels rise and proper sanitation and sewerage networks replace cesspits, the need for wastewater treatment and the opportunity for reuse will become ever greater. Israel's achievements in management, storage and reuse of treated wastewater are exemplary, and there is ample scope for productive cooperation amongst the two peoples and their institutions. The investment and running costs of a first-class system of treatment will be huge, and this could be an area of financial cooperation with Israel which will be a downstream beneficiary of the cleaner water and environment.

Environmental protection

More broadly, water security requires protection of the environment. This concerns underground water – protecting the quantity of the resource by adapting pumping to the sustainable resource and observing red lines that indicate aquifers are being overdrawn. It concerns, too, the quality of the resource which needs to be protected not only from sewage and untreated wastewater but also from agricultural chemicals. It also requires resolution of the problem of wastewater discharged to the environment, with the resulting damage to the riverine ecology and biodiversity.

Managing risks

Finally, risk management is an essential component of water security. As we saw in Chapter 1, Israel is already far advanced in appreciating and planning for the wide range of risks faced by so water-short a land. There is a big risk from climatic variability. Rising temperatures may increase demand both for agricultural water and for municipal supplies. Agricultural demand may change structurally as rainfed agriculture and pastoralism are faced with growing aridity and farmers move more into irrigated agriculture. Risks of extreme events – principally drought but also floods – will increase. Lowered precipitation and higher rates of evapotranspiration may induce a secular decline in groundwater recharge. Cooperative water management will need to take account of all these risks. One mitigating response could be 'dynamic water management' – management that would allow changes in water allocations based on the changing outlook for water resource availability, and that would provide for alternative sources when supply availability falls below demand.

Water storage, too, has a vital role to play, and here once again, Israel provides a model of risk management that Palestinians can draw from in the West Bank. Israel's integrated water system allows water to be stored either in Lake Tiberias or in artificial retention structures, or left in aquifers or reinjected into them. New infrastructure will soon even allow desalinated water to be stored in Tiberias. The West Bank Palestinians need to be able to link water sources across the West Bank and to develop needed storage, whether surface reservoirs or aquifer storage.

Water security for Palestinians in the Gaza Strip

The material conditions of water security for the Palestinians of the Gaza Strip are spelled out in Chapter 6 – reduction of groundwater pumping to sustainable levels, desalination, the development of modern water supply and sanitation infrastructure and institutions. These material considerations are in principle attainable over time, but their achievement is continually retarded and frustrated by the frequent outbreaks of hostilities and rounds of retribution. These events result in the destruction of infrastructure and in sanctions which prevent rational investment or adequate service delivery. As we sum up in Chapter 6, only a political settlement can bring the pre-conditions of water security to Gaza's hard-pressed people.

* * *

With this background, we now turn to the final part of this book, in which we will explore the conditions under which Palestinians might achieve water security, and how the water security of the Israeli people may be protected – and even enhanced – at the same time.

Part III

Towards a New Cooperation on Water Security for Israelis and Palestinians

Our companion volume *The History of Water in the Land Once Called Palestine* told the story of the two peoples who, a century ago, shared the same land, who had access to the common water resources of that land and who from the same common point were embarking on the development of water and water services to support the growth of their economy and polity. Through the extraordinary upheavals of the hundred years since the end of Ottoman sway, these two people have diverged strongly and in water no less strongly than in other spheres. The result, documented at length in Part I and II of the present book, is that today one people, the Israelis, have been dubbed a 'water superpower', while the other, the Palestinians, have almost no control over water resources, have access to only a small fraction of the water that Israelis have and receive water and sanitation services that sometimes compete with the worst in the world. The Palestinian economy and society are weakened by this water insecurity, and the environment suffers both depletion and pollution.[1]

Palestinians aspire to the same kind of water security that the Israelis have achieved – control over enough of their own water resources to meet the present and future needs of the population; the right to develop those resources to provide efficient, sustainable water services in support of the well-being of their people and the growth of a modern economy; the ability to collect, treat and reuse wastewater and to desalinate seawater in Gaza and brackish water in the West Bank; and the means to proof the economy and society against the risks of drought, water shortages and environmental degradation.

Part III of the book looks at ways to strengthen Palestinian water security while protecting that of Israel. Despite fearsome constraints on both sides, there are possibilities that a 'new deal' on water could in fact achieve this goal. In Chapter 7 we summarize first the great divide in water security that has opened up between Israelis and Palestinians; we look at Palestinian aspirations and the relevance of international water law; we assess the considerable constraints on either side and we ask whether recent developments may improve the prospects of renewed cooperation. In Chapter 8 we consider what incentives either side has to change their approach, and we also look at what lessons can be learned from other recent deals the two parties have made. Chapter 9 looks at options for cutting the Gordian Knot and also at what we can learn more broadly from this long history about the concept of water security.[2]

Chapter 7

WHAT SCOPE FOR A NEW COOPERATION ON WATER?

In practice, the Palestinians are asking for what may seem quite simple, even normal – an equitable share of the transboundary groundwater that lies beneath the West Bank and also of the Jordan River, to which they are a riparian, and to have the right to develop and manage these resources for the benefit of their people according to best practices. However, these claims have come up against Israeli policies, first because in the old zero-sum game of water, an increase in the Palestinian share in the transboundary resource was seen by Israelis as a loss, and second, in the context where for more than a century land has been at the heart of the struggle, because of the ties between water and land.

In this chapter we summarize the status quo which we have so extensively described throughout this book, and ask what has changed, or what might change. In particular, do Israel's stunning advances in desalination and wastewater reuse end the old zero-sum game? If so, what are the other constraints to a new deal on water?

Comparing the water security of Israelis and Palestinians

The failure of Oslo to achieve water security for Palestinians

A quarter of a century ago, in 1995, the Oslo II accords seemed to offer some hope of improvement of the Palestinian situation through cooperation on water management in the West Bank. A five-year deal – Article 40 – recognized Palestinian water rights and made some interim allocations, with the promise of more to come. The Joint Water Committee was set up as a mechanism of working together on development and management of the shared resource in the West Bank. However, any hopes from this arrangement were soon disappointed.

The Palestinians quickly came to regard the committee as a further means of Israeli control over Palestinian lives, a reflection of an unfair political structure and an inadequate and inequitable way to apportion and manage the resources of the watershed and aquifers of the West Bank. In the Palestinian view, the agreement gave Israel control over Palestinian water development and use, but gave Palestinians no reciprocal rights over Israeli practice. Palestinian claims to water from the Jordan

Valley system were altogether excluded. The workings of the committee appeared to the Palestinians to give Israel an effective veto over all Palestinian water projects and water use, with no counterbalancing rights of the Palestinians to prevent, for example, Israeli overpumping of the supposedly 'jointly' managed aquifers or development within the West Bank of water resources for the benefit of the Israeli settlements. The constraining Oslo agreement, which determined what Palestinians came to see as a lop-sided governance structure and which was meant to last for just five years, still governs the Palestinian water sector up to the time of writing (2021).

The results speak for themselves. With water abstractions capped by Article 40 and with growing demand for both potable water and water for agriculture and business, shortages of bulk water emerged and soon became chronic throughout the West Bank. The Palestinians found themselves with access to their own water resources of just 39 cubic metres per person each year, an eighth of the per capita resources available to Israelis (298 cubic metres per capita annually) and just 16 per cent of the minimum needed to develop and run a modern economy in a semi-arid zone such as the Mashreq – see Table 7.1.[1] Other countries of the region have more than ten times as much water per head of the population. Even arid Jordan has four times as much.[2]

Rising Palestinian demand has been met not by an equitable redistribution of access to water but by expensive water sales, limited and subject to political negotiation to obtain the consent of Israel.[3] Even these costly resources raise the Palestinian per capita water ration to only 65 cubic metres, still only a quarter of the minimum they would need as a modern economy and society. Even these smaller water rations are unevenly distributed, with many populations having much less. The development of a water carrier to link the towns of the West Bank in an efficient and rational grid fell afoul of Israeli security preoccupations, of Israel's settlement programme and of the fragmentation of Palestinian Authority amongst 165 islands of jurisdiction in the ABC mosaic.

Water services for the Palestinians in the West Bank have often grown worse, not better, particularly in towns like Yatta where public water supply seemed to come once in a blue moon and households became largely dependent on

Table 7. 1 Water Resources Available to West Bank Palestinians (2017) – in millions of m^3

	Total annual resources (in millions m^3)	**m^3 per person per year**	**Litres per capita per day**	***Percentage of target requirements***
Spring water	23			
Wells	86			
Total internal	***109***	**39**	***107***	***16***
Purchases from Israel	73	26	71	
Total	**182**	**65**	**178**	***26***

Source: PWA, based on a population of 2.8 million, which includes the population of East Jerusalem. Although population numbers are often contended, this estimate appears to accord with estimates of the Israeli Civil Administration for the West Bank which put the Palestinian population of the West Bank in May 2012 at 2.66 million (see the article *Demographic Debate Continues* by Nir Hassan in *Haaretz*, 30 June 2013.

scooping water from slopes, roads and rooftops. In the hot summers, shortages are often severe and some West Bank Palestinians feel they have reverted to third world levels of development and service. Meanwhile, wastewater projects were denied, often on security grounds,[4] untreated sewage coursed in the wadis of the West Bank and thirsty Palestinian agriculture lacked the access to either fresh water or treated wastewater with which it could have developed as Israeli agriculture has.

In 2009, when the five-year agreement was already fourteen years old, the Palestinians disengaged from the Oslo water governance arrangements. They concluded that they had no autonomy in water management and were essentially constrained to execute Israeli water strategy. Little benefit to the population had come from the arrangements. Only in 2017 did the Palestinians come back to the table to reengage in the Joint Water Committee, obliged to do so because there were too many stalled projects that required Israeli approval or cooperation.

Israeli water autonomy and world-beating water security

For the Israelis, the reality is quite different, a story of world-beating success. For years, Israel's far-sighted planners and water-aware citizens worked to turn a naturally arid country into a water superpower. Mandate Palestine was always a water-scarce country, and the Zionist leaders from the outset saw the need to secure as much water as possible in order to build a state. Through foresight, technology and the exercise of power in the region, Israel succeeded in securing the lion's share of regional water resources. Israel gained exclusive access to the water of the Upper Jordan and Lake Tiberias and, since 1967, has effectively controlled its watershed. Since the 1950s, Israel has also used – as we saw earlier – the lion's share of the water of the three Mountain Aquifers and, again since 1967, has controlled the watersheds that replenish the aquifers.

Technical, regulatory and economic measures to conserve water both in urban and domestic use as well as in agriculture reduced demand and eliminated losses while boosting the productivity of the water-based economy to levels unparalleled around the world. Technological and economic innovations hugely increased water availability by treating and recycling wastewater back into the system. Most recently, technological strides and smart implementation measures have made Israel a world leader in desalination. Creating 'new' water from the sea in this way has considerably increased Israel's water inventory. In fact, that inventory is now virtually without bounds.

All of the water Israel controls is astutely managed within a single system. From Tiberias to the Negev, the huge artery of the National Water Carrier (NWC) integrates sources, storage and uses the length and breadth of the country. This water system powers Israel's dynamic and fast-growing economy. First-class water services are delivered to agriculture, industry and households at affordable prices.[5] Even the risks of climate variability and drought are mastered by ample storage and by the ability to draw down or replenish that storage by transfer throughout the integrated national system. Recently, Israel has even been developing infrastructure

Table 7.2 Water Resources Available to Israel (2016) – in millions of m³

	Total annual resource (in millions m³)	**m³ per person per year**	**Litres per capita per day**	***Percentage of target requirements***
Natural water	1,600	184	504	*74*
Manufactured water	1,000	114	312	*46*
Total	**2,600**	**298**	**816**	***119***

Source: IWA, based on a population of 8.7 million.
Note: Target requirements assumed to be 250 cubic metres per person per year (685 lcpd).

to replenish Tiberias from the NWC. Desalinated water could actually be pumped up from the coast to restore water levels in the lake.[6]

Certainly, there are criticisms that can be made of the Israeli water economy. Chapter 1 explored the poor or absent water services to segments of the Israeli community – the 60,000 Bedouin who live in 'unrecognized' villages, for example – or the past overuse of aquifers and Lake Tiberias, which risked compromising the resource. Or the environmental impacts on rivers, most notably the Jordan, and the large carbon footprint and environmental risks of desalination. The Palestinians and Israel's neighbours may enquire whether part of the inventory of natural water that Israel controls has not been put together at their expense and to their detriment.

Yet there is no denying Israel's extraordinary achievement in water. By dint of its efforts, the country has essentially achieved de facto water autonomy, meeting the entire water demand from resources developed or manufactured within the territory that it effectively controls. It has procured assured access within the territory that it controls to 300 cubic metres of water per head each year, which is proving adequate to run a vigorous modern economy (see Table 7.2).

Nowadays, Israel has not only won water autonomy, it has the possibility of surplus – even the actuality of it. Already in 1994 Israel was water-secure enough to release 50 million cubic metres to Jordan as part of the Israel–Jordan peace treaty – see Chapter 8. Today, Israel is using water to regreen the environment, cleaning up the rivers, restoring environmental flows, even creating river parks. In that flexible inventory whose bounds can be expanded through desalination lies the truth that ***Israel is – or can be – a water-surplus nation***. This opens options, not only in the economic and environmental fields, but also in the political arena. Israel has a new power – of water diplomacy with its arid, water-short neighbours.[7]

The stark contrast in water security between Israelis and Palestinians

So here is a stark contrast in water security between two peoples who share the same land and who started from much the same point a hundred years ago. On the one hand, a people who enjoy complete water autonomy and an ample water inventory diligently managed and expandable, almost at will, first-class water and wastewater services for most of the population[8] and the ability to manage risks and shocks. On the other hand, a people who are dependent on Israel's say-so for their water management and for extra supplies which they must purchase, a people who have a water ration per capita that is a fraction of that of Israel and who lack the infrastructure that would allow them to distribute water between the source and the points of use and to correct imbalances. The water services delivered to Palestinians are poor, wastewater treatment is limited and reuse is negligible, and the environment and even health are at risk from untreated sewage. With chronic water shortages in summer and no access to storage other than the aquifers, even normal climatic variations are unmanageable, let alone extreme events. This people, the Palestinians, who we may assume can be as inventive and dynamic and resilient as their Israeli neighbours, lack the political freedom, institutional capacities and economic resources to correct the situation.

Palestinian aspirations for water security: The claim for more water

Palestinians see obtaining more water – and more water autonomy – as a vital part of their water security. In the West Bank these claims are essentially to control an equitable share of two transboundary water resources: the Mountain Aquifers and the Jordan River. At the limit, Palestinians would essentially like to claim control and use of all the water of the three aquifers that lie beneath their territory – or at least of the 85 per cent share of the aquifers' yield that arises from rainfall within the West Bank. They also lay claim, as riparians, to a share of the Jordan River.[9]

The applicability of international water law

To what extent do Palestinian claims receive support under the principles that have been applied to transboundary watercourses around the world? The assignment of rights and responsibilities on international waters is inevitably contentious as it concerns a resource which, unlike land which can be easily measured and defined, is a fluid resource that moves from one jurisdiction to another, flowing from upstream to downstream. The challenge is greater in respect of groundwater, which cannot be seen, and whose quantity, pathways and rhythm of flow are often hard to determine.

Over the years, states have asserted different principles as a basis of determining rights to international waters. These principles have been incorporated into extensive case law in the shape of treaties of various kinds – over the last two centuries about 300 international treaties have been negotiated that deal with non-navigational uses of transboundary water resources.[10]

The principle of *absolute territorial sovereignty* asserts that each jurisdiction has absolute sovereignty over the water in any international watercourse within its territory. Plainly this principle favours the jurisdiction in which the bulk of the water arises. The principle is sometimes called the Harmon Doctrine after the US attorney general who asserted in 1895 that the United States, as riparian on the Rio Grande, had sovereignty over the waters within its territory. Although Harmon did not deny the complementary responsibility of avoidance of harm to other riparians, in this case Mexico, de facto this principle of absolute territorial sovereignty has been tacitly applied by riparians to unilaterally assert rights. For practical reasons this principle is typically applied by upstream riparians with scant consideration for the interests of downstream riparians, most recently by Turkey on the Tigris/Euphrates.[11]

At the limit, this principle would give the Palestinians a green light to simply develop and use all the water within, beneath and alongside the West Bank to which it can gain access. The principle is, however, only available to jurisdictions that can impose their will on other riparians, which is hardly the case of the Palestinians.

Absolute territorial integrity differs in that it requires that riparians do not develop the portion of the shared resource within their territory if it will harm the interests of another riparian. This principle is clearly in favour of downstream riparians, who could assert the right to prevent any development upstream which altered the flow of water into their territory. De facto, this principle has been most famously applied by Egypt in its use of the lion's share of Nile waters. Although the most downstream of the Nile's eleven riparians, Egypt asserts its entitlement to a specific quantity of water and contests upstream development that could reduce that quantity.

These two 'absolute' principles essentially exclude notions of cooperative development and management, and their application is essentially for more powerful states to justify appropriation of the resource without regard to others. These principles are complemented by historical or acquired rights, often called prior appropriation or 'first in time, first in right', or, more bluntly, 'the law of capture'. Under this principle, the first to develop the resource 'captures' it and thereby acquires absolute ownership with no liability of duty of care to any neighbour.

Over time, as technology advanced and more states developed water resources, the risks of conflicting interests became clear and other principles emerged that provided a framework for more cooperative and negotiated approaches to transboundary water. The principle of *limited territorial integrity* would confirm the right of states to exploit the resource within their territory but would match it with the responsibility to avoid harm to other riparians. This principle joins a fourth, the principle of *community of interest*, which would view transboundary water resources as the common property of all riparians, to be developed and used in an equitable and reasonable way on a shared basis to the exclusion of preferential privileges of any one riparian state.[12]

These two principles are combined in the hybrid principle of *limited territorial sovereignty*, which has come to be widely accepted as the basis for cooperation on transboundary watercourses. Under this principle, all watercourse states enjoy a right to the utilization of a shared resource, and each riparian must respect the sovereignty and reciprocal rights of others. One of the main advantages of this principle is that it simultaneously recognizes the rights of both upstream and downstream nations without sacrificing the principle of sovereignty. It also reflects the principle of equitable and reasonable utilization.

UN Watercourses Convention

Based on considerable prior work and case law, the *Convention on the Law of Non-Navigational Uses of International Watercourses* was adopted by the UN on 21 May 1997 but came into force only seventeen years later, in August 2014. Although the convention has considerable suasive power with experts, it has been ratified by just thirty-six states, and key countries which might be negatively affected by its provisions have not signed up. Thus Syria and Iraq both ratified the convention but Turkey, the upstream and dominant riparian on the Tigris/Euphrates, did not. Syria and Jordan both ratified, but Israel, the upstream and dominant riparian on the Jordan, did not.

Essentially the convention provides a basis for sharing water or benefits, with its principle of 'optimal and sustainable use and benefit, consistent with adequate protection' (Article 5). In this, riparians are to take into account all relevant factors and circumstances (Article 6), including the physical characteristics of the resource, social and economic needs, including how dependent any one segment of the population is on that resource, the availability of alternatives and the efficiency of water uses. No use enjoys inherent priority apart from vital human needs (Article 10).

The convention also provides the basis for cooperative management. The parties must take appropriate measures to prevent, control and reduce any negative transboundary impact (Article 2) and take appropriate measures to prevent significant harm (Article 7). They should ensure that waters are used in a reasonable and equitable way, avoid pollution, manage water in a way that is ecologically sound, conserve the resource and protect the environment and the ecosystem. They should apply the 'polluter pays' principle, and respect intergenerational equity. There is a requirement for prior notification of any development of water or change in water management, together with a duty to negotiate on the measures (Articles 12–17).

The convention thus provides a framework within which cooperation agreements can be developed both for sharing water (or benefits) and for reasonable and equitable utilization and prevention of harm.

International law and Article 40 of the 1995 Oslo Accords

Much ink was spilled in the run-up to the Oslo II negotiations to fit the various concepts prevalent in international law to the situation of either Israel or the Palestinians. Those who argued Israel's side demanded that the Palestinians conform to the 'no significant harm' principle, while the Palestinians insisted on the requirement for 'equitable and reasonable utilization'.[13]

Neither of these lines of argument had much practical impact on the Article 40 negotiations. In these, Israel essentially asserted its rights to the Mountain Aquifers, firmly considering this resource to be their property, with the Palestinians having access on sufferance and by Israeli concessions. The agreements did provide for the recognition of undefined Palestinian water rights and set temporary (five-year) quotas dividing the resource between Israelis and Palestinians. In practice, however, these quotas largely reaffirmed the existing pattern of resource use that Israel had established through capture, with the lion's share (84 per cent) going to Israel.

The Jordan River was not included in the Oslo II negotiations. Although use of the transboundary resource of the Jordan River was the subject of the Johnston Plan, there was until that time no agreement with other riparians and Israel's development and use of the Jordan was again by capture, with other riparians strongly objecting.

This situation on the Jordan River changed around the time of Oslo II with the 1994 peace treaty between Israel and Jordan. In negotiating the treaty, Israel argued that agreement should be on 'water allocations', by which it meant the future needs of each riparian. The Jordanians asserted their historic 'water rights'. Negotiations at length concluded on 'rightful allocations', a term of constructive ambiguity which Aaron Wolf explains as 'describing both historic claims and future goals for cooperative projects.'[14] It is likely that Palestinians would not quibble at the term, provided they got the water they need, although one effect of the treaty was to confirm that neither Israel nor Jordan was one whit concerned about any Palestinian claims on the Jordan River.

Constraints to Palestinian aspirations: Palestinian–Israeli relations

Israel's protection of its water inventory

Palestinian claims to more water inevitably come up against Israeli policies on water security. Since the time of the earliest Zionists, acquisition and control of water sources has been a powerful motive and the history of the state of Israel shows how this motive has driven practice. The progressive accumulation of a water inventory in the Jordan Valley and the Mountain Aquifers has been secured by the physical control of the watershed and water bodies – Tiberias finally secured by the seizure of the Golan, the Upper Jordan secured by the state boundaries of 1948 and the gains of 1967, the Mountain Aquifers secured by the occupation of the West Bank. Israel essentially sees water autonomy as a component of national security.

Water autonomy has come to have for Israelis almost the same force as territorial independence. Not to be beholden to your neighbour for this vital resource is a political and strategic imperative. Water independence is seen as part of water security. To be reliant on a neighbour for water or subject to a neighbour's policies for access to water is considered an infringement of sovereignty.

In the old zero-sum game of water, Palestinian gains in water security would be Israel's loss, and Israel would be loath to surrender any of the water resources which it has gone to so much trouble to acquire. Of course this zero-sum game alters radically if Israel has the ability to create new water from the sea. But the advent of desalinated water has not so far encouraged Israel to meet Palestinian demands by reassigning aquifer water. To date, the offer has been of desalinated water pumped up from the coast – and not a 'right' or a 'rightful allocation' but a 'sale'. Israel has shown no signs of being willing to reallocate a quantum of the fresh water it controls to the Palestinians.

Would more Palestinian control of water require more Palestinian control of land?

The challenge of reallocating water becomes even greater when it also implies control of land. Israel has demonstrated the connection it makes between control of the land and control of water. On the same logic, the Palestinians at present control little land and little water. At Oslo, in addition to their small quota of water, they were accorded limited home rule in 165 scattered enclaves that are less than one tenth of the area of Mandate Palestine, subject to rules on movement and access established by Israel, and prey to incursions.[15] At the time, Israeli analysts made clear the connection between control of the land and control of the water: 'vital regions must never be included in a Palestinian entity because of the danger to water pumping in Israel in case that the peaceful agreement will not be kept.'[16]

And so it turned out. At first, in the years soon after Oslo, it seemed that the Palestinians might conceivably regain control over most of the West Bank, and that could have facilitated a reassignment of the groundwater there, and even of some quantum of Jordan River water. But more than two decades later, little of the land has been transferred to Palestinian jurisdiction and Israel has little need to worry about the danger to 'water pumping in Israel'.

Certainly, the current administrative arrangements and the A/B/C segregation of the West Bank make rational infrastructure planning impossible. Under the Oslo II agreement, Israel maintained full civil and security control in Area C, 60 per cent of West Bank territory. This 'temporary' arrangement has persisted now for more than twenty-five years, during which time Israel has essentially acted in Area C as though it were its own. Apart from scattered and dwindling Palestinian communities that are predominantly rural and agricultural, Area C is an area with limited access for Palestinians, as it is occupied by Israeli settlements, businesses, military zones and nature reserves. Building pipelines across these areas faces enormous obstacles, and entering these areas to maintain water infrastructure or to service Palestinian households is also a challenge. Thus, Palestinian aspirations to emulate Israel by establishing an integrated water infrastructure, with bulk carriers connecting sources to points of demand and conveying water from surplus to deficit areas, just as Israel does with the National Water Carrier (the NWC) have proved impossible in the reality that Palestinian access to Area C is strictly limited. These areas are also exactly where Palestinians need to build their wastewater treatment plants – downstream of their cities, with large open sites, and with agricultural fields below where treated wastewater can be reused, and with natural drainage.

For the future, one vital factor is Israeli policy towards the occupied territories

Since 1967, Israel has created numerous settlements in the West Bank in Area C, populating them with half a million of its citizens. It has established elaborate transport infrastructure across the territory, drilled wells and extracted groundwater, developed industrial, commercial and agricultural enterprises both in the highlands and all along the Jordan Valley, established social and educational facilities, and set up institutions for local government and security.

Policy can be inferred from actions. The Israeli settlements and the infrastructure and institutions that the Israelis have set up make it likely that Israel will continue to wish to control much of the West Bank. Palestinians have long asserted that this is a 'creeping annexation'. Even if policy is unstated, Palestinians believe that the unsaid truth is that facts on the ground, deafness to criticism and the passage of time are the mechanisms by which annexation may be consolidated. Palestinians fear that formal annexation, which has long been Likud policy, may one day be realized.[17] In this view, the future that may be offered to the West Bank Palestinians would likely be a continuation of the current home rule in their existing enclaves, perhaps with some strengthening of liberties and the offer of easier conditions for trade, investment and guest workers – essentially what is characterized by Likud as an 'economic peace'.

In summary, it is difficult to see how the Palestinians could develop and manage the aquifers without having the right to develop infrastructure and manage abstractions and use across much of the West Bank. Israel's occupation of Area C and the proliferation of settlements are likely to be a massive constraint.

Internal Palestinian politics complicate matters

For Palestinians, water is linked to other final status issues

Oslo II provided for an interim agreement for five years leading to negotiation of 'final status'. Water is one of the five issues reserved for those final status negotiations. Ever since Oslo II, all discussions and decisions about water have therefore been perceived as having implications for the final status. This has made the Palestinians extremely cautious and averse to making any new agreements on water with the Israelis. They have generally maintained the position that any arrangements for infrastructure and public services should not pre-empt their rights or represent a final solution. This follows the principle adopted long ago at the 1991 Madrid peace conference: 'nothing is agreed until everything is agreed.'

All of this aligns with the overall pursuit of sovereignty. But it makes water hostage to the resolution of much larger and thornier issues. Linking water to land makes it even more contentious, because land is the supreme issue of contention between Israelis and Palestinians. Given that rights to the land of the West Bank are a central and vital issue on which Israel shows no sign of giving away at present, claims that appear to make water rights dependent on Palestinians regaining control over the entire West Bank may put off resolution of the water issue sine die.

Water rights – or rightful allocations – that also require rights to land are likely to be a very vexed issue indeed. Might it then be better to explore ways to delink water from land, and to resolve water issues before and separately from other final status issues?

Cooperation with Israel risks the stigma of collaboration

Under current arrangements in the West Bank, water management has come to be perceived by Palestinians as a form of 'collaboration'. Article 40 set up a framework of shared governance of water in the West Bank. However, in Palestinian perceptions, not only was this arrangement one of enforced compliance intolerable beyond a short period, but it also raised concerns of 'collaboration' and of 'normalization' – see Chapter 7 of *The History of Water* for an examination of these issues. Complying with Article 40 rules and seeking Israeli approval for investments risked being understood as recognizing Israeli rights over the West Bank. Worse, some of these investments may have implied recognition or some sort of legitimization of settlements and have even provided services to these settlements. The regulatory measures applied under the Oslo agreement came to be seen as policing by the occupier of a lop-sided water agreement.

As hopes of early final status negotiations drained away, these conditions were perceived as intolerable by Palestinians. In 2007, they disengaged from the Joint Water Committee and effectively withdrew from any pretence at sharing water management. The following year, 2008, Prime Minister Salam Fayed declared a general position of 'no normalization' that reinforced this approach in the water sector.[18]

The political division between Fatah and Hamas

Political division amongst Palestinians has complicated water management. Most prominent is the division between Fatah and Hamas, and how that has splintered Palestinian institutions and efforts to manage water in the West Bank and Gaza. The Hamas victory in the election of 2006 was followed by inter-party violence and the takeover of Gaza by Hamas. Palestinian unity was fractured into two entities governed by two different political systems and leaderships. To all intents and purposes, the West Bank and the Gaza Strip have become separate water management areas with separate governance. In the Strip there are even two Palestinian water authorities, an 'official' one and a Hamas one – see Chapter 6. The natural hydrological separation between the West Bank and the Gaza Strip has been consolidated by this institutional divide.[19]

The Hamas takeover also created an additional barrier to engaging with Israel, and this has frustrated much water development in the Gaza Strip. It has made it very hard, for example, to move supplies, human resources and fuel across the border into Gaza for construction and operation of water facilities. Also, over the last decade, periodic escalations in violence between Hamas and Israel led to Israeli military operations that severely damaged water infrastructure, worsening the water and sanitation crisis there. In recent years, the PA has curtailed its fiscal transfers to Gaza.

Internal challenges and conflicts of interest

Internal challenges and conflicts of interest amongst frail but combative Palestinian institutions are slowing down implementation of water sector reforms and hence impeding investment and improvement in services. As we saw in Chapter 3, the municipal sector and the water sector within the West Bank are not of one mind over the administrative arrangements for providing water and sanitation services. These dynamics have hindered the implementation of the 2013 Palestinian Water Law, which promotes the establishment of a National Water Company and regional utilities independent of municipal government. The donors strongly support the reforms under the new Water Law, and have made some financing contingent upon its implementation. Consequently, the internal Palestinian divergence of views about the reforms is holding up investment.

Both official and popular views largely oppose cooperation with Israel on water and characterize it as, at best, collaboration with the occupier. The Palestinian official narrative continues to focus on rights to the aquifers and on the right to manage wastewater across the entire West Bank. Accompanying this negotiating goal, as we have seen, has been a policy of non-collaboration and anti-normalization. Whatever the virtue of these policies, they have had highly negative consequences for the Palestinian population, effectively curtailing water sector development, resulting in poor services and environmental damage. Yet these policies appear generally to have popular support. They are seen as fair and just and as a quest for recompense for the wretchedness and humiliations that Palestinians have endured over the years. Though, as we shall see, frustration with municipal services is now beginning to foster grievances towards local authorities, the dominant public narrative and popular opinion regarding water insecurity in the Palestinian territories place most of the blame squarely on Israel.

The added privations that result from these policies only seem to reinforce attitudes. The huge and growing disparities in water supply and services between Israelis and Palestinians increase a sense of injustice amongst Palestinians. Palestinians are aware that Israeli consumers, including those living in settlements in the West Bank, receive between three and five times more water than they do and benefit from far better services. When Palestinian consumers hear that they are to get more water but that it will be purchased from Mekorot, they furiously object to buying water to replace the resources they feel they have been deprived of by the very people who are now selling it back to them. Palestinian farmers dependent on rainfed agriculture and tanker water struggle to harvest a crop, especially in recent years of drought, while they can see neighbouring fields farmed by settlers being amply irrigated. The contrast between Israeli progress and Palestinian stagnation –

even suffering – is too obvious. Palestinians see this imbalance as further evidence of decades of injustice and proof of the flaws of the interim agreement.

There are, nonetheless, as we said, internal tensions over water. Frustration with the Palestinian Authority over the poor quality of services is considerable, and where service is particularly bad or the stench of sewage running in the wadis is too strong, the population do react, typically blaming the Palestinian Authority or the municipality and not paying their water bills. In extreme cases, customers simply disconnect from the system or hook up illegal connections. Although popular opinion may place the blame primarily on Israel, the Authority is seen at best as ineffectual or corrupt, at worst as a tacit collaborator.

Populations in poor areas in particular tend to take more radical attitudes, hostile to collaboration – but also to the Palestinian Authority. Households in the refugee camps and certain urban areas, such as the Old City in Nablus, have been sunk in poverty for decades. These areas have long been a breeding ground for resistance to the occupation. It was here that the first and second *intifada* flourished, and where clashes with the Israeli military are part of daily life. Especially in the early 2000s, these areas became fertile areas for gang activity, and, allegedly, illegal and black market activities such as drug trafficking. The Authority struggles to establish legitimacy in these neighbourhoods, which have long relied on their social networks to stay afloat and to stay safe. Although the Authority has prioritized these areas with preferential water supply, this has won them scant sympathy. Large sections of the population take a bloody-minded attitude. Payment collections are low or absent in these areas, and household water meters have not been installed. There are two sides to this – either residents refuse to pay, or, for political reasons, the municipality deliberately avoids confrontation and does not pursue these matters. The stance of these citizens is typically rooted in opposition to the occupation and strongly opposed to anything that could be seen as collaboration, but is at the same time hostile to much of what the PA strives to do, whether it can be construed as collaboration or not.

What is the problem with simple water purchases?

Water purchases from Israel have long been a fact of Palestinian life. Ever since the early days of the Israeli occupation, Mekorot has been supplying water from the Israeli water grid to Palestinians. Today, water is delivered by Israel's National Water Carrier to a series of points within the West Bank and then conveyed to Palestinian towns and villages by the Palestinian West Bank Water Department. The Israeli network also extends throughout the West Bank to bring water to the settlements. In addition, a number of Israeli-controlled wells within the West Bank are linked in to the Mekorot network and so to the National Water Carrier. The West Bank is thus patched into the Israeli water network to serve both Palestinians and the settlements. Mekorot also supplies water to points on the border of Gaza, where it is conveyed to the twenty-five municipalities by the Coastal Municipalities Water Utility (CMWU). The volumes involved have been going up. From 28 million cubic metres at the time of Oslo, the West Bank purchased 73 million cubic metres from Mekorot in 2017. In Gaza, purchases have gone from 5 million cubic metres in 1995 to 10.6 million m^3 in 2017.[20] Today water purchases from Israel represent two thirds of Palestinian potable water supply.

The reason for the increase in purchases from Israel is that West Bank Palestinians have strictly limited access to the water beneath their feet. They are limited by Oslo in how much water they can pump from the three Mountain Aquifers beneath the West Bank. In Gaza, the well water is too salty to drink, so all potable water must come from desalination. As demand goes up and shortages become pressing, the only solution – apart from some small-scale desalination in Gaza – has been to seek more water from the Israeli network. Following worsening water shortages, particularly in the summer 2016,[21] and consequent protests and increasing debate about supply insufficiencies,[22] Israel agreed in July 2017 to sell the Palestinian Authority extra water as part of the 'dividend' from the agreement that had been reached on the Red Sea–Dead Sea Project (RSDS) – on which see Chapter 8 later. The then US Middle East envoy Jason Greenblatt[23] brokered the arrangement, by which the Palestinian Authority would purchase 32 million cubic metres of water yearly from Israel's desalinated supplies. The West Bank was to purchase 22 million cubic metres for 3.3 shekels ($0.92) per cubic metre, and the Gaza Strip could purchase 10 million cubic metres for 3.2 shekels ($0.89) per cubic metre. Implementation, however, could only be gradual as the infrastructure was not in place to handle such huge quantities of new imported water.

The Palestinian leadership argued that the purchase would ease the Palestinian water crisis – but it would not compromise the Palestinian political position. Yet, there was immediate criticism amongst Palestinians of this 'deal', running along four lines of argument. The first was price – that the water purchase was at an unfairly high cost. Why should the Palestinians, amongst the poorest people of the region, pay the highest price in the region when much cheaper water was available locally?

This joined to the second thread – many Palestinians argue in principle against paying a price to replace the groundwater resources that lie beneath their feet and of which they feel they have been dispossessed. It has not escaped the Palestinians' notice that water desalinated at the coast and pumped up to altitude costs about three times as much as the cost of water pumped from within the West Bank. It is not the case that water is not available locally – after all, Israel pumps out four times as much of that Mountain Aquifer water as the Palestinians do, and has in fact over the years pumped out far more from these aquifers than was agreed at Oslo. The Palestinians also note that Israel has developed extensive wells for its own use within the West Bank, and that Israeli settlers in the West Bank are receiving and consuming three to five times more water per person than the Palestinians. Why, the Palestinians argue, in these circumstances, if there is plenty of much cheaper water close to their hand, should they be obliged to pay top dollar for desalinated water pumped all the way up from the coast?

In a third vein of criticism, there was the view that the purchase compromised final status negotiations. To this the Palestinian water minister Ghoneim responded robustly, asserting that there was no such compromise. He linked the purchase instead to the RSDS, saying that the Palestinian Authority had taken part in the whole RSDS process and Israel's consent to water purchase was part of the gains for Palestinians from the RSDS. 'The water that will be given to us as part of the deal', he explained, 'is our right because we are on the coast of the Dead Sea. This has nothing to do with negotiations on a final [settlement] with Israel.'[24] He also provided a public reminder that water is a final status issue outlined in the Oslo Accords, and that Israel was required by the agreement to recognize Palestinian water rights. 'The crisis will not be over', he said, 'unless Israel's occupation ends and we get our water rights in the three underground basins that Israel controls.'[25] The *non-dit* was simply that there was no immediate alternative to purchases in sight to relieve the chronic water shortages that were plaguing the West Bank.

Nor did the minister's views belie the reality – the fourth critique of water sales – that water purchases from Israel are not a commercial matter. They require political negotiations and clearly may come with strings attached. Palestinians sum this up as 'being able to buy back their own water at a high price – but with purchases dependent on good behaviour'.

Do recent developments improve the prospects of a new cooperation?

How desalination changes both hydro-geography and hydro-politics[26]

Desalination can remove the constraint of limited water resources. As we have seen in Chapter 1, desalination has come to form an increasingly important part of Israel's water inventory and now supplies more than two thirds of Israel's domestic water. The capacity to create new potable water from the sea at prices that are competitive with, for example, natural water transferred over long distances or pumped up to high elevation has created a situation new in the world of water. Within a country, wherever desalinated water can be economically supplied, it removes the constraint of limited water resources and it provides a buffer against climatic variations. For countries that have been dependent on others for their water, it creates the possibility of strengthened water autonomy.

Desalination could also possibly reduce or eliminate competition over water resources. Wherever there is competition for water, whether within a country or with a neighbour, desalination has the potential to change the former 'zero-sum game' in which one party's gain is inevitably another's loss. Hence, desalination can reduce or eliminate competition over water resources. At the same time, no contention over water rights can arise as desalination is plainly the property of the producer. It may also enable a water user or water-using sector or an entire region or country to weigh up the possibility of giving up water to another party without having to reduce its own consumption.

The geography of water also changes because desalination allows for greater spatial flexibility in water supply arrangements. The new water no longer arises in basins but in industrial plants. Desalinated water almost always lies at sea level, reversing the classic upstream/downstream pattern of flow and removing any chance of contention between upstream and downstream interests. This location alongside the sea advantages communities and nations that are close to the resource, but also enables water to be produced in a variety of new locations according to need. This sea-level, but flexible, location can underpin a shift in the geography of hydro-political relations.

As Aviram et al. (2014) point out, in the 1994 Israel–Jordan peace treaty water exchanges were spatially limited by the locations of supply and demand, as were the quantities exchanged. Once Israel started large-scale desalination from 2005, it was not only able to create more and more water to satisfy internal demand but was also able to locate plants to meet Jordan's need for more water in its northern areas. Israel had the technology and the raw material much closer to hand than did Jordan. Israel's counterpart agreement to purchase desalinated water in the south played to Jordan's asset of access to the Red Sea – however, as explained in Chapter 8, this eventually fell through.

That exchange would have created a neat interdependence and equivalence between the parties and furthered the idea of a new regional approach to water resources made possible by desalination. The advantage to Jordan was that the costs are lower because it does not have to transport the desalinated water to the highlands. Instead, it receives water from the Upper Jordan River.

The economics of water also changes, advantaging communities or nations that can afford to pay. Despite all the technological advances, desalinated water is still the most costly water at source. Desalination can also turn water from a national asset – or even a national trophy – into a commercial commodity. The water created has a defined cost on which to base prices and, as in Israel, producers can be private or quasi-private enterprises. In international relations this can underpin a change from a rights-based discourse to a sales orientation.

Desalination also clarifies the vexed question of the right price of water. As Aviram et al. (2014) point out, desalinated water is a manufactured good and production costs are readily available as opposed to the estimated economic price of natural water, typically based on loose definitions like scarcity value. If buyer and seller both have access to desalination, then a clear upper bound exists for water prices, making the basis for pricing water sales clearer. The value of this in transboundary negotiations is clear from the 2010 agreements between Israel and Jordan, where the prices were to be based on the costs of production at three Israeli desalination plants.[27] Thus water for the first time in the region was set to become a quasi-commercial commodity and to begin to pass out of the strictly state-controlled arena to become what Aviram et al. call the object of 'water trade' between Jordan and Israel. However, the sales would still remain a matter of inter-governmental negotiations.

This approach would clearly change the politics of water and the basis of cooperation. Israel, which can produce desalinated water efficiently in quantities more than its need, can use water in hydro-political exchanges. At the same time, it can change the basis of cooperation by shifting the discourse away from water rights to water sales.[28] We see from the Israel–Jordan deals how desalination can be the basis for new international water agreements, for example swapping fresh water for desalinated water, or swapping desalinated water in both directions but in different locations. The Jordan–Israel agreement of 2010, which was confirmed under the agreements on the Red–Dead project – on which see Chapter 8 – includes a swap of Jordanian desalinated water supplied to southern Israel in exchange for water delivered by Israel from the Upper Jordan Valley to Jordan, closer to population centres in the Jordanian highlands.

Desalinated water thus has potential for reducing the politicization of water both internally and in international relations, and these agreements can perhaps be linked to the larger theme of 'peace'. The Jordanians, for example, were able to present the 2010 agreement on fresh water/desalinated water swap as 'securing their water rights' while the Israelis were able to present it as just a water swap. The Jordanian public appeared pacific and, with no cap on availability, domestic Israeli politics also went quieter. As the spectre of drought was more or less banished for good by the availability of desalination, water users – even farmers – could not grumble. At least for the international community, these water agreements could be trumpeted as part of a longed-for 'peace' process.

In the end, the water swap between Israel and Jordan has not taken place. This is apparently due both to the difficulties in moving ahead with the Red–Dead project and to the dwindling financial viability of the swap itself.

. . . but is desalination to the advantage of the Palestinians or to their detriment?

We shall see in Chapter 8 that there are considerable differences between the Jordan–Israel deals and the position of the Palestinians vis-à-vis the Israelis. The entry on the scene of desalinated water gives the advantage to communities that are wealthy enough to buy water or where the alternatives are at a higher cost than desalinated water. The Palestinians, by contrast, are disadvantaged, as their economy is weak and household incomes are low. They do not fit the profile of consumers of desalinated water – better-off populations living close to the sea. Buying water on commercial terms is an expensive business for a poor people, and for the Palestinians the cheapest source of water lies not in desalinated water pumped up from the coast but in the aquifer water beneath their feet.

So far, the arrival on the scene of an Israeli surplus in desalinated water has been quite negative for the Palestinians. The assumption in the deals done to date has been that allocations of natural water from the Mountain Aquifers are frozen at the Oslo levels and that the Palestinians must purchase all their water needs above that level. The effect for the Palestinians of lifting the resource constraint through desalination is thus that all water at the margin has to come from desalination – water rights to the Mountain Aquifers are simply not on the table. Desalination seems to have removed any obligation from Israel to recognize any further Palestinian water rights – or even any 'rightful shares'.

Thus although the Palestinians do obtain more water, it is at a price they can barely afford to pay, it steadily and increasingly saps their water autonomy, it does nothing to resolve their claims for the right to more natural water, and far from creating interdependence makes them more and more dependent on Israel for water, with the shadow political dependence which that brings.

Commercially, the commodification of water and the entry of water into quasi-commercial transactions can only benefit Israel, the producer. Sales of desalinated water to the West Bank boost demand for the product and sales keep the desalination plants working at full capacity.

Water sales can also be used in hydro-political exchanges and the possibility that Israel has of creating a water surplus for sale can form a useful bargaining counter in regional relations. The agreements with Jordan show how water sales can form part of a wider cooperation. In the Jordan case, they were also strongly linked to 'peace' both in popular acceptance and in the reality of the interdependence so created. Here again the advantage in Palestinian–Israeli relations is clearly with Israel. Israel can present itself to the world as offering 'peace' when from a Palestinian perspective the offer combines the necessity of buying water they cannot afford with an implicit surrender of their claim to a fair share of the Mountain Aquifers.

Change in the location of the resource also clearly benefits Israel internally, as it has a long seaboard and its population is concentrated within a few miles of the sea. In the related changes to hydro-political relations, Israel is now in an even more commanding position, as all the surplus water that can be created in Israel and the West Bank is located within Israel and is its unrestricted property.[29] By contrast, the West Bank Palestinians have no access to the sea and proposals that they should have dedicated desalination from Hadera – or even a pipeline from the plant now under construction in Gaza – have proven chimerical.

Also, the advantages of water trade or water swap go to those who have something to sell or to swap – and the Palestinians in the West Bank have neither. Finally, and this is a theme we return to in Chapter 8, the 'hydro-political exchanges' between Israel and Jordan were on the basis of sovereign state to sovereign state, an arrangement that Israel would deny to the Palestinians.

Nonetheless, for the Palestinians the one big advantage of the advent of desalination is the potential end of the 'zero-sum game' of Article 40. With Israel's capacity to create new water, its water resource security and autonomy appear assured, and there is potential for surplus. With access to almost limitless new water, Israel is less dependent on the Mountain Aquifers. This creates at least the possibility of hydro-political exchanges over that resource, especially as any surrender of Mountain Aquifer resources can be replaced by desalination with Israeli consumption unaffected.

The location of the new water could also help the Palestinian case. The experience of the Jordan–Israel deals is that the surplus on offer can be variable in location within Israel's water inventory. Israel, for example, could give up fresh water to the Palestinians from the Mountain Aquifers and make good the amount from desalination. It could also 'swap' the desalinated water it currently sells to the Palestinians for fresh water from the aquifers without reducing its own water inventory.

The Palestinians' cause could also ironically be aided by the very cost of producing desalinated water and supplying it to communities in the hills relatively far from the sea, especially when there is another much less costly resource lying close to hand – the Mountain Aquifers. *Tabula rasa*, desalination creates a strong economic case for giving preference to the Palestinians in allocating water from the Mountain Aquifers.

Does the recent rebooting of the Joint Water Committee show a new way forward?

In 2016–17 the Israelis and Palestinians signed a series of agreements to give the Palestinians in the West Bank increased autonomy over their own affairs, particularly in the areas of electricity, telecommunications, postal services and water. The agreement on water that was signed on 15 January 2017 was intended to speed up project implementation, as some projects would no longer require the Israeli approval that was mandatory under the Oslo Accords. EcoPeace summarizes:

> All water projects that will not deal with transboundary wastewater, will not change current allocations of natural water, and will not deal with additional sales, will not require any JWC approval anymore. This means that water projects in Area A and B can be implemented without any approval, allowing a great deal of reconstruction and reparation projects to move forward.[30]

A 'gentleman's agreement' with Israel's Coordinator of Government Activities in the Territories (COGAT) also facilitates projects in Area C. According to Minister Ghoneim, the Joint Water Committee (JWC) set up after Oslo would be revived with a new focus on improving the water situation in Area C. In the minister's view, this revival of the JWC would 'strengthen the PWA's capacity, with the support of its partners, to implement numerous vital water projects faster — especially projects serving Palestinian communities in Area C.'[31] He also explained the new regulations as follows: 'Projects in encampments and villages in Area C do not need approval. We only need to inform the JWC. However, projects that cross through parts of Area C outside the encampments and villages need approval from the Joint Water Committee.'[32] This restriction would apply to big infrastructural projects such as wastewater treatment plants which are mostly to be located in Area C.

In the early months of implementation of this new agreement, it emerged that there was apparently a further understanding, neither written nor publicized, that the Civil Administration would not oppose the advancement of Palestinian Area C projects if the PWA reciprocated by not opposing the development of infrastructure in Area C for Israeli users. This understanding resembles the way in which the JWC used to work up to 2008, with the Palestinians being obliged to nod through Israeli settler projects in order to get agreement on their own.[33] To many Palestinian observers, this quid pro quo deal smacks too much of collaboration.

Upon signing the new water agreement, Israeli and Palestinian officials announced the revival of the JWC, so as to push forward water sector investments in the West Bank. On 16 May 2017, the committee reconvened under the guidance of Israel's energy minister Yuval Steinitz and the head of COGAT, General Yo'av Mordechai, along with the heads of the Israeli and Palestinian water authorities. There were decisions on drilling one new well and upgrading one existing well and on sharing Mekorot data to resolve past billing errors.[34] The PWA stated its intention to implement the 2014 Water Law reforms and its priority investments as set out in the 2017–22 *Strategic Development Plan* (on which see Chapter 3). The Palestinians also brought up the question of the proposed desalination facility in Gaza and announced the convening of the donor meeting to discuss its financing (see Chapter 6).

Through this agreement, the JWC would maintain its original mandate and would reconvene to discuss key issues that had long dogged the sector.[35] These issues included new drilling plans, environmental issues, water tariffs and agricultural water use. The expectation was that project approvals would be streamlined in Areas A and B, and that plans would go ahead for new water pipelines and to increase the capacity of existing lines. The committee was also to work on coordinating joint reservoir usage in preparation for expected shortages in the summer months.[36]

Water and recent 'peace' initiatives

In 2017, the Trump administration began working on a new US 'peace initiative' with the legwork being done by US special envoy Jason Greenblatt. A number of members of the US Congress sent a bipartisan letter calling upon the administration to regard water as the 'low-hanging fruit' of an ultimate peace deal. The first meeting between the Israeli and the Palestinian sides together with the special envoy took place on 26 May 2017 and bore some fruit in the shape of the water purchase agreement discussed earlier. However, subsequently talks were broken off. [37]

The United States finally came out with its plan in January 2020. However, it contains no new proposals for the 'low-hanging fruit'.[38] There is some bland language about water in Article 14 that 'the parties recognize mutual water rights and agree to equitably share existing cross-border water sources and cooperate in making additional sources available through existing and emerging technologies'. There is commitment to sustainability and water-quality protection for the aquifers, and provision for flexibility in the case of climatic variability. For extra water, priority is given to desalination and a commitment to 'reasonable prices'. Wastewater treatment and reuse is also a priority. There is no reference to a water agreement or institutional set-up, and no specifics on how the Palestinians will get any extra water other than through purchases.

The proposal is accompanied by an investment programme. This lists fourteen water and wastewater projects for a total investment of $2.3 billion. The projects, most of which are already on the table, are for desalination, wastewater treatment and water conveyance and network development, together with some rehabilitation of existing wells. The number one project is 'Water Supply: Imports from Israel – to provide immediately impactful solutions to potable water needs in Gaza and the West Bank by increasing imports from Israel'.

The proposal thus essentially confirms the current direction of travel, with extra water for the Palestinians likely to be sought mainly in manufactured water, unless the phrase 'the parties recognize mutual water rights and agree to equitably share existing cross-border water sources' could be interpreted as introducing some prospect of reallocation of groundwater. Equitable sharing is, after all, the basic principle of international water law on transboundary resources. In any case, the Palestinians showed no interest in the Trump proposals and, with the advent of the new US administration in 2021, the proposals have essentially been shelved.

Is water cooperation a pathway to peace – or a trap?

One argument that has been advanced for Palestinians to cooperate with the Israelis on water is that working together can bring understanding and forge professional relations, which may not only help to ease the water situation but also over time create the ground for movement on the political issues. In his analysis of the informal cooperation between Jordanian and Israeli professionals over the Yarmouk prior to the 1993 treaty, Jeffrey Sosland argues that 'tactical functional cooperation' can build a community and practice of trust and lead to new ideas to solve common problems.[39] Ultimately, he sees this less formal cooperation working hand in hand with political cooperation, and in the end having the potential to contribute to peace building. In the Israeli–Palestinian case, the cross-border work done on the environment under the aegis of EcoPeace also demonstrates the potential of this approach. The question for Palestinians is, however, whether tactical functional cooperation is not just another form of collaboration, accepting the normalization of the occupation of their country and working within an illegitimate framework to build relations and understanding and cooperation which simply reinforce injustice and illegality.

At a larger scale, water cooperation would increase economic interdependency – but whether this would be a pathway to peace or to a new and coercive inequity is debatable. In recent years, the Israeli leadership, and in particular Benjamin Netanyahu, has asserted that economic arrangements that benefit Palestinians financially would more readily improve security than would negotiating political concessions. Some of this thinking about 'economic peace' has seen water as one entry point. In this view, water sales would be a commercial, not a political, transaction. Ability to access adequate water would remove the impulse to pursue the political issue of 'water rights'. A network of pipes and daily flows of water would bind Israelis and Palestinians close together.

In a 2017 op-ed in *The New York Times*, Seth Siegel explored the benefits of developing economic interdependencies between the parties through water purchases. He explains 'The strategic genius of the plan is that it weaves vital economic interests of these sometimes-antagonists together. Even should Jordan or the West Bank someday fall to radical rejectionists, it would be nearly impossible for those leaders to entirely break the water ties established here without creating substantial hardship for their populations.'[40]

This is a logic that has particular appeal to business-minded Americans. It formed a strong theme of discussions brokered by the Americans during the Oslo process. The Paris Accord of 1996 was based on the tenet that prosperity would be a precursor of peace. Indeed, the idea formed a central part of the Trump 'peace initiative'. The general view of Palestinians, however, is that an economic relationship between so rich and powerful a people as the Israelis and so poor and enfeebled a people as the Palestinians is a relationship of economic subordination rather than cooperation. Even from Siegel's argument it can be deduced that Israel sees economic cooperation in terms of political control.

Nasser Abdul Karim, economics professor at Bir Zeit University, explains this point of view:

> From its economic relations, Israel seeks to preserve its security and political superiority [over the PA]. Israel is ready to establish economic ties with the PA and to alleviate economic restrictions as long as the [economic cooperation] does not undermine Israel's envisioned solution and does not allow the PA to have economic control and sovereignty. A closer economic relationship would entrench the Palestinian territories' economic subordination to Israel and does not reflect any sort of Palestinian sovereignty.[41]

Siegel does not mention another possibility, that it might be that *Israel* someday falls to radical annexationists. He may be right, that the ties of water purchase may not be broken – after all, Israel sells water to Gaza while often fighting its government and people. But the fatal logic for the Palestinians of such an arrangement is also clear. Their view is that the 'weaving together' is done by Israel as the powerful partner to tie up the Palestinians, while giving the Palestinians no influence over Israel. This possibility seems to be confirmed by the earlier 'cooperation' under Article 40 of the Oslo II accords which many Palestinians consider essentially made the PA the agent for the execution of Israel's water resource management strategy.

In this view, water cooperation from a Palestinian perspective – unless it were on a radically different basis of give-and-take cooperation between equals – is no more than the continuation of the unequal and coercive relations that Israel has established since 1967. Once the deal is done, there is no more room for manoeuvre. Any hope that Palestinians can claim water rights or reach an equitable settlement disappears. Economic 'interdependency' in this view is pure dependency and a surrender of the aspirations for which Palestinians have been making sacrifices for half a century and more. It is exchanging hopes and aspirations for justice for a mess of pottage.

Chapter 8

INCENTIVES TO CHANGE

Would the Israelis or the Palestinians change their stance? Essentially if the gains of cooperation were to benefit both parties – and the benefits outweighed the costs.

At present, many incentives facing the Palestinians in the water sector are perverse. The restrictive conditions of Article 40 and the limits on Palestinian water abstractions and infrastructure create perverse incentives *not* to cooperate on sustainable, best practice water management.

The very poor water service and low levels of potable water supply in many towns create perverse incentives *not* to pay water bills, both at the level of consumers and at the level of municipalities. As long as wastewater treatment infrastructure has been bogged down by requirements that plants treat settler sewage, and as long as reuse has been constrained by Area C limitations, the Palestinians have had neither the means nor the incentive to properly treat and reuse wastewater. The failure to collect, treat and reuse their wastewater, and the appalling state of raw sewage coursing down the wadis, polluting their own lands and streaming into Israel – this they lay squarely at the door of unreasonable and counterproductive Israeli conditions.[1] Reworking the framework to give Palestinians incentives and to empower them for good water and wastewater management would strengthen Palestinian water security.

Clearly, creating positive incentives for the Palestinians is a prerequisite to cooperation in sustainable water management. But what incentive does Israel have to change? First, there could be gains from cooperative management of the shared resource. Good practice from both parties would conserve the Mountain Aquifers and protect their quality, and it would protect Israel from what Ariel Sharon contemptuously dubbed a 'sewage *intifada*'. In addition, a water-insecure people is a restive people. Israeli cooperation would help address a humanitarian crisis, improve the well-being of a poor population and help build Palestinian institutions for good management. By helping to build Palestinian welfare and the Palestinian economy and by strengthening Palestinian institutions, cooperation would create a partnership of equality and trust, which can only be in Israel's pragmatic self-interest. It could even open up prospects for other practical agreements and broader subsequent cooperation with the Palestinian Authority.[2]

More generally, a sympathetic attitude on water would demonstrate to the world Israeli respect of law and ethics in working for solutions on a thorny issue on which Israel is exposed – see, for example, the campaign to boycott Mekorot on the international stage.[3] It would also represent a 'no regrets' step on one aspect of final status that can possibly be resolved by itself.

Israel now *can* afford to compromise on water. The nation's long struggle for water autonomy is over and the goals of which the Zionist pioneers dreamed have been attained. Today Israel can actually create almost unlimited new water, so can negotiate on other principles than its own water security. Even internal opposition to a more flexible policy on water may nowadays be limited.

On the Palestinian side, there would be important gains. Water security would become an attainable goal within a few years, but any deal would have to avoid the stigma of 'collaboration' or the perception of any compromise on other final status issues.

What has happened can happen. The recent Red Sea–Dead Sea agreement shows that Israel is prepared, when the conditions are right, to cooperate with Palestinians on water issues, and to make concessions. The 1994 peace treaty with Jordan shows that Israel can feel water-secure enough to give up water in return for some tangible gain, and can do it without raising a political furore. On the Palestinian side, recent agreements on wastewater – such as those in Wadi Nar/Kidron Valley – show some pragmatism, at least, alongside the declaration that issues of final status would not be compromised.

* * *

Why should Israel change?

The benefits to Israel of cooperative water management

We are talking here about a new scheme of cooperative management of the water resources that Israelis and Palestinians share. The old scheme of cooperation set out in Article 40 has clearly outlived its usefulness. Palestinians now reject it absolutely and endure the continuation of its mechanisms only because they are obliged to. Israelis too recognize the need for change. They recognize at least that Palestinians need more water, if not more powers. Certainly all sides recognize that the current arrangements are not conducive to the well-being of the Palestinian population and are therefore not conducive to 'peace'. Up to now, the Israeli solution has been to agree to sell more water to the Palestinians and, recently, to ease up a little on the constraints on infrastructure and water management previously encountered under the implementation of Article 40. But this is not cooperative management. It is, in the Palestinian view, the occasional leniency of a controlling power. Cooperative management is different. It is management between equal partners, in the interests of both.

Management of a shared transboundary resource requires that the partners agree on rules that assure equitable benefits for each party, share the costs and protect the quantity and quality of the resource and its environmental setting. Both of the parties need incentives to follow the rules. At present, many incentives facing the Palestinians are perverse – and this is not in Israel's interest. Too low an allocation of water gives incentives to unlicenced drilling and illicit taking of water. An imposed regulatory regime enforced by an occupying power encourages evasion. A system of water sales by a dominant power is seen as returning water earlier appropriated by that power, and this creates resentment and encourages the buyers to evade payment. A system of restrictive investment approval and denial of access for Palestinians to large parts of the West Bank gives no incentive to Palestinians to treat their wastewater and scant scope for reusing it. Ariel Sharon, in fact, believed that Israel was imposing perverse incentives *not* to treat wastewater when he made his quip about a 'sewage *intifada*'.

There is thus a case to be made for Israel to consider new institutional arrangements that would empower Palestinians to *manage the Mountain Aquifers jointly with Israel.* In line with best practices of cooperative transboundary water management, a cooperative approach based on an equal partnership between the parties would create mutual and reciprocal responsibility and give both parties the incentives to optimize benefits, share costs and work for sustainability and protection of the environment.

Benefits to Israel from Palestinian water security

Cooperation on water management would help remove some of the perverse incentives in Palestinian water management, which is in Israel's interest. As long as water over which Palestinians have even restricted control is no more than one sixth of the quantum needed to develop a modern economy and provide modern water services,[4] Palestinians have scant incentive to cooperate on sustainable management of the shared resource. Not only does their meagre ration create disenchantment with good management practice, but they believe that their partner has often departed from good practice to their detriment by overdrawing. As the Palestinians have access to only a fixed quantum, all the benefits of conservation go to the beneficiary of the residual, which again gives no incentive to good practice.[5]

By the same logic, as long as Palestinians are denied greater access to the relatively low-cost water which arises within their territory and which lies beneath their feet, they have little incentive other than desperation to pay for water pumped up from the coast. Such a water purchase contract they see as being compelled into a high-cost water market – and one with political strings attached – to replace their own resource which they see as being appropriated.

Essentially, if there were incentives for Palestinians to manage water sustainably and efficiently, this would not only strengthen their water security but Israel's also. It would certainly help to resolve what in some areas has degenerated into a humanitarian crisis. Beyond that, good water management and water security would help to build the Palestinian economy as a more equal partner to Israel. Empowerment of Palestinians as partners in managing the aquifers on a genuinely cooperative basis would help to build the Palestinian institutions and capacities which are essential to the growth of a stable, capable, prosperous people, which is in Israel's interest too.[6]

The incentive for Israel here is not only a search for good water management. It is also pragmatic self-interest. Cooperative water management can make a contribution to 'peace'. A water-insecure people is a disturbed and angry people. Israelis generally see improving the Palestinian economy as a priority – and adequate water and good water services are an important part of this. Certainly, the defence establishment sees a direct link between Palestinian hardship and security in the territories. COGAT has besought its political leadership to take steps in that direction, based on the assumption that Palestinian hardships lead to desperation, and desperation leads to violence. As IDF general Eyal Ben-Reuven said, 'the humanitarian crisis lays the groundwork for hatred.'[7]

Reputational gains

Beyond the benefits to Palestinians – and to Israel from better-off Palestinians – there could be a significant gain to Israel on the world stage. Cooperative management of a shared resource would further enhance Israel's reputation as a world-beating water manager. Where other transboundary water management arrangements have failed or produced only weak results, Israel has an opportunity to work with the Palestinians to put in place genuinely cooperative arrangements. Not only would this be a first in water management, it could also enhance Israel's reputation as a conciliator, as ardent for 'peace' as for security. Making a fair agreement on something so basic to human life and activity as water would demonstrate Israel's respect for law and ethics to the world. A fair cooperation bringing to Palestinians the possibility of the same measure of water security as Israel has achieved would do much to enhance Israel's reputation and to reduce its vulnerability to criticism by resolving a thorny issue on which it has been particularly exposed.

Economic and environmental gains

Israel would not overlook the economic and environmental benefits that a genuinely cooperative agreement would bring. Palestinians are not the only ones to be unhappy with the status quo. Israel too has many grievances from the current uncooperative arrangements. Palestinian municipalities do not pay the West Bank Water Department for much of the water that is supplied by Mekorot. Israel is obliged to deduct the amounts due from the tax revenues it collects on behalf of the Palestinian Authority. This is a source of friction between the Authority and Israel, and is capable of being perceived by Palestinians and the wider world as an act of coercive control reminiscent of the colonial era, of Anglo-French control of Egyptian tax revenues in the nineteenth century, for example. Under a scheme of genuine cooperative management, these matters would be internal to the Palestinian Authority.

There is an economic case for transferring water resources to the Palestinians because the marginal value of water is much higher in the water-short economy of the West Bank and Gaza than it is in Israel. One study estimated an overall economic gain of $59 million a year from reallocating 80 million cubic metres a year from Israel to the Palestinians.[8]

Significant economic gains are also available from cooperation which would allow economies of scale to be captured in investments, for example in desalination and bulk water distribution, or in wastewater treatment and reuse. There could also be significant economic gains from optimizing investment at the basin scale. The leading example would be to invest in developing lower-cost sources from the Mountain Aquifers for local use in the West Bank while prioritizing the use of Tiberias water and desalinated resources along the coastal plain.

A cooperative agreement would be a way to improve the protection of the environment and of human health. Sewage management has become a massive problem. Just as water flows and is no respecter of boundaries, so do wastewater and sewage flow across jurisdictions. Tens of thousands of tons of raw sewage cascade down the West Bank wadis every day and into Israel. Long-held Palestinian plans for wastewater treatment and reuse have been stymied under current arrangements. If Palestinians were empowered and enabled to manage their own water affairs within a cooperative agreement, there would be more opportunities to treat the wastewater, to recycle it to strengthen the West Bank water inventory in the way that Israel has done within its own territory and to reuse this precious resource to boost productive agriculture.[9]

Improving risk management

Moving from the 'asymmetrical' arrangements of Article 40 to a cooperative arrangement would reinforce Israel's ability to manage water-related risks. In particular, new arrangements of responsible cooperation would mitigate the current levels of risk to the shared resource from overpumping that was previously practiced by Israel or from Palestinian unlicensed drilling and abstractions within the West Bank. Responsible cooperative management by both parties would also mitigate risks to the resource and to the environment from pollution from agricultural fertilizers and pesticides and from untreated wastewater.

So might Israel consider negotiating a new water agreement?

One key factor is that it *can*. With the possibility of surplus water, this is an issue on which Israel has scope to change its stance. It can, for example, negotiate new allocations – and this is what it has recently done by agreeing new purchases by the Palestinians to be supplied by Mekorot from the NWC. But these arrangements remain within the tight corset of Article 40 and do nothing to promote genuine cooperative management, nor to build Palestinian water security – nor to reinforce that of Israel.

Could 'water diplomacy' depoliticize water? Water has been entangled with other negotiations in successive 'peace' processes as well as during the course of Oslo implementation, and has often become stuck in the old logic of the Madrid conference that started the whole 'peace' process: 'nothing is agreed until everything is agreed.' However, now that more water is a possibility, many observers see the opportunity to depoliticize it. There is certainly an option, if both sides agree, to remove the link with final status negotiations. The advantage to Israel would be both tangible – a 'water peace' – and reputational – one contentious final status issue at last agreed.

The internal political economy of water cooperation within Israel is not necessarily unfavourable. Water is less of a political issue in Israel than once it was. The lack of fuss over Israel's agreement to transfer water to Jordan in the 1994 Peace Treaty is an early testament to this – see the discussion on this treaty in this chapter. Today adequate water is available in Israel and it is very well managed. All the tough demand management measures have already been applied and all the sectors and the nation as a whole get the water they need. Conservation and efficiency are now ingrained in the national consciousness and practices. Even the threats of climate change and of growing aridity are countered by Israel's ability to create 'new' water and to store water in ample reserves. Israel is water secure and Israelis nowadays generally feel water secure. So the internal political risk for Israel to share water resources with the Palestinians is not necessarily unmanageable. Furthermore, the Israeli government and public have become proud of their leading role in the water sector. It is common amongst concerned Israelis to see water as an area of potential, where real cooperation with the Palestinians may be a possibility.[10]

In addition, the voices of environmentalists and of ordinary Israelis concerned about problems of pollution, resource depletion and ecological harms have become more clamant. Israeli action to improve resource sustainability and environmental protection would be welcomed at home, amongst neighbours, and globally. In addition, external willingness to finance projects could be significantly increased.

Of course there is a price to be paid for everything. As in all movements towards cooperation, both sides have to give way on something to attain the benefits. By contrast, unilateralism is politically expedient and does not expose thorny issues of political and economic asymmetries. There are also costs to cooperation that it is difficult to quantify. As Fischhendler maintains: 'transboundary integration entails a high potential for disagreement, high transaction costs, and infringements on sovereignty.'[11] The first step towards cooperation is to recognize equality between cooperating partners.

What conditions would change Palestinian positions?

There is no doubt that a renegotiated water agreement could bring Palestinians some important gains. In fact, a new agreement between equals on a cooperative basis could ultimately bring Palestinians the longed-for water security. In addition to resolving the current critical water problems, a 'good' agreement would bring empowerment and recognition of Palestinian institutions, both the PA and the PWA, enhancing their legitimacy. A new water agreement would make a substantial contribution not only to the economy but also to state building.

Whatever the formulation, Palestinian empowerment would be a contribution to sovereignty goals and, if that area of cooperation worked well, it could act as a first step towards a wider accord.

Provided the cooperation were not subordination – or perceived as a collaboration – the improved water availability and services, and the reality that one of the final status issues had been at least partly resolved, would lead to popular satisfaction. Empowerment of the PWA and the reality of some measure of water autonomy would change attitudes to water, sanitation and the environment. A sense of water security would strengthen incentives to the Palestinians to solve the sanitation problem and to protect the rural and urban environment. Citizen responsibility and engagement would grow and grievances reduce.

The red lines are clear, nonetheless. Nothing should be seen as collaboration, and nothing should be capable of being construed as compromising positions on other final status issues – and, above all, cooperation should not create dependency. Palestinians are most likely to have positive attitudes to options to achieve water security when those options align with political objectives and with the ultimate goals of sovereignty, security and national identity. It is not inconceivable that a separate water 'deal' could be construed as movement towards those goals.

What can we learn from other water agreements?

Does the Israel–Jordan Peace Treaty and its subsequent implementation show the possibility of relaxing the Israeli identification of water with national security?[12]

As we mentioned in Chapter 7, Israel signed a peace treaty with Jordan in 1994 in which Israel essentially traded a relatively small quantity of Jordan River water in return for a durable peace with its fellow riparian.[13] Although Israel's concessions may seem unremarkable in global terms – certainly the quantity and value of the water were small by world standards – they were striking in the context. For half a century, ever since the creation of the state, Israel had worked to build up a water inventory that would make it self-sufficient and prosperous. Internally, the pressures were strong. The highly vocal agricultural lobby, particularly the politically influential Yarmouk Triangle farmers, kept up a constant clamour to secure and increase water resources from the Jordan basin. Until the water reforms and technological advances that began in the 1980s, these lobbies were at the height of their powers. Water and state building were almost inseparable concepts. However, by the time of the Jordan treaty, Israel had effectively solved the challenge of water for agriculture – see Chapter 1 – and the agricultural lobby was quietening down. By 1994, with its water security firmly established, Israel had much more room for manoeuvre.

Over the following years the practice of cooperation between the two states strengthened and – as we saw in Chapter 7 – desalination came on the scene, changing both the hydro-politics and the hydro-geography of water in the region and creating the possibility of Israel becoming a water-surplus nation. The first result was that in 2010 Jordan and Israel signed a memorandum that proposed a joint project to swap water at different locations. Jordan would desalinate seawater in Aqaba, and deliver some of this water to southern Israel, with Israel committing to buying 30–50 million cubic metres annually.[14] In exchange, Israel would deliver water to Jordan from the Upper Jordan. This had the double advantage for Jordan of making the Aqaba desalination plant more viable and supplying water to the Jordanian heartland at much less cost than desalinating on the Red Sea and pumping up to the highlands. Although this water swap has not yet been implemented, apparently for reasons of cost and market demand on the Israeli side, the agreement showed the potential for the parties to work together.

Water cooperation with Jordan has the potential to work for a number of reasons. First and foremost, although Jordan is a state far weaker economically and militarily and with less powerful international backing than Israel, it is nonetheless a nation state nominally on an equal footing with Israel, able to declare war and peace and to assert its rights by multiple means in international fora. In the negotiations, Israel treated Jordan as an equal partner.

Second, both sides had incentives to cooperate. Israel wanted peace and normalization and the extra security which that would bring. In fact this deal suggests that Israel does have an interest in agreements on water that link to wider 'peace' themes. As Aviram et al. (2014) contend:

> While the primary motivation for the project from a Jordanian perspective is the prospect of additional water, for the Israelis it is the prospect of promoting relations with Jordan, as seen by the use of the label 'Peace Conduit', 'Peace Canal', and 'Peace Valley' in documents and proclamations describing the project in Israel.

Jordan too wanted peace and normalization but also extra water resources and the right to develop infrastructure in the basin. Israel also had something that Jordan wanted and which Israel was prepared to give up – water.

The role of an outside broker was important also. There was strong interest from the United States in a peace treaty that was fair to both sides, and this gave Israel a further incentive to cooperate because compliance would earn it further support from its principal backer. The United States played an important role for the Jordanians too because it was seen by both sides as a guarantor of some kind of fairness. This has been particularly important for Jordan as the weaker state.

Palestinian involvement in the Red Sea–Dead Sea Project showed how cooperation in a regional approach to water resources management can win concessions and bring gains

In 2013, Israelis, Palestinians and Jordanians signed a memorandum of understanding for the Red Sea–Dead Sea Conveyance Project (RSDS), marking a possible new phase in cooperation amongst Jordan Valley riparians. Founded on a concept of restoring water levels in the Dead Sea and making new desalinated water available economically, the agreement presented a regional development plan with an exchange of benefits to all parties: a desalination plant in Aqaba that would produce water for Israel and Jordan; increased quantities of water to be transferred from Lake Tiberias to Jordan; and the sale of 32 million cubic metres a year of desalinated water from Mekorot to the Palestinian Authority for use in the West Bank and Gaza.[15]

This arrangement was a first for a regional approach to water resources management. Its significance was threefold. First, it established the economic case for regional cooperation on water. The cost–benefit analysis demonstrated the 'win–win' potential of regional cooperation to yield maximum benefits for each party. However, the fragility of this arrangement was revealed when global market forces led to the collapse of Israel's previously high-value pepper farming industry in the Arava, which the desalinated water was intended to serve. Second, the RSDS project established a mechanism for regional engagement and initiated a shift of the water paradigm towards a more regional system model.[16] It showed the possibilities of a larger framework for regional water cooperation which collectively weighs and manages environmental, social and economic trade-offs at the basin scale.[17] Third, RSDS recognized the Palestinians as equal partners. For the Palestinians, this was a political gain, signalling their recognition as a riparian in the Jordan River basin and the Dead Sea. This was not something that came as an easy concession from Israel. In fact, US secretary of state John Kerry worked hard to include the Palestinians in the project, and international donors made the inclusion of the Palestinian Authority a condition of their investments.[18]

The RSDS project also provided an alternate track on which the parties could convene even when their relationship deteriorated, and when political engagement on many other levels had slowed. The agreement was signed in December 2013, during the period when the JWC was not convening. The willingness of the parties to meet even when other tracks were closed off was due in part to the fact that the World Bank and other donors served as third-party mediators, and that there was the prospect of financial incentives.

Agreements on wastewater projects show Palestinian flexibility, provided there is no clear compromise on final status issues.

In the post-Oslo period the Palestinians have resisted Israeli demands that wastewater treatment facilities inside the West Bank benefit Israeli residents of East Jerusalem and settlements – see Chapter 4 for a full discussion of this issue. When anti-normalization became official policy in 2008, this refusal became a key plank in the Palestinian political platform. For years, Israel held up approval for wastewater treatment plants in the West Bank because of the Palestinian stance. Nonetheless, there has been some cooperation between Israelis and Palestinians on the issue. At least one plant does in fact treat settler sewage and it appears that there is also agreement for the new plant at Hebron to do the same.[19] These arrangements have always been kept *sub rosa* and when news of them emerges there has been a loud outcry from Palestinians about treating 'settler shit'. Official responses from the Palestinian Authority have been muted, but the underlying policy is that nothing in this should be construed as a compromise on final status.

A similar 'constructive ambiguity' may also resolve the long-standing problem of sewage flowing in Wadi Nar (or the Kidron Valley). For decades, sewage from Israeli settlements, Palestinian towns and contested neighbourhoods in East Jerusalem has been coursing down the streambed. Managing the combined flow of wastewater has long been a hotly debated issue, with local Palestinian and Israeli leadership and national NGOs calling for solutions to mitigate the growing environmental pollution and public health risks.[20] Palestinian leadership had argued that to treat the sewage would legitimize Israeli rule of Jerusalem and the existence of Israeli settlements.

Recently, however, Israel and the PA have signed a memorandum of understanding which provides the opportunity to build a wastewater treatment scheme, and financing is being secured. The political obstacle has been averted in this case by including in the agreement, on Palestinian insistence, an explicit statement that the project does not preclude a final status agreement and that a long-term solution for wastewater management in the location would need to be determined as part of that final agreement. The tipping point seems to have been the environmental health issues associated with the raw sewage running close to village areas and to archaeological and historical sites, as well as the palpable harm to the environment of the Jordan Valley. Consequently, mayors of affected communities in the valley rallied for change. The lesson is that there is some flexibility on the Palestinian side, provided that there is also a balance of advantage and that there is no patent infringement of final status claims.

Lessons from these agreements

From the RSDS we may glean the ideas that, under pressure from the outside and where there are gains beyond the purely Israeli/Palestinian issues, Israel may be prepared to work with the Palestinians on issues of cooperative water management, and to make concessions. Both the 1994 Jordan/Israel peace treaty and the later agreements on water exchange show that Israel does set a certain store on making 'peace', at least with sovereign states. However, the fact that the water swap between Israel and Jordan has not gone ahead also shows the vulnerability of the agreements to economic, non-political drivers.

The tacit flexibility that the Palestinian Authority showed on wastewater treatment shows some willingness on the Palestinian side to take a pragmatic approach provided that the key issues of final status are not formally compromised. But the case also shows how little support the PA might expect from its people should it negotiate anything that gives away the hoped-for sovereignty, security and national identity.

The agreements between Israel and Jordan also show the potential financial benefits of cooperation. For Jordan, the original agreement for Israel to purchase water from the Aqaba desalination unit meant economies of scale for the plant, while having extra supplies for Amman and the highlands coming from the Upper Jordan valley saved all the costs of pumping water up from the coast. An additional point raised by Aviram et al. was that 'because of the cooperative nature of the project, costs will be shared among the two countries and the international donor community, which is willing to support Arab-Israeli cooperation.'

Overall, the lessons from the 1994 Peace Treaty with Jordan and subsequent agreements show the way that Israel can use water as part of a negotiation. They also show the key truth that Israel is water-secure enough to be able to give up water without compromising its water security – and without raising a political furore.

The 2010 agreement with Jordan, where Israel is swapping natural water from its north for desalinated water in the south, would have created 'interdependence' between the two states. The two states dealt on an equal footing with each other and the relationship was not asymmetric, as it would have been in the case of Jordan simply buying water from Israel. By contrast, for the Palestinians who have no water resource to trade that Israel does not already control, interdependence is not an option. The relationship is one of water sales, an asymmetric dependency that appears bound up with broader issues of subordination of the interests of one people to another.

Finally, the shape of the Israel–Jordan cooperation illustrates the potential for a game-changing role for desalination in regional hydro-politics and hydro-geography – but also some of the possible downside of these changes for the Palestinians.

New and emerging incentives: Climate change and the Covid-19 pandemic

Climate change has manifested itself in the region in hotter, drier weather and in increasing unpredictability in the timing and quantity of rainfall. Average temperatures have risen and aridity has increased. The particular vulnerability of the Palestinian territories to climate change compared to Israel is demonstrated by the drought of 2009–11. For a decade from 1997 to 2008, the cultivated area in the West Bank had remained fairly constant at around 1.8 million dunams (some 185,000 hectares), but by the 2010–11 season when the drought really hit, the cultivated area plummeted to around 1.0 million dunams (100,000 hectares), a 45 per cent drop. Food aid became necessary. The contrast with Israel is stark. Palestinian agriculture is largely rainfed – only 11 per cent of the cultivated area is irrigated, and far and away the largest area of Palestinian cultivated land is thus vulnerable to drought. By contrast, 62 per cent of the cultivated area in Israel is irrigated and hence largely protected against drought hazards.[21]

The climate situation in the region is expected to continue to deteriorate overall. Annual precipitation is expected to decrease by 10–30 per cent by 2030 and by up to 50 per cent by 2080. There will be growing potential for droughts and floods, higher temperatures leading to higher evapo-transpiration and reduced surface and groundwater availability.

Climate change is a global and regional phenomenon that requires responses beyond national boundaries. There is a possibility that the transboundary character of climate change can provide incentives for regional cooperation to reduce vulnerability, and also for wider cooperation on mitigation of the drivers of climate change. For example, in a seminal 2020 paper, *A Green-Blue Deal for the Middle East*, EcoPeace sees scope for improving adaptive capacity on both water and energy security through coordinated transboundary investments in region-wide climate smart initiatives, with the prospect that this cooperation on water and climate could contribute to conflict resolution and peace building.

EcoPeace thus sees climate change as not only a threat but also as an opportunity, and one which can be reinforced by notions of 'Build Back Better' in the wake of the Covid-19 pandemic, prioritizing climate change adaptation and mitigation as a way of 'stimulating the economy and advancing societal progress'. The target of realizing reduced and ultimately zero carbon emissions can be accompanied by programmes to invest in green jobs and infrastructure.

With the election of the new US administration, a fresh impetus for action on climate change is likely, and this could attract new investment in adaptation and mitigation in Israel and the Palestinian territories – and also in Jordan which shares the Jordan basin and which has considerable similarities and complementarities with its neighbours. We shall explore these possibilities further in the next chapter.[22]

Chapter 9

HOW COULD COOPERATION BETWEEN ISRAELIS AND PALESTINIANS BE RESET AND WATER SECURITY ACHIEVED FOR BOTH PEOPLES?

This book has shown sharply contrasted pictures of water security for two peoples who began a century ago from the same point – the limited water resources of a semi-arid land. Israel has striven for water security over many decades at a high cost of money and effort and by force of arms – and has achieved that security. Today, technology, world-beating water management practices and wastewater reuse and desalination consolidate that security and even empower Israel as a potentially water-surplus nation.

By contrast, Palestinians lack any measure of water security. In the West Bank, water resources available to them are too little and there is no integrated network to carry water from its source to where it is to be used. There is scant storage to buffer against climatic vagaries. Water management is confined to 165 separate administrative fragments with no contiguity and with limited autonomy and bound by the long outdated rules of the twenty-five-year-old Oslo Accords, which are vigorously enforced by Israel and entrenched in a situation where the parties hold tight to the notion that 'nothing is agreed until everything is agreed'. Palestinian dependence on Israel for extra water is total. Investment is limited to local infrastructure. Water plans are hamstrung by politics and restricted access, and are for the most part dependent on official Israeli approval. Households, industry and agriculture have inadequate supplies and poor services. Palestinians are excluded from the excellent agricultural potential of the Jordan Valley which Israeli settlements in the area enjoy. The Palestinians are denied the 100 million cubic metres or more of Jordan water that the Johnston Plan allocated to them over half a century ago.[1] Precious wastewater is not recycled and reused in any quantity. Instead it flows as untreated sewage in the wadis, fouling the environment on both sides of the Green Line. In Gaza, the water is undrinkable, but politics, economics and security concerns have hitherto prevented the only viable solutions, large-scale desalination and treatment and reuse of all wastewater.

One reason for the sharp disparity in outcomes in the West Bank lies in the absence of a cooperative framework that would allow an equitable allocation of the shared Mountain Aquifers and efficient, sustainable development and management of those resources. It also lies in the constraints Palestinians are under in the development of the infrastructure and institutions needed to abstract, convey and supply adequate water to the population and to economic uses. It lies too in the economic, physical and political constraints to wastewater management and environmental protection. The case of Gaza is different – there water security can be obtained only by a category shift in the political and security situation.

Palestinians have long had plans, well described in Part II of this book, for resolving these problems in the West Bank – plans for institutional reform, for infrastructure development and for environmental protection, all based on Israeli models and designed to achieve the same levels of water security that Israel has attained. These plans aim at sustainable efficient management of the Mountain Aquifers, adequate bulk water efficiently conveyed to all points of demand, efficient water supply at reasonable prices for households, businesses and agriculture, the collection, treatment and reuse of all wastewater, and protection of the environment.

Achieving these goals any time soon would require both sides to move. Palestinians would need to agree on water aside from other final status issues. Both parties would have to agree to a new scheme of cooperative water management. Israel would have to agree to a fair share of water from the Mountain Aquifers for Palestinians and to progressive reductions in its own abstractions from those aquifers, bringing in desalinated water as a substitute within its own water inventory. Both sides would have to agree to set up cooperative institutions for the management and allocation of shared water resources. Palestinian access to the resources of the Jordan Valley within a regional framework with other riparians would need at least to be on the table.

A new compact on these lines would begin to bring Palestinians the same water security as Israelis enjoy. Founded on political concessions on both sides, it could also begin to build trust where trust is rare.

Towards a new compact

Here we are not starting by talking about politics. We are certainly not talking about 'peace' or 'final status', which are way beyond the ambitions of this book. We are talking about people and their need for something so basic as water security. If we wait for the bigger picture to settle, we may yet be waiting for the Greek Kalends.

We are talking about the well-being of people and the water security that fosters that well-being through the provision of enough water to support good water services and a modern economy. We talk mainly of *Palestinian* water security as it is patent from this entire book that Israelis have already achieved that security. There is, however, a concern there because Palestinian water security is bound up with Israeli water security – both peoples share a common resource and must cooperate to protect the water security not only of themselves but of the others too. Palestinian water security must not threaten Israeli water security – and vice versa. We must not rob Peter to pay Paul. There must be advantages to both parties.

In this chapter, we propose principles; we characterize the components of water security; and we reflect on the institutions needed to gain and retain water security. We suggest practical actions for now and for later. We reflect on the risks, of which everyone will be at once aware. Finally, in a brief coda, we draw some lessons that may be of value beyond the case of Israelis and Palestinians.

Cooperation between Israelis and Palestinians in the West Bank

Principles

We propose five basic principles to shape a new agreement. First, the basis for sharing water should be spelled out clearly and fairly. Then, new arrangements should be economically efficient, taking account of the relative poverty of the Palestinians. Third, any new agreement should respect the water security of both parties and should allow for cooperation on an equal footing. Fourth, arrangements for future water management should be constructed on the basis of best practices in basin management, integrated water resource management and environmental protection and sustainability. Finally, the agreement should allow rational, least-cost development of water infrastructure for Palestinians all across the West Bank.

The basis for sharing water The argument throughout this book has been that principles of fairness demand that water should be shared on an equitable basis, that two peoples who started from a common point a century ago should have access on a basis of equity to the water resources of the land they share. The application of this principled approach would be the first step towards rebalancing water security amongst those who live side by side and share a common resource.

This argument is supported by the principle of community of interest which we discussed in Chapter 7. This principle would view transboundary water resources as the common property of all riparians, to be developed and used in an equitable and reasonable way on a shared basis. We also saw how the UN Watercourses Convention provides a basis for sharing water or benefits, with its principle of 'optimal and sustainable use and benefit'. The convention suggests that riparians of a transboundary resource take into account all relevant factors and circumstances (Article 6), including the physical characteristics of the resource, the level of dependence on the resource of any one segment of the population and the availability of alternatives, and social and economic needs.

How does the case of Israelis and Palestinians sharing the Mountain Aquifers fit into this paradigm? First the *physical characteristics* make the resource accessible to both parties. The groundwater is almost entirely recharged from precipitation on the Palestinian side of the Green Line, and the aquifers are accessible in many locations across the West Bank, although in some cases with considerable depth to water. The natural outflow is largely on the Israeli side of the Green Line and hence accessible to the Israelis, who have long used the majority of the resource from springs and wells on their side.

In the case of the Jordan River, the West Bank is a riparian for an extensive stretch of the lower river below Tiberias, and also of the Dead Sea, the terminus and sink of the river. Past plans were to irrigate the river plain of the West Bank from the Yarmouk tributary via a syphon under the main river. The proposal was never carried out but prior to 1967 the Palestinians irrigated sections of the plain by pumping directly from the river. The Jordan River is thus readily accessible from the Palestinian West Bank.

Whether the ease or cost of access of one party or another gives any weight to claims to use turns, however, on the level of *dependence* on the resource and on access to *alternatives*. Israel's main use of these aquifers has been to supply the coastal cities. The alternative source of supply has become desalination, which is readily available all along the coast and which can be distributed throughout the country. The fact that the production of desalinated water from both seawater and brackish sources can meet Israel's entire domestic water needs – and can do so at prices affordable to the well-off Israelis – demonstrates that Israel has developed a viable and affordable alternative to aquifer water and does not have to depend on the aquifer.

In contrast – and setting aside the question of Jordan River water – the West Bank Palestinians are entirely dependent on the aquifer for natural water within their territory, and they have limited access to brackish water and no access to seawater. The next alternative source of water for West Bank Palestinians is currently to purchase desalinated water from the coast and to pump it up to the highlands. The cost of buying this water is significantly higher than if Palestinians were to pump out the water from beneath their feet, even if the pumping depths are relatively deep. Desalination at the coast plus pumping over as much 100 kilometres laterally and up to an elevation of up to 1,000 metres costs roughly three times as much as pumping from a tubewell in the highlands, even if the pumping depth is 500 metres or more.[2]

Thus Israelis have an affordable and practical alternative to the use of the Mountain Aquifer – and one that lies within their own territory. In the West Bank, the Palestinians have no alternative within their own territory, and the cost of the only available alternative is as much as three times more than water from the aquifers beneath their feet.

An important related point here is *autonomy* – the extent to which water comes from within one's own territory is an important component of water security, especially within the volatile Middle East. Under the current situation, Israel enjoys complete water autonomy, with the limitless resource of desalinated seawater constantly available at the margin, whereas Palestinians are at present reliant on water purchased from their neighbour for every incremental drop. This creates a situation of structural Palestinian *dependency* on Israel.

Social and economic needs are hard to define when the two peoples are at such different stages of development – Israel is a well-off OECD member; the Palestinians live close to the edge of poverty with an economy constantly constrained and often in recession. A fundamental tenet here is equity – fair shares of water – but also equity of expectations. In fairness, why should the Palestinian economy and society not develop as Israel's has over time? Why should water demand not rise to levels commensurate with Israel's? And the complementary argument – how could the Palestinian economy and society develop to reach Israeli levels if Palestinians do not have access over time to increasing quantities of water? Do Palestinian development possibilities and Palestinians' hopes of a decent standard of living such as Israelis enjoy not in the end require the same quantum of water per capita as Israelis have?

Economic efficiency A scheme for progressive rebalancing of shares of the Mountain Aquifer would be supported by the principle of economic efficiency, which is also included in the UN Convention (Article 6). The Israelis have, since independence, invested in infrastructure and management systems that effectively costed water to reflect its scarcity price and the pressing needs for development of the country. In fact, Israel's goal of water autonomy in the two decades after independence could have made that price almost infinite – water at almost any cost.

Pumping water out of Tiberias from 200 metres below sea level uphill another 100 metres over the escarpment and into the coastal plain and then conveying it 250 kilometres to farms in the Negev was not only a fantastic nation-building project but also a very costly one. Subsequent investments have strengthened water security with similar priority to security over economics. Today, with natural resources fully developed, water security is assured at the margin by desalination. The result has been an absolute success, albeit at a price – and that success has been accompanied by continuous attention to efficiency, so that today the cost of water is affordable for Israelis and their (affluent) economy.

But Palestinians are poor, and even with the high levels of donor support they enjoy, they cannot afford water security at *any* price. Least-cost solutions are required. In practice, the 'efficiency of water uses' proposed in the UN Watercourses Convention would mean that Palestinian water supply should come from the least-cost source available to them. In Gaza, this is plainly desalination – there is no other way, and how the costs of it are shared is a question that must somehow be answered. In the case of the West Bank, the economics are the reverse. For the West Bank, desalinated water is the highest cost source, the least good choice.

At present Palestinians are being offered water from Israel's National Water Carrier, priced at the marginal cost of production – the cost of desalination – plus conveyance costs. Added to the cost of buying this water from Israel – nearly $1 per cubic metre – are other production costs that bring total supply costs for some municipalities up to more than $2 per cubic metre. Three of the largest providers – the Jerusalem Water Undertaking and Jenin and Hebron municipalities – purchase most of their water from Mekorot and all three have total operating costs of more than NIS 7, $2.20 per cubic metre. Those West Bank towns which benefit from their own wells are producing water at a fraction of that cost. Towns like Qalqilya, Salfit and Jericho which produce all their water from their own wells have total supply costs of only around NIS 2 or less ($0.50 per cubic metre).[3]

Professor Eilon Adar of Ben-Gurion University argues that 'it makes no sense for the Palestinians to incur the cost of pumping water from . . . sea level across Israel and uphill more than six hundred metres. The transportation cost would add needless expense to the water in the West Bank.'[4] The late professor Tony Allan of King's College, London, the doyen of Middle East water experts, agreed: 'Pumping desalinated water to the West Bank is not the best technical or economic option.'[5]

Clearly it makes no economic sense for the West Bank to buy Israeli water from desalination plants on Israel's coast. It would be more economic for Israel to consider the new context of water source options, agree that the Palestinians pump more water from the Mountain Aquifers and consider, alongside their Palestinian counterparts, renegotiating the arrangements laid out in the Oslo agreement. The economic solution for West Bank Palestinians is to take water from the aquifer at the points where it can be available for West Bank towns and villages at least cost.

Evidence is that even if the 'natural outflow' of the western and northern aquifers lies towards or beyond the Green Line, much of the aquifer is exploitable upstream and at much lower cost than the import of desalinated water from the coast. Professor Arie Issar, the distinguished water expert at Ben-Gurion University of the Negev, who 'helped green the Israeli desert a generation ago by finding new water sources in the [Negev]', said, 'It would be foolish to desalinate water on the coast and push it up the mountains when there are underground water resources up there, which cost only a third as much.'[6] Economics suggests that efficient allocation of water from the aquifer would prioritize Palestinian communities in the highlands. From an economic point of view, water is more valuable in the socio-economy where it is scarce. A cubic metre of water is worth much more in economic terms to a water-short Palestinian household or farmer than to their Israeli counterparts. Common sense and equity would suggest that a poor people like the West Bank Palestinians should have access to the cheapest water in the region, not the most expensive.

The principle of cooperation in management of shared water resources and the environment The principle of community of interests which we discussed in Chapter 7 underlies the practice of cooperative management, which is essential to transboundary water management. The UN Watercourses Convention in fact provides the basis for cooperative management in its requirement for notification and negotiation on any water resource development and in its provisions regarding responsibilities for water sharing and use and for environmental protection.

The basic principle of cooperation is equality between co-operators. We have seen in Chapter 7 of our companion volume *The History of Water* how the management framework established under Article 40 has failed to achieve the objective of cooperative management. This failure can be largely laid at the door of an imbalance of power between the parties which was reflected in lop-sided governance arrangements. While Article 40 may not have intended to reconcile these imbalances, as the agreement was intended only for an interim period, this problem has been compounded by the fact that a comprehensive water agreement, and the peace process in general, stalled – hence entrenching this skewed relationship. Perceived for many years now by the Palestinians as another instrument of coercion and as an extension of Israeli political control, the institutions agreed under Article 40 have essentially broken down. A restart founded on genuine cooperation should be on a basis of equal powers and mutual respect for each other's water security, aiming at a shared objective to achieve both their own and their partner's water security. A cooperative agreement is required, providing for a new beginning with new rules and new institutions, managing the Mountain Aquifers in line with best practice on integrated water resource management.

Beyond that, there is a striking community of interest in sustainability of the shared resource and in protection of its ecological setting and the broader environment. In fact, the case for cooperation and partnership approaches has become ever stronger as natural resources have been exploited to the limit and as climatic changes have intensified pressures on those resources. It is perhaps cooperation on issues like combating pollution, ensuring sustainability of the quantity and quality of groundwater, and restoring environmental flows and natural ecosystems that will help to drive – and even justify – cooperation on the management of shared water resources.

Best practice in integrated water resource management Best practice in water that has emerged over the last thirty years aims to develop a framework of water governance based on the principles of equity, efficiency and sustainability.[7] The *equity* principle is to ensure equitable access for all users to an adequate quantity and quality of water necessary to sustain human well-being and to develop a modern economy. In the case we are discussing, this would include making sure that water services are available for all uses and that the benefits of water resources development, allocation and use are shared equitably across Palestinian *and* Israeli populations and their economies.

Under the *efficiency* principle, the aim is to bring the greatest benefit to the greatest number of users with the available financial and water resources. This would mean that water is available for its highest-value economic use and that in all uses income per drop of water is maximized. Regarding *sustainability*, the goal is to sustain the ecological services provided by water and to ensure the sustainability of the resource, in both quantity and quality. This would mean, for example, ensuring that the water resource and the broader environment are not harmed and that adequate allocation is made to sustain the functioning of natural ecosystems and their services. The needs of future generations also have to be taken into account.

These three principles of integrated water resource management are supported by the UN Convention which provides for 'measures to prevent, control and reduce any negative transboundary impact' (Article 2) and 'to prevent significant harm' (Article 7). The parties should ensure that waters are used in a reasonable and equitable way, avoid pollution, manage water in a way that is ecologically sound, conserve the resource and protect the environment and the ecosystem. They should apply the 'polluter pays' principle, and respect intergenerational equity.

Translating these principles into practice requires integrated management at the basin scale across all water sources and uses within the basin. Planning and management of water resources within discrete water basins have therefore become best practice. In the case of groundwater, this indicates the need for a hydro-geographical organization of aquifer management, with regulatory and management power over the territory that lies above the recharge area and aquifer. We, therefore, suggest as a principle that institutions be empowered and take responsibility for specific hydro-geographical areas. Both parties would follow agreed arrangements for cooperative water management.

Rational infrastructure development A new water agreement should allow rational, least-cost development of water infrastructure for Palestinians across the West Bank. Palestinians have long dreamed of emulating Israel's success in creating a national water grid. The current plight of West Bank Palestinians is of islands of water abstraction with major public wells close to centres of demand and a plethora of private agricultural wells and springs scattered across the countryside. Connectivity amongst water sources at present is limited to restricted local area networks and to the multiple points at which West Bank towns are linked in to the Mekorot network and the NWC. Palestinians see this set-up as economically inefficient as they cannot transfer low-cost water between their own towns.

As West Bank Palestinians have increasing access to the Mountain Aquifers, water transfer between sources and points of use will be the most efficient solution, with the development of one or more bulk water carriers and a grid to connect up all points of demand. In addition, the development of a comprehensive and integrated wastewater collection, treatment and reuse system is a priority. As we saw in Chapter 1, Israel has pioneered a unified system and infrastructure – an integrated network of collection, treatment, storage and bulk and retail distribution which the Palestinians will need to emulate if they are to treat and reuse all their wastewater. Only this rational infrastructure development can ensure security of water services and allow the economies of scale essential to efficient service delivery. A new agreement has thus to build on the example of Israel's integrated water system and to allow for Palestinian infrastructure across the West Bank to supply water to consumers and to collect, treat and reuse wastewater.

Practical actions to implement

Agreeing principles for sharing common resources

The first practical step would be to agree principles for sharing common water on the basis of criteria for allocation. Inevitably, water sharing is a vexed issue, as vested interests, politics and national narratives clash. However, everyone can agree on one thing – that the Palestinians at present have too little water. With total per capita availability from their own resources of only 39 cubic metres each year, West Bank Palestinians have access to only 13 per cent of the 298 cubic metres that is available per head in Israel from resources controlled by Israeli.[8] Even if water purchases are taken into account, West Bank Palestinians have only 22 per cent of the water available to Israelis. The disparity is the same for domestic water supply: water available for Palestinian domestic consumption in the West Bank (65 litres per person per day)[9] is again only one quarter of the 263 litres available to each member of Israeli households each day.[10] Even if unaccounted-for water in Palestinian supply were brought down to Israeli levels, West Bank Palestinians would have only 40 per cent of the domestic water supply available to Israelis.[11]

Revisiting water allocations

So how much water do Palestinians need if they are ultimately to rival Israel's development and Israelis' living standards? Israel has demonstrated that a vibrant mixed developed economy in a semi-arid environment can get by very well on 300 cubic metres a head.[12] We may therefore take this as a benchmark for the future for Palestinians, who after all live in the same natural resource setting, have the same natural capacities, are capable of the same efforts and no doubt have similar aspirations to well-being in life.

West Bank Palestinians at present have access to 65 cubic metres per head each year, of which 39 cubic metres is natural water under their control, and the balance is expensive desalinated and pumped water which is outside their control. For the reasons given – the physical characteristics of the resource, the dependency of Palestinians on that resource and lack of alternative sources under Palestinian control, and Palestinian needs for water for their socio-economic development – the principle of equitable sharing suggests that an increasing share of water from the Mountain Aquifers should be allocated to the Palestinians.

It would be reasonable to suppose that Palestinian water use would only evolve over time, as infrastructure was developed, as the economy grew and as household demand rose gradually towards Israeli levels. Time would also be required to allow Israel to switch to alternative sources, which would be further desalination. Any transition towards increased Palestinian use of the Mountain Aquifers would therefore take place over a number of years. A reasonable first target would be to replace the current 73 million cubic metres of desalinated water purchased from Israel with Mountain Aquifer water, and then in a second phase to gradually increase the Palestinian share of aquifer water to reach 100 cubic metres per head per year. This would increase the total water available to West Bank Palestinians to 280 million cubic metres annually, compared to the 2017 quantum (see Chapter 2) of 182 million cubic metres.

This increase in the quantum of water – to just one third of Israel's per capita levels – would satisfy at least some of the current unmet demand in both municipal and industrial supply and irrigated agriculture which we have previously estimated at a minimum of an extra 200 million cubic metres.[13]

Table 9.1 shows that, after this initial increase in the share of the West Bank Palestinians, the resulting use of the Mountain Aquifers would be more or less evenly balanced between Palestinians and Israelis. Palestinian water security

Table 9.1 Hypothetical Reallocation of the Annual Potential Yield of the Mountain Aquifers (million m³)

	Palestinian share	Israeli share	Estimated potential of the Mountain Aquifers	Possible extra desalination requirement in Israel	*Palestinian share (m3 per capita per year)*
Current	109	483	679*		*39*
Aquifer water replaces Palestinian purchases	73	−73			*26*
Aquifer water to bring Palestinians to 100 m³ per capita annually (one third of Israeli levels)	98	−98		+98	*35*
Total	**280**	**312**	**679**	**+98**	***100***

* Includes 78 MCM 'unallocated' in Article 40. Note that the 'hypothetical reallocation' is based on a total yield from the Mountain Aquifers of 592 million cubic metres, 87 million cubic metres less than the potential estimated in Article 40. This reflects the possible reduction in yields due to a changing climate.

would be strengthened by the reduced cost of water – as no expensive desalinated water would be purchased – and by the increased availability of water no longer abstracted by Israel. In addition, Palestinian water autonomy would be strengthened as all of the water for Palestinians in the West Bank would be coming from the Mountain Aquifers.

When the Palestinians are able to fulfil their ambition of treating and reusing wastewater on a large scale, this too would contribute to their water inventory within their control, would drive expansion of irrigated agriculture and would strengthen their water security and autonomy. If West Bank Palestinians can reach Israeli levels of collection (95 per cent) and treatment (85–90 per cent), the extra quantum of treated wastewater for agriculture could reach 60 million cubic metres annually, doubling the current allocation to irrigated agriculture and representing 15 per cent of the increased Palestinian West Bank water inventory.[14]

Although Israel would be using 171 million cubic metres less of Mountain Aquifer water, the extra desalination production needed to replace this would be only 98 million cubic metres because Israel would have access to the 73 million cubic metres of desalinated water that it was no longer selling to the Palestinians.

. . . and in the longer term

Long-term planning is essential to the water security of both Palestinians and Israelis. This is not only because shifts in water resource management will come about over many years but also because neither the resource nor demand will stay still as climatic, demographic and socio-economic changes proceed. Israel has long since planned and allocated the resources it controls. To protect the interests of all, future allocations need to be determined fairly in tandem with long-term development plans that serve both Palestinians and Israelis, strengthening Palestinian water security step by step and protecting the water security of Israel.

It would be reasonable to assume that further increases in Palestinian access to water would be required over time as the economy develops, the population increases and living standards rise. In the long run, Palestinian demand for domestic water would presumably match that of Israelis. In the short term, Palestinian requirements would be less and would only progressively build up to Israeli levels. For years, supply would be limited by infrastructure constraints, and demand would be limited by institutional and economic constraints and by the ability to pay. Plans would need to take account of growing per capita use and of population projections. Although population estimates and trends are routinely politicized and contentious, methods for projecting population growth and calculating domestic water needs are in fact relatively straightforward and should, in a truly cooperative framework, pose no particular challenge.

How this extra demand would be met should be the object of economic and engineering analysis to determine the least cost and most practical way to meet Palestinian needs, with the principle of maximizing water autonomy respected.

The itinerary and timetable by which the Palestinians might move towards the quantum would depend on many factors – political, social and economic. But beyond the hurdles, a reasonable long-term target of the amount of water Palestinians need for a modern economy and society is clearly visible in the 300 cubic metres annually per capita on which Israel is currently thriving.

In considering transfer of water from Israel to the Palestinians, there has perforce to be consideration of the consolidation of Israel's own water security. The Israeli population is projected to increase from the current 9 million people to 15.6 million by 2050. With domestic water requirements remaining at about 275 litres per capita per day (equivalent to 100 cubic metres per year), domestic water needs alone are therefore likely to amount to almost 1,600 million cubic metres a year, up from the present 900 million cubic metres a year. Over the same period, the natural resource available to Israel from current sources is expected to reduce under climate change from the present 1,200 million cubic metres annually to around 1,000 million cubic metres by 2050 – and that quantum of fresh water would be further reduced by transfers to the Palestinians.

There are also other environmental demands on Israel's water resources. These include: restoring the aquifers and environmental flows in the streams; restoring Lake Tiberias; releasing environmental flows in the Jordan and restoring the Dead Sea.[15] All in all, Israel's long-range plans would have to include a considerable further increase in desalination capacity.

Absorptive capacity

The largest non-domestic user of water for Palestinians at present is agriculture, and water is vital for a poor, agriculture-based economy like that of the Palestinians. In fact, Palestinians argue that their needs in agriculture are more significant than those of Israelis. Agriculture accounts for a much larger share of Palestinian GDP – 5–6 per cent in the West Bank, 7–8 per cent in Gaza – in comparison to Israel's 1.5 per cent. Palestinians resist arguments that they should simply make their water use in agriculture more efficient, as Israel has done. They point to the current quite high levels of efficiency, and to the large irrigable area – more than 30,000 hectares – that is not irrigated for lack of water and distribution systems. They argue that they need water to build their economy just as Israel did from 1948 onwards. The economic benefits would be palpable – studies have estimated that access to adequate irrigation water could add nearly half a billion dollars each year to the Palestinian West Bank economy and create 100,000 jobs, boosting GDP by up to 10 per cent of GDP.[16]

In the longer term, the expectation is that the Palestinian economic structure would develop progressively towards a modern mixed economy where water is required for a wide range of industrial, municipal, commercial and leisure purposes, and for maintenance of the ecology and environmental services. As the economy grows to become as developed as Israel's, per capita water availability would grow *pari passu* towards the levels Israel enjoys.

Many questions will enter into this discussion, about what use Palestinians would make of water in building their economy, what is the scope for market-oriented agricultural growth, what is the industrial strategy and what use will future industry, commerce and tourism make of water, particularly in a context where sovereignty, governance and authority over the territory (and the economy) are so undecided.

In agriculture, likely to be the largest water-using sector of the Palestinian economy for many years, there are particular issues to be resolved. Most agricultural land is in Area C where strict movement and access controls are exercised by Israel. On top of this, Palestinians are dependent on Israel for the vast majority of their trade, where import and export checks impose significantly higher transaction costs on Palestinians than on Israeli producers. As a result, agricultural input costs are higher and export proceeds are lower.[17]

It is conceivable that a new water allocation to agriculture could be based on projections of growth in demand for water based on expansion of the irrigable area and on 'efficient' water rations, as in Israel. Common sense would return this discussion to the principle of equity, of progressively increasing allocations from the Mountain Aquifers to Palestinians and letting the Palestinian people and the forces of market-based demand determine allocations amongst competing uses.

Devising institutional mechanisms

A new cooperative approach to management of the shared water resources requires new institutions – both sets of rules and organizations. In setting rules for sharing water, a flexible approach is wisest. If history has proven anything with regard to water for Israelis and Palestinians, it is that *circumstances change*. Technology, the structure of the economy, demographics, demands on the resource – all constantly change, as does the quality and the available quantity of the resource. It may be that agreement should not simply be based on fixed quantities but rather that an agreement should lay out guidelines for apportionment of shares, so that quantities, sources and costs can be determined in a more sustainable, coherent and continuous way. On the supply side there is also the need to adapt water allocations to the risk of climatic variation, drought and consequent changes in supply and demand.

However, a dynamic system for determining allocations could increase concern amongst the parties. Is there enough trust? Would the power of the parties be balanced? On what principle of equity would it operate? Especially when operating in a context that has often been on the brink of violent confrontation, where tensions are running high and where there is scepticism about joint processes after Oslo and the JWC experience, it can be perceived as 'safer' to agree on a fixed quantity rather than on a complex process. However, this would undoubtedly result in inefficiencies. Probably it is better to try for a dynamic system. But in any case, the practice of allocating water equitably requires continuous effort.

Establishing responsive cooperating institutions to jointly manage and serve evolving demands is a tall order. Nonetheless, for both communities to prosper over the long term, it is necessary to aim so high. This was summed up in a comment by Nader Khatib, former Palestinian director of the international and regional NGO Friends of the Earth Middle East (FoEME, now EcoPeace): 'It is time to replace the failed mechanism of the Joint Water Committee . . . with an institution where Palestinians and Israelis are true partners in both water supply and management responsibilities.' A new organizational structure is needed to represent both parties in managing shared water resources sustainably and equitably.

In a study of possible arrangements, FoEME proposed a bilateral Water Commission with an equal number of Palestinians and Israelis, together with one member from outside the region. According to this proposal, the commission would make decisions on rates of abstraction and allocations based on advice from a team of science advisers appointed by the two governments. Rules would govern the allocation of water based on a common standard for per capita domestic consumption and on requirements for industry, commerce and agriculture. These rules would plainly be at the heart of the new arrangements and would need exceptionally careful consideration.[18] The common sense benchmark would be to propose to bring per capita allocations to Palestinians, progressively up to the same level as Israelis enjoy, about 250–300 cubic metres per person per year.[19]

In this, the place for third-party involvement should not be overlooked – a neutral participant to observe and uphold the five principles and to maintain transparency, for example, a multilateral institution like the World Bank, which has for fifty years facilitated the Indus Waters Treaty, and which has recent experience not only with the Red–Dead scheme (see Chapter 8) but also with fostering cooperation on several major rivers in Africa.[20]

Responsibility for water management

A second step would be to allocate responsibility for water management within a cooperative framework. As we said earlier, water management, particularly of groundwater, requires the manager to have responsibility for a joined-up hydrogeographical area – a basin or part of it, the land above an aquifer or part of an aquifer. At present, Israel controls the entire area of Mandate Palestine, with the exception of the 9 per cent or so which constitute the Gaza Strip and Areas A and B of the West Bank, where Palestinians have delegated management responsibilities under Article 40.

It is the three Mountain Aquifers which are the shared resource and which would be the object of cooperation. One approach would be a rational geographical distribution of responsibility where each party would manage a share of the aquifer according to agreed rules. In the West Bank, this would essentially give the Palestinian Authority full responsibility for managing the upstream part of the Mountain Aquifers within the West Bank. An alternative would be genuinely joint management, perhaps with a joint commission, as has been proposed by EcoPeace.[21]

Ultimately, a further agreement might be made regarding Palestinian use and management of the section of the Jordan River alongside the West Bank. Any realignment of allocations of the resources of the Jordan basin – for example, to give the West Bank Palestinians the share of Jordan water proposed in the Johnston Plan of 1955 (see Chapter 5 of *The History of Water*) – would need to be negotiated at the regional level, with the participation of other riparians, or at least of Jordan.

The clauses of the agreement to be hammered out might in fact not differ enormously from some of the provisions of Article 40. They would provide for mutual responsibilities in good practice water management, for management of wastewater and pollution, and for environmental protection. The differences would be in fair rules for water allocation, in territorial responsibility of the Palestinians for water management extending over much or all of the West Bank, for both parties and not just the Palestinians to cooperate, for water to be managed according to the rules on both sides of the Green Line and for each side to be free to develop infrastructure and use water in any way they see fit, subject to the agreed rules on allocations, environmental protection and so on. Such an agreement would require trust between the two peoples. Its successful implementation would build momentum and foster further trust.

Palestinian water development

A third step would be for the Palestinians to implement a plan of institutional improvement, infrastructure development and protection of the environment. Institutional reform plans based on the Israeli model (see Chapter 3) are well advanced, providing for the creation of a national bulk water provider on the lines of Mekorot and the establishment of efficient and autonomous regional and local utilities, managed for efficiency and at arm's length from local government. In this step, the Palestinians would also update and implement plans for investment in joined-up infrastructure for bulk water conveyance on the lines of Israel's National Water Carrier, together with the infrastructure for efficient delivery to households, businesses and agriculture. Long-held Palestinian proposals for wastewater collection, treatment and reuse would finally be put into action, and watershed management, environmental protection and clean watercourses and environmental flows would become as important a goal and practice in the West Bank as they are on the other side of the Green Line.

Financing the Palestinian water sector

Considerable investment by the Palestinians would be required. It would be expected that donors would agree to contribute, as they do at present, the lion's share of the costs of developing water and wastewater infrastructure in the Palestinian territories. In addition, the richer cooperating partner could make a contribution to the cost of environmental services, including wastewater treatment. Israel has been suffering from the flows of untreated sewage from the West Bank, and has also had apprehensions about pollution of the shared aquifer by agricultural chemicals and industrial effluent. Given the interest that Israel has in protecting its own water supplies and environment, there may be a case for Israel to finance certain protection measures. This could be done by mobilizing Israeli financing for infrastructure. Or, the Israelis could participate in joint external fundraising initiatives, as they have offered to do for the Wadi Nar/Kidron Valley Scheme.

Another approach could be to create financial incentives through an approach to cost-sharing between upstream and downstream interests that has been used with some success elsewhere in the world – payment for environmental services (PES). Under this approach, downstream beneficiaries value the services they receive from the upstream and contract with the population upstream to remunerate them for maintaining or enhancing those services. The approach is normally applied when the downstream population is considerably better off than the upstream, and so can afford to pay for the services. A typical example is a downstream water utility which contracts with upstream hill farmers and pays them to reduce erosion, enhance run-off and prevent nitrates and chemicals from entering the streamflow. This approach has the advantages of efficiency, sustainability and an automatic self-financing mechanism. It is efficient because it can make differentiated payments according to the degree to which services are provided. Sustainability is built in because PES generally requires that service providers be paid indefinitely for the services they provide. This requires that service users be satisfied that they are receiving the services they are paying for. Hence, sustainability depends on an objectively verifiable quality of service. It has an automatic self-financing mechanism because the downstream beneficiary pays, so the system generates its own funding without requiring government budgetary outlays.

There are many successful examples of PES worldwide, principally in Latin America. In Colombia, irrigation water user groups and municipalities in the

Cauca valley are paying to conserve the watersheds that supply them with water. In Ecuador, the city of Quito has created a water fund, FONAG, with contributions from the water utility and the electric power company, to pay for conservation in the protected areas from which it draws its water. In Costa Rica, the town of Heredia has established an 'environmentally adjusted water tariff', the proceeds of which are used to pay landholders to maintain and reforest watershed areas.[22]

Many hurdles exist, and it would require some creative thinking and political willingness to engage in such an arrangement for the West Bank. However, dialogue between Israel and the Palestinians could no doubt devise a workable approach to resolving a joint problem in this way.

One element in the cross-border exchange of resources may be wastewater. For example, wastewater treated in the Palestinian West Bank or in Gaza may be passed on to the Israelis for use in agriculture at an agreed valuation or in exchange for fresh water from the Israelis' inventory. Or untreated wastewater from the West Bank or Gaza might be transferred to wastewater treatment plants within Israel, at a lower valuation.[23]

A high level of risk

The final component of water security is management and mitigation of risks. We have mentioned earlier that a cooperative agreement needs to provide for management of risks to water sources: climatic variability, drought, changes in groundwater and surface water quality and quantity. But there is no doubt that the principal risks are political risks, and these risks are pervasive. Can a water agreement hold if there is no more general agreement? Will the security interests of both parties override the arrangements for cooperation on water? Is Palestinian water management over the whole West Bank risking fatal conflict with Israeli settlement policy and the facts on the ground? Is there a neutral honest broker and a reliable partner for both Israelis and Palestinians? In the absence of coercion, are the incentives enough to ensure that both sides respect the agreement? These questions are at the heart of the problems between Israelis and the Palestinians. A cooperative agreement on water is only possible if both sides agree to put aside other issues and together manage water-related risks in the interests of a fair, stable, permanent agreement to ensure water security for both sides.

Beyond water: Developing the water–energy nexus[24]

The water–energy nexus was traditionally little more than the loop between the capacity of water to produce energy in the form of hydro power and the need for energy to lift and distribute water. This nexus first arose in the region in Ottoman times when motor pumps were introduced to raise groundwater for irrigation. In Mandate times, motorized pumping grew apace and the Yishuv invested in hydro power in the Jordan basin.

After independence, Israel undertook a comprehensive and energy-intensive exploitation of all the water resources to which it had access, including lifting the entire water resource of Lake Tiberias up some 250 metres and pumping this water throughout the country as far as the Negev desert in the south. In the last two decades, energy consumption for water has shot up in Israel with the advent of desalination, where energy can make up half to two thirds of production cost.

EcoPeace, as part of its Green Deal Initiative, has proposed a 'water–energy nexus project' that would link energy for desalination with renewable solar energy through a regional partnership amongst Israelis, Palestinians and Jordanians. Under the idea, Jordan would invest in solar energy, which it would sell to Israel and the Palestinians in exchange for desalinated water from Israeli plants along the coast and from the Palestinian plant in Gaza. The pre-feasibility study found the concept to bring economic gains to all sides. If Jordanian solar power could supply 20 per cent of the energy needs of Israel and the Palestinians in exchange for desalinated water, Jordan would be able to meet all its own water needs from the purchased, water and still generate an economic surplus, possibly enough to attract private sector financial investment in the scheme.

EcoPeace records 'resistance and hesitation on all three sides' about this proposal, stemming from reluctance to enter into such an interdependent relationship, and also concerns about physical security. However, in June 2020, Israel welcomed the idea of an initial pilot cross-border solar electricity project with Jordan. Crowded Israel lacks the space for extensive solar energy farms, so buying in solar energy from Jordan would help meet Israel's target of 30 per cent solar-powered renewable energy by 2030.

This may be an idea that will go far, allowing the clean expansion of desalination, meeting the water needs of all parties and binding the three regional partners together in a scheme of productive, mutually beneficial cooperation.

Cooperation between Israelis and Palestinians for the Gaza Strip

Most of this book – and indeed most analysis of Israeli and Palestinian water issues – deals primarily with the West Bank. Yet Gaza, dependent for natural water on its highly salinized aquifer, is water insecure in the extreme. It is clear that desalination is the solution most adapted to Gaza's water supply needs, and desalination within the Strip rather than purchase of Israel's desalinated water is the approach most likely to strengthen Palestinian water autonomy.

At present, Gaza's potable water needs are met largely from small- and medium-scale desalination, topped up with purchases of desalinated water from Israel. As we saw in Chapter 6, a project has been agreed to construct a major desalination plant with infrastructure to carry potable water the length of the Strip. However, the project faces many challenges, not least Palestinian reluctance to proceed with construction of the needed power line from Israel. At the time of writing (2020), only implementation of the 'associated works' – a North–South carrier and storage – is underway. This project may serve increased water imports from Israel until or unless the desalination plant is constructed.

Yet desalination within Gaza raises many economic and practical issues. It is extremely costly, as well as energy dependent, which raises questions of whether tariffs (and cost recovery) at the required rate would be politically and economically viable. In addition, in the Gaza situation, major infrastructure projects of this kind typically encounter massive risks and implementation constraints, due both to the intermittent hostilities and to the movement and access restrictions maintained by Israel. The experience of the last two decades – see Chapter 6 – demonstrates that investment projects almost invariably get delayed or remain incomplete in the volatile political and security situation. Projects such as desalination plants and wastewater treatment plants, which are dependent on imports of energy and materials through Israel, also run major operational risks.

Could other forms of cooperation with Israel than simple water purchase help to solve the Gazan water shortages? In his book *Let There Be Water*, Seth Siegel advances the opinion that 'there is no logical solution to Gaza's water crisis without Israel playing a leading role.' He discusses several possibilities. One is indeed to build a desalination plant in Gaza – but with Israeli help, so bringing the benefits of Israel's world-beating expertise and while making possible efficient market-based delivery options and financing.

Siegel quotes Almotaz Abadi, a Palestinian official, as proposing that a Gaza desalination plant could even supply the West Bank through a water carrier. Israel would have to assure the wayleaves across Israeli territory and could also help to build and run the plant.[25] However, the economics of this would be as questionable as they are for supply of desalinated water to the West Bank from Israeli plants. A variant also mentioned in *Let There Be Water* is one proposed by Professor Eilon Adar of Ben-Gurion University that a Gaza desalination plant could supply water to the south of Israel and Israel would compensate by transferring 'more of our water from the Western Mountain Aquifer to the West Bank.'[26]

In the past, water transfer in the opposite direction had been proposed – that Israel would supply water through its National Water Carrier to Gaza in exchange for increased rights within the West Bank, either from the Mountain Aquifer or from the Jordan. However, this kind of solution now seems outdated. Today the West Bank Palestinians are very short of water and are now claiming more water, not less, from the Mountain Aquifers.[27]

Another variant mentioned in Siegel's book is an idea devised by the ever-ingenious and prospective EcoPeace – that Gaza trade its sewage to Israel in exchange for desalinated water. This could have several advantages. It buys a benefit for Gaza with something that is at present only a cost – and a menace. The financial outlays would be lower than if Gaza produced its own desalinated water. It takes advantage of Israel's skill both in desalination and in turning wastewater into a productive resource, benefitting from existing networks for distributing and using the treated effluent. It turns an environmental threat into an agricultural benefit. It can be done locally and so requires relatively little costly infrastructure and pumping. It would entail little security threat to either party, so could be done even in the absence of some more definitive political agreement.[28]

But is it true that Gaza must be dependent on Israel ad infinitum? At present this is essentially the case as Israel controls Gaza's borders and everything that enters or exits from the territory, and places extreme controls on many of the things and activities that would allow Gaza to develop alternatives. There may, however, be other solutions in which Gaza would be more autonomous. The most obvious are those which are already on the table – desalination, large or small, and comprehensive wastewater treatment and reuse, all with Palestinian infrastructure and management within the Gaza Strip. The plans are laid, even the designs are done and donors are ready and willing. But any and all of these solutions, and indeed the whole economy of the Strip, the well-being of its people and their water security depend first and foremost on a willingness on both sides to cease hostilities and to pursue a political entente.[29]

* * *

Last word

To close this long story of Israel's excellent water security and of the Palestinians' arduous and long unsuccessful striving towards the same goal, we set out in summary an agenda for the resolution of the Israeli/Palestinian water issues and the principles and powers that would assure water security for the Palestinian people alongside their Israeli neighbours.

For the Palestinians to achieve the same *water autonomy* as the Israelis, they need access under their own jurisdiction and management to adequate affordable quality water for decent domestic use, for the growth of efficient agriculture, industry, tourism and other services, and for provision of amenity and the conservation and improvement of the environment. We suggest the goal should be to bring per capita water availability for Palestinians progressively up to the level of their Israeli neighbours.

The Palestinians also need to acquire the same powers and capabilities as the Israelis in *water management*. They need the ability to manage their water resources over a discrete geographical area of the watershed and within that area to have the ability to conserve, store, withdraw or enhance those resources according to plans. They must be able to move water efficiently from source to the point of demand in an integrated and efficient system, just as the Israelis have long since achieved. They need to be able to store water between seasons and years and to be able to plan against and to mitigate short-term shocks like drought and long-term hazards like growing aridity and uncertain rainfall patterns.

The Palestinians need the same ability as the Israelis to *develop water* efficiently for the benefit of their people, for sustainability and for protection of the resource and its environmental setting. They need to be able to invest freely, as Israelis have done, in efficient, least-cost infrastructure, to develop all water sources within their jurisdiction as they see fit, consistent with any cooperative arrangements with other riparians, to develop non-conventional water sources including desalination and treated wastewater, to convey water freely to Palestinian water users, to build all necessary storage and to construct and manage efficient delivery mechanisms to all dwellings, businesses and farms.

To match Israeli achievements, the Palestinians need to be able to *manage wastewater* through efficient investment in collection, treatment, disposal and reuse, and to agree with other riparians on arrangements for any untreated or treated effluent that crosses into another jurisdiction.

They need a clear and equitable cooperative arrangement with other riparians for the *management of shared or transboundary resources*, perhaps with the involvement of a neutral third party. Where water is shared with other riparians – the Western Aquifer and the Northern Aquifer with Israel, the Jordan River with the other Jordan riparians and particularly Israel and Jordan – the principles and rules of allocation and the institutions for agreeing on plans and resolving disputes need to be clear and set up equitably as between equally empowered partners.

This is a summary list of the powers, capabilities and rights the Palestinians need if they are to achieve water security. There is nothing extraordinary in the list. It is, after all, a list of all the attributes for successful water management that Israel has enjoyed in its own achievement of water security. It is simply the list of what will need to be agreed on in order for the 'low-hanging' fruit of water security for the Palestinians to be plucked.

CODA

WHAT DO WE LEARN ABOUT THE CONCEPT OF WATER SECURITY?

This book has used as its analytical framework the concept of water security. It is reasonable, therefore, to ask what we may have learned from the analysis that might offer a commentary on the water security concept.

Inevitably there are many definitions of 'water security'. The working definition that we have employed – security of water resources, security of water services and security from water-related risks – has, in our view, proved robust. On all three criteria, the evidence demonstrates the water security of Israelis and the water insecurity of Palestinians. But what lessons are there for the concept of water security from this assessment?

We may separate local water security – of individuals and localized communities – from national water security. Issues of local water security – the access of Palestinians to adequate water and sanitation services and to water for their businesses – industry, commerce, farming, tourism, the impact of shortages and poor services and so on – all this we have discussed at length in Part II. They are the bread and butter of water management, and need no further comment from us. It is on the national level and on water resources security that we have focussed in this third part of the book, and because the only water resource of the West Bank Palestinians is essentially a shared resource, we have focussed on transboundary issues.[1]

Water security in development and nation building

A first lesson concerns the role of water security in development and nation building. We have seen throughout our century-long history of water that the interconnectedness of water resources security with national security is so close that it has in many ways come to reinforce the notion of a historical identity. The fervent commitment of the early Zionists to acquiring and developing water resources has been carried through by Israel with extraordinary dedication – by resource capture, by investment, by negotiation and agreements, and by strict regulation. The complementary loss of resources by the Palestinians has made them painfully aware of the role that water and water security could have played in their own destiny and has sharpened their aspirations to emulate the achievement of their neighbours.

The role of water autonomy in water resources security

Linked to this first lesson is a second: the role of water autonomy in water resources security. As we have seen, all of Israel's water inventory is under its physical control. For natural fresh water this includes not only the water that arises within the state's borders, which is scanty enough, but the water of the Upper Jordan and its watershed, and the water of the Mountain Aquifers and their recharge areas. Risks to this autonomy are limited at present. The allocation of Jordan water is protected not only by Israel's dominant power and its occupation of the Golan but also by treaty with the lower riparian, Jordan. The allocation of water from the Mountain Aquifers is protected not only by Israeli occupation of most of the West Bank but also by Article 40 of the Oslo II agreements.

Israel's manufactured water is even more firmly within its control as it arises either from the treatment of the effluent from internal water use or from desalination of seawater drawn from along Israel's coastline.

Water autonomy is a characteristic of many countries, particularly those with vast internal water resources such as Canada or Russia, yet more than 70 per cent of the world's population are dependent on transboundary resources for at least some part of their water resources.[2] As the development of water resources approaches its limit, competition over transboundary resources is becoming more acute and some countries are becoming vulnerable to the actions of other states. Vulnerability is felt particularly along the 260 major rivers that are shared by two or more states, and also on large transboundary aquifers.

Water autonomy is thus becoming increasingly valued, although few states have the opportunities that Israel has had to acquire and strengthen it. Singapore is one other state that has acted decisively to establish water autonomy, reducing its dependence on raw water imported from Malaysia through 'three taps' – local catchment water from rainfall, treated wastewater and desalinated water – while progressively closing off the 'fourth tap' of imported bulk supply.[3]

Desalination and water security

A third lesson is the growing role of desalination in strengthening local and national water security. With costs for desalinated water tumbling towards \$0.50 per cubic metre ex-factory, coastal communities will increasingly adopt desalination as a strategic option. Over one third of the world's population already live in urban centres alongside the feedstock, the ocean, and in many arid parts of the world the share of population along the coast exceeds 75 per cent.[4] Where these communities are experiencing water shortages and require high-quality water and complete reliability, and can afford to pay for it, they can establish complete water resources security – including autonomy and elimination of any risk of shortages – through desalination. The Israeli case demonstrates the profile: large coastal cities with high concentrations of well-off people or high-value industry, commerce and tourism which demand a quality service and which are prepared to pay for it. In some cases, as in Israel and Singapore, local water security objectives match national water autonomy objectives.

Wastewater reuse and water security

The story of Israel (see Chapter 1) also demonstrates the vital and growing role of wastewater reuse in the national water economy and security. Treating 95 per cent of all wastewater and reusing more than 85 per cent of that, Israel has demonstrated that wastewater can form a vital component of a national water inventory for water-scarce countries. Wastewater now contributes around a fifth of the nation's water and two thirds of the water used in agriculture. Techniques of injection into contained aquifers allow the treated wastewater to be stored until it is needed. Israel has complemented this technical achievement with a policy and incentive framework which has made wastewater an appreciated resource for farmers. No other country even approaches Israel's level of practice but as competition for water intensifies and, especially where demands for water transfer out of agriculture to other sectors gain traction, one path to water security will be to increase wastewater reuse in the kind of swap of wastewater for fresh water that already occurs in Israel (and in neighbouring Jordan).

The overall contribution of manufactured water to water security

Taken together, desalinated wastewater and treated wastewater – 'manufactured water' – now make up almost two thirds (61 per cent) of Israel's water inventory. They underwrite the economy and assure the country's water security and autonomy. Desalination also holds the prospect of virtually boundless supplies of potable water, at least for populations living near the sea and which are well-off enough to afford it. Let there be water! as Siegel says.

Establishing water autonomy through manufactured water is thus an option, and it is certainly one that will be increasingly adopted by cities and states which either are vulnerable because of their dependency on resources from another jurisdiction, or where the costs of bringing natural water from far afield become more and more expensive. In particular, highly urbanized and wealthy Gulf States will continue to secure water autonomy through desalination and wastewater treatment and reuse.

Storage and water security

We have seen how an integrated water system allows Israel to store fresh water in Lake Tiberias, in hill dams and retention ponds, and – through both natural recharge and injection – in aquifers. Production of desalinated water can similarly be stored, with a new pipeline now under construction to store desalinated water in Lake Tiberias. A parallel system stores treated wastewater, including in dedicated confined aquifers. These facilities can be drawn down when needed, so enabling Israel to match resources temporally and spatially to demand. Real-time management of the different types of storage can ensure that aquifers are not overdrawn and that water levels in Lake Tiberias do not drop below the 'red line' at which an irreversible salinization will occur.

Storage of fresh and desalinated water allows for satisfaction of varying demand throughout the year, especially peak demand from all sectors in the hot dry summers. Storage of desalinated water allows plants to run at optimal efficiency and capacity, for example, to take advantage of intermittent off-peak electricity prices. Storage of treated wastewater which is produced in more or less even quantities every day allows the water to be held over until the peak irrigation months of summer. The entire storage system provides a buffer against periodic drought and is designed to evolve to combat the long-term effects of climate change.

The water–energy nexus and water security

Much water development is energy intensive – pumping of all kinds, treatment and reuse of wastewater, desalination of sea and brackish water. Not only are these processes expensive in the use of energy, but they also have commensurately high carbon footprints. If desalination is to play a major part in future water security planning, as seems likely, renewable energy has to become an important complement, as in the. Green Deal that EcoPeace has proposed for Israel, Jordan and the Palestinians, based on swapping solar energy for desalinated water.

Cooperation on transboundary resources and water security

For many countries, water security will be dependent on cooperation with others. Already there are numerous agreements on transboundary waters and a growing literature on the practical, economic, legal and ethical frameworks within which interdependency can be negotiated in a way that is best for all parties. These frameworks promote best practices of integrated water resources management, particularly optimizing water management at the basin scale. The economics of transboundary cooperation similarly align on basin-wide approaches to maximize benefits at that scale and to reach agreements amongst riparians according to an equitable calculus that shares economic benefits rather than water allocations.[5]

Legal frameworks abound and best practice and case law have been consolidated in the UN Watercourses Convention which, as we have seen, incorporates the principles of cooperation, of mutual rights and obligations, of equity and minimizing harm, and of negotiated settlement of disputes.

The ethics of cooperation can be summarized in the concept of 'hydro-solidarity', which brings together the notions of interdependence on shared waters, community of interests and collective action. Falkenmark et al. 2003[6] describe hydro-solidarity as 'an ethical basis for wise water governance, balancing between upstream and downstream water use and between human use and ecosystem needs'. The concept stands specifically in opposition to fragmented approaches where the strongest tend to win. For many territories, water security in the future will depend on cooperation driven by these practical, economic, legal and ethical rationales.

The case of Israel demonstrates how desalination can strengthen national water security and reduce or eliminate competition for a previously finite resource. One party may even give up claims to a particular resource without reducing overall water availability. In addition, the change of location of manufactured water resources – to coastal zones in the case of desalinated water and to peri-urban areas in the case of treated wastewater – allows for a more flexible geography of water resources. This can, for example, reduce costs or facilitate exchange of resources, or simply make possible sales to meet the deficit of one party or another.

How much water is needed for water security?

One approach to answering this question might be to gauge the level of 'water stress' that a territory is held to experience, and a fortiori how much water they might need above the current availability. The IPCC defines 'water-stressed basins' as those having either a per capita water availability below 1,000 cubic metres per year, or a ratio of withdrawals to long-term average run-off above 0.4. To this definition we add that groundwater withdrawals should not exceed long-term average recharge.

Set against these benchmarks, the Israelis should be suffering extreme water stress. They have availability per capita of less than 300 cubic metres – and only 114 cubic metres of that is natural water. Set against the withdrawal ratio benchmark of 0.4, the Israelis (together with the Palestinians more meagre ration) are essentially withdrawing *all* run-off and *all* groundwater recharge within the basins they control in the form of either surface water diversions or pumping from the aquifers. In fact, the groundwater resource has often been overdrawn. Yet with less than one third of the 'water stress' quantum and with a withdrawal ratio' exceeding 1, the Israelis are running a vigorous modern economy. The notion of 'water stress' appears to have little power in the case we are examining for determining how much water is needed.

An alternative approach is to establish empirically the actual amount of water needed to develop a modern economy and society within the natural agro-ecological and climatic setting. In the past, such estimates were based on notions of 'carrying capacity' – we saw, for example, the calculation during the Mandate that Palestine could hold a maximum of two million people (see Chapter 4 of *The History of Water*). This calculation was based on the needs for municipal and industrial water and on a supposition that the population would be self-sufficient in basic foods.

The demonstration that this thinking is redundant is that the current population of the Mandate territory is more than 13 million people. On the one hand, water technology, particularly the tubewell and the pumping and long-distance transfer of water from Tiberias, has increased the supply of natural water, while desalination and wastewater treatment have added some 60 per cent to water resource availability. On the other hand, while demand for water has soared with population increase, urbanization, diet and lifestyle, the goal of food self-sufficiency has been set aside – by the Israelis – in favour of a 'virtual water' exchange of high-value fruit and vegetable exports and of the import of other foodstuffs in line with the comparative advantage of a water-short, warm, technically efficient country.

As a result, as we have seen, the Israeli population of some 9 million gets along very well, with a dynamic modern industrial economy, a prosperous hi-tech agriculture and efficient and affordable water services, with enough water for amenities like swimming pools and car washing, with some left over for the environment.

Is it possible to estimate water needs on the basis of managed demand? From the 1980s, there have been attempts to do this. Basing his work on the case of Israel, Falkenmark and colleagues calculated that a modern economy in a semi-arid zone would need about 500 cubic metres a head, and with good management could make do on less, with the water stress level being around 250 cubic metres. This seems to have been a pretty accurate estimate because Israel, with huge invention and investment on both the supply and demand management sides, is currently doing fine on 300 cubic metres.

So could the Palestinians, provided, of course, that all the conditions of investment, efficiencies and good governance were fulfilled.

NOTES

Introduction

1 $34,790. Source: https://tradingeconomics.com/israel/gdp. Consulted online 11 April 2020.

2 Source: Palestinian Territories Recent Development, World Bank, April 2019. Gaza per capita GDP based on a total 2014 GDP of $2.938 billion and a population of 1.816 million.

3 Source: Palestinian Territories Recent Development, World Bank, April 2019. Based on the upper–middle-income poverty rate of $5.50 a day.

4 Source United Nations Office for the Coordination of Humanitarian Assistance https://www.ochaopt.org/theme/food-security. Consulted 14 June 2019.

5 Source: 2018 Socio-Economic and Food Security Survey (SefSec) UNOCHA 2018. By contrast, food insecurity in the West Bank is lower – about 12 per cent of households are food insecure according to the same survey, down from 15 per cent in 2014.

6 The opinion of the World Bank is that only a final status agreement would bring rapid and sustained economic growth to the West Bank and Gaza. Without some economic growth and the creation of employment, the Bank has concluded that the situation will inevitably relapse into conflict. Source: World Bank. 2017. *West Bank and Gaza – Assistance Strategy for the period FY18-21 (English)*. Washington, D.C.: World Bank Group. http://documents.worldbank.org/curated/en/339871512568083583/West-Bank-and-Gaza-Assistance-Strategy-for-the-period-FY18-21.

7 Unemployment rate of 3.7 per cent.

8 According to the World Bank, only 16 per cent of Palestinian youth aged sixteen to twenty-nine have 'fully transitioned into the labour market'. Source: *Palestinian Territories Recent Development*, World Bank, April 2019.

9 Youth unemployment in Israel in 2017 was 7.3 per cent. https://www.statista.com/statistics/812121/youth-unemployment-rate-in-israel/. Consulted 14 June 2019.

10 Source: *Palestinian Territories Recent Development*, World Bank, April 2019.

11 With the exception of the Druze in the Golan, the Bedouin of the Negev and some Israeli Arab communities.

12 The phrase 'water superpower', which is from Siegel 2015, may seem overstated in view of the equity and environmental concerns raised by water policy and practice in Israel. The phrase does, nonetheless, capture both the excellence of Israel's achievements and the adversative aspects of Israeli water behaviour in the regional context.

13 The average Israeli tariff of US$2.55 is taken from *How Is the Water Industry in Israel Faring?* By Frank Coutinho, *Times of Israel*, 4 August 2018. https://blogs.timesofisrael.com/how-is-the-water-industry-in-israel-faring/

14 In Pete Seeger's version of *Michael Row the Boat Ashore*.

15 At present, for example, the Palestinians are paying top dollar for desalinated water pumped from the coast up hundreds of metres to the highlands, an arrangement that leads to amongst the highest prices of bulk water anywhere in the world. Yet the Palestinians are amongst the poorest people in the region – and yet they have beneath their feet a groundwater resource that would cost only a third as much. Common sense and equity would suggest that a poor people like the West Bank Palestinians should have access to the cheapest water in the region, not the most expensive.
16 A new agreement has thus to build on the example of Israel's integrated water system and to allow for Palestinian infrastructure across the West Bank to supply water to consumers and to collect, treat and reuse wastewater.

Chapter 1

1 Important sources for this chapter on Israel are the World Bank's 2017 study *Water management in Israel*, and Seth Siegel's 2015 book *Let There Be Water*, supplemented by interviews and fieldwork during our visits to Israel in 1996, 2008 and 2016. Comments from Dr Shimon Tal, former water commissioner of Israel, have also made an important contribution to this chapter. Siegel's work is very thorough. Based on more than 200 interviews and several years' research, it gives a panoramic view of Israel's achievements. Reviews of the book (e.g. by David Katz in *Water Economics and Policy*, 2017) appreciate the thoroughgoing nature of the work. Katz seeks to fault it as more the work of a journalist than of a water specialist but in our view that is rather missing the point, that this is a book intended for a wide audience – and it did indeed become a *New York Times* bestseller. In truth, the book does exactly what it set out to do, to showcase Israel's manifold achievements in water in an approachable way. Reviews also note that the book skates over some of the downside of Israeli water management, notably the environmental impacts of desalination and wastewater reuse, the dire condition of the Jordan Valley and the less than perfect water services to Israeli minorities. It will be evident from the frequent attributions to *Let There Be Water* in these endnotes that we have drawn considerably on it. Our own reservation about the book is principally that in its presentation of Israeli/Palestinian issues, it draws almost exclusively on Israeli sources and views the issues very much through an Israeli lens. In this sense, our own book might be seen as a humble attempt to tell the story in a more balanced way.
2 Siegel 2015: 240.
3 How Israel accumulated that inventory of natural water is discussed in our companion volume, *The History of Water*.
4 Siegel 2015: 236–7.
5 There were in fact legal precedents in both Ottoman and Mandate Palestine for public ownership of water but these had little practical application – see Chapter 3 of *The History of Water* on the Ottoman *mejelle* code and Chapter 4 on the 'nationalization' of water under the British Mandate.
6 Siegel 2015: 237.
7 Siegel 2015: 239, 242.
8 Siegel 2015: 242.
9 The institutional arrangements for water supply, as opposed to water resources management, are discussed herein, in the section on *Security of water services*.

10 Siegel 2015: 42, 44.
11 World Bank 2017; Siegel 2015: 42, 43, 241.
12 World Bank 2017: 18.
13 Sources are the Wikipedia article on Mekorot and the webpage *Main Facts & Figures* on Mekorot's new site: Mekorot, Israel National Water Co. Retrieved 31 July 2018. Also World Bank 2017.
14 As it has become a global player, Mekorot has come under criticism by international NGOs for its role in water management in the West Bank and the Jordan Valley. The 'Stop Mekorot' campaign website says: 'It is now the time to intensify pressure on public authorities to exclude Mekorot from public contracts and hold the company accountable for its water apartheid.'
15 The story of how Israel came to control the water resources of Tiberias, the Mountain Aquifers and part of the lower Jordan Valley is told extensively in our companion volume, *The History of Water in the Land Once Called Palestine*, which we refer to from now on as simply *The History of Water*.
16 Chapter 5 of *The History of Water* tells the story of this pioneering and controversial project.
17 See the section later in this chapter on '*The benefits of desalination in Israel*'.
18 Source: World Bank 2017: 27.
19 Afforestation also helps reduce erosion. World Bank 2017: 27 mentions the afforestation programme in the arid Negev 'noteworthy because it has revived old techniques for harvesting rainwater that the Nabatean people practiced from the fourth century BCE. The revived techniques focus on areas with less than 100 millimetres of annual rainfall. Groves of 0.2 to 0.6 hectares thrive from water collected from watersheds that are 10 to 100 times as large as the cultivated area they supply.' Beyond their contribution to hydrology and the environment, trees have also always had a specifically Zionist purpose in Israel. Alon Tal in *All the Trees of the Forest* (pages 86–8) calls trees 'planted flags' and describes them as 'holding the land so that it should not go back to foreign hands' and as 'erasing the evidence of Arab presence'.
20 See World Bank 2017: 25.
21 See also Chapter 2 of *The History of Water* on these salinization risks.
22 On this, see the excellent research in *Replenishment of Palestinian waters by artificial recharge* by Karen Assaf in Isaac and Shuval: 302, 307.
23 The source of much of this information is the 2018 World Bank study, *The Role of Desalination in an Increasingly Water Scarce World*. One of the authors of this present book (Christopher Ward) was also co-author of the World Bank study.
24 Desalination has been known for millennia as both a concept and later as a practice, though in a limited form. Aristotle observed in the *Meteorologica* that 'salt water, when it turns into vapour, becomes sweet and the vapour does not form salt water again when it condenses'. He also records that a fine wax vessel held long enough in seawater would be found to contain potable water because the wax acted as a membrane to filter the salt. Before the Industrial Revolution, desalination was primarily of interest to oceangoing ships. Thomas Jefferson catalogued heat-based methods going back to the 1500s, and formulated practical advice that was publicized to all US ships on the backs of sailing clearance permits. Thanks to the 2019 World Bank study and to the excellent Wikipedia article on desalination for this information.

25 Technically, all water with salinity content between 500 milligrams per litre and 30,000 milligrams per litre is considered brackish water, but brackish water desalination is usually of water with a salt content of less than 10,000 milligrams per litre.
26 *The Current State of Desalination*. International Desalination Association. Retrieved 24 April 2018.
27 See Siegel 2015: 117 for a brief discussion of this option.
28 Interview with Shimon Peres by Seth Siegel, 25 April 2013 in Siegel 2015.
29 Siegel 2015: 105.
30 LBJ had a very strong interest in desalination. According to Seth Siegel, a few days before the 1960 election in which he became JFK's vice president, Johnson wrote an article for the *New York Times*, 'If we could take the salt out of water'. Later, as president, LBJ promoted research and investment in desalination both at home and abroad.
31 Siegel 2015: 107–8.
32 Siegel 2015: 107–10.
33 Siegel 2015: 113.
34 See Chapters Six and Seven of *The History of Water*.
35 See Siegel 2015: 113 and 121. Israel has developed the technology to the point where it has constructed the world's largest and most modern plant. This plant, at Sorek south of Tel Aviv, was built by IDE and the Chinese–Israeli company Hutcheson Water. It takes in 54,000 cubic metres of raw seawater an hour. Working with 10,000 reverse osmosis modules, the plant is capable of producing a stunning two thirds of a million tons of potable water every day (624,000 cubic metres or 165 million gallons).
36 Thanks to Shimon Tal for this information (personal communication, 17 September 2019).
37 Siegel 2015: 122.
38 Thanks to Shimon Tal for this observation.
39 Siegel 2015: 124.
40 Tal was the co-author of the August 2017 World Bank study *Water Management in Israel*.
41 Personal communication from Shimon Tal to the authors, 17 September 2019.
42 Drinking water regulations worldwide usually require that potable water have TDS below 500 ppm and concentration of chlorides below 250 milligrams per litre. Israel has stricter regulations, requiring the TDS and chloride levels of desalinated water to be below 100 milligrams per litre and 50 milligrams per litre, respectively. See also Siegel 2015: 125 and the note on p 291.
43 'Desalinated water use in Israel causing alarming iodine deficiency in people' was the title of a recent article in the journal *Health* which went on to say: 'The first national iodine survey conducted in Israel revealed a high burden of iodine deficiency among Israelis.' The article pointed out the risks of iodine deficiency to the neurological development of the foetus and the intellectual functioning of young children. Was there a link to desalination? The survey suggests there may be, pointing out that iodine deficits amongst adults exposed to iodine-poor water appear to correlate with an increasing proportion of their area's drinking water coming from desalination. *Source: Article posted on March 28, 2017 by Karin Kloosterman in Health*. www.greenprophet.com/2017/03/desalinated-water-use-in-israel-causing-alarming-iodine-deficiency-in-people/.

44 The exception is the new Ashdod plant. On this case, see the discussion in the section *Project delivery method.*
45 Source: World Bank 2019a.
46 The worst conditions for SWRO are those in the hot, very salty, turbid seas of the Arabian Gulf and Red Sea, where SWRO requires extensive pre-treatment steps to make the seawater clean of biofouling matter. These conditions may also require the product water to go through costly treatment after desalination as well. It is for these reasons that the thermal treatments still prevail in those locations. Where water is hot and salty, turbid and contaminated, thermal evaporation techniques work out cheaper than SWRO.
47 The 2017 World Bank report (World Bank 2017: 22–3) tags this as the opposite of the strategy of many other countries, which use desalinated water mostly to meet peak demand. The resulting intermittent operation undermines the financial viability.
48 Siegel 2015: 118, 121–2.
49 Only in the case of the Palmachim plant had the land to be purchased by the private operator – an element that partly explains why this plant has the highest price per cubic metre – see the table *Major Seawater Desalination Plants in Israel.*
50 For example, Sorek uses just 3.6 kilowatt hours per cubic metre compared to up to 5.5 kilowatt hours per cubic metre for plants around the world (source: World Bank 2019: 40, Table 5.10).
51 World Bank 2017: 25.
52 Source: World Bank 2019a.
53 Siegel 2015: 114–5, 122; IDE website, consulted 2 January 2018.
54 Thanks to Shimon Tal for several of these points. The World Bank study *The Role of Desalination* (World Bank 2019a) provides analysis of environmental impacts and possible mitigation options. The Carlsbad example is discussed in the study.
55 Siegel 2015: 80.
56 Source: Fischhendler et al.: 40; Tal and Katz 2017: 317.
57 'Large' is defined as capacity greater than 1,500 cubic metres per day.
58 Siegel 2015: 79. See also World Bank 2017: 18; S 79.
59 Siegel 2015: 83, 84–5.
60 Thanks to Shimon Tal for this point (personal communication to the authors, 17 September 2019).
61 Siegel 2015: 252. Of the approximately, 318 million cubic metres of water used in Israeli agriculture in 2016, about 195 million cubic metres was from treated wastewater (62 per cent).
62 Siegel 2015: 85.
63 The Public Health Regulations (Effluent Quality Standards and Rules for Sewage Treatment) are popularly known as the 'Inbar standards' after the chairman of the committee which prepared them. To allow for adjustments to investment and management, the Inbar standards were introduced gradually between 2010 and 2015.
64 Siegel 2015: 83/4.
65 Wastewater is priced at the equivalent of $0.30 per cubic metre for unrestricted irrigation and $0.25 per cubic metre for restricted irrigation. This is less than half the tariff for agricultural freshwater ($0.66 per cubic metre).
66 Source: World Bank 2017: 20; Siegel 2015: 86–7.
67 Siegel 2015: 84, 86, 89.

68 Siegel 2015: 82.
69 Siegel 2015: 92–5.
70 This section draws heavily on the excellent paper *Decoupling National Water Needs*, WANA 2017.
71 Siegel 2015: 49, 55; World Bank 2017.
72 The underinvestment in Arab local authorities is evident in the poor, inadequately maintained infrastructure – roads, sewage and water connections, and so on – that is characteristic of many Arab towns and villages. See, for example, *Assessment for Arabs in Israel*, Minorities at Risk 2008; and *Shutting itself in, hoping for the best, The Economist*, 23 March 2006.
73 *The Guardian* 27 February 2003
74 See, for example *The Bedouin in Israel: Demography* Israel Ministry of Foreign Affairs 1 July 1999; *Off the Map: Land and housing rights violations in Israel's unrecognized Bedouin villages*. Human Rights Watch, March 2008 Volume 20, No. 5(E); and Bedouin information, ILA, 2007. According to the Legal Centre for Arab Minority Rights in Israel: 'With no official status, these villages are excluded from state planning and government maps, have no local councils, and receive few-to-no basic services, including electricity, water, telephone lines, or education or health facilities. [The inhabitants of these villages are viewed by the government] as trespassers on state land, although many have been living on these lands—the ancestral lands of the Arab Bedouin—since before the establishment of the state in 1948, and although state attempts to assert ownership claims on the land are vehemently disputed. Others, expelled from their ancestral lands by the state, were forced to move to their current locations by the military government imposed on the Palestinians in Israel between 1948 and 1966, and thus face the threat of expulsion for a second or even a third or fourth time.' Source: *The Inequality Report: The Palestinian Arab Minority in Israel*. Adalah, the Legal Centre for Arab Minority Rights in Israel. March 2011.
75 This first block is priced at NIS 7.676 per cubic metre ($2.26). Above this level, the cost is NIS 12.355 per cubic metre ($3.63). The overall average tariff is around NIS 10 per cubic metre ($2.94).
76 Source: World Bank 2017: 30; Siegel 2015: 90–2.
77 Siegel 2015: 45, 239.
78 Siegel 2015: 45–7, 239.
79 *Israel Water Sector – Key Issues*. The Knesset Research and Information Centre, February 2018.
80 Data from *How Much Water Do Residents of Local Cities Use?* by David Warren, Wehoville 8 December 2016. https://www.wehoville.com/2016/12/08/much-water-residents-local-cities-use/ consulted on 11 June 2019.
81 Siegel 2015: 45, 244; World Bank 2017.
82 Siegel 2015: 49, 55.
83 We owe the invaluable concept of 'virtual water' to Professor Tony Allan of SOAS and King's College, University of London.
84 Gruen in Isaac and Shuval: 275.
85 Sources: Siegel 2015: 45–7, 238; World Bank 2017: x.
86 Source: WANA 2017, and Becker and Ward 2014. Prices are those of 2010.
87 As defined by FAO, as against 75 per cent efficiency for sprinklers and less than 60 per cent for typical surface irrigation.
88 Seth Siegel has a good discussion of these innovations (Siegel 2015: 67–70 and 76–7).

89 Siegel 2015: 241–6; World Bank 2017: 26. One aspect of this is that Israel has good water data but it has not always all been in the public domain. Writing in 1994, Lonergan and Brooks (page 9) say: 'Until recently, almost all data on water in Israel were treated as state secrets.' In the same year, Kuttab and Ishaq asserted that 'Water-related articles have to be cleared by the Office of the Chief Censor'. See Kuttab and Isaac in Isaac and Shuval: 241.

90 Siegel 2015: 244.

91 World Bank 2017 mentions dedicated funds under: (i) the office of chief scientist under the Ministry of Economy (NIS 254 million 2007–15); (ii) the IWA (NIS 94 million since 2008) and (iii) the chief scientist of the Ministry of Energy and Water (NIS 20 million per year covering the R&D and pilot stages of innovative technologies).

92 Siegel 2015: 242–3; World Bank 2017: 12.

93 World Bank 2017: Note 7.

94 See Tal and Katz 2012: 318.

95 Source: Tal and Katz 2012: 319.

96 See Tal and Katz 2012: 321.

97 The former Nahr al Auja, renamed in 1948 by the new Israeli state.

98 See *And a Cleaner Yarkon River Runs through It* by Zafrir Rinat, Haaretz, 18 July 2013. https://www.haaretz.com/israel-news/sports/.premium-and-a-cleaner-river-runs-through-it-1.5292956, consulted 26 May 2019.

99 See *Water in Israel: Rehabilitation of Israel's Rivers* by Shoshana Gabbay. https://www.jewishvirtuallibrary.org/rehabilitation-of-israel-s-rivers, consulted 26 May 2019.

100 Article in the *Times of Israel* by Sue Surkes, 11 October 2017 https://www.timesofisrael.com/white-foam-covers-sections-of-yarkon-river-despite-cleanup-efforts/.

101 Tal and Katz 2012: 327 comment: 'many stream master plans stop far short of comprehensive ecological restoration and rest content with cheap and popular projects like park benches and bike and jogging trails.'

102 See Tal and Katz 2012: 325.

103 Source DNEWS 21 July 2010 https://www.seeker.com/jordan-river-too-polluted-for-baptisms-1765079616.html, accessed 25 May 2019.

104 This was in fact a year of heightened Christian awareness of the costs of environmental damage. Pope Francis published a Catholic manifesto on respect for the environment, the Encyclical Letter *Laudato Si'* Of The Holy Father Francis On Care For Our Common Home, which begins with a quotation from the beautiful canticle of Saint Francis of Assisi: '*Laudato si', mi' Signore*' – 'Praise be to you, my Lord'. The canticle reminds us that our common home is like a sister with whom we share our life and a beautiful mother who opens her arms to embrace us. 'Praise be to you, my Lord, through our Sister, Mother Earth, who sustains and governs us, and who produces various fruit with coloured flowers and herbs. This sister now cries out to us because of the harm we have inflicted on her by our irresponsible use and abuse of the goods with which God has endowed her. We have come to see ourselves as her lords and masters, entitled to plunder her at will. The violence present in our hearts, wounded by sin, is also reflected in the symptoms of sickness evident in the soil, in the water, in the air and in all forms of life. This is why the earth herself, burdened and laid waste, is among the most abandoned and maltreated of our poor; she "groans in travail" (Rom 8:22). We have forgotten that we ourselves are dust of the earth (cf. Gen 2:7); our very bodies are made up of her elements, we breathe her air and we receive life and refreshment from her waters.' http://w2.vatican.va/cont

ent/francesco/en/encyclicals/documents/papa-francesco_20150524_enciclica-laudato-si.html, accessed 25 May 2019.

105 The former Friends of the Earth Middle East. EcoPeace Middle East's three co-directors – Nader Al-Khateeb (Palestine), Gidon Bromberg (Israel) and Munqeth ## Mehyar (Jordan) – were honoured by *Time* magazine as Heroes of the Environment (2008) and the organization was granted the prestigious Skoll Award in 2009. EcoPeace Middle East also received a 2008 SEED Finalist Award (Source Wikipedia).

106 Source: *Times of Israel*, article by Melanie Lidman, 18 June 2015, accessed 25 May 2019. https://www.timesofisrael.com/baptism-by-mire-in-jordan-river-sewage-mucks-up-christian-rite/.

107 Across the river, the Jordanians claim their own baptismal site called *Bethany beyond the Jordan*.

108 Israel has long managed a popular baptism site just below Lake Tiberias called Yardenit, where the water is not yet polluted. The site, which receives up to half a million visitors every year, has twelve separate baptism pools with areas for mass baptism ceremonies and handicap accessible options.

109 This regional master plan for the Jordan River was produced by EcoPeace with the Stockholm International Water Institute and Global Nature Fund.

110 Tal and Katz 2012: 323.

111 Source: Tal and Katz 2012: 324.

112 On EcoPeace work on the Jordan, see http://ecopeaceme.org/projects/lower-jordan-river/achievements/.

113 Gidon Bromberg quoted in the *Times of Israel* article by Melanie Lidman, 18 June 2015, accessed 25 May 2019. https://www.timesofisrael.com/baptism-by-mire-in-jordan-river-sewage-mucks-up-christian-rite/.

Chapter 2

1 In 2018 a Knesset report showed 2016 total Israeli domestic consumption of 809 million cubic metres, with per capita consumption averaging 96 cubic metres (263 lcd). See *Israel Water Sector – Key Issues*. The Knesset Research and Information Centre, February 2018.

2 As we saw in Chapter Seven of *The History of Water*.

3 See Chapter Seven of *The History of Water*.

4 See Chapter Seven of *The History of Water* for a discussion of this.

5 See Chapter Seven of *The History of Water*.

6 Source: Zeitoun 2008: 74, citing Bossier 2005. Also see Zeitoun 2008: 74: Figure 4.1.

7 PWA's role was redefined in Article 8 of the 2014 Water Law to include all aspects of water resources management and development, including drafting legislation (*Section 14*); policy-making, strategies, planning (*Section 2*); water allocation and licencing of uses (*Sections 3, 4*); resource protection, monitoring and sustainability (*Sections 10, 17*); project guidelines, including for establishment of the National Water Corporation and the four regional water utilities (*Sections 6, 7*); sector capacity building; awareness raising and principles for demand management (*Sections 8, 18*); coordination of research (*Section 11*); setting standards for water quality (*Section 12*); technical cooperation (*Section 13*); promoting private sector investment

and participation (*Sections 16*); and international cooperation and management of transboundary water (*Sections 13, 19)*.

8 This shadow PWA essentially handles groundwater licencing and regulation. The original PWA branch in Gaza continues to steer investment and donor relations, and to conduct some water monitoring activities.

9 See Chapter Seven of *The History of Water*.

10 We are grateful to Mark Zeitoun (Zeitoun 2008) for this felicitous phrase. 'IWRM' is the globally accepted approach of 'integrated water resources management' which was best defined by the agreements of the International Conference on Water and Environment held in Dublin in 1992. The Conference set out three principles for forming IWRM policies and actions. These are the institutional principle, the instrument principle and the ecological principle. The *institutional principle* provides for the participation of all stakeholders, for separation of responsibility for water allocation and management from the interests of water users, and for decentralization and management of water at the lowest possible level ('subsidiarity'). The *instrument principle* provides for the efficient management of supply and demand through an incentive structure reflecting the value of water to society. The *ecological principle* provides for integrated, inter-sectoral management, with the basin as the unit of management. Since 1992, the goals and principles have been readily adopted and applied across the world. Many countries have incorporated IWRM into legislation, institutions and practice to varying degrees. See our book *Water Scarcity, Climate Change and Conflict* pp 89 ff for details.

11 A critique made by Selby (Selby 2013). See also Zeitoun 2008: 75.

12 Nonetheless, the way in which Article 40 has been implemented through the JWC had obliged the PWA to accept some derogation from these policies – see this chapter for more details.

13 See Chapter 3 for a full discussion on this. See also Zeitoun 2008: 75.

14 Source: World Bank 2019b: 9.

15 Source: Palestinian Water Authority, 2017, *Water Information System*. See the table *Annual Available Water Quantity*. Note, however, that these supply quantities include increasing amounts of overdraft groundwater in the Gaza Strip.

16 Source: WSRC Annual Report 2018.

17 Source: World Bank 2019b: 10; Zeitoun 2008: 72.

18 Zeitoun 2008: 56–7, 151.

19 WSRC was established by a decision of the Cabinet of Ministers, as mandated by the 2014 Water Law (Articles 17–28). The Council is governed by a seven-person Board appointed by Presidential Decree. Its objective is 'to monitor service providers with the aim of ensuring water and wastewater service quality and efficiency to consumers at affordable prices'. Its responsibilities are set out in Article 24 of the Law. They include: approving prices (24.1); licencing service providers (24.2); monitoring and inspecting compliance (24.3); developing performance incentives for service providers (24.4); monitoring water supply agreements (24.8); setting quality standards (24.10); publishing data (24.12); handling complaints against service providers (24.13); and regulating local authority participation in water utilities (24.16).

20 The Ministry of Agriculture oversees irrigation and provides extension advice to farmers on agricultural water management. The Ministry of Finance and Planning (MoFP) allocates and disburses sector investment finance. One particular MoFP function is managing the accounts with Israel, under which Israel makes various

deductions from the taxes it collects on behalf of the PA. In the water sector, these deductions include amounts due to Mekorot for water not paid for by the Palestinian water providers, and fees for the treatment of raw sewage flowing into Israel. The Ministry of Health is responsible for controlling health aspects of water quality, largely through inspections at the delivery point, and for licencing and control of water supply shops. The Environmental Protection Agency is responsible for overseeing environmental impact assessments for all water and sanitation projects, and for monitoring and acting on environmental issues related to water, notably wastewater issues.

21 They are also very effective in developing and testing innovative appropriate technology, for example in local-level decentralized wastewater treatment – see the examples in Chapter 4.

22 Specifically, of the total 'estimated potential' of the three aquifers, 483 million cubic metres was allocated to Israel (71 per cent) and 138 million cubic metres was allocated to the PA (20 per cent). Of the Palestinian share, 20.5 million cubic metres was to come from 'additional wells' yet to be developed. A balance of 57 million cubic metres was left unallocated and 'to be developed' from the Eastern Aquifer (see the table *West Bank: Allocation of Water Resources of the Three Shared Aquifers* in Chapter Seven of *The History of Water*. In addition, 'future needs' of the Palestinians were estimated at 70–80 million cubic metres.

23 According to Article 40 (Schedule 8.1a) increases in extraction above the Article 40 allocations 'shall require the prior approval of the JWC', but there is no record of any such approval of Israeli overpumping.

24 As we saw in Chapter Seven of *The History of Water*.

25 The Israeli State Comptroller reported in 1990 that decades of overpumping by the Israelis had led to a cumulative overdraft of 1.6 billion cubic metres and that the level to groundwater in the Mountain Aquifer had dropped 'during the period beginning in the early 1970s to 1990s by about 4 metres – each metre is equal to approximately 100 million cubic metres'. Not only was this over-abstraction unsustainable but it risked destroying the aquifer altogether as depletion brought the water level to approach the 'red line' where saline water would mix with fresh water.

26 At a public meeting in Jerusalem on 26 November 2008, the chairman of the Israeli Water Authority stated (as we noted in the section *Water abstraction* in Chapter 7 in *The History of Water*) that abstractions over the last five years had brought aquifer levels 'to the point where irreversible damage is done to the aquifer'. Source: Speech at the Water Crisis Conference organized by IPCRI, Ambassador Hotel, Jerusalem, 26 November 2008.

27 As discussed in Chapter 7 of *The History of Water*, almost no applications to deepen or replace these wells have been approved by the JWC or the Civil Administration.

28 At Bardala, in the north-eastern corner of Tubas Governorate, eight Palestinian wells were constructed before 1967 for domestic and agricultural purposes, with depths ranging from 30 to 65 metres. After the 1967 war, Israel constructed two deep wells (Bardala 1 in 1968 and Bardala 2 in 1979) a few hundred metres from the Palestinian wells. The water level in the Palestinian wells dropped at the rate of 2 metres a year, and salinity increased. Now the Palestinian wells are dry, as are most of the local springs used by Palestinian consumers for domestic and agricultural purposes. At Fasayil in Jericho governorate, Israel has drilled six production wells. The yield of the single Palestinian well in the area has fallen to zero, and the formerly abundant local springs have dried up. At Auja, the very productive Auja spring, which formerly

discharged up to 9 million cubic metres a year, has dried up for months on end through the action of five nearby Israeli production wells. A formerly water-abundant village is now buying back water from nearby settlements. Source: World Bank 2009. The case studies are from fieldwork interviews and focus groups, Jayyous, 23 November 2008.

29 Source: Zeitoun 2008: 98.

30 109 million cubic metres, made up of 85.8 million cubic metres pumped from Palestinian wells and 23.5 million cubic metres spring discharge (see the table *Annual Available Water Quantity*) divided by 2.8 million inhabitants gives per capita annual availability from *internal resources* of 39 cubic metres, divided by 365 gives daily availability of 107 lcd. *Total* water resources available of 182 million cubic metres, including 73 million cubic metres purchased from Mekorot, gives 65 cubic metres per capita annually, or 178 lcd.

31 Source: The Issue of Water between Israel and the Palestinians: 18. Government of Israel 2009. http://www.water.gov.il/Hebrew/ProfessionalInfoAndData/2012/22-Water-Issues-Between-Israel-and-the-Palestinians.pdf, consulted 27 May 2019.

32 Movement and access (M&A) restrictions refer to Israel's restrictions on movement and access of people and goods, both within West Bank and Gaza and out of those territories to the rest of the world.

33 WSRC (2015). These figures can be taken as actual supply at the tap or actual consumption, as the WSRC indicators measure 'average daily water consumption at domestic level', calculated as domestic water sales divided by the served population.

34 Many towns that depend on purchased water respond to this higher cost by not paying their bulk water bill. On this see Chapter 3.

35 See World Bank 2018 page 11 Table 1.1.

36 See Chapter Six in *The History of Water*.

37 On this see: *West Bank Water Department. Institutional reform towards national bulk supply utility* by M. Jaas in Hamdy A. and Monti R. (editors) *Food security under water scarcity in the Middle East: Problems and solutions*. Bari: CIHEAM. Options Méditerranéennes: Série A. Séminaires Méditerranéens; n. 65 2005. Pages 119–22.

38 The PA has recently re-engaged with Israel in the Joint Water Committee (JWC), and negotiations are underway for an extra 30 million cubic metres purchase from Israel and possibly a further 34 million cubic metres under the Red–Dead agreement.

39 Amongst PWA's responsibilities is that of establishing national plans, budgets and targets for water, together with the related investment programming and financing. In May 2016, it produced the *Water Sector Strategic Development Plan 2017–2022 (SDP).* The supporting *Water Sector Investment Plan (WSIP)* included a five-year investment programme that is massive in terms of the finance required ($1.25 billion for 240 projects) and in its demands on implementation capacity. These two exhaustive documents leave many questions open. Essentially it is not clear how feasible they are. In particular they do not reflect the extraordinary constraints within which the Palestinian water sector must operate.

40 Already purchases from Mekorot had risen to 73 million cubic metres in 2017.

41 Earlier, in 2004, there had been serious consideration given to a possible Palestinian desalination plant at Hadera on the coast of Israel. An article in the *New Scientist* in May 2004 reported that 'Israel has drawn up a secret plan for a giant desalination plant to supply drinking water to the Palestinian territory on the West Bank. It hopes the project will diminish pressure for it to grant any future Palestinian state greater access to the region's scarce supplies of fresh water. The new plans call for seawater

to be desalinated at Caesarea on the Mediterranean coast, and then pumped into the West Bank, where a network of pipes will deliver it to large towns and many of the 250 villages that currently rely on local springs and small wells for their water. Israel, which wants the US to fund the project, would guarantee safe passage of the water across its territory in return for an agreement that Israel can continue to take the lion's share of the waters of the West Bank. The first public hint of the plan emerged earlier in May in Washington DC. Uri Shamir, director of water research at the Technion, the Israel Institute of Technology in Haifa, told the House of Representatives Committee on International Relations that the desalination project was "the only viable long-term solution" for supplying drinking water to the West Bank. But other leading hydrologists contacted by New Scientist point out that desalinating seawater and pumping it to the West Bank, parts of which lie 1000 metres above sea level, would cost around $1 per cubic metre. "The question is whether an average Palestinian family can afford it," says Arie Issar, a water expert at Ben-Gurion University of the Negev in Sede Boker, Israel, who helped green the Israeli desert a generation ago by finding new water sources in the region. "It would be foolish to desalinate water on the coast and push it up the mountains when there are underground water resources up there, which cost only a third as much." Tony Allan of King's College London, a leading authority on Middle East water, agrees: "Pumping desalinated water to the West Bank is not the best technical or economic option."' See *Desalination: Israel lays claim to Palestine's water*. New Scientist, 27 May 2004. https://www.newscientist.com/article/dn5037-israel-lays-claim-to-palestines-water/#ixzz5ySpdLjYM.

42 In fact, there is the likelihood that some extra purchases have already agreed in the context of the Red–Dead 'water dividend', and that planning is underway for the needed new infrastructure.

43 See the table *Domestic Water Supply and Demand*. Losses of 51 million cubic metres out of gross supply of 117 million cubic metres gives a loss rate of 44 per cent.

44 See Siegel 2015: 49; S 55.

45 Chapter 3 discusses this point in detail.

Chapter 3

1 This chapter draws on material that we collected and wrote up when we took part in World Bank studies in 2008–9 and 2016–19. Some of the material is included in two World Bank reports, of which we were the principal authors, and is used here by agreement with the World Bank.

2 Source: Fieldwork interviews and focus groups, Jenin Governorate, 19–20 November 2008.

3 Source: Adapted from World Bank 2018: 5.

4 Connection rates in Gaza are also high for network water (93 per cent) and much higher for network sanitation (78 per cent) – see Chapter 6.

5 For the details and progress of these reforms see discussion later in this chapter.

6 Adapted from World Bank 2018: 6.

7 Source: Fieldwork interview, Ramallah, 1 December 2008.

8 Hebron Governorate is the most water-short of all West Bank governorates.

9 Compared to the West Bank average of 75 litres per person per day.

10 This compares to the already very low and unsustainable West Bank average of 67 per cent.
11 Municipalities do not account on an accruals basis, with debtors' and creditors' ledgers and a balance sheet. They simply record income and expenditure on a cash basis, and tot up the net inflow or net outflow of money at the end of the year.
12 On the SDP, see Chapter 2.
13 The 2013 Aqraba Town Profile by ARIJ gives a good picture of conditions before the water scheme arrived. See http://vprofile.arij.org/nablus/pdfs/vprofile/Aqraba_vp_en.pdf.
14 The mayor, however, supported the merger as 'the only viable way to get better services'.
15 Farkha is currently a member of the 'South of Salfeet JSC' along with Salfeet Municipality and three other village councils. However, villagers feel that this JSC is dominated by Salfeet and its interests. As a justification for their fears, they point to the only current activity of the JSC, which is issuing building permits. Fees collected are supposed to be divided 70 per cent for the participating local government units and 30 per cent for the JSC. However, the Farkha mayor claims that Salfeet Municipality keeps all the money.
16 On these arrangements, see Chapter 7 of *The History of Water*.
17 On the WSRC, see Chapter 2.
18 We used a version of this table in the report we wrote for the World Bank (World Bank 2018).
19 For Gaza KPIs, see Chapter 6.
20 Affordability is calculated as average water revenues per capita/GNI per capita, based on a 2014 gross national income (GNI) per capita for West Bank and Gaza of $3,060.
21 It will be recalled from Chapter 2 that *total* unaccounted-for water is 44 per cent, which includes a further 15 per cent of water missing at the bulk delivery level.
22 Source: Fieldwork interviews, Jenin, 20 November 2008.
23 Following the KfW 'German' project, unaccounted-for water (UfW) at Jenin was down from 50 per cent, but still stood at the time of our visit at 36 per cent.
24 As discussed elsewhere in this chapter, the PA ends up paying for this as the Israelis simply deduct what is due to Mekorot from the customs and tax revenue they collect on behalf of the PA.
25 Source: Fieldwork interview, Ramallah, 1 December 2008.
26 At JWU, unaccounted-for water (UfW) was better – but still relatively high at 25–30 per cent, and a marked deterioration from 2002 when the rate was 21 per cent.
27 According to the Water Law, Section 35.
28 For obscure reasons, these arrears are referred to euphemistically as 'net lending'. On deductions for sewage treatment, see also Chapter 4.
29 Source: Field visit to Yatta, 4 December 2016.
30 72.6 million cubic metres in 2017 – see Chapter 2.
31 In addition, it is likely that the deductions for untreated wastewater will continue until the West Bank can capture, treat and dispose of all its wastewater – see Chapter 4.
32 Taken together, these data cover services to about 80 per cent of West Bank households.
33 Again we used a version of this table in the 2018 report we wrote for the World Bank.
34 Adapted from World Bank 2018: 12.

35 Non-revenue water at the service provider level does not include the considerable physical losses in the bulk supply system, estimated at 15 per cent – see *Reducing losses* in Chapter 2.
36 The high rate of non-revenue water in Jordan – 36 per cent – is surprising in so water-short a country and one where water is being pumped over long distances and up to high elevations at high cost. The topography – of steep slopes – and the intermittence of supply are amongst the causes of the high losses. The Water Authority is clearly working on the issue as the rate in 2008 was even higher than in 2010 – 43 per cent.
37 In practice, only a share of these losses can be eliminated. In Chapter 2 we discussed PWA's plans to reduce losses in the bulk system to 8 per cent and in the retail system to 22 per cent. These savings could increase retail water supply by a total of 16 million cubic metres, about one quarter of present supply.
38 In 2010, the average Egyptian supplier collected only 74 cents on each dollar of cost. The average Jordanian supplier collected $1.10. Combining the working ratio and collection efficiency for these two countries, the average Jordanian provider would be at least breaking even on an income and current expenditure basis. The average Egyptian supplier would be well in deficit.
39 This section draws on World Bank 2019: 97.
40 While full-cost recovery is an essential longer-term objective, there may be a need to progressively increase cost recovery as services improve and efficiencies increase. An immediate goal is to cover the costs of operation and maintenance so that the service provider remains solvent. Over the longer term, recovery of depreciation and ultimately financing of capital investment may be the objective.
41 On all the hurdles to Palestinian investment in the water sector, see Chapter 7 of *The History of Water*.
42 Source: Fieldwork interview Ramallah, 1 December 2008.
43 Source: Fieldwork interviews, 18–20 November 2008.
44 Including investment in Gaza.
45 PWA's longer-term target is to reduce losses to 22 per cent by 2030 – see Chapter 2 *Reducing losses*.
46 *IBNET Water Supply and Sanitation Blue Book 2014*. World Bank, Washington DC.
47 This section draws on World Bank 2018: 63. Although the reform programme covers the whole water sector, it is discussed in detail in this chapter because the great bulk of the reforms concern the restructuring of water supply.
48 On the SDP, see Chapter 2, *PWA's blue skies planning*.
49 This section draws on World Bank 2018: 65.
50 PWA/Hydroconseil 2016.
51 On the statute of JSC, see the section on *Service provision* earlier.
52 According to the Orgut study, these proposals are based on successful reorganizations of the solid waste and electricity sectors in Palestine (PWA/Orgut 2017: 7).
53 PWA/Orgut 2017: 9.
54 PWA/Orgut 2017: 48–9.
55 'Fictitious' because, as we have seen, almost no local government service provider covers its full costs, including depreciation. Many run deficits even on O&M costs alone. The fictitious surplus consists of money that is owed to WBWD but not paid. It is difficult to justify 'compensating' a municipality for what is effectively a diversion of public funds.

56 'Full' cost recovery would include depreciation to build up reserves for asset replacement.

Chapter 4

1 Source: *Jerusalem Post*, 26 May 2011.
2 Gidon Bromberg quoted in *The Jerusalem Post* article by Sharon Udasin: *PA to get $45 million wastewater treatment facility in Hebron*. 26 May 2011.
3 The *Stormwater, Domestic Wastewater and Industrial Wastewater Master Plan for Hebron* (2001). This plan was developed with financing from the United States Agency for International Development (USAID).
4 A principal source for this section is the World Bank appraisal report: World Bank. 2015. *West Bank and Gaza – First Phase of the Hebron Regional Wastewater Management Project (English)*. Washington, DC: World Bank Group. http://documents.worldbank.org/curated/en/978051468309360810/West-Bank-and-Gaza-First-Phase-of-the-Hebron-Regional-Wastewater-Management-Project.
5 Source: *Disclosable Version of the ISR – Hebron Regional Wastewater Management Project – Phase 1 – P117449 – Sequence No: 09 (English)*. Washington, DC: World Bank Group. http://documents.worldbank.org/curated/en/809911561059624782/Disclosable-Version-of-the-ISR-Hebron-Regional-Wastewater-Management-Project-Phase-1-P117449-Sequence-No-09.
6 Bromberg is Israeli director of EcoPeace, the former Friends of the Earth Middle East.
7 Source: *PA to get $45 million wastewater treatment facility in Hebron* by Sharon Udasin, *Jerusalem Post*, 26 May 2011.
8 This section draws on work we did for the 2009 World Bank report *Assessment of Restrictions on Palestinian Water Sector Development* (World Bank 2009).
9 On Article 40, see Chapter 7 of *The History of Water*.
10 Source: PECDAR 87ff.
11 Source: Fieldwork interviews, Tel Aviv, 26 November 2008 and Jerusalem, 27 November 2008.
12 Source: B'tselem report on three study cases.
13 This is documented in a twenty-minute film made by the French aid organization AFD.
14 See Chapter Seven of *The History of Water* for a full examination of this level of constraints.
15 The source for the current situation in Salfit is largely the article *Drowning in the waste of Israeli settlers* by Jaclynn Ashly, 18 September 2017 al Jazeera. https://www.aljazeera.com/indepth/features/2017/09/drowning-waste-israeli-settlers-170916120027885.html.
16 Source: Nablus Municipality: *Wastewater Treatment Plant Nablus West Annual Report for Operations and Reuse 2017* February 2018 http://wwtp.nablus.org/wp-content/uploads/2018/02/Final-2017-report-20-2-2018.pdf. Accessed online 4 August 2019.
17 The plant is located in El Ein wadi 12 kilometres north of Jerusalem and two kilometres south of the town of El Bireh.
18 The plant was constructed between 1995 and 2000 at a cost of 7 million euros, financed by German aid. It is designed to treat 5,000 cubic metres of effluent daily to

meet Palestinian standards for recharge: BOD levels below 20 milligrams per litre and total suspended solids below 30 milligrams per litre.

19 Palestinian critics refer to this less politely as 'refining the shit of Zionist colonies'.

20 Source: http://www.kawther.info/wpr/2013/04/19/german-scandal-18-million-dm-for-treatment-of-colonists-waste-water.

21 USAID/EHP/Save the Children Report – Village Water and Sanitation Program Phase II, June 2003.

22 Source: World Bank 2007a: 1.

23 Source: World Bank 2009: 99.

24 Fieldwork interview, 26 November 2008.

25 2003/4, WaSH MP 2004.

26 Source: WaSH MP 2004: 64.

27 Source: WaSH MP 2004: 63.

28 Source: MAS 2009 citing the Pan Arab Project for Family Health (PAPFAM) Survey 2006.

29 The Local Government Performance Assessment (LGPA) Survey. The LGPA Survey and PWA data provide the information basis for this section.

30 Source: IBNET 2014.

31 See Chapters 2 and 3.

32 On the investment programme, see the section 'Bridging the gap' in Chapter 2.

33 Source: ARIJ 2016: 65–6.

34 Source: Fieldwork interviews, Jerusalem, Ramallah, November 2008.

35 The Germans had initially been interested in financing this project, which was a complement to the wastewater treatment plant which they had financed – see the section earlier in the chapter on the al Bireh wastewater treatment plant. However, the Germans eventually withdrew. KfW wrote to the Israeli authorities in February 2002 to say they were not prepared to finance the preparatory studies for the reuse pilot because of the high risk that the project 'would not materialize at all due to rejection'. Source: World Bank 2009: 111.

36 Source: World Bank 2009, based on Meerbach, Abdo, Itleib and Hind, 2003.

37 According to what we were told on-site during our fieldwork in 2008, 'the technical demonstrations were poorly handled – using a sprinkler on vegetables, for example', and the process of confidence building seems to have been mishandled: 'The problem is that the people were not consulted, nor were they connected to the plant. In fact they were insulted. There is a need to go in phases: economic feasibility, public awareness, and training.'

38 *Water-driven Palestinian agricultural frontiers: the global ramifications of transforming local irrigation* by Julie Trottier and Jeanne Perrier, CNRS and Université Paul Valéry, France. Journal of Political Ecology Vol. 25, 2018: 304.

39 One problem in this approach has been explored by Julie Trottier, who argues that all or almost all springs and wells that are used for irrigation in the West Bank are privately controlled and there is no mechanism by which they could be converted to urban water supply, other than by voluntary sales which are already, in fact, taking place on a large scale in the form of sales to tankers. Dr Trottier also argues that reusable wastewater can rarely be used in exchange for surrendered fresh water as the farmers involved in the two parts of the transaction are likely to be quite different – different locations, different resources.

40 Source: Trottier and Perrier; and *Environmental and Social Impact Assessment for Al-Bireh Reuse Trunk Line to Al-Auja Area 2016.*

41 See the article 'Innovative wastewater recycling' in Nablus at https://www.cdmsmith.com/en-EU/Client-Solutions/Projects/Wastewater-Management-Nablus.

Chapter 5

1 Much of this section draws on fieldwork we did for our 2009 report to the World Bank.
2 Over 6,000 hectares. Marj Ibn Amr is known to the Israelis as the Plain of Esdraelon.
3 Some of these numbers are correct, others not. We are only recording the perceptions and grumbles of farmers.
4 This would be equivalent to $70 per hectare.
5 As we noted in Chapter 3, the PWA maintains that all these unlicensed wells in the West Bank are drilled into the shallow aquifers (either Eocene in Jenin, or Pleistocene in the Jordan Valley) and therefore are not part of the Mountain Aquifer system regulated under Oslo. The PWA asserts that 'these wells only draw on Palestinian resources and do not impact Israeli wells'.
6 With value added per worker dropping from NIS 16,000 ($4,500) in the 1990s to under NIS 10,000 ($2,800) since the mid-2000s. Source: PCBS (2012a) and PCBS Labour Force surveys, cited at World Bank 2013: 38.
7 Source: whc.unesco.org. 2014, cited in the Wikipedia article *Olive production in Palestine*.
8 Recall the identical Israeli view cited earlier of trees as 'planted flags'.
9 The PA Ministry of Agriculture (2004a) described this factor in its *Strategy for Sustainable Agriculture* as 'psychological hope related to the retention of Palestinian land.' [World Bank 2009: 23 Note 47]
10 Jordan irrigates 40,000 hectares out of the 270,000 hectares cultivated. Israel irrigates about 190,000 hectares out of 430,000 hectares cultivated.
11 See the table *Sources and Uses* in Chapter 2.
12 Source: PWA 2008.
13 Source: Fieldwork interviews and focus groups, Jenin, November 2008.
14 Mark Zeitoun's luminous phrase, Zeitoun 2008: 15. On settlement agriculture, see the discussion later in this chapter.
15 Where the right to use water is part of the land title, usually where a permanently flowing spring is exploited jointly by a group of farmers, the landowners have time-shares – the right to use the whole flow of a canal or a part of the flow for a certain number of hours. A local committee is elected to manage the system, arrange maintenance and resolve disputes. In other cases, the water – a well or a spring – can be separated from land ownership, in which case the individual or group who owns the source might divide up the water between them or simply sell the water to the farmers around. Where a market in irrigation water exists, prices were in the past relatively low, little more than cost. The average sale price of irrigation water from wells in 1990 was $0.172 per cubic metre, while the average cost was estimated at $0.16. Today, as we saw in Jenin, prices have gone sky-high – between $1 and $3 per cubic metre.
16 These basically restricted farmers to average water use levels slightly below those of 1970–3.
17 Hisham Awartami, Economic Aspects of the Agricultural Sector in the Occupied Territories, 1986 (3): 78–89.

18 Source: World Bank 1993: 1.7.
19 See Chapter 6 of *The History of Water*.
20 Source: Shuval 2007: 124.
21 Source: Awartami 1986: 143.
22 Source: Agricultural Statistics Indicators, 1981–8, Amman; Ministry of Agriculture, Amman, 1989.
23 Source: Awartami 1986: 147–8.
24 Source: Awartami 1986: 148.
25 Source: Awartami 1986: 143.
26 Awartami 1986: 149 gives the comparative figures in Jordanian dinars: West Bank JD 0.100 per cubic metre; Israel JD 0.020 per cubic metre; and JVA JD 0.003 per cubic metre.
27 Source: World Bank 1993 4: 3.11 Note 27.
28 Source: Fieldwork interview, Ramallah, 16 November 2008.
29 Source: UNCTAD 2015: 25.
30 Source: UNCTAD 2015: 22 citing ARIJ 2011.
31 *Effects of Movement and Access Controls on Water for the Palestinian Agriculture Sector, preliminary assessment by MAS 2009 (draft).*
32 World Bank. 2013. *West Bank and Gaza – Area C and the future of the Palestinian economy (English)*. Washington DC; World Bank Group. http://documents.worldbank.org/curated/en/137111468329419171/West-Bank-and-Gaza-Area-C-and-the-future-of-the-Palestinian-economy.
33 Based on an irrigated area of 190,000 hectares and water use in agriculture of 1,200 million cubic metres.
34 Source: Siegel 2015: 57–71.
35 It was Professor Anne Lambton who said this in her *Persian Land Reform*.
36 Source is our field visit to Jayyous in November 2008.
37 See Chapter 6 of *The History of Water.*
38 See Chapter Seven of *The History of Water*. An article by Gideon Levy and Alex Levac published in *Haaretz* on 20 September 2019 – 'Down in the Jordan Valley, the Cruel Wheels of the Israeli Occupation Keep on Turning' – describes the case at Mount Tamoun: 'Two days after Prime Minister Benjamin Netanyahu declared, on Tuesday last week, his intention to annex the Jordan Valley after the election, forces of the Civil Administration carried out the uprooting of hundreds of olive trees that were about to yield their first fruit, and demolition of the cisterns holding the water that was used to irrigate them. The first crop of these seven-year-old trees was set to be harvested in another few days. The Civil Administration also uprooted in full some large olive trees, about 50 years old, from this privately owned grove and buried them under the rubble of the reservoirs. The affair began last Thursday morning at about 7:30. Mursheid Bani Odah and Jihad Bani Odah [spotted] . . . four bulldozers, two power shovels and two excavators, escorted by three jeeps of the Israel Defense Forces and three more belonging to the Civil Administration . . . moving from the direction of Atouf toward the dry hill of Mount Tamoun . . . above the verdant, budding settlements of Ro'i and Beka'ot. When the two reached their property on the hill, they saw workers using electric saws on their olive trees while bulldozers laid waste to the cisterns they had built. [Now all that is left are shallow graves in the thorny, rock-strewn area, where the young olive trees were buried and the demolished concrete walls of the six reservoirs, each of which held 70 cubic metres of water].' The following week Haaretz published an article on a similar case of uprooting, this

time in the Hebron area: *In the South Hebron Hills, a Quiet Population Transfer Is Underway.* https://www.haaretz.com/israel-news/.premium-in-the-jordan-valley-the-cruel-wheels-of-the-israeli-occupation-keep-turning-1.7867122?=&utm_source=Push_Notification&utm_medium=web_push&utm_campaign=General&ts=_1569149378675.

39 The Ein al Fashka springs lie within the West Bank above the north-western shore of the Dead Sea, about 3 kilometres south of Qumran, which also lies within the Palestinian West Bank. The Israelis have declared the area a nature reserve and archaeological site.

40 Source: UNCTAD 2015: 16, citing UNOCHA 2012b.

41 El Musa citing David Kahan (page 113): *Agriculture and Water Resources in the West Bank and Gaza (1967-1987).* Elmusa also cites the West Bank Data Project.

42 Source: UNCTAD 2015: 15.

43 The JNF financed the building of the Tirza, Og and Naama reservoirs, all of which are used for the irrigation of Israeli agriculture in the Jordan Valley. See: Amira Hass, 'PA Farmers Hung out to Dry while Israelis Flourish in Jordan Valley' Haaretz 2 December 2012, accessed at http://www.haaretz.com/news/diplomacy-defense/pa-farmers-hung-out-to-dry-while-israelis-flourish-in-jordan-valley. premium-1.481797105.

44 In 2012, the World Bank estimated 93,000 dunams (9,300 hectares) of settler agriculture, largely irrigated, and with productivity higher than that of their Palestinian neighbours. Sources: UNCTAD 2015: 19, World Bank 2013: *Area C and the future of the Palestinian economy.* Report No. AUS2922. Of settler agriculture, 10,195 dunams were within 'closed military zones and firing zones'; 11,046 dunams were on lands under military service orders; 1,851 dunams were within designated nature reserves; and 760 dunams were on 'lands expropriated for public use' (source: Kerem Navot: *Israeli Settlers' Agriculture As A Means Of Land Takeover In The West Bank* (2013)).

45 See, for example, the following 2019 article in Haaretz: *A Bedouin Family Got Evicted by Israel* by Amira Hass. Haaretz, 18 August 2019: 'Salem Ka'baneh and his Bedouin family are no stranger to seasonal wandering between two permanent sites and searching for food for the sheep. For about seven or eight months a year they live in a neighbourhood of simple structures – tin shacks, huts, pens and tents – in the farming village of al-Jiftlik in the Jordan Valley, some 15 kilometres (9 miles) from their second permanent site at al-Hadidiya. But this time the wandering was premature, forced. On August 4, 2019, a Civil Administration inspector appeared at the family's encampment near al-Hadidiya in the Jordan Valley.'

'He ordered the family to move away from the place where they and their herd stay several months each year during the warm weather. About half an hour earlier, Odeh says, a settler from the settlement of Ro'i showed up and also ordered them out. They decided to spare themselves what they had undergone in May and July this year – the destruction of their tents and sheep pen.'

'Salem's parents were born and lived in the Negev, before being forced out to the West Bank after 1948. "I was born in al Naqab (Negev)" he says. "After, I lived in al-Auja" – a village north of Jericho. He recalls a house that the authorities tore down in 1973, then wandering north to Marj Najeh and at the end of the '90s – a forcible eviction from there too. The family gradually built a house in Jiftlik– a 200-square-meter (2,150-square-foot) stone house with a balcony. Nice furniture and ornaments. In 2016, the Israelis demolished the house. Everything was thrown outside, a pile of stones and concrete are the remains of the house. The authorities also demolished the new pen.'

'The first demolition [in 2019] of the Ka'abneh family's tent and pen at al-Hadidiya was on May 30. Seven structures were torn down, including a pen and a mobile toilet. On June 12 "they" came again and the demolition was shorter, because there was only one tent and one pen. Male and female members of the Border Police accompanied the Civil Administration inspector, and workers accompanied the bulldozer: seven workers the first time and four the second.'

'Ruwaida was born and raised at al-Hadidiya, and helped raise the family's sheep and make cheese, the way her sons and daughters help her and her husband with today. She witnessed the demolition of her childhood's encampment, as her children have experienced the demolitions these days. "Twenty years ago they came in helicopters to collect the debris [to prevent the tents' sheets and boards from being used again]. Today they bury them and we don't know where," she says. Her father, about 80, lives in the village of Tammun today. "Resting from the demolitions," she says.'

'In the past 25 years the pasture areas remaining for the Palestinians in the Jordan Valley (a third of the West Bank) have been decreasing due to the expansion of the settlements and outposts. But despite all Israel's bans on grazing, construction and linking homes to infrastructure in most of the valley, despite the declared firing zones and all the demolitions and forced evictions, about 50 communities still live there and preserve their traditional way of life centred around herding and raising sheep.'

'"Was it ever different?" I ask Salem Ka'abneh . . . He ponders and says: "Until the '80s we still felt there could be a little justice. They let us stay in the place they evacuated us to. But today they can change their mind every time."'

46 The phrase is the World Bank's. See World Bank 2013.

47 Area C was defined under the Interim Agreement as 'areas of the West Bank outside Areas A and B, which, except for the issues that will be negotiated in the permanent status negotiations, will be gradually transferred to Palestinian jurisdiction in accordance with this Agreement'. According to the Interim Agreement, the gradual transfer should have been completed by 1997.

48 Source: World Bank 2013: 31.

49 Source: World Bank 2013. LRC was founded in 1986. It is a Palestinian NGO dedicated to researching Palestinian land issues.

50 Source: Fieldwork interviews and focus groups, Jayyous and Falamiya 23 November 2008.

Chapter 6

1 Judges 16.23 tells of the travails of the Israelite Samson in Philistine Gaza. Milton's Samson Agonistes opens with Samson's lament:

> Ask for this great Deliverer now, and find him
> Eyeless in Gaza, at the mill with slaves

2 Source: Intervention at the Sderot Conference on the Gaza Water and Sanitation Crisis, EcoPeace Conference Summary, 6 March 2018.

3 On the Beit Lahiya saga, see the section *Sanitation and wastewater* below.

4 *Population and Demographic Developments in the West Bank and Gaza Strip until 1990*. UNCTAD/ECDC/SEU/1 United Nations Conference on Trade And Development. https://unctad.org/en/docs/poecdcseud1.en.pdf.
5 Estimates from Wikipedia for the population of Palestine in 1947 are 1,970,000, citing Sergio Della Pergola (2001), who draws on the work of Bachi (1975), the founder of the Israeli Central Bureau of Statistics. See Bachi, Roberto (1974): The Population of Israel, Institute of Contemporary Jewry, Hebrew University of Jerusalem. pp. 133, 390–4.
6 Source: Siegel 2015: 179.
7 Overdraft of an aquifer occurs when abstractions exceed the recharge, leading to depletion of the groundwater reserves stored in the aquifer. Because the Gaza aquifer lies below sea level and is immediately adjacent to the sea, depletion of the aquifer draws in seawater which progressively advances inland beneath the surface, causing the whole aquifer to become salty and undrinkable over time. Ultimately, the water will be unusable, without desalination even in agriculture.
8 3,000–5,000 ppm.
9 Military Order no. 291 of 1968. This order overruled the prevailing Egyptian law in the Gaza Strip under which surface and groundwater on and beneath the land belonged to the landowner.
10 Annual agricultural water quotas per dunam were: citrus 1,000 cubic metres; vegetables 700 cubic metres; strawberries 1,000 cubic metres; and olives or almonds 300 cubic metres (Isaac and Shuval 1994: 256).
11 Source: Ziad. According to Sosland, in 1988–9, the settler population, then numbering fewer than 1,000, consumed 2 million cubic metres of Gaza's groundwater, whereas the more than 1.5 million Palestinians consumed only 92 million cubic metres. For 1986, Sosland makes consumption of Gazans 142 cubic metres per capita, that of settlers 2,240 cubic metres (Sosland 2007: 153, 257–8).
12 Grey in Isaac and Shuval 1993: 223.
13 On the NWC, see Chapter 1.
14 Sources: Grey in Isaac and Shuval 1993: 222–4; Siegel 2015: 180.
15 Interview of Jeffrey Sosland with Shaul Arlosoroff, July 1995 – see Sosland 2007: 153 and note 62 on page 257.
16 Zeitoun 2008: 92, 101.
17 See World Bank (2003). West Bank and Gaza update. World Bank Report on Impact of *Intifada (PDF)*. p. 27.
18 On the similar situation in the West Bank, see Chapter 3.
19 The two plants are financed respectively by KfW, and by Japan and the Islamic Development Bank.
20 Oslo designated 5 million cubic metres of potable water to meet 'immediate needs', to be supplied by Mekorot – see Chapter 7 of *The History of Water*.
21 See the table *Domestic Water Supply* in Chapter 2. In Israel, domestic consumption in 2016 was 263 lcd (Chapter 1).
22 Sources: World Bank 2009 27; PWA Gaza database, CMWU database; communications from Ahmed al Yaqoub and Rebhy Sheikh, PWA, February 2009.
23 Source: PWA communication to the authors, May 2017.
24 PWA 2015a; PWA 2015c.
25 PWA Gaza database; CMWU database; communications with Ahmed al Yaqoub and Rebhy Sheikh, PWA; Messerschmid 2008.

26 Only 3 per cent of the water pumped from the aquifer complies with World Health Organization drinking water-quality standards.
27 Source: World Bank 2018.
28 This supply level is slightly above the 2014 level recorded in the table *Total Water Availability*.
29 Professor David Grey (Isaac and Shuval: 224) also raises the question of ownership of water resources. If the Gaza Strip has reverted to Egyptian law which applied between 1948 and 1967, then 'water on the land belongs to the landowner', so that the kind of state-led command and control measures that Israel applied so successfully may not be legal in the Gaza Strip. Even if new Palestinian water law applies – see Chapter 2 – it is doubtful that expropriation of private water wells could be practiced.
30 In the world, only a handful of high-governance territories have really recovered control over groundwater – Israel, a handful of US states, countries in Europe. Thanks to Jeremy Berkoff for sharing this insight many years ago.
31 Source: Mekorot responds to Gisha's Freedom of Information application regarding water supply to the Gaza Strip. 2 September 2015. https://gisha.org/legal/5016.
32 Several of which are explored by Siegel in *Let There Be Water*.
33 Based on the studies for the central desalination plant.
34 Compared to the 85–90 million cubic metres a year of barely potable and non-potable water supplied through the network from municipal wells and 8 million cubic metres a year of potable water supplied by Mekorot.
35 PWA/WASH Partners/GIZ 2015.
36 PWA/Hydroconseil (2016).
37 Sources: PWA/Hydroconseil 2016; PWA/GIZ 2015; PWA 2015a; PWA/WASH Partners/GIZ 2015; GIZ/PWA/CEP 2015.
38 The power cuts also interrupt municipal water supply. Low water pressure in the network makes the filling of rooftop water tanks a challenge, and the frequent power outages mean that household-level water pumps cannot do the job either.
39 Source: Israel Advances Gaza Water Project: Passage of equipment to construct desalination plant and water reservoirs okayed by Defense Ministry, by Yaniv Kubovich, *Haaretz*, 2 August 2018.
40 Sources: UNICEF 2019. *UNICEF seawater desalination plant helps head off Gaza water crisis.* https://www.unicef.org/stories/unicef-seawater-desalination-plant-helps-head-gaza-water-crisis and *Searching for clean water in Gaza* by Gregor von Medeazza, 10 January 2019 https://blogs.unicef.org/blog/searching-clean-water-gaza/. The UNICEF source also says that 'with USAID funding, UNICEF . . . partnered with the Massachusetts Institute of Technology (MIT) to develop a new desalination prototype based on electro-dialysis, which extracts salt particles from the water by running an electric current through it. A potential game-changer for water in the Gaza Strip, the prototype reduces energy use by up to 60 per cent and operates with solar power; it can transform up to 90 per cent of the water from the aquifer into drinking water and lowers cost.'
41 The principal source for this section is: Palestinian Water Authority: Gaza Central Desalination Plant and Associated Works Program. Donor Information Handbook. Ramallah, 2018.
42 Based on a population of 1.9 million.
43 On non-revenue water and collection efficiency, see later, this chapter.
44 This will be a new grid connection from Israel via a 161-kV line with a dedicated power line from El Matahen substation (within Gaza) to the project site.

45 The 'associated works' are considered a 'no regrets' option even if the desalination plant is not constructed. Essentially, these associated works would comprise a water carrier that would distribute desalinated water, either locally produced or imported, throughout the Strip.
46 Source: World Bank press release 10 February 2020 World Bank and partners invest $117 million in water for Palestinians in Gaza. https://www.worldbank.org/en/news/press-release/2020/02/10/world-bank-and-partners-invest-us117-million-in-water-for-palestinians-in-gaza.
47 Demand estimates are from the studies for the desalination plant.
48 Source: World Bank 2007b: 8.
49 Communication from World Bank staff based in Gaza, 19 February 2009.
50 For West Bank comparator figures, see the table *Water Service Key Performance Indicators* in Chapter 3.
51 PCBS 2015; PWA 2015c.
52 Affordability is calculated as average water revenues per capita/GNI per capita. Based on a 2014 gross national income (GNI) per capita for West Bank and Gaza of $3,060, Gaza's percentage is as follows: 92 lcd × 365 days × NIS 1.90 per cubic metres average price/3.83 × 1,000 = $16.66 per year/$3,060 per capita GNI = 0.6 per cent.
53 As we saw in Chapter 3, non-revenue water is the difference between the water that is supplied and the water that is billed. It has three components: actual physical losses from the system, theft of water through illegal connections and water supplied to customers who are not billed. Depending on the service provider's policy, this may include refugee camps, surviving family of martyrs, mosques and public buildings.
54 Source: Fieldwork interview, WHO, Gaza City, 24 November 2008. See also Isaac and Shuval 1994: 263: *The Gaza Strip Water Problem* by Ephraim Ahiram and Hanna Siniora.
55 Source: Fieldwork interviews, Khan Younis, 24 November 2008.
56 Source: Interview with World Bank staff based in the Jerusalem Office, November 2008.
57 Source: *Israel to build pipeline to absorb sewage from Gaza*. Ynetnews, Matan Tzuri, 7 January 2017. https://www.ynetnews.com/articles/0,7340,L-4983174,00.html.
58 The source for much of this discussion is the World Bank. See: https://www.worldbank.org/en/news/feature/2018/03/12/north-gaza-communities-will-finally-benefit-from-sewage-treatment-services.
59 Source: LGPA. See also *The Gaza Strip Water Problem* by Ephraim Ahiram and Hanna Siniora in Isaac and Shuval 1994: 263.
60 World Bank 2018: 45.
61 Source: Fieldwork interview, WHO, Gaza City, 24 November 2008.
62 Sources: Centre on Housing Rights and Evictions Position Paper (2008) 'Hostage to Politics: The impact of sanctions and the blockade on the human right to water and sanitation in Gaza'; and Abu Naser, A., et al. 'Relation of nitrate contamination of groundwater with methaemoglobin level among infants in Gaza', Eastern Mediterranean Health Journal, Volume 13, No. 5 (September–October 2007), http://www.emro.who.int.
63 Source: Intervention at the Sderot Conference on the Gaza Water and Sanitation Crisis, EcoPeace Conference Summary, 6 March 2018.
64 Sources: UNESCO World Heritage Sites Tentative List https://whc.unesco.org/en/tentativelists/5722/, consulted 20 March 2020; and *Once a vibrant natural reserve, Gaza's coastal wetland is now a health hazard*. Amjad Yaghi, +972 Magazine, 5 March 2019.

65 Intervention at the Sderot Conference on the Gaza Water and Sanitation Crisis, EcoPeace Conference Summary, 6 March 2018. See also *The Jerusalem Post*, 6 July 2017 'Gaza sewage forces shutdown of Israeli beach: Israel may build a pipeline to Sderot to treat waste', article by Sharon Udasin and Tovah Lazaroff.
66 Sources: EcoPeace Conference Summary 6 March 2018; speech of Rotem Caro Weizman from EcoPeace (rotem@foeme.org]. An article in *Haaretz* on 15 May 2019 about tourism visits to the Israeli border with Gaza says: 'From here, we can see the Ashkelon power plant that supplies electricity to Gaza. Despite all the bad blood between the two sides, McLean (the tour guide) explains why Israel has an interest in supplying electricity to the enclave: During power outages, Gaza can't operate its sewage treatment facilities and the effluent starts flowing north onto Israel's beaches. "We're all in this together", he notes, "and whether for selfish or humanitarian reasons, we have to care about what's going on there. You can't just build a wall and throw out the key."'
67 Source: Speech of MK Maj. Gen. (res.) Eyal Ben-Reuven at the Sderot Conference on the Gaza Water and Sanitation Crisis, EcoPeace Conference Summary, 6 March 2018.
68 Source: Shawa Issam *Water situation in the Gaza Strip*, in Isaac and Shuval: 251; and Ziad.
69 When we were there in 2008, about 100 of these wells had been rehabilitated.
70 Source: Fieldwork, Khan Younis, 25 November 2008 and Donald MacIntyre *Gaza: Preparing for Dawn*. London 2018.
71 Source: World Bank. https://www.worldbank.org/en/news/press-release/2015/05/21/gaza-economy-on-the-verge-of-collapse.
72 The main source here is State of Palestine Ministry of Agriculture *National Agricultural Sector Strategy 2017-2022*. November 2016.
73 Part of a $50 million USAID project launched in May 2016 called Envision Gaza, a five-year project focussing on improving the employment rate, with an emphasis on areas like technology, textiles and agriculture. Kamhawi told *The Jerusalem Post*: 'We want to work with firms so they can become more competitive in the local and export market.' The project has worked with 300 different farmers or farming companies in Gaza and 'more than 30 Palestinian firms have signed contracts with international buyers, bringing $34 million to the local economy.'
74 See: *In Gaza, using agriculture to grow the economy* by Melanie Lidman, *Times of Israel*, 17 May 2016. https://www.timesofisrael.com/in-gaza-using-agriculture-to-grow-the-economy/.
75 As we write this, a headline from the *Times of Israel* on 30 April 2019 flashes up on the screen: 'IDF accuses Islamic Jihad of Gaza rocket fire, cuts fishing zone as punishment.'
76 The decision may also have been influenced by shortages of fresh produce in the Israeli market.
77 Source: Al Jazeera 15 August 2018. https://www.aljazeera.com/news/2018/08/israel-reopens-gaza-commercial-crossing-month-long-closure-180815074300410.html.
78 See: *In Gaza, using agriculture to grow the economy* by Melanie Lidman, *Times of Israel*, 17 May 2016. https://www.timesofisrael.com/in-gaza-using-agriculture-to-grow-the-economy/.
79 Source: The Netherlands Representative Office (NRO), Palestinian Territories 'Gaza Exports to Europe with Dutch Support' by Market Insider, Wednesday, 18 December 2013. http://www.intracen.org/Gaza-exports-to-Europe-with-Dutch-support/#sthash.lS3FO1Dl.dpuf.

80 See: *In Gaza, using agriculture to grow the economy* by Melanie Lidman, *Times of Israel*, 17 May 2016. https://www.timesofisrael.com/in-gaza-using-agriculture-to-grow-the-economy/. On the *High Value Crops Export Programme* see http://www.intracen.org/Gaza-exports-to-Europ-with-Dutch-support/.

81 Source: Fieldwork interviews, PWA, CMWU, Gaza City, 24–25 November 2008.

82 Source: Fieldwork interviews, Gaza City, 24–25 November 2008.

83 Source: Fieldwork interviews, Khan Younis, 24 November 2008.

Part III

1 Israeli commentators have suggested that aspects of the present Palestinian polity, particularly weak governance, restrictions on the press and on freedom of speech, and the frailty of accountable institutions make drawing parallels between the Israeli and Palestinian situations problematic. However, here we are simply pointing out the fundamental disempowerment of the Palestinians in respect of water. What really empowered Palestinian people and institutions might achieve if they gained the fundamentals of water security is a question that has not yet been put to the test.

2 In Part III of the book, there is a fortunate congruence of thinking with many of the ideas of the visionary EcoPeace organization. We have discussed these ideas with Gidon Bromberg, the Israeli director of EcoPeace, and are grateful to him for guidance and for pointing out identities and similarities of views, as well as occasional divergences. However, we take full responsibility for everything that we have written, which is based on our own research in the West Bank and Israel, on the vast documentation on the topic and on our attempts to think through the often apparently intractable issues.

Chapter 7

1 On the question of how much water a population actually requires to provide it with water resources security, see endnote 415.

2 Citing 'eight hours supply per week in Amman', commentators point out that water services in Jordan are sometimes poor. However, that is not the point here, where we are discussing how much natural fresh water there is per head of the population.

3 Some analysts argue that water purchases may be convenient to the PA. Not only is it a ready resource but it avoids the challenges of transferring water from other uses in the West Bank, which would not only harm the agricultural economy but also run up against the fact that much rural water in Palestinian hands is private or communal property. However, all new sources – whether from wells developed in the West Bank or water purchased from Mekorot – is in public hands.

4 There may also be 'NIMBY' issues. It is said that at one stage the proposed Hebron wastewater treatment plant was derailed because a mosque was constructed on the site. During our visit to Yatta in 2018 we heard the vocal opposition of local people to the proposed siting of the plant and transmission main. This opposition apparently put a brake on the project for up to seven years.

5 Farmers may grumble about these prices. Where in the world do farmers not grumble? But by and large Israeli agriculture has prospered on its water ration – see Chapter 1.

6 Personal communication from Shimon Tal to the authors, 17 September 2019. See Chapter 1.

7 The idea that Israel's capability to desalinate, and desalination more generally, may be a game-changer has long been mooted. See, for example, *Desalination as a Game-changer in Transboundary Hydro-politics* by Ram Aviram, David Katz and Deborah Shmueli (*Water Policy* 16 (2014) 609–24) which takes Israel–Jordan cooperation on water as its example. The paper argues that 'the option of desalination allows states to pursue both unilateral and collaborative policies that were not practical in the period prior to desalination'.

The authors maintain that 'the widespread adoption of desalination is already causing a significant shift in transboundary hydro-politics, and this can only be expected to increase in significance as desalination becomes an increasingly important source of water supply'. This is because 'with desalination water allocation is perceived less and less as a zero-sum game. Water scarcity is no longer exogenously deterministic'.

They argue, thus, that 'geographic and spatial dynamics are no longer merely a function of upstream-downstream placement. Access to the sea, rather than upstream position, is now much more important. Secondly, desalination allows for greater spatial flexibility in terms of water supply arrangements.'

One added advantage, according to the paper, is that 'more avenues for cooperation are feasible and reasons for conflict are fewer. Just having the option of desalination changes the relative bargaining power of parties and their incentives for cooperation.'

However, power relations are still important. Although their expression may change: '[Desalination] may still increase the power of the economically stronger nation. The discourse of water relations changes from one of imposing political and military might to one of promoting national and regional economic development.'

8 'Most of the population' except for some Israeli Arab and Bedouin communities and the Druze in the Golan.

9 Until 1967, the Jordan River had always been a potential water source for the Palestinians. As discussed in Chapter Five of *The History of Water*, the Johnston Plan had envisaged an annual supply of 100–150 million cubic metres to the West Bank from the Yarmouk to be delivered via siphons beneath the main river Jordan. However, this project was never realized and following the Occupation, West Bank Palestinians have been denied any access to the river or its waters. Nonetheless, the notion that West Bank Palestinians have some rights on the Jordan River did not completely die. As late as 1992, a UN report suggested that 120 million cubic metres of Jordan River water that could be used by the Palestinians in the West Bank was in fact in use by Israel. A regional UN agency, ESCWA, in the same year estimated the 'Palestinian share' of Jordan water to be 320 million cubic metres, although the basis of this is unclear. See: The Centre for Engineering and Planning, Report for ESCWA Land and Water Resources in the Occupied Palestinian Territory, 1992.

10 Source: Aaron T. Wolf, Trends in Transboundary Water Resources: Lessons for Cooperative Projects in the Middle East. IDRC.

11 See *The Harmon Doctrine One Hundred Years Later: Buried, Not Praised* Stephen C. McCaffrey Natural Resources Journal Volume 36 Issue 4 Fall 1996.

12 According to Wouters, the principle of community of interest 'finds its legal foundation in the *River Oder* case decided by the Permanent Court of International Justice (1929), which referred to "the community of interests in an international

watercourse"'. Patricia Wouters. *Water Security: Global, regional and local challenges*. Institute for Public Policy Research. May 2010.

13 See Zeitoun: 147.

14 See Aaron T. Wolf, *Trends in transboundary water resources: Lessons for cooperative projects in the Middle East*: 10.

15 Areas A and B are about 2,250 square kilometres, 40 per cent of the West Bank area of 5,640 square kilometres Even in Area A the IDF has often felt free to enter. The area of the Gaza Strip is 365 square kilometres. Together, Areas A and B and the Strip are about 9 per cent of the 28,000 square kilometres area of pre-1948 Palestine.

16 Source: H. Gvirtzman, *Groundwater Allocation in Judea and Samaria*.

17 This was Binyamin Netanyahu's policy going into the September 2019 elections. See also *Haaretz*, 17 April 2019.

18 See *The New York Times*, 25 August 2009. https://www.nytimes.com/2009/08/26/world/middleeast/26mideast.html?mtrref=www.google.com&gwh=42C2F96FB9749EF55E962EBB757B0A14&gwt=pay&assetType=REGIWALL.

19 World Bank 2017. On water management in Gaza, see Chapter 6.

20 Source: Palestinian Water Authority, 2017. Water Information System. Ramallah – Palestine.

21 https://www.al-monitor.com/pulse/originals/2016/07/palestine-bethlehem-water-shortage-israel.html.

22 http://www.independent.co.uk/news/world/middle-east/ramadan-2016-israel-water-west-bank-cuts-off-a7082826.html.

23 Greenblatt announced his resignation in September 2019.

24 https://www.al-monitor.com/pulse/originals/2017/07/israel-palestine-economic-peace-water-agreement.html#ixzz55xHPWAXZ.

25 https://www.al-monitor.com/pulse/originals/2017/07/israel-palestine-economic-peace-water-agreement.html#ixzz55xGyZEC8.

26 Much of the material and ideas in this section are drawn from *Desalination as a game-changer in transboundary hydro-politics* by Ram Aviram, David Katz and Deborah Shmueli (*Water Policy* 16 (2014) 609–24)

27 The 2010 'minutes of meeting', quoted in Aviram et al. 2014, specify '*The price payable by Jordan . . . will be the average price payable by the Government of Israel for desalinated water produced at the . . .* [three desalination plants] *less the actual costs incurred by Jordan for filtration treatment of the . . . Sold Water*' (MOM 2010, part 1.2). These prices are also the basis for the purchase of water by Israel from the planned Aqaba plant.

28 Aviram et al. 2014 say, for example, that one new factor in the 2010 agreement is that the water to be supplied is not on a basis of 'rights' or rightful allocations' but of 'sold water'. Where the 1994 peace treaty referred to rights or rightful allocations, the 2010 minutes of meeting (4 October 2010), for the first time, refers to 'sold water'.

29 With the possible exception of the saline Ein Feshka springs above the Dead Sea, which presumably could be desalinated.

30 EcoPeace *Water diplomacy* 2017.

31 http://www.al-monitor.com/pulse/originals/2017/06/palestine-israel-joint-water-committee-dispute-meeting.html#ixzz55lZayu1P.

32 http://www.jpost.com/Arab-Israeli-Conflict/Israel-gives-Pal-Authority-limited-water-autonomy-in-West-Bank-478672.

33 See the discussion on this in Chapter 7 of *The History of Water*.

34 In this meeting, the Israeli counterparts specifically agreed to the following: (i) drilling of the Janzour well, providing 150 cubic metres per hour for Jenin; (ii)

upgrading of Um Safa well to provide additional capacity for Ramallah; and (iii) providing information on past bulk supply and to retroactively review past bulk water billings from Mekorot and to consider a refund in case of overcharging.

35 For the mandate of the JWC, see Chapter Seven of *The History of Water*.

36 On 16 January 2017, the Palestinian Water Authority issued a press release: 'The revised working mechanism of the Joint Water Committee comes into force. Ramallah – The Palestinian Water Authority (PWA) announced today the signing of a new mechanism for the work of the Joint Water Committee. The implementation of the infrastructure projects requires the approval of the Joint Committee, which has been stalled for seven years due to the Israeli side's insistence on providing projects for the settlements. The new amendment stipulates "granting the water authority the right to execute all infrastructure projects without returning to the joint committee". The Water Authority explained that through this amendment, it will be able to move forward in its plan to develop the water sector, especially the delivery of water projects to marginalized areas that lack water and sanitation services in order to strengthen the resilience of citizens to face the Israeli measures aimed at displacing them and seizing their land in order to expand and establish settlements on them.' (http://pwa.ps/ar_page.aspx?id=OgQtCCa1462844361aOgQtCC)

37 Source: https://www.reuters.com/article/us-israel-palestinians-usa-water/trump-envoy-announces-israeli-palestinian-water-deal-silent-on-peace-prospects-idUSKBN19Y1EZ.

38 The water and wastewater treatment section of the US Plan (Section fourteen) reads:

- The parties recognize mutual water rights and agree to equitably share existing cross-border water sources and cooperate in making additional sources available through existing and emerging technologies.
- Shared aquifers will be managed for sustainable use to prevent impairing the groundwater quality or damaging the aquifers through over-extraction. Hydrological and climatic conditions, amongst other factors, will be considered when managing extraction.
- The parties will prioritize investing in desalination and other emerging technologies to produce substantial additional quantities of water for all uses and jointly seek to provide easily available, reasonably priced water to both parties.
- The parties agree to also focus investment in wastewater treatment and wastewater recycling and reuse to control and minimize pollution of the shared groundwaters.
- The parties will work together in good faith to manage the details with respect to water and wastewater treatment issues.

Source: *Peace to Prosperity: A Vision to Improve the Lives of the Palestinian and Israeli People*. January 2020.

39 See Sosland: 202.

40 https://www.nytimes.com/2017/07/13/opinion/israelis-and-palestinians-water-deal.html.

41 https://www.al-monitor.com/pulse/originals/2017/07/israel-palestine-economic-peace-water-agreement.html#ixzz55xLaJ3VN.

Chapter 8

1 Gidon Bromberg pointed out to us instances of NIMBY-ism on the Palestinian side regarding wastewater management. Under a high-governance Palestinian

institutional set-up, NIMBY issues would presumably be handled through democratic processes as, for example, environmental issues such as those over desalination in Western Galilee may be in democratic Israel.

2 See EcoPeace 2018 report.

3 See, for example, *Why boycott Mekorot?* (stopmekorot.org/6-reasons-to-boycott-mekorot/), which appealed for support for the First International Week of Action Against Mekorot on World Water Day 2014, with the slogan *Take a stand for water justice!* The appeal catalogues grounds of complaint against Mekorot, including 'water apartheid', 'supplies to illegal settlements', 'pillage of natural resources and wanton destruction of Palestinian infrastructure', 'turning off the tap on Palestinians during the dry summer months', 'partnering the JNF in the *Negev Blueprint* plan, which will evict 40 000 Palestinian Bedouins from their homes', and 'turning the Jordan River into a sewage pit'.

4 Based on Palestinian access to natural water of 40 cubic metres per capita annually against Falkenmark's stress level of 250 cubic metres per capita.

5 A point raised in the 2018 EcoPeace report.

6 This is presumably the goal of those who talk of an 'economic peace'. But the logic is that this peace is not possible unless the Palestinians are empowered as equal partners.

7 Source: Speech of MK Maj. Gen. (res.) Eyal Ben-Reuven at the Sderot Conference on the Gaza Water and Sanitation Crisis, EcoPeace Conference Summary, 6 March 2018.

8 See Becker and Ward 2014: 8.

9 On the impediments to Palestinian wastewater treatment, see Chapter 5, and on progress and options on wastewater reuse, see Chapters 5 and 6. Reuse would have to overcome not only the infrastructure constraints but also institutional and incentive constraints. Israel has demonstrated how wastewater can go from being an environmental problem to becoming a valued water resource (see Chapter 1) and, other things being equal, the Palestinians could follow suit.

10 http://ecopeaceme.org/projects/water-the-peace-process/.

11 See Fischhendler et al. 2011: 53.

12 This section draws heavily on Sosland 2007: 206.

13 The treaty (Annex II Article 3) calls for both parties to seek additional means to supply Jordan 50 million cubic metres a year. This was partially implemented in 1997 when Israel agreed to supply Jordan with 25–30 million cubic metres annually from Tiberias as an interim arrangement until Israel had constructed a desalination plant. Additionally, Israel was to withdraw an extra 20 million cubic metres from the Yarmouk in the winter period and return the same quantity to Jordan from Lake Tiberias in the summer. This was effectively a mechanism for Jordan to store winter flood waters in Tiberias. The agreement also provided for what was essentially a swap under which Jordan was to get an amount of desalinated water (10 million cubic metres) from saline springs in the Upper Jordan while Israel was entitled to abstract an equivalent amount from wells in the Arava Valley (Article IV(3)). Aviram et al. (2014) hold that this swap of water from desalination in the north for abstraction in the south demonstrates the potential for desalination to allow parties to agree to forgo shares of natural sources without reducing overall consumption, and also shows that the potential for desalination was already beginning to influence parties' willingness to share water. Sources: Aviram et al 2014; Haddadin, 2001; 2002, Haddadin and Shamir, 2003.

14 MOM, 2010, clauses 3–7.

15 http://www.worldbank.org/en/news/press-release/2013/12/09/senior-israel-jordanian-palestinian-representatives-water-sharing-agreement.
16 RSDS admittedly does not include all Jordan Valley riparians at this time, as Lebanon and Syria were not involved.
17 It was reported that former US special envoy Jason Greenblatt was a supporter of the RSDS approach, believing that the project is a model of how regional water cooperation can provide economic benefits and promote trust between the parties. See http://www.al-monitor.com/pulse/originals/2017/07/israel-palestinians-us-jason-greenblatt-red-dead-sea-canal.html#ixzz55x9vvNc7.
18 http://www.al-monitor.com/pulse/originals/2017/07/israel-palestinians-us-jason-greenblatt-red-dead-sea-canal.html#ixzz55x5zNhYF.
19 See the discussion on the al Bireh and Hebron wastewater treatment plants in Chapter 4.
20 http://www.sipprojects.org/projects/kidronnar-basin/, https://www.generosity.com/community-fundraising/water-treatment-in-the-kidron-al-nar-valley, https://www.csmonitor.com/World/Middle-East/Olive-Press/2013/1206/Palestinian-mayor-recruits-global-village-to-clean-up-sewage, https://www.csmonitor.com/World/Middle-East/2013/1206/How-sewage-is-bridging-the-Israeli-Palestinian-divide-in-Jerusalem, https://www.reuters.com/article/us-israel-palestinians-environment/reign-of-sewage-in-biblical-valley-may-be-coming-to-an-end-idUSKBN1AN0S1.
21 Source: Beltrain and Kallis: 23, 66.
22 Source. Bromberg et al. 2020: 3.

Chapter 9

1 On the question of Johnston Plan allocations, see the note on Chapter 7, and also Chapter 5 of *The History of Water* where the Johnston Plan is discussed in detail.
2 A joint project of the British Geological Survey and the PWA calculated the all-up cost of providing groundwater around Tulqarem and Qalqilya from depths to water of up to 250 metres (and from up to a further 200 metres drilling depth inside the aquafer) to be around 10 cents per cubic metre (2001 prices), equivalent to 15 cents per cubic metre in current prices at the well head. The equivalent delivered to bulk storage close to the point of use would be in the region 20–25 cents per cubic metre at current prices. This compares with an ex-factory cost of desalinated water of a minimum of 54 cents per cubic metre and a bulk delivered cost to the West Bank of the order of $1 per cubic metre. The study priced pumping from depths of 250–500 metres in the north of the West Bank at around 20 cents per cubic metre, equivalent to 30 cents per cubic metre in 2020 terms. For pumping in the southern West Bank west of Hebron, where depths can be as much as 750 metres, costs could be 25 cents per cubic metre in 2001 terms, equivalent to 38 cents per cubic metre currently. Thus even water pumped from deep in the southern West Bank would come in at only half the cost of bringing desalinated water up from the coast. See *Mapping groundwater development costs for the transboundary Western Aquifer Basin*, A.M. MacDonald et al. Hydrogeology Journal 2009 17: 1579–87.
3 Source: Performance Monitoring of Water Service Providers in Palestine, Water Sector Regulatory Council Ramallah.
4 Siegel 2015: 190/191.

5 See *Desalination: Israel lays claim to Palestine's water*. New Scientist, 27 May 2004. https://www.newscientist.com/article/dn5037-israel-lays-claim-to-palestines-water/#ixzz5ySpdLjYM. See also the discussion in Chapter 6 on this point.

6 See *Desalination: Israel lays claim to Palestine's water*. New Scientist, 27 May 2004. https://www.newscientist.com/article/dn5037-israel-lays-claim-to-palestines-water/#ixzz5ySpdLjYM.

7 Best practice on integrated water resource management was set out in the principles agreed at the 1991 Dublin Conference. See Christopher Ward and Sandra Ruckstuhl (2017) Water Scarcity, Climate Change and Conflict in the Middle East. 2017. I.B. Tauris, London.

8 The metric here is water under control, which in the case of the West Bank Palestinians would exclude water purchases from Israel. In the case of Israel, it includes both natural and manufactured water, as both are entirely under Israel's control. See the table *Water Resources Available* in Chapter 7.

9 Source: Chapter 2. Table *Domestic Water Supply and Demand for Palestinians in the West Bank 2016.*

10 *Israel Water Sector – Key Issues*. The Knesset Research and Information Centre, February 2018.

11 If West Bank unaccounted-for water were reduced to 10 per cent of gross domestic supply of 115 litres per person per day, each person would receive on average 104 litres, 40 per cent of the Israelis' 263 litres. See the table *Domestic Water Supply and Demand* in Chapter 2.

12 Empirically 300 cubic metres per person of annual water availability is a low ration compared to other countries in similar semi-arid environments. Greece has 1,260 cubic metres, Syria 1,778 cubic metres, Iran 1,526 cubic metres, and Lebanon 571 cubic metres. Only Jordan has less than Israel – 235 cubic metres. Source *The National Water Footprint Explorer*, The Water Footprint Network. Consulted online 2 April 2020. https://waterfootprint.org/en/water-footprint/national-water-footprint/.

13 We saw in Chapter 5 that a 2013 World Bank study suggested that agriculture could do with a further 189 million cubic metres of water. A 2018 World Bank study cited in Chapter 2 found a supply/demand gap for domestic water of at least 40 million cubic metres – the actual gap in 2016 was 88 million cubic metres, but with very high levels of unaccounted-for water, which should be discounted from the calculus – see the table *Domestic Water Supply and Demand* in Chapter 2.

14 Assuming that 50 per cent of an increased municipal and industrial supply of 150 million cubic metres annually (2016 was 117 million cubic metres – see the table Domestic Water Supply in Chapter 2) is recovered as wastewater and 85 per cent of that is treated and reused in agriculture.

15 Sources: IWA 2012 *Master Plan for the National Water Sector*; and Becker and Ward 2014: 13.

16 See the discussion *Costs to the West Bank economy of lost opportunities in agriculture* in Chapter Five.

17 See; Beltram and Kallis: 23; and Selby 2011.

18 Source: FoEME.

19 How much water a population actually requires to provide it with water resources security is a subject of much debate. Here we take as a benchmark the rule of thumb developed by Falkenmark in the 1980s, that an industrialized country in a semi-arid zone has a gross water demand of approximately 500 cubic metres per capita per year, and that a population with secure access to half of that amount – 250 cubic

metres – *could be considered as 'relatively water-stressed'. Falkenmark in fact developed his idea based on his analysis of the Israeli economy.* See: *The measurement of water scarcity: Defining a meaningful indicator* by Simon Damkjaer and Richard Taylor at https://www.ncbi.nlm.nih.gov/pmc/articles/PMC5547033/. They quote from: Falkenmark M, Lindh G. *How can we cope with the water resources situation by the year 2015?* Ambio. 1974;3:114–22; and from Falkenmark M. *Fresh water: Time for a modified approach.* Ambio. 1986; 15: 192–200. In 2017, West Bank Palestinians had access to water that lies within their notional control of just over 39 cubic metres per person per year (see the table *Water Resources Available to West Bank Palestinians* in Chapter 7). This quantum is equivalent to 8 per cent of the gross water demand of 500 cubic metres defined by Falkenmark or 16 per cent of the 'relatively water stressed level' of 250 cubic metres. This compares to Israelis, who have nearly eight times as much water as the West Bank Palestinians (298 cubic metres per person per year), a quantum per capita that lies between Falkenmark's upper and lower bounds. Even if water purchases from Israel are taken into account, Palestinians have access to only 65 cubic metres per capita, only one quarter of the 'stress level' and less than one quarter of the total resources available to Israel.

For comparison, residents of Lebanon, Syria and Egypt all have access to internal water resources of over 700 cubic metres a year. Even residents of the dry land of Jordan have access to about 170 cubic metres a year, only half of Israel's quantum but over four times the per capita volume available to West Bank Palestinians from internal sources.

By this measure, West Bank Palestinians are very water stressed and hence water insecure, particularly where this insecurity of water resources is joined by insecurity in water supply, sanitation and risk management. Set against the same metric, Israel has only about two thirds of Falkenmark's benchmark of 500 metres but is clearly efficient at both supply and demand management and does very well on what it has, which is after all many multiples of what is available to the Palestinians. But what chance of meeting gross water demand to build a modern economy and society for the West Bank Palestinians with less than one fifth (16 per cent) of even the 'water stress' level?

20 'The Indus Waters Treaty was signed in 1960 after nine years of negotiations between India and Pakistan with the help of the World Bank, which is also a signatory. The negotiations were the initiative of former World Bank President Eugene Black. Seen as one of the most successful international treaties, it has survived frequent tensions, including conflict, and has provided a framework for irrigation and hydropower development for more than half a century. Former US president Dwight Eisenhower described it as "one bright spot . . . in a very depressing world picture that we see so often."' Source: Fact Sheet - The Indus Waters Treaty 1960 and the Role of the World Bank. 11 June 2018. https://www.worldbank.org/en/region/sar/brief/fact-sheet-the-indus-waters-treaty-1960-and-the-world-bank.

21 See Friends of the Earth Middle East 2008. *Draft Agreement on Water Cooperation.*

22 See Ward and Ruckstuhl 2017.

23 According to Gidon Bromberg, proposals along these lines have been made by the Israelis but rejected.

24 The source for this section is the seminal paper *A Green-Blue Deal for the Middle East* by Gidon Bromberg and his colleagues.

25 Source: Siegel 2015: 181–3; 190–1.

26 Source: Siegel 2015: 190–1.

27 Source: Grey in Isaac and Shuval 1994: 226.
28 Source: Siegel 2015: 182–3.
29 That political entente would clearly need to have the endorsement of both Hamas and Fatah.

Coda

1 Even soil moisture – the precipitation that remains in the soil profile and neither evaporates nor drains to watercourses or groundwater – is in a sense a transboundary resource in the West Bank because most of the land that is not built up is controlled by Israel.
2 Reference: Wouters: 4.
3 Source: *Singapore plans for water autonomy through desalination and wastewater reuse* in World Bank 2019: 78.
4 See World Bank 2019a.
5 In a seminal 2005 paper, Dale Whittington and colleagues argued that there was a strong economic case for cooperation amongst Nile riparians to manage and develop the Nile at the basin scale rather than in segments determined by the decision of each of the eleven riparian, and to share benefits rather than quotas of water. This approach would increase the economic benefits from irrigated agriculture and hydropower generation, reducing risks and costs of floods, drought and sedimentation, and maximizing the availability of water for economic use the length of the river. The study concluded that the total potential direct gross economic benefits in irrigation and hydroelectric power would be of the order of $7–11 billion annually and net benefits of the order of $9 billion annually, $5 billion more than at present. See Whittington D, Wu Xun and C. Sadoff. *Water resources management in the Nile Basin: the economic value of cooperation*. Water Policy 7 (2005): 227–52. See also the discussion in Ward and Ruckstuhl pp 194 ff.
6 Falkenmark, M., Grey, D., Kasrils, R. and Lundquist, J. (2003) Hydrosolidarity through Catchment Based Balancing of Human Security and Ecological Security, Contribution to the Virtual World Water Forum, Kyoto, March 20.

BIBLIOGRAPHY

Aaronsohn, Aaron. *Agricultural and Botanic Explorations in Palestine*. Washington DC: US Government Printing Office, 1910.

Abed, George T. *The Palestinian Economy: Studies in Development under Prolonged Occupation*. Edited by George T. Abed. London: Routledge, 1988, 358.

Abu Nasar, A. 'Relation of Nitrate Contamination of Groundwater with the Haemoglobin Level Among Infants in Gaza'. *Eastern Mediterranean Health Journal* 13 (September–October 2007). http://www.emro.who.int.

Ahiram, Ephraim and Hanna Siniora. *Water and Peace in the Middle East. Proceedings of the First Israeli-Palestinian International Academic Conference on Water*, edited by J. Isaac and H. Shuval, 10–13 December 1992, Zurich: Switzerland, 1994.

Albright, W. F. *The Archaelogy of Palestine: A Survey of the Ancient Peoples and Cultures of the Holy Land*. London: Penguin Books, 1949, 171.

Al Khatib, Nader and Karen Assaf. *Palestine Water Supplies and Demands*. Zurich: Isaac and Shuval, 1994.

Al Jazeera. 'Israel Reopens Gaza Commercial Crossing'. Article in *al Jazeera*, 15 August 2018. https://www.aljazeera.com/news/2018/08/israel-reopens-gaza-commercial-crossing-month-long-closure-180815074300410.html.

Aliewi, Amjad. 'Water Resources: The Palestinian Perspective'. In *Water Wisdom*, edited by Alon Tal and Alfred Abed Rabbo. New Jersey: Rutgers University Press, 2010, 231–52.

Aliewi, Amjad, Karen Assaf, and Anan Jayyousi, eds. *Sustainable Development and Management of Water in Palestine*. Ramallah, Palestine: House of Water and Environment, 2008, 567.

Allan, J. A. *Water, Peace and The Middle East: Negotiating Resources in the Jordan Basin*. London: I.B. Tauris, 1996, 250.

Allen, Tony. *Virtual Water: Tackling the Threat to Our Planet's Most Precious Resource*. London: I.B. Tauris, 2011.

Attili, Dr Shaddad. *Statement by the Head of the Palestinian Water Authority*, January, 2008, 4.

Al Yaqoubi, Ahmed S. *Country Paper: Water Resources Statistical Records in Palestine*. United Nations EGM on the Production of Statistics on Natural Resources and Environment, June, 2007.

Aqraba. *Town Profile* by ARIJ. 2013. http:///vprofile.arij.org/nablus/pdfs/vprofile/Aqraba.

ARIJ. *Status of the Environment in the State of Palestine*. Applied Research Institute, Jerusalem, 2016.

Ashly, Jaclynn. 'Drowning in the Waste of Israel Settlers'. *Al Jazeera*, 18 September 2017. https://www.aljazeera.com/indepth/features/2017/09/drowning-waste-israel-settlers170916120027885.htm.

Assaf, Karen. *Replenishment of Palestinian Waters by Artificial Recharge*. Isaac & Shuval, 1994, 302, 307.

Associated Press. *Press Release on World Bank Statements on Easing Israeli Restrictions*. 6 November 2008, 2.

Aviram, Ram, David Katz and Deborah Shmueli. 'Desalination as a Game-changer in Transboundary Hydro-Politics'. *Water Policy* 16 (2014): 609–24.

Avitsur, Shmuel. 'The First Project for the Intensive Exploitation of the Yarkon Waters (The Frangija-Navon Scheme of 1893)'. *Haaretz Museum Bulletin* 6 (1964): 80–8.
Avnieri, Arie L. *The Claim of Dispossession – Jewish Land Settlement and the Arabs 1878–1948*. Efal, Israel: Yad Tabenkin, 1982.
Awartami, Hisham. 'Economic Aspects of the Agricultural Sector in the Occupied Territories'. 3 (1986): 78–89.
Bach, Roberto. *The Population of Israel*. Institute of Contemporary Jewry of the Hebrew University of Jerusalem, 1974, 133, 390–4.
Bard, Mitchell G. *Myths and Facts: A Guide to the Arab-Israeli Conflict*. American-Israeli Cooperative Enterprise (AICE), 2012.
Bargouth, J. M. and R. M. Y. Al-Saed. 'Sustainability of Ancient Water Supply Facilities in Jerusalem'. *Sustainability* 1 (2009): 1106–19.
Becker, Nir and Frank A. Ward. 'Adaptive Water Management in Israel: Structure and Policy Options'. *International Journal of Water Resources Development* (2014): 1–18.
Beltrain, Maria and Giorgos Kallis. 'How does Virtual Water Flow in Palestine? A Political Ecology Analysis.' *Ecological Economics* 143, issue C (2018): 17–26.
Ben-Gurion, David. *Diary*. Sede Boker, Israel: The Ben-Gurion Archive.
Ben-Porat, Miriam. *Special Report of the State Comptroller of Israel*. 1987.
Ben-Reuven, MK Maj Gen. Eyal. Sderot Conference on the Gaza Water and Sanitation Crisis, EcoPeace Conference Summary. 6 March 2018.
Benvenisti, Meron. *The West Bank Data Project: A Survey of Israel's Policies*. Washington and London: American Enterprise Institute for Public Policy Research, 1984, 97.
Benevenisti, Meron. *Sacred Landscape: The Buried History of the Holy Land since 1948*. London and Los Angeles: University of California Press, 2000, 366.
BIMKOM. *Under the Guise of Security: Routing the Separation Barrier to Enable the Expansion of Israeli Settlements in the West Bank*. BIMKOM/B'tselem. 2005. August 2004, 93.
Biswas, Asit K., John Kolars, Masahiro Murakami, John Waterbury and Aaron Wolf. *Core and Periphery: A Comprehensive Approach to Middle Eastern Water*. Oxford India Paperbacks, Water Resources Management Series, New Delhi: OUP 1997, 160.
Black, Ian. *Enemies and Neighbours: Arabs and Jews in Palestine and Israel, 1917–2017*. Penguin, Random House, 2018, 606.
Bouillon, Markus E. *The Peace Business: Money and Power in the Palestine-Israel Conflict*. London, 2004, 247.
Bromberg, Gidon (Israeli Director), Nada Majdalani (Palestinian Director), Yana Abu Taleb (Jordanian Director). *A Green Blue Deal for the Middle East*. December 2020, Tel Aviv, Ramallah and Amman.
Bunton, Martin. *The Palestinian – Israeli Conflict: A Very Short Introduction*. Oxford and London: OUP, 2013, 132.
B'Tselem. *Forbidden Roads: Israel's Discriminatory Road Regime in the West Bank*. B'Tselem. Israeli Information Center for Human Rights in the Occupied Territories. August, 2004, 55
B'Tselem. *Means of Expulsion: Violence and Harassment in the Southern Hebron Hills*. July, 2005, 59.
B'Tselem. *A Wall in Jerusalem: Obstacles to Human Rights in the Holy City*. Tel Aviv: B'Tselem, 2007a.
B'Tselem. *Ghost Town: Israel's Separation Policy in Hebron*. Tel Aviv: B'Tselem, May 2007b, 107.

B'Tselem. *Ground to a Halt: Denial of Palestinian's Freedom of Movement in the West Bank*. August, 2007c, 118.
B'Tselem. *Human Rights in the Occupied Territories: Annual Report 2007*. January, 2008, 57.
Caponera, Dante A. *Principles of Water Law and Administration: National and International*. Rotterdam, Netherlands: A. A. Balkema Publishers, 1992, 71; Z74; IS 97.
Carey, John. *The Unexpected Professor: An Oxford Life in Books*. London: Faber & Faber, 2014, 361.
Centre of Housing Rights and Evictions. *Policies of Denial: Lack of Access to Water in the West Bank*. December 2008, 37.
Centre of Housing Rights and Evictions. *Position Paper. Hostage to Politics: The Impact of Sanctions and the Blockade on the Human Right to Water and Sanitation in Gaza*. 2008.
CIHEAM. *Options Mediterraneennes: Serie A, Seminaires Mediterraneens*. Bari: CIHEAM. No. 65, 2005, 119–122.
Chomsky, Noam. *Occupy*. London, 2012, 121.
Chomsky, Noam and Ilan Pappe. *Gaza in Crisis: Reflections on Israel's War against the Palestinians*. London: Haymarket Books, 2011, 242.
Conder, C. R. *Tent Work in Palestine*. USA: Jefferson Publication, 2015, 133.
Consulate of Spain. *A Review of the Palestinian Agricultural Sector*. Spain, 2007, 76.
Coutinho, Frank. 'How is the Water Industry in Israel Faring?'. *Times of Israel*, 4 August 2018. https://blogs.timesofisrael.com/how-is-the-water-industry-in-Israel-faring/
Dajani, cited in Lane, 1994: 4, Development as a Gift: Patterns of Assistance and Refugees Strategies in the Jordan Valley by Mauro van Aken. *International Symposium on the Palestinian Refugees and UNRWA in Jordan, the West Bank and Gaza*, 1949–1999.
Dershowitz, Alan. *The Case for Israel*. Hoboken, NJ: Published by John Wiley and Sons, 2003, 265.
Dillman, Jeffrey D. 'Water Rights in the Occupied Territories'. *Journal of Palestine Studies* 19, no. 1 (Autumn 1989): 52. http://www.jstor.org/stable/2537245 (accessed 18 October 2010).
Eastern Mediterranean Health Journal. 'Relation of Nitrate Contamination of Groundwater with Methaemoglobin Level among Infants in Gaza'. *Eastern Mediterranean Health Journal* 13, no. 5. http//www.emro.who.int.
Eaton, J. W. and D. J. Eaton. *Water Utilization in the Yarmouk-Jordan*. Zurich: Isaac and Shuval, 1994.
EcoPeace. *Speech of Rotem Caro Weizman*. EcoPeace Conference Summary 6 March 2018. http://ecopeaceme.org/projects/lower-jordan-rotem@foeme.org.
EcoPeace. *Let the Dead Sea Live*. Tel Aviv: B'Tselem, 2000, 31.
El Musa, Sharif S. *Water Conflict: Economics, Politics, Law and the Palestinian-Israeli Water Resources*. Washington, DC: Institute for Palestine Studies, 1997.
Ehrenreich, Ben. *The Way to the Spring: Life and Death in Palestine*. London, 2017, 428.
Environment and Security in the Middle East. The Effects of the Israeli-Palestinian Conflict on the Hydraulic Resources of the Jordan Basin.
ESCWA. *Inventory of Shared Water Resources in Western Asia*. Beirut: ESCWA, 2013. https://waterinventory.org/surfacewater/jordan-river-basin.
EWASH (Emergency Water and Sanitation-Hygiene Group). *EWASH Concerned by Water Restrictions in the West Bank Resulting from Israeli Discriminatory Policies*. EWASH Press Release, 21 June 2016.
Falkenmark, Malin and Carl Folke. 'Ecohydrosolidarity: A New Ethics for Stewardship of Value-Adding Rainfall'. In *Water Ethics: Foundational Readings for Students and*

Professionals, edited by Peter G. Brown and Jeremy J. Schmidt, 247–64. Washington, DC: Island Press, 2010.
Fallon, Michael. 'Stability in the Middle East Now Depends on How Serious We Are about Tackling Climate Change'. *The Independent*, 12 April 2021.
Faruqui, Naser, Asit K. Biswas and Murad J. Bino, eds. *Water Management in Islam*. USA: United Nations University Press, 2001, 147.
Feitelson, Eran and Marwan Haddad, ed. *Management of Shared Groundwater Resources: The Israel-Palestinian Case with an International Perspective*. USA: Kluwer Academic Publishers, 2000, 496.
Fischhendler, Itay, Shlomi Dinar and David Katz. 'The Politics of Unilateral Environmentalism: Cooperation and Conflict over Water Management along the Israeli-Palestinian Border'. *Global Environmental Politics* 11, no. 1 (2011): 36–61.
Fisher, Franklin M. and Annette Huber-Lee, et al. *Liquid Assets. An Economic Approach for Water Management and Conflict Resolution in the Middle East and Beyond.* Washington, DC: Resources for the Future, 2005, 242.
Fischhendler, Itay. *The Politics of Unilateral Environmentalism: Wastewater Treatment along the Israeli-Palestinian Border*. Hebrew University, 20.
Flappan, Simha. *The Birth of Israel: Myths and Realities*. New York, 1987, 277.
Folke, Carl. 'Freshwater for Resilience: A Shift in Thinking'. *Philosophical Traditions of the Royal Society (B)* 358 (2003): 2027.
Friends of the Earth Middle East. *A Seeping Time Bomb*. February 2004a, 24.
Friends of the Earth Middle East. *Conservation and development of the Dead Sea*. March 2004b, 71.
Friends of the Earth Middle East. *Advancing Conservation and Sustainable Development of the Dead Sea Basin – Broadening the Debate on Economic and Management Issues*. March 2004c, 71.
Friends of the Earth Middle East. *Crossing the Jordan: Bringing Peace to the Lower Jordan*. March 2005a, 32.
Friends of the Earth Middle East. *Pollution of the Mountain Aquifer by Sewage: Finding Solutions*. July 2005b, 8.
Friends of the Earth Middle East. 'Good Water Neighbors: A Model for Community Development Programs in Regions of Conflict'. *FoEME*, August 2005c, 40.
Friends of the Earth Middle East. *A Seeping Time Bomb: Pollution of the Mountain Aquifer by Solid Waste*. January 2006a, 30.
Friends of the Earth Middle East. *Health Crises in the Making: Protecting Water Resources requires Cooperation with the PA*. April 2006b, 4.
Friends of the Earth Middle East. 'Good Water Neighbors: Identifying Common Environmental Problems and Shared Solutions'. *FoEME*, February 2007a, 55.
Friends of the Earth Middle East. *Nature, Agriculture and the Price of Water in Israel*. November 2007b, 16.
Friends of the Earth Middle East. *Environmental Peacebuilding Theory and Practice*. January 2008a, 35.
Friends of the Earth Middle East. *Draft Agreement on Water Cooperation*. June 2008b, 34.
Gabbay, Shoshana. *Water in Israel: Rehabilitation of Israel's Rivers*. https://www.jewishvirtuallibrary.org/rehabilitation-of-israel-s-rivers.
German Technical Cooperation Programme for the Water Sector in the Palestinian Territories. *Factsheet* (In cooperation with the German Financial Cooperation). February, 2007.

Ghosheth, Adnan Farouq Saad Aldin. *Disclosable Version of the ISR – Hebron Regional Wastewater Management Project – Phase 1 – P117449 – Sequence No: 09 (English).* Washington, DC: World Bank Group, 2019. http://documents.worldbank.org/curated/en/809911561059624782/Disclosable-Version-of-the-ISR-Hebron-Regional-Wastewater-Management-Project-Phase-1-P117449-Sequence-No-09.

Gilbert, Martin. *The Routledge Atlas of the Arab-Israeli Conflict.* 10th ed. Oxon: Routledge, 2012, 227.

Gilbert, Martin. *The Story of Israel from Theodor Herzl to the Dream for Peace.* London, 2018, 160.

Gilmour, David. *Dispossessed: The Ordeal of the Palestinians 1917–1980.* London, 1980, 218.

Gisha. *Mekorot Responds to Gisha's Freedom of Information Application Regarding Water Supply to the Gaza Strip.* 2 September 2015. https://gisha.org/legal/5016.

GIZ/PWA/CEP (Deutsche Gesellschaft für Internationale Zusammenarbeit, Palestinian Water Authority, and Centre for Engineering and Planning). *Survey of Private and Public Brackish Desalination Plants in Gaza Strip.* Final Analysis Report, September 2015.

Government of Israel. *The Issue of Water between Israel and the Palestinians.* 2009. http://www.water.gov.il/Hebrew/ProfessionalInfoAndData/2012/22-Water-Issues-Between-Israel-and-the-Palestinians.pdf (accessed 27 May 2019).

The Government of Israel. *Israel's Chronic Water Problems.* Israel Ministry of Foreign Affairs, n.d. https://mfa.gov.il/MFA/IsraelExperience/AboutIsrael/Spotlight?Pages/Israel-s%20Chronicle%20Water%20Problem.aspx.

The Government of the United Kingdom. *Report of the 1937 Palestine Royal Commission* Cmd. 5479. 1937.

Green, Stephen. *Taking Sides: America's Secret Relations with a Militant Israel. The 1953 Aid Cut-off: A Parable for Our Times.* New York: William Morrow & Co, 1984, 76–83.

Grey, David. *The Development of the Water Resources of the Occupied Palestinian Territories: Some Key Issues.* Isaac and Shuval, 1994, 220ff.

Gruen, George E. *Contribution of Water Imports to Israeli-Palestinian-Jordanian Peace.* Isaac and Shuval, 1994.

GTZ. *Training Needs Assessment: Water Supply and Wastewater Service Providers.* November 2006, 65.

Guyatt, Nicholas. *The Absence of Peace: Understanding the Israeli-Palestinian Conflict.* London and New York: Zed Books, 1998, 188.

Gvirtzman, H. *Groundwater Allocation in Judea and Samaria.* Isaac and Shuval, 1994, 214ff.

Haddad, Toufic. *Palestine Ltd. Neoliberalism and Nationalism in the Occupied Territory.* London: I.B. Tauris, 2016, 338.

Haddadin, M. J. 'Negotiated Resolution of the Jordan-Israel Water Conflict'. *International Negotiation* 5, no. 2 (2000): 263–88.

Haddadin, M. J. *Diplomacy on the Jordan: International Conflict and Negotiated Resolution.* Norwell, MA: Springer, 2001.

Haddadin, M. J. *Diplomacy on the Jordan: International Conflict and Negotiated Resolution.* Boston: Kluwer Academic Publishers, 2002a, 535.

Haddadin, M. J. 'Response to commentary by Uri Shamir'. *Natural Resources Forum* 26, no. 3 (2002b): 254–55.

Haddadin, Munther. 'Evolution of Water Administration and Legislation'. In *Water Resources in Jordan. Evolving Policies for Development, the Environment and Conflict Resolution*, edited by Munther Haddadin, 29–42. Resources for the Future, 2006. ISBN 1-933115-32-7.

Haddadin, M. J. 'Cooperation and lack thereof on management of the Yarmouk River'. *Water International* 34, no. 4 (2009): 420–431.

Haddadin, M. J. and U. Shamir. The Jordan River Basin, Part I: Water Conflict and Negotiated Resolution Jordan River Case Study, Part II: The Negotiations and the Water Agreement Between the Hashemite Kingdom of Jordan and the State of Israel. 2003. PC-CP Series, No. 15 UNESCO / IHP / WWAP, Paris, France.

Hamdy, A. and R. Monti, eds. *West Bank Water Department: Institutional Reform towards National Bulk Supply Utility*.

Hammond, Jeremy R. *Obstacle to Peace. The US Role in the Israel-Palestinian Conflict*. Michigan: World View Publications, 2016, 508.

Harrington, Cameron. *Fluid Identities: Toward a Critical Security of Water*. PhD thesis. The University of Western Ontario. November 2013.

Hass, Amira. 'PA Farmers Hung Out to Dry while Israelis Flourish in Jordan Valley'. *Haaretz*, 2 December 2012.

Hass, Amira. 'A Bedouin Family Got Evicted by Israel'. *Haaretz*, 18 August 2019. http://www.haaretz.com/news/diplomacy-defense/pa-farmers-hung-out-to-dry-while-israel is-flourish-in-jordan-valley.premium-1.481797105.

Helman, J. *Cleanliness and Squalor in Inter-War Tel-Aviv*.

Herzl, Theodore. *The Old New Land*. German: Altneuland. Original edition 1902, republished by CreateSpace Independent Publisher, 2012.

Hirsch, Dafna. '"We are Here to Bring the West, Not Only to Ourselves": Zionisst Occidentlism and the Discourse of Hygiene in Mandate Palestine'. *International Journal of Middle East Studies*. https://doi.org/10.1017/S0020743809990079 (accessed 26 October, 2009).

Hodgkin, Thomas. *Letters from Palestine, 1932 – 36*. Edited by E. C. Hodgkin. London, 1986, 202.

Hourani, Albert. *Arabic Thought in the Liberal Age 1798–1939*. Oxford Paperbacks, 1970, 403.

Hull, Edward. *Mount Seir, Sinai and Western Palestine*. London: Richard Bentley & Son, 1885.

Husseini, Hiba. *The Palestinian Water Authority: Developments and Challenges Involving the Legal Framework and Capacity of the PWA*. 7.

Hydrological Service of Israel (HIS). *Development of Utilization and Status of Water Resources*. 211, 296–8.

IBNET. *Water Supply and Sanitation Blue Book 2014*. World Bank, 2014.

The International Conference on Water and the Environment (ICWE). 'The Dublin Statement on Water and Sustainable Development'. ICWE Secretariat, World Meteorological Organization, 1992. Web. 16 April 2011. http://www.wmo.int/pages/prog/hwrp/documents/english/icwedece.html#p4.

Institute for Palestine Studies. *Supplement to Survey of Palestine. Notes Compiled for the Information of the United Nations Special Committee on Palestine*. June, 1947, reprinted 1991 Washington, DC, 153.

International Desalination Association. *The Current State of Desalination*. Retrieved 24 April 2018.

Isaac, Jad and Hilel Shuval. *Water and Peace in the Middle East. Proceedings of the First Israeli-Palestinian International Academic Conference on Water*, Zurich, Switzerland,

10–13 December 1992 Studies in Environmental Science 58 Published by Elsevier, 1994.
Government of Israel. *Israel Water Sector – Key Issues*. The Knesset Research and Information Centre, February 2018.
Government of Israel. *The Issue of Water between Israel and the Palestinians*. http://www.water.gov.il/HebrewProfessionalinfoAndData/2012/22-Water-Issues-between-Israel-and-the-Palestinians.pdf (accessed 27 May 2019).
Israel Water Authority (IWA). *Water Supply to the Settlements*. October 2008c, 10.
Israel Water Authority (IWA). *The Natural Water Resources Between the Mediterranean Sea and the Jordan River*. Jerusalem – 2012 Authors are Gavriel Weinberger (Head of Israel Hydrological Service), Yakov Livshitz and Amir Givati.
Israel Water Justice: Water as a Human Right in Israel By Tamar Keinan, Friends of the Earth Middle East, Israel Editor: Gidon Bromberg, Friends of the Earth Middle East Series' coordinator: Simone Klawitter, Policy Advisor.
Israeli-Palestinian Interim Agreement. Article 40. 1995.
Jaas, M. *West Bank Water Department. Institutional Reform towards National Bulk Supply Utility*. Edited by A. Hamdy and R. Monti.
Jad, Isaac and Atif Kubursi. *Dry Peace in the Middle East*. Applied Research Institute of Jerusalem and Dept of Economics McMaster University, Ontario, Canada.
Jayyousi, Anan. *Israeli Water Crimes on Palestinian Water Resources*. Mimeo, 2008, 12.
Jayyousi, Anan and Omar Zimmo. *Good Practice Case Studies on the Palestinian Water Sector Donor Coordination*. 9.
Johnston, Penny. 'Witness in Jerusalem: Re-Readings'. In *Palestine Studies* Issue 51 2012.
Kahan, David. *Agriculture and Water Resources in the West Bank and Gaza (1967–1987)*. 1987.
Kally, Elisha, with Gideon Fishelson. *Water and Peace. Water Resources and the Arab-Israeli Peace Process*. USA: Praeger Publishers, 1993, 127.
Karlinsky, Nahum. *The Limits of Separation: Jaffa and Tel Aviv before 1948: The Underground Story*. In: *Tel-Aviv at 100: Myths, Memories and Realities*, edited by Maoz Azaryahu and S. Ilan Troen. Indiana University Press.
Karlinsky, Nahum. *California Dreaming: Ideology, Society, and Technology in the Citrus Industry of Palestine, 1890–1939*. Albany, 2005.
Kark, Ruth. *Jaffa: A City in Evolution, 1799–1917*. Jerusalem: Yad Izhak Ben-Svi Press, 1990.
Kerem Navot. *Israeli Settlers' Agriculture As A Means Of Land Takeover In The West Bank*. 2013.
Khalidi, Rashid. *The Iron Cage. The* Story of the Palestinian Struggle for Statehood Oxford, 2006, 281.
Khalidi, Rashid. *Palestinian Identity The Construction of Modern National Consciousness*. New York: Columbia University Press, 1997, 310.
Khalidi, Rashid. *Resurrecting Empire*. Western Footprints and America's Perilous Path in the Middle East Boston, USA, 2004, 223.
Khouri, Rami G. The Jordan Valley. *Life and Society below Sea Level*. London and New York: Association with the Jordan Valley Authority, 1981, 238.
Kislev, Yoav. *The Water Economy of Israel*. LAP LAMBERT Academic Publishing 2014, 126.
Kloosterman, Karin. *Desalinated Water Use in Israel*, in Health, posted 28 March 2017. www.greenprophet.com/2017/03/desalinated-water-use-in-israel-causing-alarming-iodine-deficiency-in-people.

Kubovich, Yaniv. 'Israel Advances Gaza Water Project: Passage of Equipment to Construct Desalination Plant and Water Reservoirs Okayed by Defense Ministry'. *Haaretz*, 2 August 2018.

Kuttab, Jonathan and Isaac, Jad. *Approaches to the Legal Aspects of Conflict on Water Rights in Palestine/Israel.* Isaac and Shuval, 1994, 241.

Lambton, Professor Ann K. S. *The Persian Land Reform 1962–1966.* Oxford: Clarendon Press, 1969, 386.

LeBor, Adam. 'Zion and the Arabs. Jaffa as a Metaphor'. *World Policy Journal*, 24, no. 4 (Winter 2007/2008): 61–75.

LeBor, Adam. *City of Oranges. Arabs and Jews in Jaffa.* London, 2006, 357.

Lemire, Vincent 2000, *Water in Jerusalem at the End of the Ottoman Period (1850–1920)*, Bulletin du Centre de recherche français à Jérusalem [En ligne], 7 | 2000, mis en ligne le 13 mars 2008, Consulted 4 February 2019. http://journals.openedition.org/bcrfj/2572.

LeVine, Mark, 2005. *Overthrowing geography: Jaffa, Tel Aviv and the struggle for Palestine 1880–1948.* University of California Press, 2005.

Levy, Gideon and Levac, Alex. 'Down in the Jordan Valley, the Cruel Wheels of the Israeli Occupation Keep on Turning'. *Haaretz*, 20 September 2019. https://www.haaretz.com/israel-news/.premium-in-the-jordan-valley-the-cruel-wheels-of-the-israeli-occupation-keep-turning-1.7867122?=&utm_source=Push_Notification&utm_medium=web_push&utm_campaign=General&ts=_1569149378675.

The Local Government Performance Assessment (LPGA) Survey.

Lidman, Melanie, 'In Gaza, Using Agriculture to Grow the Economy.' *Times of Israel*, 17 May 2016. https://www.timesofisrael.com/in-gaza-using-agriculture-to-grow-the-economy/.

Lidman, Melanie. 'Baptism by mire in Jordan River'. *Times of Israel*, 25 May 2019. https://www.timesofisrael.com/baptism-by-mire-in-jordan-river-sewage-mucks-up-christian-rite/.

Likhovski , Assaf. 'Is Tax Law Culturally Specific? Lessons from the History of Income Tax Law in Mandatory Palestine'. *Theoretical Inquiries in Law* 11, no. 2 (2010): 43–70.

Lonergan, Stephen C. and Brooks, David B. *Watershed: The Role of Fresh Water in the Israeli-Palestinian Conflict*. Ottawa: IDRC, 1994.

Lowdermilk, Walter C. *Palestine, Land of Promise*. London, 1944, 167.

MacDonald et al. 'Mapping groundwater development costs for the transboundary Western Aquifer Basin, Palestine/Israel. A.M. MacDonald, B. É. Ó Dochartaigh, R. C. Calow, Y. Shalabi, K. Selah, and S. Merrett'. *Hydrogeology Journal* 17 (2009): 1579–87.

MacIntyre, Donald. *Gaza: Preparing for Dawn*. London, 2018, 352.

Marie, Amer and Imad Abu-Kishk. 'Review of Water Legislation from the Pre-British Mandate Period through the Israeli Occupation'. *Palestine-Israel Journal* 19, no. 4 & 20, no. 1 (2014) / Natural Resources and the Arab-Israeli Conflict.

MAS. *Effects of Movement and Access Controls on Water for the Palestinian Agriculture Sector*. Preliminary Assessment. 2009 (draft).

MAS-Palestinian Economic Policy Research Institute. *Economic Impacts of Water Restrictions in Palestine*. Preliminary Estimates. March 2009, 74.

Masterman, E. W. G. 'Agricultural Life in Palestine'. *The Biblical World* 15, no. 3 (March 1900): 189. http://www.jstor.org/stable/3137064.

Matthews, Elizabeth, Ed. With Newman, David and Daoudi, Mohammed S. Dajani. *The Israel-Palestine Conflict. Parallel Discourses*. Oxford, 2011, 276.

Mekorot, Israel National Water Co. *Main Facts & Figures*. 31 July 2018.
Messerchmit. 2008.
Minorities at Risk 2008 *Assessment for Arabs in Israel.*
Montefiore, Simon Sebag. *Jerusalem, the Biography*. London: Weidenfeld and Nicolson, 2011, 638.
Morris, Benny. *Righteous Victims: A History of the Zionist-Arab Conflict 1881–1999*. London, 2000, 751
Nablus Municipality 2017. *Wastewater Treatment Plant Nablus West Annual Report for Operations and Reuse 2017* Eng. Suleiman Abu Ghosh Eng. Yousef Abu Jaffal Mr. Sameh Bitar Eng. Mohammad Homeidan Eng.Yazan Odeh. http://wwtp.nablus.org/wp-content/uploads/2018/02/Final-2017-report-20-2-2018.pdf (accessed 4 August 2019).
Netherlands Representative Office (NRO). 'Palestinian Territories: Gaza Exports to Europe with Dutch Support' by Market Insider'. *Wednesday*, 18 December 2013. http://www.intracen.org/Gaza-exports-to-Europe-with-Dutch-support/#sthash.lS3FO1Dl.dpuf.
New Scientist. 'Desalination: Israel Lays Claim to Palestine's Water'. *New Scientist*, 27 May 2004. https://www.newscientist.com/article/dn5037-israel-lays-claim-to-palestines-water/#ixzz5ySpdLjYM.
Abu Nasar, A et al. 'Relation of Nitrate Contamination of Groundwater with Methaemoglobin Level Among Infants in Gaza'. *Eastern Mediterranean Health Journal* 13, no. 5 (September–October 2007). http://www.emro.who.int.
Niksic, Orhan, and Nur Nasser Eddin. *Public Expenditure Review–Palestinian Territories*. Washington, DC: World Bank Group, 2016. http://documents.worldbank.org/curated/en/320891473688227759/Public-Expenditure-Review-Palestinian-territories.
Norris, Jacob. 'Toxic Waters: Ibrahim Hazboun and the Struggle for a Dead Sea Concession, 1913–1948'. *Jerusalem Quarterly* 45: 25–42. ISSN 1565-2254. Available from Sussex Research Online https://sro.sussex.ac.uk/id/eprint/43631.
Oren, Michael *Six Days of War June 1967 and the Making of the Modern Middle East* OUP, 2002, 446.
Owen, E. R. J. *Economic Development in Mandatory Palestine 1918–1948 in The Palestinian Economy*. Edited by George T. Abed. London: Routledge, 1988.
Palestinian Central Bureau of Statistics (PCBS). *Agricultural Statistics* 2005/6. December 2007, 39.
Palestinian Central Bureau of Statistics (PCBS). *Survey on the Impact of the Expansion and Annexation Wall on the Socio-Economic Conditions of Palestinian Localities which the Wall Passes Through*. September 2008, 19.
Palestinian Central Bureau of Statistics (PCBS). 'Poverty Profile in Palestine, 2017'. *Palestine*, 2017. http://www.pcbs.gov.ps/Document/pdf/txte_poverty2017.pdf?date=16
Palestinian Central Bureau of Statistics (PCBS) and the World Bank. *Deep Palestinian Poverty in the Midst of Economic Crisis*. October 2004. In English and Arabic. 71.
Palestinian Hydrology Group. *Water for Life. Israeli Assault on Palestinian Water during the Intifida*. 2004 Report, 204.
Palestinian Hydrology Group. *Water for Life. Water, Sanitation and Hygiene Monitoring Program*. 2005 Report, 204.
Palestinian Water Agenda 2008–2010. *Strategy Notes for Short-term Priority. Investments in the Water Supply and Wastewater Sector in Palestine*. May 2008.
PASSIA. *Water and Environment*: *Water Data*. No date.
Palestine Authority, Ministry of Agriculture. *Strategy for Sustainable Agriculture*. 2004.

Palestine Authority, Ministry of Agriculture. *National Agricultural Sector Strategy 2017–2022*. November 2016.

Pappe, Ilan. *History of Modern Palestine. One Land, Two Peoples* Cambridge: Cambridge University Press, 2004, 333.

Pappe, Ilan. *The Ethnic Cleansing of Palestine*. Oxford: One World, 2006, 313.

Pappe, Ilan. *The Making of the Arab-Israeli Conflict 1947–1951*. London, 2006, 324.

Pappe, Ilan. *The Rise and Fall of a Palestinian Dynasty. The Husaynis 1700–1948*. London: Saqi Books, 2010, 399.

Pappe, Ilan. *The Idea of Israel. A History of Power and Knowledge*. London, 2015.

Pappe, Ilan. *The Biggest Prison on Earth. A History of the Occupied Territories*. London: Oneworld Publications, 2017, 273.

Pappe, Ilan. *Ten Myths about Israel* London, 2017, 171.

Peake, A. S. *Peake' Commentary on the Bible*. Edited by by Matthew Black, Harold Henry Rowley and Arthur Samuel Peake. Thomas Nelson: London, 1962.

PECDAR. *Palestinian Water Strategic Planning Study*. 2001, 140.

Plant, Steven. 'Water Policy in Israel'. *Policy Studies* 47 (July 2000). Jerusalem: Institute for Advanced Strategic and Political Studies.

Pope Francis. http://w2.vatican.va/content/francesco/en/encyclicals/documents/papa-f rancesco. 20150524 enciclica-laudato-si.html (accessed 25 May 2019).

PNA/PWA. *Letter from PWA to B'Tselem*. 14 August 2008, 5.

PWA. *Water Strategy 2000*. Ramallah, 2000.

PWA. *An Audit of the Operations and Projects in the Water Sector in Palestine: The Strategic Refocusing of Water Sector Infrastructure in Palestine*. Final Report, 18 November 2008a. Funded by the Norwegian Representative Office in Palestine, 90.

PWA. *Water Sector Status in West Bank. Summary Report with West Bank Governorates Emergency and Development Plan*. Draft, October 2008b, 50.

PWA. *Water Governance Programme: Building the Capacity for Institutional Reform of the Water Sector*. Ramallah, Report prepared by the PWA with support from the United Nations Development Programme, 15 March 2009.

PWA. *White Paper on Water Sector Reform in Palestine*, April 2012.

PWA. *Status Report of Water Resources in the Occupied State of Palestine*. Ramallah: PWA, 2013. http://www.pwa.ps/.

PWA. *PWA Water Tables 2014*. Palestinian Water Authority Water Information System. 2014.

PWA. *Desalinated Water Chain in the Gaza Strip "From Source to Mouth."* Analysis Report. PWA, GiZ, Norwegian MFA, ECHO, NRC, ACF, GVC, IOCC, Islamic Relief, Oxfam, and Save the Children, 2015a.

PWA. *Gaza Strip: Desalination Facility Project: Necessity, Politics and Energy*. PWA, 2015b. http://www.pwa.ps/userfiles.

PWA. *Water Crisis in Gaza: The Future Depends on Sustainable Solutions* (in Arabic). Ramallah: PWA, 2015c. http://www.pwa.ps.

PWA/Hydroconseil. *National Water Company Draft Action Plan*. 2016.

PWA/Orgut. *Roadmap for the Creation of Regional Water utilities in the Frame of the Water Sector Reform in Palestine. Draft Phase 2*. Completion Report. Palestinian Water Authority/Orgut Consulting AB, February 2017.

PWA/Hydroconseil. *National Water Company Draft Action Plan* (2016). PWA/ Hydroconseil. 2016.

PWA/WASH Partners/GIZ (Palestinian Water Authority, WASH Partners, and Deutsche Gesellschaft für Internationale Zusammenarbeit). *"Surveying Private & Public Brackish*

Water Desalination Plants in the Gaza Strip & Studying the Water Supply Chain." Dissemination Workshop PowerPoint, September 2015.

PWA/Norway. *Audit of the Operations and Projects of the PWA*. Draft, 5 October 2008, 73.

PWA. *Gaza Central Desalination Plant and Associated Works Program. Donor Information Handbook*. Ramallah, 2018.

Rinat, Zafrir. 'And a Cleaner Yarkon River Runs Through It'. *Haaretz* 18 July 2013. https://www.haaretz.com/israel-news/sports/premium-and-a-cleaner-river-runs-through-it 1.5292956 (accessed 26 May 2019).

Ring, Kenneth PhD. Abdullah Ghassan Letters *from Palestine. Palestinians Speak Out about Their Lives, Their Country, and the Power of Nonviolence*. Tucson, Arizona, 2010.

Rogan, Eugene and Avi Shlaim. *The War for Palestine: Rewriting the History of 1948*. Cambridge: Cambridge University Press, 2001.

Rogan, Eugene. *The Fall of the Ottomans. The Great War in the Middle East 1914–1920*. Allen Lane, Great Britain, 2015, 485.

Ed. Rogers, Peter and Lydon, Peter. *Water in the Arab World. Perspectives and Prognoses Eleven Essays*. Harvard, 1994, 369.

Romeo, Leonardo G. *Assessment of the Strategic Development and Investment Planning (SDIP) Process: A Rapid Assessment of Policy and Selected Technical Issues*. LDI (Local Development International LLC), 2017.

Rouyer, Alwyn R. *Turning Water into Politics: The Water Issue in the Palestinian-Israeli Conflict*. Palgrave Macmillan, 1999.

Sadoff, C. and Grey D. '(Sink or swim? Water security for growth and development'. *Water Policy* 9, no. 6 (2007): 545–571.

Said, Edward W. *Orientalism*. London, 1978, 368.

Said, Edward *Peace and Its Discontents: Essays on Palestine in the Middle East Peace Process*. With a Preface by Christopher Hitchens. New York, 1995, 188.

Said, Edward W. and Hitchens, Christopher, eds. *Blaming the Victims. Spurious Scholarship and the Palestinian Question*. London, 2001, 296.

Salah, John S. 'Jaffa Drainage Scheme'. *Municipal Corporation of Jaffa* 18, no. 6 (1935).

Samuel, Edwin. *A Lifetime in Jerusalem: The Memoirs of the Second Viscount Samuel*. Jerusalem: Israel Universities Press, 1970.

Sand, Shlomo. *The Invention of the Jewish People*. London and New York: Verso, 2009, 332.

Sayigh, Yusuf A. 'The Palestinian Economy under Occupation'. In *The Palestinian Economy*, edited by George T. Abed. London: Routledge, 1988.

Schama, Simon. *Belonging. The Story of the Jews 1492–1900*. London: Penguin, Random House, 2017, 790.

Schlaim, Avi The Iron Wall. *Israel and the Arab World*. London, 2000, 670.

Schlaim, Avi. *Israel and Palestine. Reappraisals, Revisions, Refutations*. London, 2010, 392.

Schoenfeld, Stuart, Eric Abitbol and Francesca de Chatel. *Retelling the Story of Water in the Middle East: Reflections on and about a Conversation at the Dead Sea*. Ontario, Canada: York University, 2007.

Schwarz, J. *Management of Israel's Water Resources*. Isaac and Shuval, 1994.

Schwartz, J. *Israel Water Sector Review*. Report prepared for the World Bank, Tel Aviv 1990.

Segev, Tom. *Israel and the War that Transformed the Middle East*. Little, Brown, 1967.

Selby, Jan. *Water, Power and Politics in the Middle East*. I.B. Tauris, 2003, 275

Selby, Jan. '"New Security Thinking" In Israeli-Palestinian Water Relations'. *Facing Global Environmental Change: Environmental, Energy, Food, Health, and Water Security Concepts*. Edited by Hans, 2009.

Selby Jan. *Dependencies, Independence, and Interdependence in the Palestinian Water Sector,* 2011.

Selby, Jan. 'Cooperation, Domination and Colonization: The Israeli Palestinian Joint Water Committee'. *Water Alternatives* 6, no. 1 (2013): 1–24. ISSN 1965-0175.

Selby, Jan and Messerschmid, Clemens. 'Misrepresenting the Jordan River Basin'. *Water Alternatives* 8, no. 2 (2015): 258–79. ISSN 1965-0175.

Shamir, Uri. 'Water Agreements between Israel and its Neighbours'. In *Transformations of Middle East Natural Environments,* edited by Jeff Albert, Magnus Bernhardsson and Roger Kenna. Yale F & ES Bulletin 103, 1998.

Shapland, Greg. *Rivers of Discord. International Water Disputes in the Middle East.* London: C. Hurst & Co., 1997, 183.

Shawa, Issam R. *Water Situation in the Gaza Strip,* Isaac & Shuval, 1994.

Shehadeh, Raja. *Palestinian Walks: Notes on a Vanishing Landscape.* London, 2008.

Shehadeh, Raja. *Occupier's Law: Israel and the West Bank.* Washington, DC: Institute for Palestine Studies, 1985.

Sherman, A. J. *Mandate Days: British Lives in Palestine 1918–1948.* London: Thames & Hudson, 1997, 264.

Shuval, Hillel. 'Meeting Vital Human Needs: Equitable Resolution of Conflicts Over Shared Water Resources of Israelis and Palestinians'. In *Water Resources in the Middle East,* edited by Shuval and Dweik, 3–16. Berlin: Springer, 2007.

Shuval, Hillel and Hassan Dweik, eds. *Water Resources in the Middle East* .Israel-Palestinian Water *Issues – From Conflict to Cooperation.* Volume 2, Hexagon series on Human and Environmental Security and Peace. Berlin: Springer, 2007, 454.

Shuval, Hillel. *Evaluating the WHO 2006 Health guidelines for wastewater reuse in agriculture for Palestinian requirements* Power point presentation. 5 November 2008, 4.

Siegel, Seth M. *Let There Be Water.* New York: St Martin's Press, 2015, 337.

Siegel 2015: 252. Of the Approximately, 318 Million m^3 of Water Used in Israeli Agriculture in 2016, about 195 Million m^3 was from Treated Wastewater (62 Per Cent).

Smilansky, David. *What is the Water Supply Situation in Tel Aviv?* Yedi.ot.Iriyat. Tel Aviv.5.8.9. (1934).

Smith, Charles D. *Palestine and the Arab-Israeli Conflict. A History with Documents* Bedford/St Martin's, USA 2017, 597.

Society for Austro-Arab Relations. *Development Perspectives for Agriculture in the Occupied Palestinian Territories.* 1992.

Soffer, Arnon. *The Relevance of the Johnston Plan to the Reality of 1993 and Beyond.* Isaac and Shuval, 1994.

Sokmen, Muge Gursoy and Ertur Basak, eds. *Waiting for the Barbarians.* A Tribute to Edward W Said. Verso, 2008.

Sosland, Jeffrey K. *Cooperating Rivals: The Riparian Politics of the Jordan River Basin.* Albany: State University of New York, 2007.

Surkes, Sue. 'White Foam Covers Sections of the Yarkon River'. Article in the *Times of Israel,* 11 October 2017. https://www.timesofisrael.com/white-foam-covers-sections-of-yarkon-river-despite-cleanup-efforts.

A Survey of Palestine Prepared in December 1945 and January, 1946. For the information of the Anglo-American Committee of Inquiry. Volume I and Volume II Reprinted by The Institute for Palestine Studies, Washington, DC, 1991 Volume I, 534 Volume II, 1139.

SUSMAQ. *The Susmaq Project: Sustainable Management of the West Bank and Gaza Aquifers: Summary Report,* 2006, 44.

Sutcliffe, Claud R. 'Palestinian Refugee Resettlement: Lessons from the East Ghor Canal Project'. *Journal of Peace Research* 11, no. 1 (1974): 57–62.

Tal, Alon. *The Evolution of Israeli Water Management: The Elusive Search for Environmental Security*. Chapter 5.

Tal, Professor Alon and Abed-Rabbo, Dr Alfred. *Water Wisdom: Preparing the Groundwork for Cooperative and Sustainable Water Management in the Middle East*. Rutgers University Press, September, 2010, 371.

Tal, Alon. *All the Trees of the Forest. Israel's Woodlands from the Bible to the Present*. Yale University Press, 2013, 348.

Tal, Alon and David Katz. 'Rehabilitating Israel's Streams and Rivers'. *International Journal of River Basin Management* 10, no. 4 (2012): 317–30.

Talmon, J. L. *The Origins of Totalitarian Democracy*. London: Sphere Books, 1970, 355.

Templin, Julia S. *Zababdeh: A Palestinian Water History*. Julia S. Templin, MSc thesis, Utah State University, 2011. *All Graduate Theses and Dissertations*, 911. https://digitalcommons.usu.edu/etd/911.

Thomson, W. M. *The Land and the Book*. Thomas Nelson & Son, 1911.

Trottier, Julie and Perrier, Jeanne. 'Water-Driven Palestinian Agricultural Frontiers: The Global Ramifications of Transforming Local Irrigation'. *Journal of Political Ecology* 25 (2018): 304.

Tuchman, Barbara W. *Bible and Sword. England and Palestine from the Bronze Age to Balfour*. New York, 1984, 412.

Tzuri, Matan. 'Israel to Build Pipeline to Absorb Sewage from Gaza'. *Ynet News*, 7 January 2017. https://www.ynetnews.com/articles/0,7340,L-4983174,00.html.

Udasin, Sharon and Lazaroff, Tovah. 'Gaza Sewage Forces Shutdown of Israeli Beach: Israel May Build a Pipeline to Sderot to Treat Waste'. Article in the *Jerusalem Post*, 6 July 2017.

UNCTAD. *Population and Demographic Developments in the West Bank and Gaza Strip until 1990*. UNCTAD/ECDC/SEU/1 United Nations Conference on Trade and Development, 1990. https://unctaf.org/en/docs/poecdeseudi1.en.pdf.

UNCTAD. *The Besieged Palestinian agricultural sector*. New York: UNCTAD, 2015.

UNDP. *West Bank and Gaza Environment Priorities Note (P169628)*.

UNICEF. *UNICEF Seawater Desalination Plant Helps Head Off Gaza Water Crisis*. 2019. https://www.unicef.org/stories/unicef-seawater-desalination-plant-helps-head-gaza-water-crisis.

UNISPAL *Water Resources of the Occupied Palestinian Territory*. Committee on the Exercise of he Inalienable Rights of the Palestinian People, New York, United Nations, 1992. https://unispal.un.org/UNISPAL.NSF/0/296EE705038AC9FC852561170067E)5F

UNOCHA. Unitedd Nations Office for the Coordination of Humanitarian Assistance. 2019. https://www.ochaopt.org/theme/food-security (accessed 14 June 2019).

UNOCHA. Socio-Economic and Food Security Survey (SefSec). 2018.

UNOCHA. *WBG Closure Maps*. April 2008, 19.

UNOCHA. *Gaza Strip Inter-Agency Humanitarian Fact Sheet*. June 2008, 2.

UNOCHA. *Gaza Humanitarian Situation Reports*, 29 April, 2008, 17 November, 2008.

USAID /EHP. Save the Children Report – *Village Water and Sanitation Program Phase II*, June 2003.

Van Aken, Mauro *Development as a Gift: Patterns of Assistance and Refugees Strategies in the Jordan Valley*. In International Symposium on the Palestinian Refugees and UNRWA in Jordan, the West Bank and Gaza, 1949–1999.

Vishwanath, Tara, Brian Blankespoor, Faythe Calandra, Nandini Krishnan, Meera Mahadevan, and Mobuo Yoshida. *Seeing is Believing: Poverty in the Palestinian Territories*. Washington, DC: World Bank Group, 2014.

von Medeazza, Gregor. *Searching for clean water in Gaza*, 10 January, 2019.

WANA. *Decoupling National Water Needs for National Water Supplies: Insights and Potential for Countries in the Jordan Basin*. West Africa-North Africa Institute, June 2017.

Ward, Christopher and Sandra Ruckstuhl. *Water Scarcity, Climate Change and Conflict in the Middle East*. London: I.B. Tauris, 2017, 343.

Weinthal, Erika and Sowers, Jeannie. *Targeting Infrastructure and livelihoods in the West Bank and Gaza*. OUP.

Weizman, Rotem Caro. *Speech at EcoPeace Conference* Summary, 6 March 2018.

Weizman, Eyal. *Hollow Land: Israel's Architecture of Occupation*. New Edition. London: Verso, 2017, 318.

World Bank. *The Economic Development of Jordan*. Washington, DC: World Bank, 1955.

World Bank. *Developing the Occupied Territories: An Investment in Peace* Vol 1: Overview and Key Findings Vol II: Strategic Choices at the Macro Level. Vol III: Performance of the Private Sector. Vol IV: The Agricultural Sector Vol V: Infrastructure sectors Vol VI: Human Resource Development, 1993.

World Bank. *Peace and the Jordanian Economy*. 1994, 62.

World Bank. *The Hashemite Kingdom of Jordan: Agricultural Sector Adjustment Operation and Agricultural Sector Technical Support Project*. Working Papers Volume II (Papers 9 –14 Statistical Annex and Bibliography) 30 March 1995.

World Bank. *Poverty in West Bank and Gaza: Summary*. May 2001, 21

World Bank. *Palestinian Economic Crisis*. March 2002a, 141.

World Bank. *Long Term Policy Options for the Palestinian Economy*. July 2002b, 129.

World Bank. *Report on the Impact of the Intifada*. Washington, DC: World Bank, 2003.

World Bank. *West Bank and Gaza Infrastructure Assessment*. December 2004a, 43.

World Bank. *Palestinian Economic Crisis*. October 2004b, 93.

World Bank. *Socio-Political Structures, Development and State-Building in West Bank and Gaza: A Country Social Analysis*. Washington, DC: The World Bank, June 2006a, 46.

World Bank. *Country Economic Memorandum: Growth in WBG: Opportunities and Constraints*. September 2006b. Vol I 80 Vol II 72.

World Bank. *West Bank and Gaza Public Expenditure Review: From Crisis to Greater Fiscal Independence*. March 2007a. Vol I 50.

World Bank. *West Bank and Gaza Water Sector Update*. Draft Final, 1 November 2007b. Text: 37 Tables: 40.

World Bank. *Two Years after London: Restarting Palestinian Economic Recovery*. Report to the Ad Hoc Liaison Committee. 24 September 2007c, 35.

World Bank. *West Bank and Gaza Update*. March 2008a, 24.

World Bank. *West Bank and Gaza Update*. June 2008b, 24.

World Bank. *Political Economy of Policy Reform – Issues and Implications for Policy Dialogue and Development Operations*. Report No. 44288-GLB, Social Development Department (SDV). Washington, DC: The World Bank, 2008c.

World Bank. *WBG Water Sector Institutional Support Study*. February 2008d, 39.

World Bank. *Economic Effects of Restricted Access to Land in the West Bank*. 2008e, 41.

World Bank. *Issues Paper: Interim Technical Assistance Note on Water*, June 2008f, 13.

World Bank. *West Bank and Gaza. Palestinian Trade: West Bank Routes*. December 16, 2008g. Report No. 46807, 22.

World Bank. *West Bank and Gaza: Assessment of Restrictions on Palestinian Water Sector Development*. Washington, DC: World Bank, April 2009, 134.

World Bank. *West Bank and Gaza: Coping with Conflict? Poverty and Inclusion in the West Bank and Gaza*. Report No. 61293-GZ, July. Washington, DC: World Bank, 2011.

World Bank. *Area C and the future of the Palestinian economy*. Report No. AUS2922. Washington, DC: World Bank, 2013.

World Bank. *Water Management in Israel*. Washington, DC: World Bank, 2017.

World Bank. *Towards Water Security for Palestinians. West Bank and Gaza Water Supply, Sanitation, and Hygiene Poverty Diagnostic*. Washington, DC: World Bank, 2018, 131.

World Bank. *The Role of Desalination in an Increasingly Water-Scarce World*. Washington, DC: World Bank, March, 2019a, 97.

World Bank. *Palestinian Territories Recent Development*. Washington, DC: World Bank, April, 2019b.

World Bank/TATF. *Building Palestinian Institutional Capacity*. March 2003, 64.

WSRC (Water Sector Regulatory Council). *Bridge to Sustainability: Water and Wastewater Service Providers in Palestine*. Ramallah: WSRC, 2017.

Zeitoun, Mark. *Power and Water in the Middle East: The Hidden Politics of the Palestinian-Israeli Water Conflict*. London: I.B. Tauris, 2008, 214.

INDEX

www.ingramcontent.com/pod-product-compliance
Lightning Source LLC
Chambersburg PA
CBHW070901080426
R18103400001B/R181034PG41932CBX00004B/7

* 9 7 8 0 7 5 5 6 3 7 9 8 0 *